Engaging the Community
in Decision Making

Engaging the Community in Decision Making

*Case Studies Tracking
Participation, Voice and Influence*

Roz Diane Lasker *and*
John A. Guidry

McFarland & Company, Inc., Publishers
Jefferson, North Carolina, and London

Illustrations by Rosemary Chasey, Capitola Design.

LIBRARY OF CONGRESS CATALOGUING-IN-PUBLICATION DATA

Lasker, Roz Diane.
Engaging the community in decision making : case studies tracking
participation, voice and influence / Roz Diane Lasker and John A. Guidry.
p.   cm.
Includes bibliographical references and index.

ISBN 978-0-7864-4312-3
softcover : 50# alkaline paper ∞

1. Group decision making—United States—Case studies.   2. Political participation—
United States—Case studies.   I. Guidry, John A.   II. Title.
HM746.L37   2009   361.80973—dc22   2008050990

British Library cataloguing data are available

Cover image ©2008 Shutterstock

Manufactured in the United States of America

*McFarland & Company, Inc., Publishers
Box 611, Jefferson, North Carolina 28640
www.mcfarlandpub.com*

Acknowledgments

This book, which was written on behalf of the large and diverse group of people involved in the Pathways to Collaboration Workgroup, reflects what all of us learned together over a period of four years. Neither the learning nor the book would have been possible without the generous support of the W. K. Kellogg Foundation. Barbara Sabol, in particular, made sure the Workgroup had the time and flexibility to discover what we and others in the field of community participation didn't know and to fill that gap by conducting a rigorous investigation. Because of her vision and commitment, we now know how to tell if the promise of community participation is actually being achieved and what practitioners, funders, and evaluators need to pay attention to in order to achieve that goal. We hope that communities around the world will be supported in applying this new knowledge.

As we describe in the first part of the book, this was a deeply collaborative effort, involving people associated with five community partnerships and a technical support team. Although these individuals, listed below, played various roles and participated for varying lengths of time, all made important contributions to the work. Coming from very different backgrounds, they brought an array of ideas, skills, and experiences to the Workgroup, which they continually shared with each other. They also brought a generosity of spirit, which made it possible for us to let go of what we thought we knew and support each other in exploring the unknown.

These gifts, as valuable as they were, would not have sufficed if the participants in the Workgroup had not also been incredibly dedicated to what we were doing together. Over the years, as work continued at an unrelenting pace, we depended on each other to get the job done, and people came through for each other in spite of many other demanding obligations at work and at home. When illness or tragedy struck, Workgroup participants were there for each other and found ways to compensate for each other. At some point, we realized we had created a community. That is the greatest gift we gave each other, and it is what made it possible for the Workgroup to accomplish what none of us could have done alone.

Community Leadership Team of Beyond Welfare (Story County, Iowa): Steve Aigner, Gabriel Arato-Smidt, Mark Barrett, Tyler Barrett, Jan Beran, Louis Harris Bey, Cindy Blessing, Julie Bradley, Bruce Carroll, Jenell Clarke, Jan Cook, Joanna Courteau, Antoinette Eichhorn, Salwa Elbasher, Randy Gabrielese, Shawna Garrey, Wes Hamstreet,

Jessica Heath, Nancy Huewe, Jeana King, Noumoua Lynaolu, Linda Manatt, Joyce Matters, Holly McDonald, Joe Melcher, Matt Michael, Christina Oldfield, Terry Pickett, David Sahr, Keith Schrag, Lois Smidt, Alissa Stoehr, Cindy Weigel, Mechelle Williams, Jocelyn Wilson.

Humboldt Park Empowerment Partnership (Chicago, Illinois): Eduardo Arocho, Christine Badger, Ruth Dominguez, Raul Echevarria, Ruben Feliciano, Kathleen Gems, Juanita Irizarry, Noah Temaner Jenkins, Magdalena Martinez, Abdi Maya, Eliud Medina, Melissa Morales, Bethsaida Nazario, Roberto Nieves, Miguel Palacio, Sam Pearson, Limaris Pueyo, Niuris Ramos, Riccadona Rivera, Gabriela Roman, Nydia Roman, the Reverend Onix Rosado, Enrique Salgado, Lucia Tellado, Jocelyn Wilson.

MIRACLE Group (Cass Lake, Minnesota): Ardean Brasgalla, Jake Chernugal, Melissa Chernugal, Dan Evans, Randy Finn, Shirley Fisher, Sharon Gieseke, Eileen Gothman, Janice Harper, Rebecca Laesch, Mike Meyers, Dennis Parker, Dayne Sather, Donna Sather, Patricia M. Singleton, William Stocker.

Southeast Oklahoma Champion and Enterprise Community (Choctaw, McCurtain, and Pushmataha counties, Oklahoma): Albert Alexander, Carla Bonner, Pamela Briley, Jay Bee Burner, Eugenia Butler, Greg Campbell, Billy Covington, Henry Edwards, Aimee Frost, Kristi L. Frost, Patty Frost, Irvin Jones, JoAnn Karlen, Dianne McColister, Tonya McKnight, Cynthia Morgan, Jerry Poole, Beatrice Royal, Lila Douglas Swink, Rhonda Teague, Stacy Teague, Wallace Walker, Deborah Weehunt, Jim Wood.

Tri-County Workforce Alliance (Coahoma, Quitman, and Bolivar counties, Mississippi): Laura Allhands, Charles Barron, Judy Bland, Charles Butler, Lillie V. Davis, Alkie Edwards, Gloria Goins, Jordan Goins, Sophia Golden, Dr. John Green, Dr. Val Hinton, Elizabeth Johnson, Charles Langford, Fredean Langford, Valerie Lee, Sarah Leonard, Shirley Morgan, Charles Reid, Josephine P. Rhymes, Victor Richardson, Shawanda Russell, Dorothy Stamps, Tana Vassel, Wayne Winter, George Walker.

Support Team: Quinton Baker, Dorothy Benson, Oscar Bernal, Ruth Nicole Brown, Carol Coulter, John Guidry, Norge Jerome, Judy Jones, Rachel Koster, Roz Lasker, Nicole Lezin, Paulina Lopez, Janice Perlman, Larry Turns, Nadia Van Buren, Elisa Weiss, Abigail Wiener.

Table of Contents

Preface   1

Introduction: Are We Actually Doing What We Want to Be Doing?   5

Case Narratives

  1. Community Voices Against Violence in Cass Lake, Minnesota   21

  2. Housing for Single Mothers in Humboldt Park, Chicago   40

  3. A "Poor Man's Bank" in the Southeast Oklahoma Enterprise Community   54

  4. A Workforce Alliance Minigrant Program in the Mississippi Delta   68

  5. The Community Leadership Team of Story County, Iowa   80

  6. Developing a Professionalization Curriculum in the Mississippi Delta   93

  7. Revitalizing Cass Lake, Minnesota   108

  8. Community Centers in Southeastern Oklahoma   123

  9. The Incorporation of Beyond Welfare in Ames, Iowa   141

10. Saving a Mural in Humboldt Park, Chicago   156

Cross-Case Analysis

11. The Pathway of Ideas   170

Application to Practice

12. Realizing the Promise of Community Participation   200

Chapter Notes   221

References   231

Index   237

Preface

This book is about a promise — the promise of community participation to give people who have been excluded from decision making an influential voice about issues that affect their lives. It is also about an extraordinary journey that more than 100 people who aspire to realizing that promise took together. Over the course of four years, the members of the Pathways to Collaboration Workgroup came face-to-face with the "black box" of community participation —fundamentals we thought we knew, but actually didn't know — and developed the relationships, methods, and tools we needed to look inside.

Readers who open that black box with us will be going on a journey, too. There are a lot of discoveries to be made along the way — discoveries about the barriers that are inadvertently preventing us from realizing the promise we care about so much and discoveries about how those barriers can be overcome. But we know from our own experiences that these discoveries don't come easily. To realize the promise of community participation, we need to be willing to look at ourselves, our communities, and our work in new ways. For our Workgroup, the questions and challenges started early. It was only by grappling with who, and what, community participation is all about that we discovered the black box that needed to be opened.

Community participation holds out a promise to people who have been excluded from decision making, and our journey forced us to take a long, hard look at our relationship to the members of those groups. Everyone in the Workgroup — the people involved in the community partnerships and the technical support team — has had his or her own personal experiences with exclusion. At various points in our lives, we have been left out of decisions that mattered to us, and suffered as a result, because of our race, ethnicity, age, gender, religion, sexual orientation, disability, income, level of formal education, or perceived lack of relevant knowledge. Many of us have worked hard to gain more influence by acquiring acknowledged expertise through formal education and training, developing relationships within and beyond our communities, and advancing to positions where we are listened to and have some power. Our goal is to use that influence and power for the benefit of people in our communities, particularly those who are more disadvantaged than ourselves.

One way of benefiting our communities is by identifying and addressing issues that matter to community members through participation processes. But in disadvantaged communities where many people have a history of exclusion, whose voices need to be

1

heard directly and whose voices need to be influential? We didn't have an answer to this question when we started our journey, but we recognized that it wouldn't be possible to get to the answer unless we were willing to pay special attention to the role and influence of people who are usually spoken for by others and who are the targets of community programs and services: the poorest, least educated, and most marginalized residents in communities.

We found this difficult for a number of reasons. Many of us had been in the position of these residents earlier in our lives, and through our work and other associations, we interacted regularly with people who currently were. Consequently, we identified strongly with them; when we spoke, we felt that our words were speaking for them. We also struggled a lot with acknowledging distinctions among people in communities. Everyone in the Workgroup is committed to running participation processes that remove society's labels and treat people equally. Focusing attention on the least powerful among us seemed to reinforce a form of stigmatization that we vehemently oppose.

It's fortunate that we were able to resolve these difficulties, because our journey wouldn't have gotten very far if we hadn't. After numerous, and sometimes heated, discussions, we recognized that not talking candidly about the social reality of people in certain groups doesn't change that reality for them. Our participation processes have the potential to do that, by giving the most disenfranchised members of communities an influential voice, but we'll never be able to tell if that is happening, or figure out how to make it happen, unless we look at their participation directly.

To move forward, we also needed to clarify the nature of the distinctions we were willing to make. When we use the term "marginalized"—which appears frequently as an adjective in this book—we are not describing intrinsic qualities of the people to whom it is applied. Instead, we are describing how people are treated by society. In the course of our discussions, we recognized that society marginalizes some people more than others and that people can be marginalized under some circumstances but not others. Community participation holds out a promise to anyone who is marginalized, under any circumstances and to any extent, but it holds out the greatest promise to the poorest, least educated, and most marginalized community residents who have no other way to raise issues that matter to them or to get those issues addressed in ways that work for them.

Our willingness to acknowledge distinctions among people in communities bought us half the ticket for our journey. We obtained the other half when we committed to tracking the influence of the various kinds of people in participation processes. The promise of community participation is all about influence, and everyone in the Workgroup had been using the term a lot. But we discovered, to our surprise, that we had no way of knowing whose voices were actually influential. The reason was straightforward (although astounding in retrospect). Neither we, nor anyone else in the field, had been looking at the influence of participants directly. Instead, we had been focusing our attention on the involvement of community members—giving them opportunities to participate in the process and "seats at the table." Hidden in the black box, influence was something we had been taking for granted.

One of the major accomplishments of our journey was the development of methods to assess the influence of the various people in community participation processes, and these methods were the foundation for everything we learned. But making the decision to look at influence directly was difficult because it took us out of our comfort zone. We had been feeling good when an array of community members were involved in our participation processes. Shifting our focus from opportunity to influence would raise the bar for success and take us into unknown territory. It made us ask ourselves: How seriously do we want to achieve the promise of community participation? Readers of this book will face that question, too.

Roz Diane Lasker
New York City
January 2009

Introduction:
Are We Actually Doing What
We Want to Be Doing?

In 2006, five of the most community-driven partnerships in the United States embarked on an unprecedented investigation. They decided to take a fresh look at some of their experiences working with members of their communities to find out how influential different people had been and how the pattern of influence affected what the partnerships had been able to accomplish.

When the partnerships began working together in 2004, no one anticipated the need for such an investigation. The partnerships' strong track records engaging a broad range of community members had been the basis for their selection — out of a field of more than 750 applicants — to participate in the Pathways to Collaboration Workgroup. For two years, the partnerships had been working with a technical support team to explore their community participation processes in detail. The Workgroup's goal was to document exactly what the partnerships were doing to promote meaningful community engagement and to understand and share how they were doing it so that they and other interested partnerships could strengthen their work.

In the course of this exploration, the Workgroup kept hitting a major stumbling block. It was clear that community members were driving what the partnerships did. But the partnerships' communities, like most others, were not homogeneous; they encompassed people who differed from each other in various ways. Of the people in these different groups, who was actually doing the driving and who was going along for the ride?

This question was important to the partnerships because they were committed to maximizing the voice and influence of the people who were experiencing problems in their communities, especially the poorest, least educated, and most marginalized residents. The partnerships' community participation processes certainly created opportunities for these residents to be involved. But no one knew how effective the opportunities were in giving them an influential voice in the partnerships' work.

The reason for this uncertainty was that the partnerships hadn't been assessing the extent to which they actually were doing what they were committed to doing. To figure out how well their participation processes were working to promote the voice and influence of different kinds of community members, and to identify what the partnerships could learn from each other to optimize influence, they would need to open up a "black box" in their work and look at influence directly.

This was a courageous step for the partnerships to take. While it had never occurred to them (or anyone else in the Workgroup) to assess influence before, doing so now raised the possibility that the partnerships would find out that they were not enabling the influence of marginalized residents as much as they thought they had been doing or wanted to be doing. Nonetheless, it was only by opening up the black box that they and others could learn how to achieve that goal.

The Pathways partnerships that decided to undertake this investigative journey were the Community Leadership Team of Beyond Welfare in Story County, Iowa; the Humboldt Park Empowerment Partnership in Chicago, Illinois; the MIRACLE Group in Cass Lake, Minnesota; the Southeast Oklahoma Champion and Enterprise Community in southeast Oklahoma; and the Tri-County Workforce Alliance in the Mississippi Delta. The Workgroup's investigation was organized by the Center for the Advancement of Collaborative Strategies in Health at The New York Academy of Medicine and was funded by the W. K. Kellogg Foundation.

The Promise of Community Participation

As the members of the Pathways to Collaboration Workgroup soon discovered, they weren't the only ones who could benefit from taking a closer and more direct look at the pattern of influence in community participation processes. The extensive literature in the field suggests that the need for the Workgroup's investigation is considerably broader.

Interest in community participation has exploded over the last 40 years, both in the United States and internationally.[1] These processes go by many names and take many forms, such as public and citizen participation, civic engagement, participatory and deliberative democracy, community collaboration, comprehensive community initiatives, and participatory research. But they all share a common promise: *giving people who have been excluded from decision making an influential voice about issues that affect their lives.*

Many people fall into the "excluded" category. Those who are poor, have little formal education, or are marginalized on the basis of race, ethnicity, gender, religion, age, sexual orientation, or disability have a long history of being excluded from the inner circles of power that influence decision making in representative democracies.[2] Outside the political process, members of these groups have often been spoken for by others, particularly when they are perceived as being vulnerable, impaired, or in need of programs or services.[3]

There has been a growing sense among many mainstream or "ordinary" community residents that their voices don't count, either. Their ability to influence issues that matter to them has waned as elections have become more partisan, policy makers have become increasingly beholden to special interests, and important decisions have been delegated to technical experts and bureaucrats who are not directly accountable to the public.[4] Traditional forms of involvement have left them little room to have a meaningful impact.[5]

Having a more direct and influential voice is obviously critical for the people who have been excluded from public discourse and decision making. Over time, their lack of influence has led to profound inequities and injustices in society. To get issues they care about on society's agenda and to have those issues addressed in ways that work for them, the persistent imbalance in influence must be corrected.

Although it may seem counterintuitive, people who have had a lot of influence also stand to gain by giving more voice and influence to historically excluded groups. Increasingly, experts and decision makers have become specialized classes, shut off from the people they are supposed to serve.[6] That's a problem because those people—comprised largely of members of historically excluded groups—have knowledge that experts and decision makers need in order to do their work effectively. As the literature repeatedly emphasizes, ordinary and marginalized residents have the most accurate and direct knowledge of their own concerns, needs, and values; the particularities of their local contexts and cultures; and the ways that problems and solutions (in the form of plans, policies, programs, and technologies) affect their lives.[7] When experts and decision makers lack this "lay" knowledge, serious consequences have been reported to ensue: incorrect assumptions about the public; the development of plans and policies that inadvertently put people at risk; insufficient understanding of problems; inability to solve problems; and lack of public trust and confidence in plans, policies, and decisions.[8]

Finally, giving historically excluded groups a more influential voice is essential for a healthy democracy. All people living in democratic societies have a right to be part of decisions that affect their lives.[9] Equally important, progress in a free society depends on the unfettered entry and exchange of ideas among its members. As John Stuart Mill pointed out over a century ago, restricting people's voices has negative consequences for the general public. It prevents good ideas from being heard and enables damaging ideas to gain adherents because others can't oppose them with better alternatives.[10]

Over the last 40 years, numerous processes have been developed to bring marginalized and ordinary residents together with experts and decision makers and to give historically excluded groups a more influential voice in decision making.[11] Spurred by governments and philanthropic organizations around the world, these processes have been implemented by thousands of government agencies, community-based organizations, academic institutions, and partnerships, often as a requirement for funding. Community participation processes have been used for a variety of purposes, including public policy development and budgeting, community development, technology and environmental risk assessment, health and social welfare, community-based research, deliberative discourse, and civic engagement.

From the outset, however, serious concerns have been raised about the extent to which the rhetoric of community participation is actually being realized in practice. Writing in 1969 about "maximum feasible involvement of the poor" in the Community Action Programs and Model Cities Programs in the United States, Sherry Arnstein noted that in most cases, participation was not associated with a redistribution of power or significant social reform, making it "an empty and frustrating process for the powerless."[12] To distinguish "sham" participation from meaningful participation, she described a Ladder of Citizen Participation, with rungs corresponding to the extent of power that poor people have in affecting the outcome of the process.

In the ensuing years, the field of community participation has evolved considerably. Participatory processes have been incorporated in an ever-growing number of programs around the world. To support this work, experts have developed and promoted a broad array of inclusive practices. Handbooks, reports, and evaluations of community participation processes and practices have appeared in a rapidly expanding literature, which encompasses many disciplines.

In spite of this vast experience, we don't seem to have made much headway in realizing the promise of participation. Community participation can't give historically excluded groups an influential voice in decision making unless they are involved in the process, but engaging low-income populations, minority groups, and young people has been very challenging. No one knows how extensive the problem is because the demographics of participants is not commonly reported in the literature and does not appear to be tracked in many processes.[13] When processes obtain and report demographic information, people who are better off in terms of income, education, and status are usually overrepresented.[14]

As Arnstein noted in 1969, even when historically excluded groups are involved in a participation process, that is no guarantee that their voices will be heard or heeded. Since then, many new inclusive practices and evaluation methods have been introduced and implemented. Nonetheless, concerns about "sham" or "phony" participation have not dissipated.[15]

The literature describes numerous ways that organizers, facilitators, and powerful participants can control community participation processes—both intentionally and unintentionally—and their control appears to have curtailed the influence of historically excluded groups considerably.[16] Reports repeatedly describe participation processes that were used to legitimize what powerful players wanted to do. Yet there is scant evidence in the literature of processes where the participation of marginalized and ordinary residents had a significant impact on plans or actions or—even more importantly—led to outcomes that were explicitly desired by people in those groups. Processes that have not given community residents an influential voice have been associated with increasing levels of skepticism, cynicism, and mistrust.[17] Residents have been reported to drop out of such processes or to be unwilling to participate again.[18]

Many people involved in community participation aspire to making their processes "real," "genuine," and "resident-driven."[19] But given the current state-of-the-art, they face serious obstacles in doing so. Most fundamentally, *the field lacks direct methods to determine whose voices are influential in participation processes*. Consequently, it is not possible to determine the extent to which the promise of community participation is being achieved for historically excluded groups. Influence is included as an indicator in some evaluation frameworks, but it is generally assessed by seeing if the product of a participation process—such as a plan or a report with recommendations—is adopted by policy makers.[20] An extensive review of the literature failed to identify any evaluation frameworks that focus on *who* influences the development of the product or *who* influences the actions that policy makers and others ultimately take. Some processes that seek to achieve consensus explicitly avoid identifying individual voices.[21]

The field also has a limited understanding of how participation processes enable the voices of historically excluded groups to be influential. Consequently, practitioners don't really know what to do to optimize influence. Many of the evaluation criteria in the literature focus on attributes of participation processes that are believed to be necessary in order to give historically excluded groups an influential voice, such as inclusiveness, representativeness, fairness, independence, early involvement, diverse control, transparency, broad framing and scope, interactivity and interrogation, deliberation, empowerment, and neutral, professional staff.[22] But it isn't possible to determine how important these (or potentially other) attributes are without directly assessing the influence of the various kinds of participants in the process. Only by looking at that relationship can we understand the conditions that enable the voices of historically excluded groups to be influential.

Finally, ***the field has limited evidence about the effectiveness of community participation processes***.[23] Consequently, it is difficult to make a strong case for continuing or increasing the current investment. As any practitioner knows, community participation processes entail a lot of drawbacks. They have been reported to slow things down and to make work more messy, contentious, and costly than traditional top-down approaches.[24] These drawbacks are only justifiable if they lead to better results.

While there are no widely held criteria for judging the success of community participation processes, it would be reasonable for the outcome measures to reflect the compelling reasons for giving historically excluded groups an influential voice in the first place: (1) to address inequities and injustices in society by getting issues that matter to marginalized groups on the agenda and addressing those issues in ways that work for them; (2) to provide experts and decision makers with the additional knowledge they need to develop more effective and legitimate plans, programs, and policies; and (3) to promote progress in a healthy democracy through the unfettered entry and exchange of ideas. A key question for funders, practitioners, researchers, and community residents is whether processes that fulfill the promise of community participation can succeed in achieving these outcomes. To answer that question, we need to be able to track the influence of the different kinds of participants in community participation processes and relate those patterns of influence to what the processes are able to accomplish.

The Study

Clearly, many other people are in the same predicament as the Pathways partnerships were when the Workgroup decided to open up the "black box" of community participation and look at influence directly. To do that, the Workgroup chose a retrospective case study approach. By investigating a set of cases from the partnerships' past experiences, the Workgroup would be able to learn about influence under the particular circumstances of each case and, hopefully, draw generalizable conclusions by combining and comparing findings across the cases.

The diversity of the partnerships is an advantage in this kind of study, because conclusions that apply to all of the partnerships are likely to be broadly applicable. Although all of the partnerships are located in the midsection of the country, their communities range from very urban to very rural, and their dominant populations vary, encompassing people who are African American, Hispanic/Latino, Native American, and Caucasian.

The partnerships also differ in the way they are structured and in the kinds of practices they have used to involve community members in their work.

The study, which took two years to complete, was a deeply collaborative effort, involving 125 people in the five partnerships and 15 people on the support team. The terms "Pathways to Collaboration Workgroup" and "we" refer to all of these participants. Collaboration was critical because the study required different kinds of knowledge and skills and thousands of person/hours to complete. Partnership members brought an extensive understanding of the history and functioning of their partnerships and communities, and they had strong relationships with other people who would need to be involved. The support team included researchers from various disciplines who trained partnership members in the qualitative methods they would need to use to investigate the cases, such as interviewing techniques and document review.

The support team was also responsible for organizing and facilitating the collaborative research process. Over the course of the study, a core group of people from all of the partnerships and the support team interacted frequently through biweekly conference calls and 13 cross-case meetings. The individuals investigating each partnership's cases met regularly on their own and engaged in case-specific work with the support team through additional telephone calls and meetings. Learning from each other at every step, the Workgroup selected a set of cases to study, developed a way to assess influence in the cases, investigated the cases, and analyzed the case evidence.

Selection of the cases. In March 2006, the Workgroup selected a set of ten cases to study — two per partnership. We decided these cases "fit the bill" because they met three important criteria: they varied in the extent to which different kinds of people had been involved; the partnerships were excited about investigating them; and sufficient evidence was likely to be available to carry out the investigation.

In the study, the Workgroup wanted to pay particular attention to the voice and influence of people who were experiencing problems directly — especially the poorest, least educated, and most marginalized residents in the partnerships' communities. The purpose of the investigation was *not* to evaluate the partnerships on the basis of how influential these residents had been, however. That goal wouldn't have been helpful or even meaningful, since the involvement of different kinds of participants had varied quite a lot in the partnerships' work. Consequently, the pattern of influence was likely to have varied, too.

Instead, the purpose of the study was to learn what had been supporting and hindering the influence of people in various groups so the partnerships could institute changes in their practices that would help them optimize influence in the future. For this kind of study, the lack of consistency in the partnerships' past experiences was extremely valuable because we needed a set of cases that varied in terms of the extent to which different kinds of people had been involved, how they had been involved, and how their involvement influenced what the partnerships ultimately did. To be sure the set of cases spanned this range, each partnership investigated one case where the poorest, least educated and most marginalized members of their community were thought to have had substantial influence and another case where more advantaged community members were thought to have been the main drivers.

To make the work worthwhile, the cases had to be meaningful to the people from the partnerships and exciting for them to investigate. Although the purpose of the study was to help the Workgroup learn about the voice and influence of different people in community participation processes, the cases that the partnerships selected were not about the implementation of a "community participation process," per se. Instead, they were about ways that members of the partnerships' communities grappled with serious and challenging issues over time. This frame of reference — which is how the Pathways partnerships think about their work — is very different than most of the reports about community participation in the literature, which deal with the implementation of a particular inclusive practice (such as a community visioning session or a citizens jury) or participatory program (such as a community-based participatory research project or a comprehensive community initiative). Using the partnerships' case-based frame of reference meant that we would not define "community participation process" in advance. Instead, the investigation would search for all of the opportunities people had to be involved in each case. The sum of these opportunities would constitute that case's community participation process.

Finally, we needed to be sure that sufficient evidence would be available to investigate each of the cases. This evidence would need to come from two sources: documents that recorded the critical events of the case as they were happening in real time; and people who could provide their knowledge of past events through interviews or group discussions during the course of the investigation. When critical documents or participants could not be found, otherwise attractive cases were knocked out of the running.

The Workgroup's approach to assessing influence. To embark on the study, the Workgroup needed a clear way to think about whose voices had been influential in the partnerships' cases. We did this in the most direct way possible — by focusing on the ***ideas*** of the various people in community participation processes. This approach would enable us to determine who had a voice in the cases, who had an influential voice, and whether the pattern of influence mattered.

- *Who had a voice?* People use their voices to express ideas they want others to hear. So if the study could ***identify the ideas that particular people expressed*** in the cases, we would be able to determine who had a voice in the process as well as what they said with their voices.
- *Who had an influential voice?* To find out whose voices had been influential in the cases, we would need to ***track different people's ideas over time to see what happened as a result of their ideas being expressed.*** For example, if an idea was about an issue that mattered to certain people in the community, was something proposed or undertaken to address that issue? If an idea described how an issue should be addressed, was that idea incorporated into a plan that was developed or an action that was taken? In our study, ideas that were used to make something happen would be considered to be influential; other ideas would not. The extent to which different participant's ideas were acted upon would reflect the extent to which they had influence in the process.
- *Did the pattern of influence matter?* To find out how the pattern of influence mattered, we would need to ***relate the ideas that were and were not used in***

each case to what the community participation process was ultimately able to accomplish.

Looking at their cases in this way involved some fundamental shifts in thinking for the Pathways partnerships. One of the reasons they hadn't thought to look at the influence of different participants before was because they — like many other partnerships — had a unitary notion of community. Each of the partnerships was community-driven. The leaders and members of the partnership, and the people who participated in the partnership's work in other ways, were from the community. Therefore, the partnership spoke with one voice — the voice of the community. If we think of that unitary community voice as white light, the Workgroup's approach to assessing influence is akin to introducing a prism. The different colors that emerge from the prism are the voices of the individual participants, which were previously hidden.

Another fundamental shift — for virtually everyone in the Workgroup — was paying close attention to the ideas of different participants. These ideas are the focal point, or unit of observation, of our study. To assess influence in each of the cases, we would need to look for information that had not been included in the partnerships' original narratives of the cases: what all of the ideas were; who expressed them; when and under what conditions; whether the ideas were used; and how that mattered.

We would also need to think about potentially missing ideas. We could do that by identifying people with relevant connections to each case who either didn't have opportunities to participate in the process or didn't contribute ideas during the opportunities they had.

Investigation of the cases. We recognized from the outset that this would be a challenging investigation. Because the work involved such fundamental shifts in thinking, we would need to be very clear about the information we were looking for in each case. We would need to avoid making subjective interpretations of that information and be willing to accept solid, corroborated evidence, even if it differed from what we initially thought we

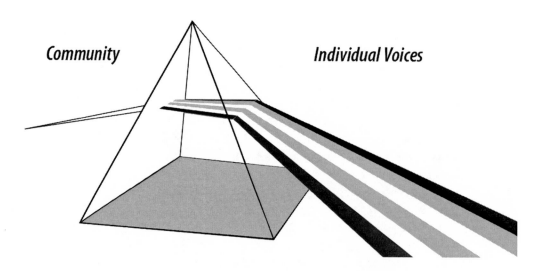

Individual Voices Emerging from the Prism

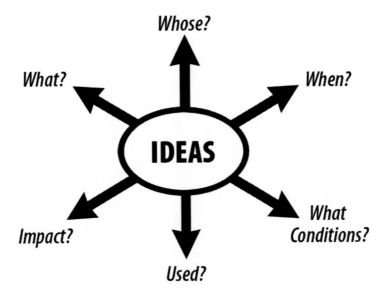

Tracking Ideas

would find. Since our goal was to conduct a comparative case study, we would need to be sure that the investigation was carried out consistently across all the partnerships and cases.

To meet these challenges, the Workgroup developed a number of tools to support the investigation of each case: an initial set of questions to guide the search for evidence; timelines laying out key events; catalogues to keep track of all of the source material; guides for designing interviews and group discussions; work sheets to record relevant information from individual documents and transcripts; and tables to record all of the case evidence.

The original set of questions that we prepared for each case used several strategies to help us find needed information about different people's ideas. One strategy began with the ***main ideas*** in the case. If the case was about a problem, such as a need for more suitable housing or escalating levels of crime and violence in the community, we asked: Who said this was a problem? When? What did they say about it? Who was experiencing the problem directly? What do we know about those people's ideas? If the case was

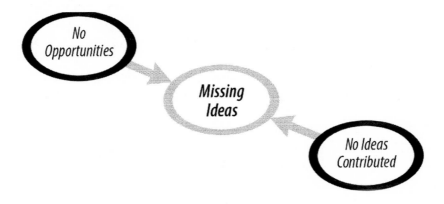

Missing Ideas

about an action, such as establishing community centers, a minigrant program, or a "Poor Man's Bank," we asked: Who proposed this action? When and why? What was the problem they were trying to address? Who were they trying to help? What do we know about those people's ideas? Who was involved in designing the action that was eventually carried out? What ideas did they contribute?

A complementary strategy began with the *opportunities* that people had to contribute ideas in the case. In addition to the structured mechanisms that were used to engage community members in many of the cases— such as visioning sessions, summits, focus groups, and surveys— we looked for other venues where people came together to express ideas, make decisions, and take action, such as formal and informal meetings, conversations, rallies, and protests. For each opportunity, we asked: When did it take place? Who was involved? Were there any limitations on who could attend or what they could say? Is there evidence about what different people said?

The third strategy began with the different groups of people — or *"players"* — who were involved in the case. We paid close attention to the poorest, least educated, and most marginalized residents in the community, who were frequently experiencing the main problems in the case or were the targets of its main actions. We also looked for other individuals, groups, and organizations—from both within and outside the community — who stimulated or organized what happened in the cases or contributed to the events in other ways. For each player, we asked: What do we know about their ideas? When and where did they have opportunities to contribute their ideas? How did the actions that were taken in the case affect them?

These questions led us to numerous sources of needed information in the 10 cases. Over the course of the investigation, we reviewed 1,025 documents and conducted 130 interviews and group discussions.

Initially, we displayed our evidence in case-specific tables that helped us track different players' ideas. The tables had vertical columns for each of the players in the case and horizontal rows for each of the opportunities in the case where players could contribute ideas, arranged in chronological order. The cells in the table were filled with the ideas that particular players expressed during particular opportunities. Different kinds of ideas— ideas about problems, actions, and process— were represented by different colors.

These tables helped us in a number of ways. They showed us when different players in a case had opportunities to contribute their ideas and what their ideas were at those times. Looking across a horizontal row, we could see which players participated in each opportunity and the range of ideas those players expressed. Tracking ideas over time, we could see how ideas about problems led to proposals for action, and how actions that were proposed or taken led to new problems. Tracking ideas across players, we could see when different players shared ideas and when one player acted on another player's idea.

We created another set of tables to record the impacts that were experienced by the different players in each case. These tables were organized in the same way as the idea tables except that the cells were filled with impacts rather than ideas.

Analysis of the case evidence. The goal of our analysis was to identify:

• Whose ideas were influential at the points that determined what happened in each case

- The factors that affected the potential for different players' ideas to be influential
- How the ideas that were, and were not, influential were related to what was ultimately accomplished in each case.

The case tables were too unwieldy to use for this purpose, so we presented the evidence in the tables in a complementary format — as a set of case lists. In these lists, we identified and defined the various categories of players in the case. We organized all of the problem ideas in the case into thematic groupings so we could appreciate similarities in the ideas that different players expressed, even if the ideas were expressed at different times and opportunities. We presented all of the action ideas that were proposed by the players in chronological order, distinguishing actions that were taken from those that were not. We also presented the impacts that were experienced by the players.

Since every entry in the case list was linked to a particular player, we were able to create player-specific lists that presented the problem ideas, action proposals, and impacts that related to each of the players. We also prepared player-specific opportunity grids that identified the opportunities each player had to contribute ideas in the case and described the conditions of those opportunities. These player-specific lists and opportunity grids demonstrated the power of our investigative prism. For the first time, we could clearly see each case from the perspective of its different participants.

We used the lists and opportunity grids to conduct our analysis of each case. First, we distinguished the ideas in the case that were influential from those that were not. We defined a problem idea as being influential if it was addressed by any of the actions that were taken in the case or if it could be linked to an untaken action that was proposed by someone other than, or in addition to, the player who expressed the problem. We defined an action idea as being influential if the action was ultimately carried out. Then we used the player-specific lists to see which of each player's ideas were influential and which were not, to determine the extent to which each players' ideas were influential, and to characterize differences in influence among players.

Next, we compared the opportunity grids for the various players in the case, looking for differences in the timing, number, or conditions of their opportunities that could account for differences in the influence of their ideas.

Finally, we looked at how the case impacted each of the players. To gauge the extent to which each player's problems were addressed, we related the problems they expressed to the impacts they experienced. We also characterized the other impacts each player experienced and compared players according to the extent to which their problems were addressed and the extent to which they experienced other beneficial and adverse impacts.

Influence Revealed

We thought our work was nearly done when we had completed the investigation and analysis of the cases, but, in fact, we had only laid the foundation for understanding voice and influence in community participation processes. Our exploration continued, moving from the particular to the general, as we wrote narratives of each of the cases, conducted a rigorous cross-case analysis, and considered how we and others could apply what we had learned to optimize influence in practice. In the subsequent sections of this book, we share our findings—which turned out to be a lot more than any of us expected. Below is an overview of what's to come.

Case Narratives

In the first stage of our exploration, we used the evidence from our investigation to learn about influence under the particular circumstances of each of the ten cases in our study:

- Community Voices Against Violence in Cass Lake, Minnesota
- Housing for Single Mothers in Humboldt Park, Chicago
- A "Poor Man's Bank" in the Southeast Oklahoma Enterprise Community
- A Workforce Alliance Minigrant Program in the Mississippi Delta
- The Community Leadership Team of Story County, Iowa
- Developing a Professionalization Curriculum in the Mississippi Delta
- Revitalizing Cass Lake, Minnesota
- Community Centers in Southeastern Oklahoma
- The Incorporation of Beyond Welfare in Ames, Iowa
- Saving a Mural in Humboldt Park, Chicago

The evidence enabled us to write vivid, detailed stories, which reveal—for the first time—the voices of all of the players in the case. These reconstructed narratives make up the next section of the book. Each story is followed by our analysis of the case, which identifies who was involved; what the major impacts were; whose ideas were influential at the critical points that determined what happened; and how the accomplishments and limitations in the case were related to ideas that were, and were not, influential.

Cross-Case Analysis

The individual case stories and analyses were interesting and valuable, but our larger objective was to see if we could identify any generalizable findings by looking at the ten cases as a whole. Since there was so much information to get our arms around, it took longer than expected to conduct this cross-case analysis. But the effort was worth it because it led to an important and unexpected discovery. Comparing and combining findings across the cases, we uncovered a common pathway that players' ideas need to travel in order to be influential in community participation processes.

This pathway explains how participation processes give players an influential voice — through opportunities that enable them to express ideas they care about, to communicate

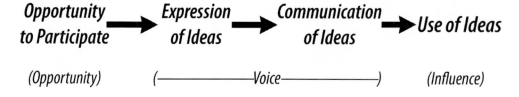

| Opportunity to Participate | → | Expression of Ideas | → | Communication of Ideas | → | Use of Ideas |

(Opportunity)   (——————Voice——————)   (Influence)

The Pathway of Ideas

their ideas to others who can help move them forward, and to have their ideas be used as a basis for decisions and actions. We found that players' ideas need to get through all of the steps of the pathway in order to be influential. If they are blocked at any step along the way, they lose their potential for influence.

In Chapter 11, we discuss this pathway in detail, presenting the case evidence on which it is based. Using the analogy of a track meet to describe how the ideas in the cases moved along the pathway, we identify the factors that determined which players' ideas moved forward at each step and how the impacts in the cases related to the ideas that did, and did not, advance.

We—and many others who aspire to realize the promise of community participation—want our participation processes to promote the voice and influence of historically excluded groups. But our study found that the ideas of marginalized and ordinary residents are far less likely to get through all of the steps in the pathway than the ideas of other players. In other words, participation processes are inadvertently recreating the inequities they were intended to address in the first place! If we want to realize our aspirations, we need to level the playing field.

Application to Practice

In the final chapter, we return to the questions that spurred our study, identifying ways that we and others can use what we learned to make the playing field more level for historically excluded groups and, by doing so, move toward realizing the promise of community participation.

When we began the study, neither we nor anyone else in the field had methods to determine if, or to what extent, our processes were promoting the voice and influence of historically excluded groups. Now we know how to tell if we're doing what we want to be doing—by tracking the ideas of different players over time.

We learned that it's worth investing more effort to assure that marginalized and ordinary residents have an influential voice in our processes, and we now have knowledge and tools that can help us do that. Our study identified numerous hurdles that block the ideas of marginalized and ordinary residents from being influential in participation processes. But for every hurdle we identified in the cases, we found examples in other cases—or in other opportunities in the same case—where supportive strategies moved ideas across the barrier. Consequently, we know all of the hurdles can be overcome.

The hurdles and supports in the pathway provide us and other practitioners with a framework for distinguishing what we want to keep on doing in our processes from what we need to change. This framework also enables us to learn from other practitioners who are using supportive strategies that address the particular hurdles that our own processes need to overcome.

We learned that opportunities are the places where improvements can be made in participation processes and that the opportunities that comprise a process go well beyond specially constructed participation exercises. Our study shows how the voice and influence of historically excluded groups can be enhanced by changing who is involved in opportunities, the kinds of opportunities in which they are involved, the conditions of those opportunities, and the relationship among the opportunities in the process. Based on these findings, we have developed tools that practitioners can use to anticipate problems in processes they are planning so they can institute needed supports beforehand.

The findings and tools from our study show us what we need to do to realize our aspirations. But in the course of conducting our study and reflecting on the findings, we recognized that applying what we've learned involves changes in mindset as well as practice. We close the book by discussing four ways that our thinking about community participation is changing:

- From involving marginalized and ordinary residents in the process to giving them influence through the process
- From seeking to speak in one voice to eliciting many voices
- From making assumptions about the people we want to help to hearing their ideas directly
- From giving historically excluded groups influence at the margins to assuring they have influence that counts.

* * *

The case narratives in Chapters 1 through 10 can be read in any order. We have ordered them in a way that flows for us:

- Community Voices Against Violence in Cass Lake, Minnesota
- Housing for Single Mothers in Humboldt Park, Chicago
- A "Poor Man's Bank" in the Southeast Oklahoma Enterprise Community
- A Workforce Alliance Minigrant Program in the Mississippi Delta
- The Community Leadership Team of Story County, Iowa
- Developing a Professionalization Curriculum in the Mississippi Delta
- Revitalizing Cass Lake, Minnesota
- Community Centers in Southeastern Oklahoma
- The Incorporation of Beyond Welfare in Ames, Iowa
- Saving a Mural in Humboldt Park, Chicago

But they can be read in other ways as well, for example, by pairing the cases related to each of the five community partnerships:

Community Leadership Team of Beyond Welfare (Story County, Iowa)
- The Community Leadership Team of Story County, Iowa
- The Incorporation of Beyond Welfare in Ames, Iowa

Humboldt Park Empowerment Partnership (Chicago, Illinois)
- Housing for Single Mothers in Humboldt Park, Chicago
- Saving a Mural in Humboldt Park, Chicago

MIRACLE Group (Cass Lake, Minnesota)
- Community Voices Against Violence in Cass Lake, Minnesota
- Revitalizing Cass Lake, Minnesota

Southeast Oklahoma Champion and Enterprise Community (Choctaw, McCurtain, and Pushmataha Counties, Oklahoma)

- A "Poor Man's Bank" in the Southeast Oklahoma Enterprise Community
- Community Centers in Southeastern Oklahoma

Tri-County Workforce Alliance (Coahoma, Quitman, and Bolivar Counties, Mississippi)
- A Workforce Alliance Minigrant Program in the Mississippi Delta
- Developing a Professionalization Curriculum in the Mississippi Delta

To support such flexibility, each case was written to stand on its own. Familiarity with any of the other cases is neither expected nor required. We believe the benefits of providing readers with this flexibility outweighs the trade-offs involved. Readers will find that some of the same contextual information is provided in both of the cases from each community and that we use the same language to explain the organization of the analysis section in each of the cases.

1

Community Voices
Against Violence
in Cass Lake, Minnesota

The Story

On August 1, 1998, a group of about 150 people marched through the streets of Cass Lake in north-central Minnesota.[1] The march ended in a "Peace Rally" at Dreamcatcher Park, where the participants wrote the names of loved ones who had been lost to violence on a banner that had been specially made for the occasion. The event that precipitated the rally was the brutal murder and rape of a 54-year-old woman who had been out for a walk in the early morning of May 14. The crime was committed by a 19-year-old man who had been drinking and partying with some friends the previous night. He was a member of the Leech Lake Band of the Ojibwe, whose reservation surrounds the small city of Cass Lake. The victim, who was white, had owned a resort on the western edge of the reservation.

Vivid reports of the incident in newspapers around the state sent shockwaves through the local community. But crime and violence had been prominent features of everyday life in the area for some time and, as the names on the banner documented, many households had experienced some form of violent death directly. About a month before the rally, 40 people, including white and Ojibwe residents, had gathered at the Cass Lake Family Resource Center to "take back our community we have lost to crime, violence, drugs, gangs, and alcohol...." Believing that "the common values of mutual respect and courtesy are traditional in all cultures," they created "Community Voices Against Violence" as a way to "stand together to save our children, parents, elders and loved ones from the sorrow and fear caused by acts of violence in our community."[2]

The Peace Rally was the group's first action. It gave Ojibwe and white residents of the city and the reservation an opportunity to come together publicly to commemorate their losses and express the emotions they had in common: outrage, sadness, fear, and anguish. It also allowed them to stand alongside their neighbors and say "we're not going to take this anymore."[3]

"People like me ... were actually scared"

The Leech Lake Reservation was established in 1855 when the Leech Lake Band of the Ojibwe signed a treaty giving a large portion of north-central Minnesota to the United States, retaining 670,000 acres for themselves.[4] Over the next 150 years, the Band lost control over much of this land, along with its valuable resources. Beginning in 1887, the federal government allowed parcels of land to be granted or sold to timber and railroad companies, profiting the non–Natives who owned and worked in those industries. In 1908, concerns about overly aggressive logging prompted the federal government to incorporate more than 40 percent of the reservation's land in the Chippewa National Forest. A homesteading boom brought white families to the reservation — so many, in fact, that they eventually outnumbered the Ojibwe, who now directly own less than 5 percent of the land under reservation jurisdiction. Most of the resorts that dot the shores of the reservation's 40 lakes are owned by white families.

Along with the loss of land and physical resources, the Leech Lake Band also faced the dismantling of its tribal culture and authority.[5] From the late 19th century to the mid–20th century, the federal government tried to "de–Indianize the Indians" in order to assimilate them into the mainstream. Ojibwe traditions and ceremonies were prohibited by federal policies. Children were sent to English-speaking boarding schools, hundreds of miles away from their parents, tribe, and native language. The Band also lost the right to control many of its own activities. States and counties assumed legal authority over Native Americans on and off the reservations. Until 1972, members of the Band could not even hunt or fish on their own reservation free of state regulation.

Deprived of the means to support themselves, many members of the Band fell into poverty. In the mid–1990's 32 percent of the 4,400 Ojibwe on the reservation were living in poverty, compared to 12 percent of the reservation's 5,200 white residents. Band members were scattered across the reservation in a patchwork of small, isolated villages and towns. Some lived in low-income housing that had been funded by the federal government. The most notorious of these developments was known as "Tract 33."

At that time, the city of Cass Lake was also in a state of decline. Situated in the midst of the reservation, the city had been incorporated almost 100 years before by white settlers involved in timber and railroad companies. For many years, the city flourished as a logging and wood processing center and as one of the largest railyards in northern Minnesota. During that period, it was home to over 2,000 residents, most of whom were white. Once the old-growth forest was logged out, however, and the associated industries and the rail terminal closed down, hundreds of good-paying jobs were lost. By the mid 1990's, only about 800 people lived in Cass Lake, and Native Americans comprised two-thirds of the population. Twenty-nine percent of the city's residents were living in poverty — more than three times the state average. The proportion of Native Americans in poverty (34 percent) was more than twice that of whites (15 percent).

As poverty and a general sense of hopelessness became more pervasive, both the city and the reservation experienced growing problems with alcoholism, drug abuse, crime, and violence. Gangs began to form, and the area became a major drug-trafficking distribution point.[6] By the mid–1990's, the rates of murder, nonfatal shootings, beatings, rapes, domestic violence, school violence, breaking and entering, thefts, vandalism, and driving under the influence of alcohol or drugs made the area, per capita, "more dangerous than the worst neighborhood in Minneapolis or New York City."[7]

In this environment, many people were living in fear. As one resident recalled, "I didn't feel safe in town, you know I was always looking over my shoulder and always when I parked my vehicle outside I was always checking on it to make sure nothing was happening."[8] A woman who worked in the local hospital at the time said that break-ins and destruction to cars and the buildings was so great that "the hospital hired security guards to cover every shift and all doors were really locked. We were kind of in lock up from then on...."[9] A former Chairman of the Leech Lake Band described the situation on the reservation: "We started to see more beatings take place and more violence taking place ... Track 33 was bad and it just seemed to be something like a wildfire." Another member of the Band told him: "At night you can't sleep around here. There are cars racing up and down the street, and there are gunshots periodically and people coming to my door and knocking and wanting to come in, so I have to stay up and watch my house."[10]

Much of the crime was being committed by youth — particularly Native American males — and some of them were afraid, too. As an Ojibwe man who was a teenager at the time recalled: "I was involved, you know, in a lot of car thefts, just about anything from beatings from fighting to getting in the, starting to sell drugs.... Some of the people I grew up with, they are doing prison time for murder and I got other friends sitting in prison for attempted murder and these are the ones I grew up with and called, you know, my brothers... It was a rapid change just from when I was growing up ... how bad it picked up.... People like me at the time ... were actually scared."[11]

The MIRACLE Group's Public Safety Committee

In 1996, a group of community leaders in Cass Lake came together to do something about the city's decline. They called themselves the MIRACLE Group — an acronym for "Moving Ideas and Relationships for the Advancement of Cass Lake's Economy." The members of the MIRACLE Group were very concerned about crime and violence in the area because they believed these issues were integral to rebuilding the economy. Concerns about safety in the community and the schools were driving families away and discouraging others from moving in.[12] Crime and violence were also contributing to the loss of business by area resorts and stores. To achieve two of the group's main objectives — strengthening tourism and revitalizing the downtown business district — the situation would need to be brought under control.

The members of the MIRACLE Group recognized that the multiple overlapping jurisdictions in the Cass Lake area complicated everything they were trying to do, including their efforts to address crime and violence. Within a five-mile radius of the city there were six governing bodies (Cass County Board, Cass Lake City Council, Leech Lake Reservation Tribal Council, Pike Bay Town Board, U. S. Forest Service, and Beltrami County Board); three court systems (Cass County, Beltrami County, and Leech Lake Reservation); six law enforcement agencies (Cass County Sheriff, Beltrami County Sheriff, Cass Lake Police, Leech Lake Law Enforcement, Leech Lake Department of Resource Management, and U. S. Forest Service), and two school districts (Cass Lake/Bena and Bug-O-Nay-Ge-Shig Schools).[13] Going out a little further, two more counties came into play: Hubbard and Itasca. The entities in these numerous jurisdictions didn't have a strong record of cooperating with each other, and relations between the reservation and the federal and local jurisdictions were strained by the long history of mistreatment of Band members by the white community and recent changes in legal authority. To make sure that offenses were covered throughout the area, including the "corners," people needed to start talking to each other across jurisdictional boundaries.

In late 1996, the MIRACLE Group formed a "Public Safety Committee," inviting law enforcement professionals from the various jurisdictions in the area to become members. Invitations were also extended to providers of social services, including Louise Smith, the director of the Cass Lake Family Resource Center.[14] The "Family Center," as it was known, had opened in 1994, and Smith became director a year later. She was a white woman who married into the Leech Lake Band and lived on the reservation with her family. Most of the Center's clients were also Band members, living on the reservation or in the city. Smith was a good choice for the committee because she was very aware of the problems with crime and violence in the area—both from her own personal experiences as well as those of her clients. She was also close to Randy Finn, an Ojibwe man who owned property and businesses in Cass Lake and was soon to become the MIRACLE Group's leader.

Community Voices Against Violence

In 1998, when people in the area heard about the rape and murder of the resort owner and were trying to grapple with the vicious crime, Louise Smith and some of the other service providers at the Family Center got together to talk about it. As she recalled: "When this lady died, we knew that there were white people that were just blaming Native people because the community didn't control the majority of the violence that was happening among the Native people. Native people were feeling so bad, because it was one of their own that did this terrible thing. I remember gathering together with this group that had been meeting ... at the Family Center in our conference room. From what I remember, [the group asked] what can we do?"[15]

They decided to invite more people to a meeting at the Family Center on July 1, and to have Randy Finn—Smith's friend who was the leader of the MIRACLE Group—facilitate the meeting. About 40 people came, white and Ojibwe; most worked for social service organizations and other agencies around the area. The participants gave themselves a name, "Community Voices Against Violence," and created a brief mission statement[16]:

Community Voices Against Violence believes that common values of mutual respect and courtesy are traditional in all cultures. We stand together to save our children, parents, elders, and loved ones from the sorrow and fear caused by acts of violence in our community. The purpose of Community Voices Against Violence is to take back our community we have lost to crime, violence, gangs, drugs, and alcohol and create an atmosphere of zero tolerance. Through decisive leadership, education, community support, and interactions, we demand strict accountability and swift justice for those who commit crimes and violent acts in our community.[17]

As their first action, the members of the new organization—called "CVAV" for short—planned the Peace Rally that would be held on August 1. According to Smith, they were hoping the rally would "make a statement to the community that there were people who cared, that there were people who wanted to get something done and make this community able to turn around ... [and] with that statement we would draw people in. I think that we were just operating as a bunch of service providers that came together to do the best that we could."[18] Mary Helen Pelton, superintendent of the Cass Lake/Bena school district, created the banner for community members to record the names of loved ones who had been lost to violence.

The Peace Rally had a strong impact on the 150 people involved. It was the first time that many had ever seen whites and Native Americans participating together in a public event. As Eli Hunt, who was Chairman of the Leech Lake Band of the Ojibwe at the time, recalled: "What stands out in my mind, is that there's a gathering of citizens that got together both Native and non–Native to just kind of lay the cards out on the table to say, 'This is what we see happening in the area. I want to organize and try to identify some things that we can do to respond or to curb some of this nonsense that's going on.'"[19] The rally also helped participants emotionally. "The people that were involved felt really good" said Smith. "It always helps when somebody is out there expressing their pain for somebody else, and they're showing it. It helps them come to terms with their own feelings, their own pain and to start the healing because they've done something."[20]

After the rally, CVAV members continued to meet — weekly at first, then monthly — to talk about their experiences with crime and violence. Sharing these experiences was never easy; it also wasn't safe for many people to do. From years of conversations with clients at the Family Center, Louise Smith knew that people risked retaliation by perpetrators or family members if they talked about specific criminal acts. Even worse, in some of the incidents, the perpetrators were the police. Smith had heard numerous stories of Native American women who had been raped by the police and Native American youth who had been violently threatened and harassed by the police. Fear had prevented all of these victims from reporting the crimes. In addition, Smith had heard rumors that members of the Cass Lake police force were involved in trafficking drugs and stolen goods. It was very dangerous to talk publicly about that.[21]

In CVAV meetings at the Family Center, which was perceived as a relatively "safe" place, people in the community began to share their stories with each other.[22] Having such an opportunity was very important to the service providers, community residents, and public officials who participated. According to a city official who was a regular participant in CVAV from its inception, "...the big thing with the violent situation [is that] people want to hear their story, people want to tell their story. Because if you are victim of a violent crime, you want to be able to tell somebody, and it's really important that somebody listens to you. They may not be able to solve any of your problems, but long as you can listen, if you can get it off your chest, you are going to feel better."[23]

CVAV members also planned further actions at their meetings, including another Peace Rally and a series of community forums about law enforcement and the judicial system. The idea for these forums came from service providers and officials in CVAV who believed that "we needed to educate the community, because people don't understand why they do what they do. They don't understand why the courts make the judgments that they do. They don't understand what happens in between in the probation arena...."[24] If residents understood how the system worked and the constraints that law enforcement officials faced, they would be able to tell if the conduct of police, prosecutors, and judges was appropriate or inappropriate.

The forums took place at the Palace Casino, a small establishment just a few miles outside the city of Cass Lake, which was owned by the Leech Lake Band. In the first, held on September 30, 1998, officers from the various jurisdictions in the area talked about law enforcement. In the second, held on November 20, 1998, judges spoke about the adult and juvenile court systems. In the third, on March 30, 1999, prosecutors discussed "What Happens between an Arrest and the Court Sentence."

In addition to providing useful information to the 50 to 100 community residents who attended, the forums gave the area's law enforcement professionals opportunities to talk about the jurisdictional problems they were facing and what might be done to resolve those problems. At the time, the Leech Lake Band was beginning to establish its own police force and judicial system to enforce the civil regulatory authority it had recently acquired over its members on the reservation. The Band also wanted its tribal police force to play a role in enforcing criminal law on the reservation, which previously had been under federal authority but was now being transferred to the states. The law enforcement officials at the forums supported the development of the reservation's tribal police force and judicial system. They also discussed the need to develop more consistent regulations across the jurisdictions—for example, around youth curfews, truancy, and housing eviction policies—and to cooperate in enforcing those regulations.[25]

The Youth Summits

Young people were at the heart of the problems with crime and violence in the Cass Lake area. Youth—particularly Native American males—were committing many of the crimes. In 1997, there were over 1,100 youth arrests for offenses ranging from assault, burglary, theft, property damage, weapons, and drug possession to disorderly conduct, underage alcohol use, and trespassing.[26] Youth were also victims of violence, inflicted by themselves as well as others. One resident recalled that adults around Cass Lake were "mostly concerned about the kids ... there were suicides, a lot of drugs, there was gangs. People were seeing their kids kind of getting out of control and being very self abusive in different ways. The ... greatest concern was about the kids...."[27] A social service provider working with youth described the gangs as "something to belong to for these kids that have never belonged to anybody or anything.... They think its cool, but then ... they get to a point where they have to ... beat up somebody or steal a car, whatever their initiation thing is.... But if they don't do it, then they get the trouble and they get beat up ... like that one that got his fingernails ripped off. He was trying to leave the boys [the gang]. So that was their fear."[28] With so many Native American youth involved in crime, prejudice extended to those who weren't. "Everybody ... turns and walks on the other side of the street ... if they saw them coming."[29]

Members of CVAV cared about youth, but youth had not been included in CVAV's meetings, and CVAV was not focusing particular attention on youth issues. Others in the community were, however—the MIRACLE Group and the Leech Lake Tribal Council. In late 1996, Randy Finn put the establishment of a Boys & Girls Club on the agenda of the MIRACLE Group's Community Development Committee. A MIRACLE Group member recalled that they saw the Boys & Girls Club "as an answer, especially for the young kids. If we can get the young kids early before they have problems or if they have problems, that there is a safe place that they can be."[30] On the Leech Lake Reservation, the

Tribal Council was drawing up plans to develop its own youth services division. The need for youth programming was supported by a report on the developmental assets of 6th to 12th graders in the Cass Lake/Bena school district that was released in February 1997.[31] This report, prepared by the Search Institute for the school district, documented that the majority of these students lacked critically needed supports from their parents, teachers, and other adults in the community. Most of the students also lacked social competencies, a positive identity, positive values, and a commitment to learning.

In November 1998, two youth summits were held in the area. On November 2, the school system held a summit for students at the Cass Lake/Bena High School, and on November 20, the Leech Lake Tribal Council held a summit for about 200 reservation youth at the Leech Lake Palace Casino.[32] Prior to the high school summit, 59 students completed a survey that explored their community concerns, willingness to volunteer and serve on committees (for a Boys & Girls Club, Youth Service Advisory Council, and Community Education Advisory Council), and preferences for programming. At both summits, the youth broke out into smaller groups to talk about the problems they were facing and to propose possible solutions. Youth were actively involved in collecting and analyzing the data from the high school survey and in organizing and facilitating the discussions at the summits.

In the survey and both of the summits, the young people expressed many of the same concerns. The problems they identified most frequently included not having anything to do, violence, and drug and alcohol abuse by young people and adult family members. The notes from the breakout sessions at the summits paint a vivid picture of the kinds of crime and violence they were concerned about at the time: murder, suicide, rape, physical and emotional abuse by family members, stealing, vandalism, graffiti, shooting out street lights, car accidents related to drunk driving, truancy, and cheating. The youth related problems with crime and violence to boredom, substance abuse, peer pressure, and racism, which they said was causing fighting, arguing, name calling, and low self-esteem. They also mentioned the prejudice and harassment they were experiencing at the hands of the police.

Describing the environment in which they were living, the young people spoke about not having someone to talk to or something positive to believe in. Some were living in homes where they were neglected or abused by parents who had problems with alcohol, drugs, or gambling. In families like these, they lacked emotional support and discipline. The problems they identified in the broader community included poverty, dilapidated housing, unemployment, lack of spirituality, and "we live in all different communities!!!"[33] The emotional consequences were serious—the youth described deep feelings of depression, grief, and loss.

The young people who participated in the survey and the two summits in November 1998 proposed many possible solutions to address crime, violence, and the other problems they were experiencing. From the available records, it appears that some form of recreation center was at the top of the list. Repeatedly the youth proposed a place that would be open after school, in the evenings, and on weekends where they could "hang out," eat, and engage in a variety of activities, including sports, games, and entertainment. Some wanted these "rec centers" to include cultural programs, arts and crafts, tutoring, and a place for homework as well.

In the breakout sessions at the summits, the young people emphasized the importance of having good role models. Toward that end they requested adult mentors, peer mentors (including youth who had left gangs), more Native American teachers in the public schools, more people who practiced cross-cultural respect, and people who could educate others about different cultures and respect. To strengthen their families, they wanted more activities that family members could engage in together as well as rehabilitation and counseling programs to help their parents deal with alcohol and drug abuse, gambling, domestic abuse, separation, divorce, and unemployment. For further support, the youth asked for counselors to help them deal with grief and crises. They also proposed expanding youth involvement in traditional practices, like talking circles.

To help them stay and succeed in school, the youth requested that schools provide them with more help, including tutoring and more class time for homework. To help deter crime, they proposed having locker checks and cameras in the schools. About 60 percent of the students who responded to the high school survey said that a "safe house" was needed for youth in the community.

In addition to enabling youth to identify problems and potential solutions, the summit that had been convened by the Leech Lake Tribal Council on November 20 also created a mission statement: "We are united for the purpose of encouraging youth to have a voice in their reservation, community, schools, and home. To create opportunities for all youth to be more involved in their own community so they can see a chance for their future. To help them in their struggles against alcohol, drugs, and violence. We are dedicated to making changes in the community to help youth and their families see that a positive future is possible." Following that summit, the Leech Lake Tribal Council passed a resolution to "prioritize, identify, and fund youth activities on the Leech Lake Reservation for the years 1999 and 2000."[34] The resolution established a Youth Committee consisting of representatives of the reservation's Social Service Division, Housing Division, and the Veteran's Memorial Programs. The Council also began looking for an outside consultant to run another reservation-wide youth summit.

On April 16, 1999, the Leech Lake Tribal Council held a summit for youth 10–18 years old from each district area of the reservation. During the summit, the youth elected two of their peers—one male and one female—to represent them on the Tribal Council's Youth Committee. The youth also formed a committee to begin the process for developing Youth Councils in each of the reservation's communities.[35]

After that summit, the Youth Committee submitted a proposal to the Tribal Council for a "Youth Activity Program." The proposal recommended restructuring the Leech Lake Veteran's Memorial Recreation and Sports Program to hire new staff residing in each of the reservation's communities to provide the following activities for youth: a recreation/sports activity at least two times each week; a health/fitness activity at least two times each week; a cultural activity once a week; and a tutoring or counseling session twice a month. It also stated that transportation would be provided to make it possible for youth to participate in these activities.[36]

During the same period, Randy Finn, other members of MIRACLE Group, and other adults in the community moved forward to establish a Boys & Girls Club in the area, which opened in January 2000. They wanted to be connected to a national organization (Boys & Girls Clubs of America) "so that it [youth programming] won't be a political hot potato" in the community.[37] Reservation officials, on the other hand, viewed Boys & Girls as an "outside" organization; "We don't need them coming in here telling us how to raise our kids."[38] The Tribal Council's desire for independent control over programs affecting youth on the reservation led to the development of its Youth Activity Program.

As both of these initiatives were underway, five Ojibwe youth wrote the following letter "to the Cass Lake Community:"

> We are a group of youth from different communities who all attend the Cass Lake-Bena School district and who are asking for help from you. There are many of you who say you are concerned about the youth who are getting in trouble. These few are the ones that are giving all Cass Lake youth a bad name. There are many of us who are not getting into trouble and are trying to be community leaders, but we need your help to succeed. We have talked to a lot of other youth, and we all agree we need a building while we wait for the Community Rec Center to be built. We need a place to go so we can stay away from negative activities. It doesn't have to be anything fancy for now, but big enough to hold 35 to 40 youth. It could have a pool table, foosball table, board games, etc. We want to have a place where we can get together, a place to meet our friends and have somebody to talk to when we have problems. We think it is time that people stop talking about how bad we are and start doing something to help us. If anybody can help us, we can be reached through Naomi at the Cass Lake Family Center. Thank you.[39]

Joint Assistance and the Community Survey

In the spring of 1999, CVAV seemed to run out of steam. According to Louise Smith "...we didn't know what to do next. We truly just didn't know where to go. We now had people working together. The law enforcement agencies were beginning to work together, which was always a problem before — the reservations ... the city ... counties."[40] Other groups in the community were focusing on youth. So CVAV members decided to get outside help. They requested and received joint assistance from two nonprofits that often worked together: the Center for Reducing Rural Violence (CRRV) and the Upper Midwest Community Policing Institute (UMCPI). CRRV "helps rural communities develop and implement comprehensive, holistic strategies for reducing and preventing violence." UMCPI works with law enforcement agencies regionally and nationally, "building bridges between law enforcement professionals and the communities they serve in order to create safer neighborhoods and reduce the fear of crime."[41]

The CRRV organizer who worked with CVAV and others in the Cass Lake area explained how the joint assistance worked:

> We walk in and work with a small group to identify what we called an initial priority — trying to get the group to narrow their focus to something manageable. We start off with an organizing process with selecting stakeholders, a broad representative group from the community, anyone who has an investment in the process. We take them through a learning phase. During that time what they're doing is trying to learn more about the reality of violence in their community using data and research. And also working on learning more about best practices and what has worked in other communities to address the particular priority that they want to work on. After the learning phase ... is a data collection and what we call the data dump, that's part of the learning where we're looking at real live data

rather than perceptions or fears. We go into an action planning process, [then it] moves into an implementation phase, and ends up with celebration and monitoring.[42]

The focus on stakeholders changed the nature of CVAV meetings. The CRRV organizer defined stakeholders as "agency people" — representatives of the governmental and nonprofit organizations in the area that could have an impact on violence and crime. People involved in many of these agencies had been members of CVAV all along. The application for assistance from UMCPI was prepared by CVAV members who were working for the Cass County Sheriff's Department, the Cass Lake Police Department, the Leech Lake Reservation Department of Public Safety, the Cass Lake Family Center, the Family Safety Network, Youth and Family Services, the Leech Lake Family Violence Prevention/Intervention Program, Cass Lake/Bena Community Education, and the Law Enforcement Task Force. CVAV members were also among some of the other "potential stakeholders" listed in the request: the Mayor of Cass Lake; the Chairman of the Leech Lake Reservation; the Superintendent of the Cass Lake/Bena School District; the Chairperson of the Leech Lake Reservation Housing Authority; the Chief of the Leech Lake Reservation Police Department; and the pastor of the Christian & Missionary Alliance Church.[43] Once they were formalized as a stakeholder group, however, they came to CVAV meetings as representatives of their agencies rather than as an expression of personal concern. Since attendance was now part of their jobs, the meetings were held during the day instead of in the evening. That made participation more difficult for community residents who worked for organizations other than the stakeholder agencies.

With CRRV's "systems approach," the content of CVAV meetings shifted from sharing experiences of violence and organizing rallies and forums to priority setting and planning. Many of the residents who had participated in CVAV previously weren't interested in developing action plans, particularly when an issue that was important to them was eliminated from CRRV's "achievable" agenda. People who weren't representing agencies stopped coming, and Louise Smith recalled that was when "I saw, personally, the life kind of go out of the group."[44]

The stakeholders who continued to be involved in CVAV — and new ones who joined — worked with UMCPI to survey people in the Cass Lake area about their perceptions of violence. Based on the experiences that community members had shared in the earlier CVAV meetings, the stakeholders identified the kinds of information they wanted to obtain, and staff from UMCPI, working with a researcher from the University of Minnesota, developed the questionnaire.

In the fall of 1999, 14 community members took the survey door-to-door to people who lived within a five-mile radius of the city of Cass Lake. This area included the city itself, Pike Bay Township, and the parts of the Leech Lake Reservation that were closest to the city, including Tract 33. The survey explored people's perceptions about the quality of life in the community, perceived community problems, their involvement in the community, and perceptions about law enforcement. Overall, 338 residents completed the survey; 83 percent were Native American (which matched the demographics of the area), and most were adults (only 4 percent were 21 or younger).

Almost everyone who responded to the survey thought that crime and violence were serious problems in the area. Other problems that more than half of the residents believed to be serious included alcohol and drug abuse, unsupervised children and teenagers, lack of recreational activities, lack of economic opportunity, and poor relations between the community and law enforcement. Most of the people said they didn't feel safe — even within walking distance of their home in the day or night — and many had been a victim of a violent crime within the past year (26 percent overall, and 42 percent in Tract 33). More than half had had some contact with law enforcement in the past year; of those, half were dissatisfied with the encounter. Specifically, they said that law enforcement was doing a poor job responding quickly to calls for service, helping people to feel safe, helping people who were crime victims, enforcing laws consistently, and working with the community to prevent crime and solve problems. Two-thirds thought that a lack of cooperation or consistency among the different law enforcement agencies in the area was hindering effective law enforcement. Responding to questions about their personal connection to the Cass Lake community, more than half of the people said they didn't really feel they were a part of the community; they thought of the area just as a place to live.[45]

The survey documented that many people in the community — not just those who had attended the early CVAV meetings — were having problems with the police. That information made Louise Smith realize that educating people about law enforcement through the kinds of forums that CVAV had organized was not going to be enough — "the survey obviously had law enforcement as one of the top problems of people. It wasn't the lack of education. It was these other things that were going on...."[46] To fix the problem, something would need to be done about police officers in the area.

On December 16, 1999, the survey findings were presented publicly at a CVAV community forum at the Cass Lake American Legion Hall. CVAV members knew that the findings would not be easy for some police officers to take, so they arranged to have people in law enforcement make the presentations: Randy Fisher, the Chief Deputy of the Cass County Sheriff's Department and Gina Gabrielle, Chair of the Department of Justice at the Leech Lake Tribal College. The results had leaked beforehand, however, and some police officers — particularly on the city police force — were angry; they saw the survey as "a shot at law enforcement rather than part of a snapshot of a community."[47] When the findings were presented at the forum: "...the room was full. All of the chairs were full. The police officers came in and lined the rooms standing up. Do you think that they were upset? They said, 'Well, who put this together?' Actually, the presentation I think was done well, but they were unhappy, but none of this other little stuff came out. The little stuff meaning, it was a general tone that the people did not trust them. They did not respect them. That came out in that room."[48]

Although the findings were contentious, they couldn't be ignored. The survey was rigorous and representative of the adults in the area. Moreover, it had been conducted under the auspices of UMCPI — a policing organization. Public presentation of the findings created a strong momentum for change. On June 30, 2000, Cass Lake's police chief announced his retirement, and a new chief, Larry Johnson, was recruited, who began working to create a more responsive and respectful relationship with the community.

On October 5, 2000, the Leech Lake Band, the city of Cass Lake, and the counties of Beltrami, Cass, Hubbard, and Itasca entered into a cooperative law enforcement agreement. The agreement's stated goals were to "(1) coordinate, define, and regulate the provision of law enforcement services and to provide for mutual aid and cooperation between the Band, Counties, State, and City relating to enforcement of laws of the State of Minnesota and laws of the Leech Lake Band; (2) establish a process by which the Band, Counties, State, and City will work together cooperatively to enhance public safety efforts on the Leech Lake Reservation, and (3) preserve the parties' respective jurisdictions on the Leech Lake Reservation so that neither the Band, State, Counties, or City is conceding any claim to jurisdiction by entering into this cooperative agreement."[49] Everyone involved in CVAV regarded this agreement as one of their major achievements. Law enforcement officials were finally "working together with one mind" to address issues of crime and violence.[50] As a result, the system was much less confusing to residents and people working in the various law enforcement agencies; it would also be more effective.

In early 2001, some current and former officers of the Cass Lake police department made allegations against the new police chief, putting his position in jeopardy. At a Cass Lake Council hearing on February 14, Louise Smith and other members of CVAV testified in support of Chief Johnson, saying that it was important to have someone with his character and integrity to counteract the deep distrust and discontent with law enforcement in the area, which had been documented in the 1999 community survey. At that hearing, CVAV members also gave testimony about police abuse and corruption, particularly among members of the city force — rapes of Indian women, children that officers had fathered out of wedlock, harassment of Native youth, use of undue physical force in interactions with Native Americans, and leaks from officers warning drug traffickers in the area of sting operations by other law enforcement agencies. Stating that "people need to be protected, not intimidated," they convinced the Council to have the "moxie" to stand up to its original decision to hire Johnson.[51] Shortly thereafter, corrupt members of the city police force were the target of an FBI sting operation.[52]

In the spring of 2001, the CRRV organizer nominated CVAV for the Minnesota Peace Prize, which was awarded by the Minnesota Office of Drug Policy and Violence Prevention. He said that he wanted to recognize the "remarkable progress" the group had made and give them "some outside recognition that would help them continue the momentum to do the work they started doing."[53] The prize cited CVAV for "facilitating town forums, involving youth and seniors in violence reduction, creating safe places and other actions."[54]

From CRRV to Weed & Seed

CRRV continued to provide assistance to CVAV until 2005, but although a number of action plans were developed, the group does not appear to have taken many actions. There is no evidence that the group engaged in any coordinated effort to address the first priority it identified under CRRV's guidance: youth assaults. Independently, the Cass Lake/Bena school district developed a policy of "zero tolerance to violence," the Leech Lake Tribal Council implemented its Youth Activity Program, and the MIRACLE Group established Boys & Girls Clubs around the area, providing structured programming to 1000 youth on the reservation and in the city. The unstructured "rec center" that youth requested repeatedly — in the high school survey, summits, and letter to the community — was not built. In addition, there is no evidence that any of the other actions youth proposed to strengthen their families, address racism, or deal with grief and loss were developed or implemented.

According to the CRRV organizer, domestic violence was the second priority that CVAV identified with his assistance.[55] The idea for the "Women's Advocacy Group" that was formed appears to have originated in conversations between a CVAV stakeholder and the new Cass Lake Police Chief. The stakeholder, who joined CVAV in 1999 to represent the Leech Lake Police Force, was the mother of the Ojibwe man who had been convicted of raping and murdering the resort owner. At the time the Women's Advocacy Group was formed, she was working with the Leech Lake Domestic Violence Program and wanted to improve relations between women's advocates and the police force.

In October 2002, CVAV stakeholders became the steering committee of a newly formed Weed & Seed program in the area. Weed & Seed is a federal program, sponsored by the Department of Justice and overseen by the relevant U. S. Attorney's office. Using four strategies—community policing; law enforcement; prevention, intervention, and treatment; and community restoration — the program is designed to "weed out" violent criminals and drug abusers and "seed" needed community services. The city of Cass Lake had submitted unsuccessful applications for a Weed & Seed designation in 1998 and 2000. An application that Randy Finn and city and school officials submitted in October 2001 was successful. The designation came with $225,000 per year for five years. Finn, other members of the MIRACLE Group, and CVAV stakeholders wanted to use these resources to do what "we want to do instead of what the Feds want us to do."[56] But many elements of the Weed & Seed program — such as drug task forces and "safe havens" that provide services to youth and adults— are required of all designated sites.

In retrospect, the involvement of CVAV stakeholders in Weed & Seed had a damaging effect on CVAV. Receiving Weed & Seed funding was "like dropping a bomb of money into the community...."[57] As the program's steering committee, CVAV stakeholders were on the front line as agencies in the area began competing and fighting with each other for their share of the funding. In addition, Weed & Seed was even more agency-focused and agency-driven than CRRV. Many of the founding members of CVAV — people who worked at agencies in the area and people who didn't — were not very interested in Weed & Seed's bureaucratic agenda. By 2003, the CVAV stakeholders on the steering committee stopped referring to themselves as "CVAV" because they didn't want CVAV to be identified with Weed & Seed. In March of that year, Randy Finn — who at that time was the leader of the MIRACLE Group, CVAV, and Weed & Seed — resigned from the latter two organizations. As one CVAV member who was on the Weed & Seed steering committee recalled, after that, "we never had another CVAV meeting...."[58]

Weed & Seed has been involved in a number of activities in the area, including a community policing program and the development of the Paul Bunyan Gang and Drug Task Force and the Leech Lake Police Department Weed & Seed Unit. Arrests and seizures of guns and drugs have increased, but residents don't perceive much of an improvement in the levels of crime and violence in the community. In December 2005, Minnesota Public Radio broadcast a program entitled "Cass Lake community struggles with increase in violence."[59] The program revealed that sixteen people had been murdered in this sparsely populated area from 2000 to 2005. Many others had died from suicide or had experienced nonfatal beatings, shootings, and stabbings. All of these violent incidents were "Indian against Indian;" many involved youth.[60]

Other forms of violence continue to kill youth in the area. On August 18, 2002, a 15-year-old Ojibwe girl died of a drug overdose in a house on Tract 33 owned by her boyfriend's grandfather. Elaine Fleming, a member of the Leech Lake Band, professor at the Tribal College, and future mayor of Cass Lake (2003–2007) led several "healing walks" to commemorate the girl's death and to make people more aware of Native American victims of crime. But the community's reaction was not the same as it had been for the murdered resort owner in 1998. In Fleming's experience, "generally if European Americans have a gathering, they support their gathering. If an Anishinabe [Ojibwe] person is an organizer, generally you don't have that bridge."[61]

The Case Analysis

Community Voices Against Violence involved numerous players, almost all of whom were affected by crime and violence in some way: members of CVAV; members of the MIRACLE Group; other people involved in the area's local and tribal governments, law enforcement agencies, and schools; other people living on the reservation and in the city of Cass Lake — youth and adults, Ojibwe and white; and consultants from the Center for Reducing Rural Violence and the Upper Midwest Community Policing Institute. To understand how the ideas of these different players influenced what happened, we (1) looked at the major impacts of the case; (2) identified whose ideas were influential at the critical points that shaped CVAV; and (3) explored how the accomplishments and limitations in the case were related to ideas that were, and were not, influential.

Major Impacts

Community Voices Against Violence benefited residents of the Cass Lake area in important ways. Through its meetings, rallies, and forums, CVAV brought people together across racial, sectoral, and jurisdictional divides, facilitating conversations and actions among individuals and groups who otherwise would not have talked to each other or worked together. Through CVAV, residents were able to express their painful feelings about the escalating problems of crime and violence in the community, tell their personal stories, demonstrate their support for others, and start a community healing process, which was sorely needed after the 1998 rape and murder of the resort owner.

The process gave people hope and courage, focusing attention on issues that residents were afraid to discuss publicly before: inadequate police response (particularly in the poorest sections of the reservation), abuse of Native American residents by police, and police corruption. Officials involved in CVAV spurred actions to address these problems. The Cass Lake police chief and other officers were replaced, making the force more responsive to, and respectful of, community residents. The police force on the Leech Lake Reservation was strengthened. Law enforcement agencies in the various jurisdictions entered into a cooperative agreement, making the overall system more effective and much less confusing. Relations between women's advocates and members of the area's police forces were improved.

Through parallel efforts, Native American youth — a group centrally connected to crime and violence in the community — were given opportunities to talk about the problems they were facing and what they wanted to be done to address those problems. Two young people were also elected to represent their peers on the Leech Lake Tribal Council's Youth Committee. Many youth are benefiting from the structured programs offered at the Boys & Girls Clubs that have been established around the area and from the reservation's youth activity program. Adults in the community are pleased that more youth are being supervised. Nonetheless, many of the important issues that young people identified in the youth survey and summits have not been addressed, and most of the actions they proposed have not been taken. Young people still lack places to "hang out" and engage in unstructured activities after school, in the evenings, and on weekends. Poverty, racism in the community, and serious problems with the adults in their families persist.

Over time, CVAV was not able to sustain the process that made participation in the group so meaningful to its members, and CVAV meetings were ultimately discontinued. The area is continuing to experience high levels of crime, gang-related activity, and violence; as a result, adults and youth are losing the hope they once had that something can be done to resolve these problems. Longstanding racial divisions in the community have not been overcome. Native Americans and whites were able to come together around an extreme case of cross-race violence, but that has not been repeated as successfully in cases of "Indian-against-Indian" violence.

Critical Points of Influence

Looking at the events and impacts in this case, there appear to be four points at which the influence of players' ideas mattered: (1) creating CVAV; (2) determining the future direction of CVAV; (3) deciding how the community would be involved; and (4) deciding which actions would be taken.

Creating CVAV. The decision to create CVAV was made by the 40 people — Ojibwe and white — who participated in the meeting at the Family Center on July 1, 1998. Most of them worked for social service organizations and other agencies around the area. That meeting would not have taken place, however, if Louise Smith had not brought some of the other professionals at the Family Center together beforehand to talk about the murder of the resort owner and its impact on the community. CVAV's mission statement expressed the group's commitment to cross-cultural respect and support. Additional people were drawn into CVAV at the first Peace Rally. The community residents, public officials, service providers, and law enforcement professionals who participated in CVAV's subsequent meetings developed a group dynamic that made people feel safe and comfortable sharing their personal experiences with crime and violence.

Determining the future direction of CVAV. The decisions to request assistance from the Center for Reducing Rural Violence and the Upper Midwest Community Policing Institute were made by the members of CVAV after they had organized the Peace Rallies and law enforcement forums and didn't know what to do next. The CRRV organizer appears to have suggested bringing in UMCPI.

UMCPI's primary form of assistance was to help CVAV design and conduct a community survey, and the results of that survey had a strong influence on CVAV. The documentation of the extent to which residents were experiencing problems with the police enabled CVAV members to act effectively to address those problems.

CRRV had a profound influence on the way CVAV functioned. With the organizer's restructuring, CVAV members no longer came together informally to share their personal concerns about violence in the community. Instead, a formal stakeholder group was created, in which people participated as representatives of their agencies. Meeting times were shifted from the evening to working hours, and the meetings, themselves, became bureaucratic, concentrating on setting priorities and developing action plans. CVAV members who weren't representing stakeholder agencies stopped coming to the meetings when it became inconvenient for them to do so and when issues and activities that were important to them were eliminated from CVAV's "achievable" agenda. The stakeholders who continued to participate as part of their jobs didn't have their hearts in it, and the group took very few actions. With these changes, the founding CVAV members felt something important had been lost, but they apparently had no way to influence what was happening.

The decision to serve as the steering committee of Weed & Seed was made by the members of CVAV's stakeholder group. Taking on that role further distanced CVAV from the process that had made participation meaningful to its members. The only option for influence at that point was to discontinue CVAV's meetings.

Deciding how the community would be involved. Over the course of this case, many intentional efforts were made to involve adults and youth in the area in addressing the community's problems with crime and violence — CVAV's rallies, meetings, and forums; the CVAV/UMCPI survey of community residents; the Cass Lake/Bena school district's survey of high school students; and the three youth summits.

CVAV members decided how they and other people in the community would be involved in CVAV activities. The Peace Rallies gave residents opportunities to commemorate their losses, express the emotions they had in common, show their support for each other, and state, as a group, that they were going to take back the community that had been lost to crime and violence. In CVAV's early meetings, residents had opportunities to tell the stories of their experiences with crime and violence and to hear the stories of others. The purpose of this story-telling was primarily emotional — it enabled people to be heard, to recognize they were not alone, to deal with their pain, and to begin to face what was wrong. At the CVAV forums, community residents had opportunities to listen to presentations and ask questions of the law enforcement professionals who made the presentations. The potential for residents to influence the way the community addressed the problems of crime and violence depended on how their stories and questions affected other people at the meetings or forums who were in positions to develop and take actions.

CVAV members, staff from UMCPI, and a researcher from the University of Minnesota determined how the community would be surveyed about crime and violence. The way they designed the survey gave residents the potential to have a considerable amount of influence over an issue that mattered to them — their relationship to law enforcement. The survey was targeted to people living within a five-mile radius of the city. A substantial number of adults responded to the survey, and those who did were representative of the area's various neighborhoods and the population's racial make-up. The questions — which appear to have been influenced by the stories people told in CVAV meetings—probed deeply and specifically into the impact of crime and violence on people's lives and the nature of their interactions with law enforcement. In the analysis, all of the data were presented, and responses among people in different neighborhoods were compared. The survey was conducted under the auspices of a policing organization (UMPCI); to further strengthen the survey's credibility, the findings were presented by local law enforcement officials at the public forum.

Young people appear to have been actively involved in organizing and facilitating the two youth summits in November 1998. Their role in designing the November 1998 survey of students at Cass Lake/Bena High School is unknown, although they participated in collecting and analyzing the data from the survey. The other players who determined how youth were involved in these activities were the teachers and staff at the high school, the members of the Leech Lake Tribal Council, and Randy Finn.

The survey and breakout sessions at the summits gave youth opportunities to talk about the problems they were facing and what they wanted to be done to address those problems. The ideas they expressed were documented at the time. The potential for those ideas to be influential, however, depended on how they would be used by the adults in the community who were in positions to develop and implement actions. The summits did not give youth opportunities to develop their ideas into feasible actions or to work with adults in that regard.

Youth appear to have been far less involved in organizing the April 1999 youth summit, for which the Leech Lake Tribal Council contracted with an outside consultant. The record of that summit provides little documentation of young people's ideas about crime and violence. The summit's primary purpose appears to have been to elect two youth representatives to the Tribal Council's Youth Committee. There is no evidence that the youth representatives influenced the Youth Activity Program that this committee produced.

Deciding which actions would be taken. The community engagement activities described above generated many ideas about problems that were contributing to crime and violence in the area and actions that could be taken to address those problems. In addition, some people and groups in the community had ideas of their own, which predated the broader community engagement activities. From its inception, the MIRACLE Group was committed to fostering intergovernmental cooperation, and in 1996, Randy Finn and the MIRACLE Group's Community Development Committee began working to establish Boys & Girls Clubs in the area. Prior to CVAV, the Leech Lake Tribal Council had begun to establish a police force and legal system on the reservation and was exploring the development of some form of youth division.

Decisions about which ideas would move forward were made by a number of players—CVAV; officials from the area's local and tribal governments and law enforcement agencies; and the MIRACLE Group. CVAV focused public attention on problems with police response, abuse, and corruption and created conditions that made local governments and law enforcement agencies accountable for addressing these problems. Ultimately, the local and tribal governments and law enforcement agencies took the actions that led to the replacement of the Cass Lake police chief, the expansion of the reservation's police force, and the area's cooperative law enforcement agreement.

The MIRACLE Group and the Leech Lake Tribal Council determined the actions that would be taken to address youth issues. Although Randy Finn and the Tribal Council were very influential in giving young people voice through the youth summits, the only ideas that moved forward were those that the MIRACLE Group and the Tribal Council had proposed beforehand.

Relating Impacts to Influence

The people who started CVAV believed that residents needed opportunities to come together and talk about their experiences in order to deal with the rape and murder of the resort owner and address the escalating levels of crime and violence in the community. In its early meetings, CVAV was very successful in creating an environment where people from different backgrounds felt safe and comfortable telling their stories— anguishing stories about family members involved in crime and potentially dangerous stories about police who were unresponsive, corrupt, and abusive. This story-telling had great emotional value, but the experiences people related also revealed serious problems in the community. In retrospect, the challenge that CVAV faced was figuring out how to transform these experiences into accepted knowledge.

The service providers in CVAV initially thought that people in the community needed to be educated about law enforcement; if they understood how the system worked, they would be able to distinguish appropriate from inappropriate police conduct. The law enforcement forums that ensued provided residents with this information, but their greater value appears to have been in bringing law enforcement professionals from different jurisdictions together, which contributed to the development of the cooperative law enforcement agreement.

After the forums were completed, CVAV members didn't know what to do next, so they looked to outside experts for advice. The staff from UMPCI turned out to be very helpful. With support from UMPCI, CVAV developed a survey that was grounded in the experiences that people had been sharing in their stories at CVAV meetings. As a result, CVAV was able to quantify the extent to which community residents were having problems with the police and document the specific nature of those problems. By doing so, they transformed people's stories— which some officials might previously have considered to be anecdotes or the complaints of marginalized residents— into data that needed to be taken seriously. Conducting the survey under the auspices of a policing organization, and having the data presented by members of local law enforcement agencies, gave further credibility to the survey's findings.

By contrast, CRRV's advice does not appear to have been helpful. The organizer's restructuring of CVAV was designed to enable stakeholders representing agencies to contribute their expert knowledge to accomplishing something achievable. There was no explicit recognition of the value of people's experiential knowledge, however, and CVAV's meetings no longer provided people with opportunities to contribute that kind of knowledge. This was a critical loss for ordinary residents of the community because CVAV's rallies and early meetings had provided them with their only means of expression.

The involvement of youth in this case demonstrates that having opportunities to express ideas does not necessarily mean those ideas will be influential. Although youth were not involved in CVAV's meetings or community survey, the efforts of other groups gave young people several opportunities to talk about the problems they were facing and what they wanted to be done to address those problems. Nonetheless, no action appears to have been taken in direct response to the ideas that young people expressed. The MIR-ACLE Group and the Leech Lake Tribal Council interpreted the findings from the youth survey and summits as support for their plans to establish Boys & Girls Clubs and a youth activity program in the area. But neither the Boys & Girls Clubs nor the youth activity program have provided young people with the unstructured "rec center" they repeatedly requested. Equally important, youth were never given opportunities to work with adults to find ways to address issues that matter to them so much — poverty, racism, and the dysfunctional behavior of many of the adults in their lives.

2

Housing for Single Mothers in Humboldt Park, Chicago

The Story

On October 26, 1998, two senior staff members of the Latin United Community Housing Association presented a proposal at a meeting of the Humboldt Park Empowerment Partnership. LUCHA — which is the Spanish word for "struggle" as well as the acronym for the association — had been developing housing in the area for more than ten years. To address the problems of low-income single mothers, the association now wanted to construct 55 apartments in two buildings on the 3200 block of Division Street that would provide tenants with child care and other supportive services on site. The purpose of this presentation was to obtain the community support that LUCHA would need to obtain tax credits and other financing for the project.

The monthly meetings of the Humboldt Park Empowerment Partnership were an appropriate venue for discussing local development issues. LUCHA was one of about 80 members of the partnership, which included other affordable housing developers, social service agencies, block clubs, cultural organizations, businesses, clergy, hospitals, schools, and other neighborhood associations and groups. Created in 1994 by the Near Northwest Neighborhood Network, one of the partnership's earliest actions had been to involve the community in creating a land use plan to guide future development in ways that would stem the tide of gentrification and improve conditions for the people who were already living in the area around Humboldt Park. At the partnership's monthly meetings, member organizations and outsiders had opportunities to offer their proposals for future development in the area and to build support and constituencies for their ideas.

When LUCHA made its presentation to the Humboldt Park Empowerment Partnership on October 26, it was ready to move forward with its housing project. The association had already invested three years developing the idea and pursuing available lots. It had also begun to organize single mothers in a group called "Mothers United in Action." But when the community groups at the partnership's monthly meeting heard what LUCHA's representative had to say, some were staunchly opposed to LUCHA's proposal.

Poverty and Gentrification in Humboldt Park

The Humboldt Park area on the northwest side of Chicago surrounds one of Chicago's largest parks, named for Alexander von Humboldt, the German naturalist, explorer, and advocate for human rights. Within its boundaries, the park contains stony brooks, a large lagoon, a boat house in the Prairie School design, a field house, ball fields, and gardens. Different neighborhoods surround the park — West Town to the east, Logan Square to the north, and Humboldt Park to the west. The housing styles mix single-family frames and two-family brick "two-flats," along with larger apartment and commercial buildings on the main avenues. An industrial area and rail corridor are south of the park. The Humboldt Park Empowerment Partnership focuses predominantly on the areas that are nearest the park on its east and west sides.[1]

This part of Chicago was settled in the nineteenth century by Germans and Scandinavians, followed later by Poles, Italians, and Russian Jews. In the 1950s, immigrants from Puerto Rico began to settle in the area, and in the 1960's, Puerto Ricans displaced from other parts of Chicago moved there as well. In June 1966, after a white police officer shot a Puerto Rican youth, riots erupted on Division Street, the east-west thoroughfare that has long served as the heart of the Puerto Rican community. As the pace of white migration from Humboldt Park picked up and the eastern parts of Chicago underwent gentrification, more Puerto Ricans and African Americans moved in. By the late 1980s, most of the residents on the west side of the park were African American, and Puerto Ricans were dominant east of the park. Large numbers of Mexican immigrants were also settling in the area, adding to its identity as a Latino neighborhood.

At this time, and continuing through the 1990's, the area around Humboldt Park was economically depressed and socially distressed. Most of the manufacturing companies had closed their plants, and unemployment rates were as high as 30 percent in some of the census tracts. About 45 percent of the area's 125,000 residents were living at or below the poverty level. The park and streets were dirty and many houses were abandoned or in disrepair.[2] One resident described what he and others faced: "There was rampant drug selling — illegal drugs, prostitution, gang banging. We had two liquor stores on ... the 3200 Block of West Division [Street] that were selling liquor and cigarettes to anybody regardless of age.... It wasn't safe to walk down the block at night, and it wasn't safe to walk down the block on Division in the morning." Another resident described problems with crime: "...it was a rough neighborhood.... There was guys selling drugs out of the house on either side of where I lived. Hanging out their windows selling drugs. Drugs on every corner. There were cars getting burned on the street occasionally."[3]

Many organizations were working to address neighborhood crime problems and to meet the basic needs of the community. Among these were numerous block clubs, which sometimes consolidated — into the Block Club Federation or the United Blocks of West Humboldt Park, for example — to give residents in particular neighborhoods a greater voice. The community also had three nonprofit organizations committed to providing adequate housing for people in the area: Bickerdike Redevelopment Corporation, the Hispanic Housing Development Corporation, and LUCHA. Beginning in the late 1980's, LUCHA had rehabilitated four buildings to create 47 apartments for low and moderate income families and had constructed a 68-unit single room occupancy building with integrated support services for previously homeless individuals.[4]

The Near Northwest Neighborhood Network was established in 1986 to coordinate the efforts of the many organizations in the community. Originally, the Network focused on crime prevention; later it developed into an "organization of organizations," along the lines of the model created by Saul Alinsky with the Industrial Areas Foundation. By the mid–1990's, when the area was facing the double threats of encroaching gentrification from the east as well as poverty and crime within, the Network formed the Humboldt Park Empowerment Partnership to "unite groups that have traditionally been operating on their own into a cooperative grassroots planning process."[5]

The partnership originally wanted the Humboldt Park area to be included in Chicago's Empowerment Zone. When that bid failed in 1994, the partnership obtained $35,000 from the city to engage community organizations and residents in developing a land use plan. This plan, and the partnership's accompanying community development plan, provided a framework for controlling land and securing investment to make Humboldt Park a better place for the people who were already living there and to prevent residents from being displaced by gentrifiers.

Around this time, Billy Ocasio—a Puerto Rican community organizer and former building rehabilitation specialist with LUCHA—became Alderman for the 26th Ward, which included sections on the east and west sides of Humboldt Park. At his suggestion and with his assistance, the partnership obtained a Redevelopment Area designation for parts of Humboldt Park in 1998, which gave the city control over vacant land and blighted buildings in the designated area and provided up to $3 million to secure these lots for redevelopment.[6]

"Very hard to find an apartment"

In the late 1980's, LUCHA staff members became aware that many single mothers were having difficulty obtaining suitable housing. One-quarter to one-third of the households in the area were headed by single mothers, and two-thirds of these single-mother households were living at or below the poverty level.[7] A staffer from that period remembered "...some single moms coming in and complaining ... that they were being treated unfairly, and it was too expensive for them because they were by themselves. They were being mistreated by the landlord."[8] Mistreatment by landlords included physical abuse and rape, as well as pressure for rent payments.[9] A single mother who eventually became involved in LUCHA's project said, "for a single person it is very hard to find an apartment because they [landlords] think we are not going to pay, that we won't have the money and, when you're alone and you don't have money for the deposit, all that piles up...."[10] Another recalled how she had been paying rents that were too high in various apartments in the area when her son came from Puerto Rico to live with her: "This was when I was living on California [Avenue], where they were discriminating against me in the rent. So I said to the priest at my parish, 'Father Mike, do you want me to leave the community?' He said, 'No, of course not,' and I told him I needed an apartment and he thought of LUCHA right away."[11]

In 1992, when Billy Ocasio was working as a building rehabilitation specialist at LUCHA, another group of single mothers came to his office to talk about these kinds of issues. This time, in addition to describing their problems, the single mothers suggested that LUCHA create housing for households like theirs. The women and Ocasio had several conversations, and he later came up with a concept for a large housing project that would integrate affordable housing with social services for the single mothers and their children. In his view, developing housing and support services separately was part of the problem the single mothers faced. As he put it, "nobody was coordinating the efforts."[12] Ocasio talked about the idea with other staff members at LUCHA, but it was placed on the backburner, since the association had other housing developments in progress and couldn't take on an additional project at the time. In 1993, Ocasio was appointed Alderman of the 26th Ward and left LUCHA.

A few years later, in 1995, LUCHA conducted an assessment of the tenants in their housing projects and learned that 73 percent were single mothers.[13] At this point, the association was able to take on another endeavor, and the staff began developing a housing concept for families headed by single mothers. The idea was to build a structure that would house about 100 of the poorest single mothers and their children and to provide these families—who would all be facing similar problems—with an array of supportive services right in the building.[14] Some of these services, like a playground on the premises and after school programs, would shield the children from the gangs, drug traffic, and violence on the street.[15] Living closely together in a protected space, the single mothers would be able to support each other and build community.

Once the housing concept was defined, LUCHA's Executive Director and Board began to organize single mothers who were living in existing LUCHA housing as well as others in the community who needed affordable housing. The group, which was led by an organizer on LUCHA's staff, was called "Mothers United in Action" or "Madres Unidas en Acción" (MUA).[16] At the start, the role of the MUA organizer appears to have been similar to the kind of support that LUCHA envisioned case managers would provide to single mothers in the planned housing project. During MUA meetings, the single mothers talked about some of the problems they were facing, like needing to find child care close to their house so they could go to work, having to "put up with their partners" in order to afford housing, not having finished high school, and not knowing English.[17] MUA conducted informational sessions for the mothers on going back to school, obtaining Section 8 vouchers (which low-income people could use to subsidize rent payments in privately owned housing),[18] dealing with domestic violence, and generating more income (by learning hairstyling, for example).[19] The group also linked the single mothers to other support services in the community.

The First Proposal: Logan Square

LUCHA identified a site for its housing project in the Logan Square neighborhood, northwest of the park, and in February 1998, the association submitted an application to the Chicago Department of Housing to secure the tax credits and loans that would be necessary for financing the "Single Mothers Housing Project."[20] LUCHA proposed acquiring and rehabilitating a building with a grocery on the ground floor to create 100 two- and three-bedroom apartments that would be rented to families with incomes lower than 60 percent of the area's median income. The application stated that "the project will take a holistic approach by addressing housing and the social-economic needs of women and their children" by providing "housing and a full range of support services. During the mother's stay, follow-up will be conducted by case managers with expertise in family care to assure [that] residents achieve their goals in obtaining education, job training, life skills, and health care related information and services. The ultimate goal is to promote self-reliance by developing skills and resources to enhance the lives of single mothers and their children." The application also stated that LUCHA would acquire nearby vacant lots to provide tenants with off-street parking.

The site was in the 35th ward, and in June, LUCHA staff and supporters of the project from the Association of Ministers met with Vilma Colom, the Alderman from that district, to gain her support for the application.[21] When Colom refused to endorse the project, LUCHA began to explore other options, including lots in the 26th Ward, where Billy Ocasio was Alderman and where the Humboldt Park Empowerment Partnership was very active.

"Support the project, but not the site"

LUCHA found vacant lots in that ward, and on October 26, 1998, William Acevedo and Jonathan Levy went to the monthly meeting of the Humboldt Park Empowerment Partnership to present LUCHA's proposal for developing housing for single mothers on the 3200 block of West Division Street. Acevedo was a building rehabilitation specialist at the association, and Levy was the Associate Director. At the meeting, they distributed a "Single Parents Project Fact Sheet" with a hand-drawn diagram that described LUCHA's plan to construct a 38-unit apartment building at one end of the block, near Spaulding, and a 17-unit apartment building at the other end, near Kedzie.[22] All of the apartments would have either two or three bedrooms. The architect for the project was listed as Peter Landon, whose firm had worked with LUCHA before and had a lot of experience in affordable housing. The single mothers in LUCHA's housing would have access to social services, and the on-site child care might be open to other families in the community as well as the tenants.[23]

The presentation met with stiff opposition from the partnership's organizational members, led by United Blocks of West Humboldt Park, a group of people who lived or owned property in the neighborhood where LUCHA was proposing to build its housing project. "United Blocks," as the group is known, had been aware that LUCHA was working on this project, and its members accounted for one-fourth of the 47 people who attended the meeting. In its opposition to the proposal, United Blocks was supported by other community groups, including the Block Club Federation, a group that had organized residents in other parts of the area and had a powerful voice in the Humboldt Park Empowerment Partnership.

Repeatedly during the meeting, the community groups said that they supported the general concept of housing for single mothers, but not the site.[24] Their underlying reason was that LUCHA's housing project — which they saw as concentrating a large number of low-income people on one block — would exacerbate the very problems they were trying to address.[25]

For many in the room, there was already far too much subsidized low-income housing and too many social services in the Humboldt Park area,[26] and members of United Blocks didn't want their neighborhood to become a "dumping ground" for more.[27] They believed that LUCHA's single room occupancy building—which was very near the proposed site for the single mothers' housing—had brought many problems to their neighborhood. The previously homeless men and their friends were hanging around outside the building "to do drugs, drink in the alley, drink in the parking lot.... They urinate in the alley and throw their bottles down there and get drunk and pass out in the parkway."[28] In the eyes of United Blocks, a large concentration of single mothers would do much of the same. LUCHA's new project would bring in "150 kids," overwhelming their neighborhood's overcrowded schools.[29] Too many teenagers in one place raised concerns about gangs.

Another reason that members of United Blocks opposed the project was that it offered "no opportunities for people to purchase housing." They wanted to promote home ownership because they believed renters weren't as invested in the neighborhood: "Renters in general ... if you're renting a house, which you're not paying for, and if you trash it, it doesn't cost you anything...." In their eyes, people like single mothers, who receive housing for "free" (i.e. subsidized housing), would be even less responsible.[30]

The Block Club Federation supported United Blocks because "we let the community decide and then we back whatever the community decided."[31] A leader of the Block Club Federation who was at the meeting recalled that no one there was "against the program" for single mothers—"They said they loved the idea of having a building for single moms, but that was not the good area." In addition to LUCHA's single room occupancy building, the Chicago Housing Authority was planning to build a lot of public housing in West Humboldt Park, and an HIV clinic was being proposed, too.[32] Neither United Blocks nor the Block Club Federation wanted "all of this in one area."

At the end of the meeting, the Humboldt Park Empowerment Partnership passed a motion to "support the project but not the site." Eliud Medina, the Executive Director of the Near Northwest Neighborhood Network—who had also been on LUCHA's staff in the past—said he would work with LUCHA to find another site.[33]

The Third Proposal: Christiana Street

On September 1, 1999, LUCHA filed a new tax credit application with the Chicago Department of Housing to construct eight buildings with 49 three-bedroom apartments on a block of North Christiana Street. This site was also in the 26th Ward, very near the West Division Street location that LUCHA had proposed at the Humboldt Park Empowerment Partnership meeting the year before. The application stated that the housing would be for families with incomes of $19,000 or less, with "special emphasis on single mother headed families." The design would be "consistent with the current architecture features of the surrounding area."[34]

Support services were integral to the project: "Using the community space available within the buildings, community social service organizations will help families develop skills, find jobs, develop businesses and better educate their children. In order to reach families that are currently homeless, LUCHA will work with shelters, churches and other community organizations and institutions which serve them. Every family living in the project will be required to develop a set of self improvement goals that will become the bases for the support services. The network of support organizations will help assure that families achieve their goals and become empowered to get out of poverty and dependency."

The application included "linkage agreements" with 26 organizations providing support services and said that the services "will be coordinated by our Single Mother Organizer."[35]

In 1999, a new organizer was hired for MUA, and part of her job was to attend meetings of the Humboldt Park Empowerment Partnership's steering committee and housing action team. When the Christiana Street proposal came up, she recalled a representative from United Blocks saying "They [single mothers] don't belong there. I don't want them there. I mean the community doesn't want them there. They're creating a problem. There are too many on one block, you know?" She was struck that no one else at the partnership meetings was trying to defend LUCHA: "The one that we presented the project to, he would get up and interrupt in the meeting. 'No, just forget about it. They're not going on Christiana. That's too many and that's not fair.' It was a constant argument, to a point where I had to literally stop going to meetings, because the arguments were so bad."[36] In November, representatives from United Blocks and the Block Club Federation informed the steering committee that they were writing a letter to the partnership and the Alderman stating that their organizations were opposed to LUCHA's project because it "does not present any room for home ownership."[37]

In December, the MUA organizer and dozens of single mothers from MUA participated in a rally that LUCHA organized in support of the Christiana Street housing. Some of the project's opponents also showed up and vied with the single mothers for the attention of the press. The MUA organizer recalled these people saying things like: "No. They're single moms, you know? They're in the streets. They're going to take our husbands." The negative stereotyping and misconceptions about single mothers were very painful to the MUA members and to the organizer, who had been a single mother earlier in her life. One of the women responded by saying, "Hey, I'm a single mom. I work and I'm a nurse." Another said, "Hey, I'm an administrative assistant and I work hard to keep my kids in school." At the end of the rally, the organizer remembered a member of United Blocks getting in front of the television camera and saying "No, it should be single homes and the moms should leave."[38]

United Blocks and other organizations were successful in getting Billy Ocasio, the 26th Ward Alderman, to oppose LUCHA's project at the Christiana Street site. Ocasio wrote LUCHA saying that he would not go against the community organizations' position, though he would work with other Aldermen to find sites for smaller-scale housing that would be distributed throughout the area.[39] On December 6, Ocasio's chief of staff was quoted in the Chicago Sun-Times, saying "There has been too much low-income housing dropped in Humboldt Park, and that has to stop. We want stable home ownership." In the same article, United Blocks leader Miguel Nogueras was reported as saying "Why would we want to build 49 apartments and saturate one block with all these families?"[40]

The dispute put the Near Northwest Neighborhood Network — which was responsible for organizing, convening, and coordinating the Humboldt Park Empowerment Partnership — in an awkward position with its member organizations. According to the Executive Director, Eliud Medina, "we were caught in the middle, because then LUCHA basically accused us of manipulating the [partnership] process [against them]. The block clubs basically accused us of trying to bring large numbers of government housing into their area."[41] The relationship with LUCHA was so strained that the association withdrew itself from the partnership's mailing list for a while. Ultimately, Medina tried to resolve the tension by writing to the Chicago Department of Housing in support of providing tax credits to LUCHA for this project, but not at the Christiana Street site, which he stated was the position that the partnership's organizations had voted to support. He pledged to work with the LUCHA and the city to find another site.[42]

At this point, LUCHA dropped the idea of developing housing that would bring large numbers of single mothers together with comprehensive support services on site. Instead, the association took up Ocasio and Medina on their pledges to find sites for multiple small buildings, with a few apartments in each, spread around the community. After 15 years, home ownership would be incorporated in the project; tenants at that time would have an option to buy their apartments.[43] LUCHA mobilized the single mothers in MUA to put pressure on Ocasio, who had the power to give LUCHA access to vacant or city-owned lots in his ward. LUCHA also began to work on purchasing some lots in the area from private owners.

"A long process"

From early 2000 through the completion of construction of the housing in the summer of 2006, LUCHA and the single mothers in MUA endured what LUCHA's Executive Director called, simply, "a long process." Many of the single mothers participated in MUA's meetings and advocacy activities because they wanted to live in the housing themselves. As the years passed, some of these women became discouraged.[44] Others stayed motivated by the prospect that the housing would eventually benefit other single mothers like them,[45] and by being part of "a strong group ... to let the community know that we're there. We need something to happen."[46]

Negotiating for land with Ocasio was a drawn-out and contentious process. As the negotiations progressed, the Alderman stipulated that he would only provide lots to LUCHA if some of the housing for single mothers was also located in other wards. He felt that his overall support for affordable housing had wound up concentrating too many of these developments in his ward, and he wanted to see Aldermen in other wards take on some of the responsibility. The single mothers in MUA put pressure on Ocasio in a variety of ways. They organized telephone campaigns, registered single mothers to vote, and met with State Senator Miguel del Valle. Eliud Medina was also in contact with Ocasio.

As potential lots were identified, the project's architect looked at them to make sure they would be appropriate for family housing. Lots near industrial sites, too far from playgrounds, or on very busy streets were not good places for young children. Ultimately, LUCHA obtained 11 lots—four provided by Ocasio in the 26th Ward, two provided by Alderman Granato in the 1st Ward, and the rest purchased by LUCHA from private owners—as well as tax credit approval from the Chicago Department of Housing to construct 11 buildings with 36 apartments overall.

LUCHA contracted with Peter Landon's firm to design the housing, requesting that a female architect work with members of MUA to find out what single mothers wanted. On February 23, 2000, four of the women in MUA met at the firm's office, where they reviewed "a packet of information with different types of housing proposals—two-flats, three-flats, group housing with community spaces, larger types of buildings and kind of more of an apartment type of complex with probably a play space."[47] The women were asked what they preferred and discussed their preferences with a female staff member. According to Catherine Baker, the architect who was eventually assigned to the project, "the overriding theme" in the responses "was that all of the women wanted privacy and they wanted individual spaces, and none of them were interested in a larger complex."[48]

The single mothers also filled out a survey to obtain their views about specific design elements. The exterior features of the housing that mattered to them most related to privacy and safety. The women wanted private entrances to their own apartments, private keys to the front door of the building, no common stairwells, and no bushes near the building where people could hide. They also wanted to live in a building with a backyard, parking, and outside storage space for bicycles. For the apartments, the women wanted space — two or three bedrooms, a living room and dining room, and walk-in closets. It was very important for them to be able to see their children from the kitchen, which meant that the apartments would need to be laid out with lines of sight from the kitchen to both the living room and the backyard. For amenities, the women wanted washers and dryers inside the apartment, fireplaces, dishwashers, and central air conditioning. The architect was able to incorporate most of these preferences in the design of the housing, with the exception of fireplaces, dishwashers, and air conditioners, which were too expensive.

Baker was committed to having the housing blend in with the prevailing style of the neighborhood, which was the trend in affordable housing construction. Most of the buildings on the blocks where the lots were located were two to four stories high. Some were single family homes, and others had one apartment per floor. The exteriors were mostly brick, and the buildings were close together, situated toward the front of the lots. To blend in, the housing for single mothers would need to use regular size bricks (instead of larger ones or cinder blocks) and have higher ceilings than most subsidized housing. Ten of the 11 buildings for single mothers are in this style, with one apartment on each of three floors. One of the units is larger and sits on a double lot; it has six floor-through apartments, two on each floor. LUCHA requested community space in one of the buildings. Some of the women were agreeable to this, and it was included in the basement of the double-lot building. The original intent was to provide child care in this space, but the building code prohibits using rooms below ground for this purpose.

Construction of the housing began in 2005 and was completed in the summer of 2006. Ten of the 36 apartments have two bedrooms, and the rest have three. The housing was targeted to families with incomes between 31 and 50 percent of the median in the area — families in this income range tend to headed by single mothers in Humboldt Park. LUCHA received hundreds of applications for the housing, and almost all of the apartments are occupied by single mothers and their families, including two women who were members of MUA during the late 1990s, when the controversy between LUCHA and the other community groups was at its height. LUCHA is the landlord of the buildings, and tenants will have the right to purchase their apartments after 15 years.

Current Perspectives about the Housing

The single mothers who are currently living in LUCHA's housing appear to be very pleased with it. When they talk about why, the main reasons are safety, the small-scale of the housing in multiple buildings around the area, and the affordability of the rent. The women like the interior design of the apartments and the way the buildings blend into the neighborhood. As one put it: "I definitely like the way it's set up ... it's modern ... and it's actually nicer than I thought it would probably be. I didn't envision it being like a nice building.... I think it definitely does affect the neighborhood probably more positively because you have people moving in that are working and ... they want to make the neighborhood nicer. And even the buildings look very nice."[49] Dealing with LUCHA is also an improvement over the private landlords who have exploited some of the single mothers in the past.

Magdalena Martinez, who is a leader in the Block Club Federation and also co-chair of the Humboldt Park Empowerment Partnership, is also pleased with the outcome — for the neighborhood and for single mothers. She said, "I think it worked out very well because [the buildings are] within the area, and they're scattered. So nobody even knows that they're single moms' apartments...." She credits the partnership's process with enabling the community to prevent a large housing development that would have had a "big commotion of people outside the building." She added, "we visited them and the apartments are beautiful. They're ample. They have a beautiful yard. It's just beautiful for a single mom and their kids. I'm hoping that they're very happy with it." She would like to see more housing like this built in the community for single mothers.[50]

United Blocks was able to prevent LUCHA from building the large housing project for single mothers in its neighborhood, but its members are more circumspect about the role of the Humboldt Park Empowerment Partnership in development in the area. Based on their experience with this and other projects, the members of United Blocks tend to regard the partnership and local affordable housing developers as running roughshod over the rights of the neighborhood's homeowners. In their view, the partnership's land use plan and the Humboldt Park Redevelopment Area ignore the voices of homeowners.

For the women who were involved in MUA, the reaction is mixed. During the 13-year period that it took to develop and construct the housing, some of the single mothers became disillusioned with LUCHA, primarily because they felt the association wasn't keeping its promises. Others were "turned off" by the advocacy and organizing that MUA engaged them in. One of the single mothers felt "threatened" when she was told that she needed to be actively involved in MUA in order to be on the list of potential applicants for the housing. In addition, one of the MUA organizers was disappointed when LUCHA's initial concept didn't go forward: "I wanted them to have the hundred units and the social worker. I wanted to work in that building with them. I wanted to continue helping them out."[51]

Many of the women who participated in MUA benefited substantially, however. Not surprisingly, the single mothers who live in the housing feel it was "definitely worth [it] ... even though it took a while. [MUA] definitely put that idea in people and it was something to look forward to."[52] For some of the other women, being involved in MUA gave them a sense of power and leadership in their lives — the knowledge that they could "fight for what [they] believe in."[53] They learned a lot about housing, which enabled a number of women to obtain more suitable housing through other means, such as Section 8 vouchers or standing up to their landlord. As an MUA organizer who had been a single mother put it: "I wasn't afraid to tell the landlord that I have my right as a mom, as a tenant, you know? There are tenant rules, and we have our rights. Anyone who would try to mess with me, I would pull out that little pamphlet and tell that these are my rights. I never had anyone else step on me. They couldn't race me around on that, so they just respected me for who I was." Participation in MUA made some of the women recognize that they could do more than they were doing at the time, which encouraged them to continue their education. MUA also helped some of the women get jobs. After obtaining housing in a Bickerdike development in Humboldt Park, one of the single mothers was recruited by Bickerdike as a community organizer because of her previous experience in MUA.

The Case Analysis

The development of LUCHA's housing for single mothers involved numerous players: the staff of LUCHA, including the organizers of MUA; the single mothers who spoke with LUCHA staff and participated in MUA; the Executive Director of the Near Northwest Neighborhood Network; the organizational members of the Humboldt Park Empowerment Partnership, including representatives of United Blocks and the Block Club Federation; the Aldermen of three wards in the area; and the architects who worked on the project. To understand how the ideas of these different players influenced what happened, we (1) looked at the major impacts of the case; (2) identified whose ideas were influential at the critical points that shaped the housing for single mothers; and (3) explored how the accomplishments and limitations in the case were related to ideas that were, and were not, influential.

Major Impacts

The housing that LUCHA constructed is clearly benefiting the single mothers who live there with their families. The women feel better off than they did before in terms of the housing's affordability, privacy, safety, and design. The housing also appears to be acceptable to the other people in the neighborhoods where the buildings are located, which is an important accomplishment considering the prevalence of negative stereotypes about single mothers in the area and the concerns of residents and Aldermen about increasing the number of subsidized housing developments.

Participation in MUA appears to have been of value to many of the single mothers involved, even if they didn't receive an apartment in LUCHA's new housing project. The group's informational and skill-building activities gave them — and at least one of MUA's organizers— a new sense of power over their own lives, which opened opportunities they hadn't considered before. Some of the women were able to obtain more suitable housing through Section 8 vouchers, by standing up for their rights with landlords, or other means.

The accomplishments in this case came at a price, however. The process to create the housing entailed a substantial amount of tension and conflict — between LUCHA and the Humboldt Park Empowerment Partnership, between LUCHA and other community groups (particularly United Blocks and the Block Club Federation), between LUCHA and area Aldermen, between single mothers and other neighborhood residents; and between the Executive Director of the Near Northwest Neighborhood Network and some of the Network's community groups. These conflicts added years to the prolonged period of time that it took to build the housing—13 years from the original idea to completion of the project. Ultimately, the housing was able to accommodate only a small fraction of the hundreds of single mothers who wanted to live in the apartments.

Critical Points of Influence

Looking at the events and impacts in the development of LUCHA's housing for single mothers, there appear to be six points at which the influence of players's ideas mattered: (1) developing the original concept for the housing; (2) establishing MUA; (3) preventing the original housing concept from moving forward; (4) designing the housing; (5) obtaining the tax credits and lots for the project; and (6) deciding who would live in the housing.

Developing the original concept for the housing. The need for more suitable housing for single mothers was first expressed by single mothers, themselves. Had they not approached LUCHA staff on two occasions (the late 1980's and 1992), it is unlikely that the project would ever have gotten underway. At the time, single mothers said they wanted housing that was affordable, available to them without discrimination from landlords, safe from neighborhood crime and mistreatment by landlords, and close to child care. When he was employed at LUCHA, Billy Ocasio believed that single mothers were also experiencing problems because social services were not coordinated with housing. He developed the concept of bringing large numbers of single mothers together in a big housing complex with comprehensive support services on-site. This idea was later embraced and turned into specific housing proposals by LUCHA's Executive Director and other LUCHA staff members.

We do not know what single mothers knew about LUCHA's first three proposals, and there is no evidence to suggest that LUCHA staff consulted them in developing the proposals. Information obtained from single mothers by the architect later in the case (see "designing the housing," below) suggests that LUCHA's original concept was "out of sync" with the preferences of single mothers in important ways. In particular, the features that the women wanted in order to assure their privacy and safety were incompatible with the large, collective housing complex that LUCHA originally envisioned. There is no evidence that single mothers ever requested "case management" to be included with their housing, and we do not know how they would have reacted to a housing requirement to "develop a set of self-improvement goals."

Establishing MUA. LUCHA's Executive Director and Board decided to create MUA and to staff the group with a "single mother organizer." The Executive Director decided when and how MUA would advocate for LUCHA's housing proposals—by having the organizer attend meetings of the Humboldt Park Empowerment Partnership and by involving the single mothers in rallies and other campaigns. The informational and skill-building activities at MUA meetings were influenced by the various organizers and the single mothers, themselves. The single mothers in MUA do not appear to have been involved in any aspect of the design of the housing until LUCHA's original concept had been altered and the architect had been hired.

Preventing the original housing concept from moving forward. LUCHA was repeatedly prevented from realizing its original concept of housing for single mothers by community groups, who were supported in their opposition by the Humboldt Park Empowerment Partnership, the Near Northwest Neighborhood Network, and area Aldermen. The specific objections of these players determined not only the location of the housing that LUCHA ultimately built, but also the smaller size and broad distribution of the buildings, the potential for tenants to own their apartments after a period of time, and the elimination of comprehensive on-site support services.

Consistent with common practice at the time, LUCHA prepared a well-developed proposal before meeting with community members and organizations. The first public opportunity that United Blocks and other groups had to express their ideas was to react to a fully developed proposal that LUCHA presented at a Humboldt Park Empowerment Partnership meeting. At that time, it became apparent that LUCHA's proposal would create problems for them. LUCHA's ideas did not become influential until the association altered its original concept in ways that addressed those problems.

Designing the housing. LUCHA was instrumental in assuring that a female architect would work with members of MUA to determine their preferences in housing. The views of the single mothers who participated were very influential — most of the features that were important to them were incorporated in the ultimate design. Although only four of the single mothers in MUA actually completed the architect's survey, it is likely that many more provided input through MUA meetings.

None of the single mothers involved in these surveys and discussions were interested in living in a large complex, but their ideas did not influence LUCHA's decision to construct small buildings instead of a large housing complex. That decision had been made beforehand, in response to objections raised by other players.

Obtaining the tax credits and lots for the project. LUCHA needed the support of the Aldermen in whose wards the housing would be built to obtain tax credits from the Chicago Department of Housing. LUCHA also depended on Aldermen to obtain access to vacant or city-owned lots for the project. Support from the Alderman for the 26th Ward was predicated on developing housing for single mothers that would be acceptable to other groups in the community and to locate some of the buildings in other wards. Once these conditions were met, the Executive Director of the Near Northwest Neighborhood Network worked with Alderman Ocasio to identify potential lots. The architect eliminated lots that were not suitable for family housing.

Deciding who would live in the housing. More than 500 people applied to live in the housing. Among those satisfying the income requirements, most were single mothers. Decisions about which of the applicants would receive one of the 36 apartments were made by LUCHA according to a government-approved tenant selection plan.

Relating Impacts to Influence

The important accomplishments in this case appear to be related to all of the critical points of influence — *including* the blocking actions that prevented LUCHA's original concept from moving forward. Some of the changes that LUCHA made in response to objections raised by United Blocks, the Block Club Federation, and other community groups led to the development of housing that was more closely aligned with what single mothers actually wanted. This outcome was fortuitous, however, since the objections of the community groups were based on their own interests rather than those of the single mothers.

The potential for creating housing that would not have worked out as well for the single mothers—and the tension and conflict in the case, which added years to the time it took to complete the housing—can be related to the way the original concept for the housing was developed and subsequently refined. After the single mothers expressed a general need for more suitable housing, LUCHA created a solution for them. Most likely, LUCHA staff thought they knew what the single mothers wanted, and the single mothers probably assumed that LUCHA knew what they wanted, too. In presenting its proposal to the Humboldt Park Empowerment Partnership, LUCHA does not appear to have anticipated that its solution for single mothers might cause problems for people living in the neighborhood where the housing would be built. The only option these groups had to influence LUCHA's proposal was to oppose it.

In retrospect, it appears that two kinds of knowledge were missing early on, when the original concept for the housing was being developed. Some of the knowledge LUCHA lacked was from the very people it was trying to help: single mothers. At the start of the case, LUCHA was aware of some of the problems that single mothers were experiencing with their current housing, but it did not really know what single mothers envisioned more suitable housing to be. Without such information, it was not possible to develop housing that would work as well as possible for single mothers or even to know if LUCHA's proposals were "on the right track." Single mothers could have contributed their ideas about housing features that mattered to them through MUA, but the group does not appear to have been used for this purpose until much later in the case, when the architect was hired.

In the early stages, LUCHA also lacked the knowledge of the community residents who would be living in the neighborhoods where the housing for single mothers would be built. As the opposition to LUCHA's proposals revealed, some community groups did not want another large subsidized housing complex in their neighborhood because they believed such a project would exacerbate many of the problems they were trying to address. Negative attitudes about single mothers and their children heightened some people's concerns about the project. As it turned out, the housing that was ultimately constructed—small buildings that blend into the neighborhood and are distributed across the area—met the needs of single mothers as well as the community groups. There was no way to identify this alignment early on, however, because neither single mothers nor the community groups were actively involved in developing LUCHA's proposals.

3

A "Poor Man's Bank" in the Southeast Oklahoma Enterprise Community

The Story

The Poor Man's Bank was a loan program that operated in rural Oklahoma from 1995 through 2000. It provided loans of up to $5,000 for the purpose of starting or expanding a business, and its intended clientele were people who were very poor and had little or no access to commercial banking opportunities. The Poor Man's Bank came out of a larger process of economic and community development in the area — the "Southeast Oklahoma Champion and Enterprise Community," which was established with a $2.9 million grant from the federal government in 1995. "The EC," as people in southeast Oklahoma called it, also gave the area competitive advantages for other government funding for the ten years from 1995 to 2004, as long as the projects could be tied to the EC's strategic plan. The area won the EC designation as the result of an Empowerment Zone/Enterprise Community application in 1994. Enterprise Communities were smaller versions of Empowerment Zones — the "second prize" as some of the people who participated in the process called it.

Although the EC and the Poor Man's Bank served several communities in Choctaw and McCurtain Counties, the story of the Poor Man's Bank began in Idabel, Oklahoma.[1] Idabel is the seat of McCurtain County and is home to about 6,500 people. Like the rest of the area in the EC, Idabel is remote and quite rural, about three hours by car from Dallas, Oklahoma City, or Tulsa, which are the nearest large cities. The railroad tracks that run through Idabel used to form the historical boundary between the white, African American, and Native American (mainly Choctaw) communities in the city — whites to the east of the tracks, African Americans and Choctaws to the west. Over time, this boundary has become less rigid, but most of the city's African American residents continue to live in West Idabel.

West Idabel and the EC

Irvin Jones, a local community leader in West Idabel, was actively involved in the planning process that led to the EC. Jones had grown up in West Idabel in the 1950s and early 1960s when the community's segregated high school — Booker T. Washington High School — was still open. Before desegregation, Booker T. Washington was an important place for young people to build connections to their elders, especially the teachers and educators in the community, who became mentors to whole cohorts of young people. In the early 1960s, Jones left West Idabel for a career in the Army. With desegregation, Booker T. Washington closed, and African American students began to attend Idabel High School, which had previously been restricted to white students. By the time Jones returned to Idabel in 1992, his former school was deteriorating. Its ample grounds had become a hangout for people engaged in drug use or other illegal activities, as well as for young people with nothing else to do. The community had lost the vibrancy Jones recalled from his youth. Trash was piled in heaps here and there, and the economic activity that had existed before in the central part of the community seemed to have dried up.

Jones began to talk to others about doing something to address the situation he'd returned to, and the Idabel Minority Action Committee — IMAC for short — was born. In 1992 and 1993, IMAC organized some community clean-up events that were very successful in terms of bringing people out and beautifying the area, but the community needed more than this.

In March 1994, Jones was invited to a meeting convened by the Little Dixie Community Action Agency. Little Dixie was the local federally funded "CAP agency," which provided services to low-income people in southeastern Oklahoma. At the time, Little Dixie was relatively small, with an annual budget of about $600,000. It was noted for providing a local transportation service that enabled people, especially the elderly, to access services in the spread-out area. Little Dixie was also involved in other activities, including an affordable housing program. The purpose of the meeting that Jones attended was to discuss the federal Empowerment Zone/Enterprise Community (EZ/EC) program, which had just been enacted in 1993 to "create jobs and business opportunities in the most economically distressed areas of inner cities and the rural heartland."[2]

Jones recalls telling the group of community leaders, public officials, and agency staff that he didn't think "27 white men in suits" would do anything for his community, a statement that people involved in the EC recall vividly. Although Little Dixie operated throughout the area, it had little presence in West Idabel; residents there were barely aware of the agency's programs or their eligibility for them. The agency's name also did little to endear it to the African American community. Nonetheless, Jones was convinced to stay involved in the EZ/EC process, which offered him and other grassroots leaders from West Idabel a chance to contribute their ideas to the EZ/EC application's central feature, the strategic plan.

EZ/EC applications were based on geographic areas that met certain criteria. Each participating area was a census tract — one of the basic demographic units in the United States Census. In a rural EZ/EC application, half of the participating census tracts had to have a poverty rate above 35 percent, and none could have a poverty rate lower than 20 percent.[3] There were several areas in southeastern Oklahoma that fit these criteria, though none more than West Idabel, where 50 percent of residents were living at or below the federal poverty level. The census tract on the western side of Hugo, the Choctaw County seat, was also predominantly African American and had a poverty rate of 45 percent. Another census tract around the town of Boswell in western Choctaw County had a rate of 37 percent, and one around the town of Ft. Towson in eastern Choctaw, 35 percent.

Community leaders, including public officials, gathered again in late March to establish "steering and planning committees" for each census tract (hereafter referred to simply as steering committees). Jones became the leader of the committee in West Idabel. The leaders also needed to create a community planning process because the EZ/EC announcement stated that successful applications would reflect "community participation." To develop a process for engaging the broader community, the group brought in an outside consulting firm, National Training Associates, from Sebastopol, California. They were to provide the steering committees and other interested residents with training in a participatory strategic planning process.[4]

A training workshop for about 100 people was held on April 7–8, 1994 in Hugo, where Little Dixie was headquartered. The "system," which the workshop participants would later use to involve many other residents in their local communities, involved two breakout sessions. The first was designed to help people understand the need for change through discussions that explored how community needs had been addressed in the past.[5] In a second round of breakouts, participants were asked to write their ideas about current community needs, problems, and potential solutions on "sticky notes." These notes were posted around the meeting hall for everyone to see, grouped into categories, such as economic development, social and human development, infrastructure, public safety, and education.

Excited about the prospect of getting a $40 million Empowerment Zone grant, large numbers of residents participated in local planning meetings throughout the area in April and May of 1994. These meetings were organized by local steering committees, which were also responsible for reviewing the sticky notes from the planning meetings in their census tract, deciding on their census tract's priorities, and developing specific action proposals.

We don't know how specific the ideas on the sticky notes were, or how they were used by the local steering committees, because the sticky notes have either been lost or destroyed. As far as ideas about economic development were concerned, participants in the process recall only that the residents were interested in "jobs." In West Idabel, the economic priorities of the community and the steering committee were initially rendered in general terms—"jobs" and "industrial development." To make these priorities actionable, the West Idabel steering committee appointed a locally known civic leader, Dr. Walter Frey, as their economic advisor.

"The way they did it in Africa"

Dr. Frey was an administrator for the McCurtain County campus of Southeastern Oklahoma State University and had been involved with the Idabel Chamber of Commerce. He was generally regarded as a community leader in economic matters, and the Poor Man's Bank was his idea. As Jones recalls,

Dr. Frey presented the idea to the steering committee [in West Idabel]—our local steering committee. And [he] explained it to us—told us it was an idea he read in a magazine or something about the way they did it in Africa. It would loan small amounts of money to very poor people, and the village boss or whatever would kind of oversee it. They would make trinkets and sell it to the tourists or whatever. And these people were not bankable or had no other source of getting any funding. And it was very successful; they paid the money back. And when they paid theirs back somebody else could [borrow money]— 'cause they had limited amount of money, so when they paid theirs back somebody else could borrow it. He thought that maybe West Idabel could do the same thing. With peer pressure and people knowing that you couldn't get any until somebody paid theirs back.... And he thought it might work in West Idabel.[6]

A proposal for "Grameen Banks (Poor Man's Bank)" was one of three economic projects submitted by the West Idabel steering committee for inclusion in the EZ/EC strategic plan.[7] Recognizing that "economic development in West Idabel is greatly dependent upon available and accessible finances," the proposal stated that "the creation of Grameen Banks will increase the possibilities of high risk borrowers getting loans for skill training, small business establishment, and improving current businesses." More specifically, the proposal identified the problems that needed to be addressed as "barriers to commercial businesses in West Idabel, lack of sufficient training and knowledge about business operation, lack of sufficient finances and support to take the chance" caused by the "lack of a central business district in West Idabel, lack of needed business skills, and negative perception about the west side." The purpose of the Poor Man's Bank would be to "provide easy access to loans for prospective trainers, and small businessmen." For a proposed budget of $1 million, the program would "provide training in the census tract area, plan and implement seminars for those persons interested in starting a business or expanding and improving an existing business." In doing so, it would "utilize resources of the community ... chamber of commerce, law enforcement, civic and religious groups, and work center to beautify, improve, upgrade, and enhance West Idabel the track area."[8]

The Grameen Bank, to which the proposal referred, began in Bangladesh in 1976.[9] It lends mainly to women (97 percent), recovers over 98 percent of the loans, and has about 2,500 branches in almost 80,000 villages. Projected disbursements for 2007 were almost one billion dollars, all financed by the Grameen Bank's own deposits and loan repayments. In 2006, its founder, Dr. Muhammad Yunus, was awarded the Nobel Peace Prize.

The Grameen Bank is a large, formalized version of a "revolving loan fund."[10] Smaller, informal arrangements exist throughout the world, often involving members of a close-knit group whose mutual dependence and relationships tend to enforce repayment and compliance with the agreed-upon rules. In the rural Andes, for example, housewives in small villages, or otherwise bound by family relations, pool resources so that each member can obtain a sum (say, $200) once a year for a major household purchase; repayment ensures that the next person will be able to draw their sum, and so on.

The key to high repayment rates among many revolving loan funds is that the participants are members of the same close-knit community and the people who borrow the money also control it. In the case of informal funds that involve village members or family members, the fund itself is often contributed by those people. After one person borrows some amount and pays it back, the next person can borrow. In the case of the Grameen Bank, borrowers are organized into five-member groups that are chosen because of their pre-existing relationships and solidarity. Although the group is supervised by Grameen officials at the start, eventually the local groups control their resources, make their decisions, and together ensure the repayment of their own loans.

We don't know how much Dr. Frey knew about the operation of the Grameen Bank or other revolving loan programs,[11] and members of the West Idabel Steering Committee had not been aware of these programs before learning about them from Dr. Frey. But the general idea of peer pressure made sense to committee members, and they supported the idea of a program that would bring financial resources directly to people in their community.

Dr. Frey came with the members of the West Idabel steering committee to present the Poor Man's Bank proposal to the overall steering committee, which included all of the members of the other local census tract steering committees (five per census tract) and one member each from Little Dixie, the Kiamichi Economic Development District of Oklahoma (KEDDO), and the Choctaw Nation.[12] West Idabel's proposal was consistent with the federal government's EZ/EC guidelines, which stated that the "funds may be used to promote economic independence for low-income residents, such as capitalizing revolving or micro-enterprise loan funds for the benefit of residents."[13] Little Dixie was interested in using the EZ/EC application to stimulate small business entrepreneurship across the entire area and, at the meeting, the overall steering committee decided to make the Poor Man's Bank a program that would be available for all the census tracts, not just West Idabel.

Action A-21

Little Dixie was responsible for translating the priorities from the local steering committees into the actions of the EZ/EC strategic plan. Action A-21 proposed the creation of a "Poor Man's Bank" for "economic development and growth in the target [EC] area."[14] Describing the problem, Action A-21 stated that "economic development in the target area is greatly dependent upon available and accessible financing." But "many residents of the target area do not have the collateral for a loan to get a business enterprise started or to expand an existing business. They also may not have sufficient information on available financing, may not be considered credit-worthy by local banking institutions, or may not know how to deal effectively with lending institutions.... The creation of a Poor Man's Bank will increase the possibilities of high risk borrowers getting loans for skill training, small business establishment or improving current businesses."

Action A-21 recognized that "the ability to make future loans is dependent on past loans." Referring to unidentified experiences elsewhere, it noted that "it has been proven in other such programs that 'Poor Man's Banks' have a repayment rate of more than 98 percent" and that "these micro-enterprise 'banks' are actually a committee of local residents, including a banker, business people and citizens." Action A-21 also stated that "detailed procedures for loan approval, servicing and other operational matters" would be developed by "the lead agency [Little Dixie], the local [steering] committees, chambers of commerce and local banks."

The EZ/EC application was sent to the federal government on June 30, 1994.[15] The budget for a $40 million Empowerment Zone grant included $1 million for the Poor Man's Bank. In the accompanying budget for a smaller, $2.9 million Enterprise Community grant, $100,000 was allocated for the Poor Man's Bank. In percentage terms, the Poor Man's Bank fared better in the smaller budget, going from 2.5 percent of the Empowerment Zone funds to 3.4 percent of the Enterprise Community funds. On December 21, 1994, the census tracts in southeast Oklahoma were designated as an Enterprise Community.

The Poor Man's Bank Committee of the EC

The overall steering committee of the EC was chaired by Sonny Victor, who was also on the West Idabel steering committee; the vice-chair of the overall steering committee was Irvin Jones. Victor, who ran an educational services and consulting firm in Idabel, had been a prominent supporter of the EZ/EC process from the beginning. He had grown up in the Choctaw section of West Idabel, and had developed a close working relationship with Jones over the course of the EC designation.

When the overall steering committee met to move forward with the Poor Man's Bank in April 1995, Victor proposed the establishment of a "Poor Man's Bank Committee" (PMBC) of the EC to design the program — subject to the overall steering committee's ultimate approval — and to oversee its implementation. The PMBC would include one person from each of the local census tract steering committees, one from Little Dixie, and one each from the Hugo and Idabel chambers of commerce (at least one of whom would be a banker). At this time, Dr. Frey was no longer involved with the EC, and the representative from West Idabel on the PMBC was Irvin Jones, head of the West Idabel steering committee and vice-chair of the EC.

According to Jones, Little Dixie presented the group with a proposal for structuring the Poor Man's Bank at the first meeting of the PMBC and everyone just "signed up."[16] There would be one Poor Man's Bank fund for the entire EC. Each local census tract steering committee would form its own Poor Man's Bank subcommittee, and applications to the Poor Man's Bank would originate in the census tracts. The local steering committees would hear the loan proposals in a public meeting, after which they would decide which applications to support. From there, the recommended applications would go before the PMBC and then to the overall steering committee for final approval. Loan applicants would need to demonstrate that their individual income did not exceed $9,000 annually. The maximum amount of a loan would be $5,000, repayable within 2 years at a 5 percent interest rate. Little Dixie would administer the Poor Man's Bank loans, disbursing funds to approved recipients and receiving repayment directly from them. This management role would be folded in with Little Dixie's other loan programs, which initially included a Small Business Administration loan program and, later on, "SEEDS" loans[17] funded by a subsequent grant associated with the EC.[18]

At the time the PMBC adopted Little Dixie's proposals for structuring the Poor Man's Bank, many revolving loan funds had been established nationally as well as internationally, ranging from large scale government-funded programs to smaller models operated by community based organizations. The language in Action A-21 shows that Little Dixie knew something about these programs, but it does not appear that Little

Dixie researched the broader experience with revolving loan funds to see how successful programs achieved their high repayment rates. The initial procedures for the Poor Man's Bank did not address the potential issue of delinquent loans.

Making the Loans

The West Idabel steering committee seized the opportunity to provide these loan funds directly to community members. The first Poor Man's Bank loan was made in West Idabel on October 10, 1995. The next set of loans were made in April 1996 — six in West Idabel and two in Central Choctaw. By July 1997, 24 loans had been disbursed: 19 in West Idabel, 4 in Central Choctaw, and 1 in West Choctaw.

The 19 loans in West Idabel funded the opening of 13 new businesses and the expansion of 6 existing businesses:

- 4 for beauty/hair businesses (2 to open new salons, 2 for existing salons)
- 3 to open new auto work businesses (mechanics, body shop, etc.)
- 3 for restaurants (2 to open new restaurants, 1 to expand an existing restaurant)
- 2 for cleaning services (1 to open a new business, 1 to expand)
- 1 to expand a construction business
- 5 to open other new businesses (Cisco store, welding, plumbing, variety shop, and "pagers, etc.")
- 1 to "buy tools for existing business"

The 5 loans in Central and West Choctaw funded the opening of 2 new businesses and the expansion of 3 existing businesses:

- 2 to expand construction-related businesses (Central Choctaw)
- 1 to expand a trucking business (Central Choctaw)
- 1 to open a variety shop (Central Choctaw)
- 1 to open a new "dog kennel" (West Choctaw)

A number of informal procedures and practices developed as the Poor Man's Bank were implemented. In West Idabel — a small community of 1,600 residents where the level of familiarity was high — the steering committee approved loans from applicants who were known to members, had income and skills that members knew about, and who were "already doing something" (i.e. working).[19] The members sometimes provided advice to help applicants make a good impression during their public presentation to the West Idabel steering committee. At Little Dixie, one of the managers in charge of Little Dixie's loan programs said that he sometimes worked with Poor Man's Bank recipients, partnering them up with other loan programs to develop businesses.[20]

The Poor Man's Bank was important in raising the profile of the EC and the local West Idabel steering committee in the community. For West Idabel, these loans represented $92,000 of direct investment, almost the entire amount of the original Poor Man's Bank loan fund.[21] It was proof to local residents that the EC wasn't just using the high poverty rates in the African American section of Idabel to justify spending for programs elsewhere. As Jones recalled, this was "the first time anybody in West Idabel ever touched, put their hands on, spent, or saw any grant money."[22] Eighteen of the loans in West Idabel went to African American community residents who spent the money in the community.

The single loan to a white recipient provided a valuable local plumbing service to people in the community for a couple of years. Four of the businesses in West Idabel continue to operate ten years after the original loans were made.

The Poor Man's Bank also generated interest in other programs and services that the EC made available to West Idabel. For example, a substantial amount of "self-help housing"[23] was constructed there through programs that Little Dixie developed or expanded with the EC. Throughout the process in 1995, 1996, and 1997, the local steering committee members grew as community leaders, and the participation of Irvin Jones and other IMAC members increased that organization's profile in the community as well.

The Poor Man's Bank was apparently perceived to be less important outside of West Idabel. Only four loans were made in Central Choctaw, one in Western Choctaw, and none in Eastern Choctaw or Western Hugo. While the predominantly white residents of some of these communities may have had easier access to conventional loans than the residents of West Idabel, that is unlikely to have been the case in Western Hugo—the African American section of Hugo with a poverty rate almost as high as that in West Idabel. The chief difference between West Idabel and Western Hugo appears to have been the composition of their local steering committees. West Idabel's committee was dominated by the "grassroots" members of IMAC. In Western Hugo, the committee was dominated by prominent people in Choctaw County, only one of whom was from the western part of Hugo.

Delinquent Loans: "Complicating things in the community"

The Poor Man's Bank was one of several loan and small business programs that Little Dixie was developing with the EC designation. The Poor Man's Bank loans were very small by comparison, and in the event of nonpayment, Little Dixie's interpretation of "peer pressure" meant calling on the local steering committee to make loan recipients fulfill their obligations. As Irvin Jones described the process:

> They [the PMBC] really wanted the local steering committees to decide who gets the loans. Because it was a local steering committee and the community's peer pressure that was supposed to be responsible for making sure these people pay these loans back.... [The public application process] was going to be part of the peer pressure. Everybody would know who would get the loans. Everybody would know what the status was. It felt like we needed to do it in public if there was going to be any peer pressure applied at all.[24]

By late 1996, several Poor Man's Bank loans were delinquent, meaning that they were not being paid or were behind the payment schedule, and Little Dixie's loan manager began to call Irvin Jones, asking him to collect the loan payments in West Idabel. Problems with repayment continued through 1997, and loans to people in Central Choctaw were also becoming delinquent.[25] According to a Little Dixie loan manager, it was difficult to collect the loans:

> A lot of the people we couldn't find. They had moved away from the area. Even if we could find them, well, the program was for the very poor and they just didn't have anything. They didn't have any money to pay the loans back. And the few that maybe could have paid the loans, there wasn't any collateral so they didn't have much of a reason to pay back money if we couldn't take back collateral.[26]

Not only were the loans difficult to collect, Jones recalls that "my attempts to collect monies were complicating things in the community."[27] Some loan recipients accused Jones of keeping the money for himself; when Little Dixie's loan manager contacted them, they said they had paid Jones, causing friction between Little Dixie and Jones. As a leader of the overall EC as well as the process in West Idabel, Jones found his integrity questioned. A program that had at first been an important support for the EC in West Idabel quickly became a problem, both for the EC and for Jones's own leadership position in the community.

In retrospect, Jones admits that from the beginning of the Poor Man's Bank, when the PMBC was designing the program, he didn't think the proposed terms of repayment were possible for the intended recipients, since paying back a $5000 loan over 2 years at 5 percent interest would require payments of about $220 per month. Nonetheless, even though Jones was member of the PMBC and vice-chair of overall EC steering committee, he chose not to say anything:

> I just couldn't believe that if I sat up and said these people are not going to be able to pay it back at that rate — I just didn't feel like they were going to try to change the rate. I felt like they were going to probably not make the loans.[28]

Without Jones's input, the PMBC imposed a repayment schedule on loan recipients that amounted to $2,640 per year. The maximum income allowed for a Poor Man's Bank loan recipient was $9,000, barely above the federally established poverty level of $7,470 for one person in 1995. The required loan repayment was close to 30 percent of $9,000 — the equivalent of a second rent, under the rule of thumb that rent make up no more than a third of a household's income.

In creating this repayment schedule, the PMBC did not consult anyone in West Idabel or elsewhere who would be in the potential applicant pool, and committee members never discussed how a person in poverty might be able to make payments equal to about 30 percent of their income. They probably assumed that "peer pressure" would be sufficient to ensure repayment.

By mid–1996, as Jones's experiences trying to collect the Poor Man's Bank loans were turning sour, the PMBC recommended changes in procedures for future loans. The maximum income level for loan recipients would be raised to $12,300 annually (the poverty rate in 1997 was $7,890.00). Recipients would need to provide proof of income and proof of citizenship and would need to adhere to minimum wage and other labor standards for anyone who was employed with loan funds. In addition, the PMBC recommended adopting Little Dixie's suggestion that recipients of approved loans receive business training prior to the disbursement of funds.[29] The collection procedure remained the same — asking the local steering committee members to pursue delinquent loan recipients.

Jones brought the PMBC's recommendations back to the West Idabel steering committee for discussion. Concerned about up-front costs and hurdles for loan recipients, he recommended against supporting business training prior to loan disbursement. Jones explained his rationale:

> [If] the requirement to go to training before the loan was approved, we felt like most people probably wouldn't apply for the loans anymore. Because, you know, it's easy to say go to training [but] the only place you can get training is ET Dunlap or the Vo-Tech. And you have to have money to go to ET Dunlap or the Vo-Tech.[30]

The West Idabel steering committee recommended against the requirement for business training, but that change as well as all of the others proposed by the PMBC were approved by the EC's overall steering committee. This led to a rethinking of the Poor Man's Bank in West Idabel. As Jones recalls, "...in West Idabel at a steering committee meeting ... we entertained a motion to temporarily suspend operations until [loan recipients] ... came current on their loans. That never happened, so we never made any more...." On November 11, 1997, the West Idabel steering committee formally closed its Poor Man's Bank application process. The steering committee told the community "that the people who borrowed the money didn't pay it back, so we didn't have any money. And it was designed to renew itself after people paid it back, but it wasn't working that way. And so we no longer have money to loan because people didn't pay it back."[31]

The Poor Man's Bank continued to operate in the other census tracts in the EC, but no further loans were made until late 1999, after Little Dixie's loan manager was replaced. At that point, according to the new loan manager, the overall steering committee voted to cede Poor Man's Bank operations to Little Dixie, ending the local steering committees' involvement in the process:

> Most of the local steering committees had stopped having regular meetings by the time I came to work for Little Dixie in October of 1999.[32] I believe at the beginning the local steering committees found applicants and brought them in to Little Dixie. The loans that I made, the people came to me for a loan and I told them about the program. If they qualified I helped put together their loan packet and I presented their application to the loan committee for approval.[33]

From October 1999 to November 2000, five more Poor Man's Bank loans were disbursed to applicants from Central Choctaw. The records show only one of these being paid in full, so delinquency — and ultimately, default — continued to be a problem.[34] After that, the Poor Man's Bank ceased to function. Little Dixie deposited the remaining Poor Man's Bank funds, about $50,000, into its Loan Loss Reserve Account that guarantees a percentage repayment on other Small Business Administration loans made by Little Dixie.[35]

The Case Analysis

The Poor Man's Bank involved numerous players: community residents who participated in the EZ/EC process; recipients of Poor Man's Bank loans; members of the West Idabel steering committee; members of the PMBC; members of the overall steering committee; and staff of Little Dixie. To understand how the ideas of these different players influenced what happened, we (1) looked at the major impacts of the case; (2) identified whose ideas were influential at the critical points that shaped the Poor Man's Bank; and (3) explored how the accomplishments and limitations in the case were related to ideas that were, and were not, influential.

Major Impacts

The Poor Man's Bank benefited the residents of the EC in important ways, particularly those living in West Idabel. The program invested $138,000 in communities in the area, with the lion's share of $92,000 going directly to West Idabel — a "first" for that African American community. As a result of this investment, 30 loan recipients were able to start, expand, or improve businesses. One of these businesses provided plumbing services that had not previously been available locally in West Idabel, and five of the businesses continue to operate years later: two beauty salons, a barber shop, and an auto body shop in West Idabel and a bricklaying business in Central Choctaw.

The way the Poor Man's Bank was structured created serious problems, however, making it unsustainable. As a result, a revolving loan program that was supposed to last at least 10 years operated for only 18 months in West Idabel and for less than 5 years in Central Choctaw (where the program was much less active). When the Poor Man's Bank stopped functioning, the loan funds were no longer available to people in the EC communities. Although the program enhanced the stature of the West Idabel steering committee, the imposed responsibility for collecting delinquent loans impacted the chairperson of that committee adversely.

Critical Points of Influence

Looking at the events and impacts in the Poor Man's Bank, there appear to be five points where the influence of players' ideas mattered: (1) getting the Poor Man's Bank into the EZ/EC strategic plan; (2) designing and redesigning the operating procedures for the program; (3) deciding who would receive the loans; (4) deciding how the loan funds would be used; and (5) deciding whether (or to what extent) a census tract would participate in the program.

Getting the Poor Man's Bank into the strategic plan. The opportunity to get any proposal into the strategic plan came about as a result of the EZ/EC application process. In the case of the Poor Man's Bank, four players were very influential: Dr. Frey, the West Idabel steering committee, the overall steering committee, and Little Dixie.

The idea for the Poor Man's Bank originated with Dr. Frey — without his idea it is unlikely the Poor Man's Bank would ever have been created, since we have no evidence that anyone else in the area was thinking along these lines. Dr. Frey's opportunity to be influential arose when the members of the West Idabel steering committee brought him on as their economic advisor. That committee, in turn, moved the Poor Man's Bank idea forward by supporting Dr. Frey's recommendation and by including his proposal in its submission to the overall steering committee. The overall steering committee made the decision to include the Poor Man's Bank in the strategic plan as a program that would be available throughout the EC area. Little Dixie wrote Action A-21, setting the basic parameters for program.

It does not appear that ideas from the local planning meetings influenced the creation of the Poor Man's Bank. While a broad spectrum of residents participated in the meetings — including poor residents who could potentially have benefited from having access to a revolving loan program — there is no evidence that problems related to obtaining credit were explicitly raised or discussed. Our best understanding of community residents' concerns about economic issues — gleaned from interviews with some of the people involved in the process — is that they wanted "jobs," which was not one of the reasons for establishing the Poor Man's Bank.

Designing and redesigning the operating procedures for the program. Action A-21 specified who would be involved in the design of the Poor Man's Bank, and the PMBC provided all of its members — representatives from the local steering committees, the two chambers of commerce in the area, and Little Dixie — with a *potential* opportunity to influence how the program would operate. That potential was not realized, however. All of the ideas adopted by the PMBC appear to have been introduced by Little Dixie, with little, if any, discussion or debate among other PMBC members. Little Dixie's influence over Poor Man's Bank loans and loan funds expanded over time. In 1999, the EC transferred control of the application process to Little Dixie. By late 2000, Little Dixie transferred the remaining Poor Man's Bank funds to another account in its loan programs.

It does not appear that the PMBC sought the ideas of local steering committee representatives, even though they would be responsible for operating the loan program locally. The chair of the West Idabel steering committee (and vice-chair of the overall steering committee) was "at the table" and fairly certain that many loan recipients would not be able to meet the proposed payback terms. But his ideas had no opportunity to be influential since he chose not to express them (for fear that the PMBC would respond by adopting qualifying criteria that would have excluded most of the potential loan recipients in West Idabel).

The people the Poor Man's Bank was trying to help — potential and actual loan recipients — were not on the PMBC. They had no other opportunity to influence the structure of the program since they were not consulted in the initial design or later on when delinquent loans were becoming common, threatening the viability of the Poor Man's Bank.

Deciding who would receive the loans. Procedures adopted by the PMBC gave each of the local steering committees complete control over the application process in its community. Their recommendations had to be approved by the PMBC, but we have no evidence that any local recommendation for a loan was ever overturned.

Deciding how the loan funds would be used. Although loan recipients did not have any influence over the way the Poor Man's Bank was structured, the program gave them a great deal of influence over what they did with their loan money. Applicants created their own proposals for Poor Man's Bank loans, and recipients carried out their proposals according to their own designs. Members of the West Idabel steering committee helped some applicants make their presentations more effective, and some applicants may have received business training or planning advice from the loan manager at Little Dixie. But as far as the evidence shows, these external influences were minimal.

Deciding whether (or to what extent) a census tract would participate in the program. Although the Poor Man's Bank was an EC-wide program, decisions about participation were left to each of the local steering committees. There was very little interest in the program outside of West Idabel. The West Idabel steering committee ended its participation when the problems of collecting delinquent loans became too burdensome for Irvin Jones.

Relating Impacts to Influence

We can relate the important accomplishments of the Poor Man's Bank to three of the points of influence in the case: getting the program into the EZ/EC strategic plan; deciding who would receive the loans; and deciding how the loan funds would be used. None of the players involved in contributing the idea of the Poor Man's Bank or moving it forward were people who would actually need such a loan, and the program was not developed in response to any problem that potential loan recipients expressed during the local planning meetings at the start of the process. Nonetheless, the Poor Man's Bank was very valuable to community members, especially in West Idabel. This was due, in large part, to the creation of domains where two groups of players could exert influence. The Poor Man's Bank enabled the West Idabel steering committee to select loan recipients in its community, and it enabled the recipients of loans to put their business ideas into action.

Many of the problems that emerged over the course of the Poor Man's Bank, and ultimately led to its demise, can be related to a single point of influence — the design and redesign of the program. The maximum amount of the loan, $5,000, was not sufficient to start a business, and the repayment schedule was not realistic for the intended recipients. As a result, delinquency and default rates were very high. The 19 recipients in West Idabel repaid only 33 percent of the $92,000 loaned; the 9 recipients in Central Choctaw repaid 56 percent of the $41,000 loaned; and the single recipient in West Choctaw repaid only 24 percent of his $5,000 loan. A revolving loan program with such repayment problems is not sustainable.

Although the PMBC provided all of its members with the potential to influence design decisions, the only influential player was Little Dixie. Other PMBC members may have deferred to Little Dixie on the assumption that its staff had the requisite expertise. But we also know of at least one occasion when a member of the PMBC recognized a critical payback problem and didn't express his concerns because doing so might have jeopardized Poor Man's Bank funding for members of his community.

In retrospect, it appears that several kinds of knowledge were missing in the design and redesign of the Poor Man's Bank. Although the language in Action A-21 indicates that Little Dixie was aware of the high repayment rates in other revolving loan programs, there is no evidence that Little Dixie consulted with the people who developed or ran such programs to find out how high repayment rates were achieved. Instead, it appears that Little Dixie and the other members of the PMBC relied on the general notion of peer pressure without knowing what was actually required to make peer pressure work.

Little Dixie and the PMBC also lacked the knowledge of the people the Poor Man's Bank was trying to help — poor people who wanted to start or expand businesses and who would be responsible for paying back the loans. Interviews with loan recipients in 2007 showed that they recognized structural problems with the program which were making the repayment of loans difficult or impossible. One recipient stated simply that "payments were too high."[36] Another said "Having to pay monthly was a problem for me. I can't work when it rains, or if the weather is too cold. I paid when I could. When I couldn't work, I couldn't pay."[37] Others commented on the inability of their businesses to make enough profit to repay the loan or even to stay in business: "At the end of the month when it came time to pay on the loan, I hadn't earned enough."[38] "It [the $5,000 loan] was enough to get you started but not keep a business."[39] Had potential loan recipients been consulted initially — or had actual loan recipients been consulted midstream — the PMBC might have had a better understanding of the amount of funding that poor people needed to start or expand businesses and how much they could afford to pay back monthly.

Finally, the PMBC lacked the knowledge of people on the local steering committees who were responsible for operating the Poor Man's Bank locally and for applying the necessary peer pressure to assure the repayment of loans. Each of the local steering committees had representatives on the PMBC, but their ideas about the problems they might face — or later, were facing — in carrying out their responsibilities were not actively sought.

Lacking influence on the PMBC, the representatives of the local steering committees were not able to prevent or correct structural problems with the Poor Man's Bank — particularly those related to delinquent loans. Since the Poor Man's Bank was most active in West Idabel, these problems were most serious for the West Idabel steering committee, particularly Irvin Jones. Ultimately, the only option for influence that was available to that committee was to end West Idabel's participation in the program.

4

A Workforce Alliance Minigrant Program in the Mississippi Delta

The Story

In 1996, the Foundation for the Mid South awarded grants to six "Workforce Alliances" in the Delta region of Mississippi, Louisiana, and Arkansas. Part of a larger initiative to revitalize the struggling economy of the Delta, the workforce alliances were created "to raise the skills of the Delta's labor pool." The Workforce Alliances would do this by "upgrading the current workforce and integrating the unemployed into the labor market through literacy and skills training; preparing students to enter the workforce by facilitating the transition from school to work; and providing post-secondary training."[1] The partnership in Coahoma, Quitman, and Bolivar counties—one of the poorest and least industrialized areas of the Mississippi Delta—called itself the Tri-County Workforce Alliance.

Prior to receiving the $400,000 implementation grants, members of the various alliances had participated in an intensive training program to learn about strategies for promoting workforce development. The Foundation's "core model" had been developed with MDC, an organization that had been working since the 1960's to help communities in the south "transition from a segregated, agricultural workforce to an integrated, industrial workforce."[2] During the training sessions, the leadership of the alliances worked with staff from the Foundation for the Mid South to explore how the core model could be used in each of their communities. The group also expanded on the model, coming up with new strategies that some of the alliances might want to use. One of these strategies was a "minigrant program," which would enable alliances to award small amounts of their implementation grants to other people or organizations in their community for specific purposes.[3]

A Foundation staff member actively involved in the Workforce Alliance program at the time recalled the minigrant strategy as "a small part of the overall initiative."[4] In its original implementation plan, the Tri-County Workforce Alliance hardly mentioned minigrants at all. But a year later, Tri-County (as that alliance is known) began a minigrant program that would last seven years, becoming a centerpiece of its workforce development efforts.

Linking Equity to Economic Development

Workforce alliances were one arm of the "Delta Partnership" that the Foundation for the Mid South created in 1993 to "revitalize the economy of the Delta by promoting racial, social, and economic equity." The other arm of this initiative was the Enterprise Corporation of the Delta, an independent organization created by the Foundation to provide capital and technical assistance to small- and medium-sized Delta businesses in workforce alliance communities and to increase local and national demand for Delta-produced goods and services.[5]

The history of the Mississippi Delta gave the Foundation a strong case for linking the goals of equity and economic development. Before the Civil War, the Delta was a sparsely settled wilderness of dense forest and swamps. The annual flooding that made the soil very fertile also made it difficult to cultivate, so the region didn't have much of a plantation economy. After the war — when African Americans achieved the right to work as free laborers, own property, vote, and hold political office — many purchased or rented land in the Delta, establishing their own autonomous communities and livelihoods in places that were "back there among the wolves and other wild things."[6] The town of Mound Bayou in Bolivar County, created by former slaves, held the promise of a world where African Americans were able to govern themselves and control their own destinies.[7]

In the late nineteenth century, the area became attractive to white planters. With federal resources allocated by the Mississippi River Commission, a levee system was constructed to control the flooding in the Delta. The Illinois Railroad integrated the region into the nation's industrial transportation network, bringing loggers who cleared forested areas for agricultural production. With these changes, the large-scale cultivation of cotton became economically feasible, and white planters established cotton plantations in the Delta.

As the plantation economy began to thrive, African Americans migrated to the Delta to take advantage of the opportunity. But without sufficient resources of their own — and with the end of Reconstruction — most became sharecroppers on white plantations, incurring more debt than profit for their efforts. With the mechanization of agriculture in the mid–20th century, far fewer laborers were needed to produce cotton. Lacking other skills, and with little education, many African Americans in the Delta had no way to support themselves. Some sought work in Memphis or Chicago. For those who stayed, dependence on the welfare system became commonplace.

Although most of the plantations and other businesses in the Delta were owned by whites, African American leadership emerged in other areas. In the era of "Jim Crow" segregation, African American churches functioned as strong social networks that held the black community together. The area's ministers became leaders in the black community, along with African American educators who were nurtured in the segregated school system. In the post civil rights era, African Americans became political leaders as well, eventually comprising most of the Delta's mayors, city council members, and county officials.

In spite of this leadership, African Americans in the Delta continued to be among the poorest people in the country. In Coahoma, Quitman, and Bolivar Counties—home of the Tri-County Workforce Alliance—more than two-thirds of the population is African American. When Tri-County began its work in 1996, one-third to almost one-half of these people were living in poverty, a rate three to four times higher than whites. The unemployment rate among African Americans in the area was almost four times that of whites, and fewer than half of the African American population had completed high school. The situation in places like Jonestown, in Coahoma County, was extremely dire. As a former mayor said in 1993, "We have 1,476 people, but we may have 100 who actually work. Almost all the stores have closed. The town is basically broke."[8]

The Origins of Tri-County's Minigrant Program

The work of the Foundation for the Mid South, like that of MDC, has been grounded in a belief that communities can be stronger if their members reach across lines of race and class to solve problems of poverty.[9] In developing its Delta Partnership initiative, the Foundation saw the workforce alliances as local hubs of a change process that could bridge these boundaries. To achieve that goal, the Foundation required each alliance to establish an "Implementation Team" comprised of people from different races, social classes, sectors, and counties in its region. It also required the alliances to establish task forces around each of the Foundation's objectives for the program: an Out-of-the-Workforce Task Force to integrate the unemployed into the labor market through literacy and skills training; a Current Workforce Task Force to raise the skills of the area's current labor pool; and a Future Workforce Task Force to prepare youth to enter the workforce by facilitating the transition from school to work.

Tri-County met the Foundation's diversity requirement, although the social and historical "fault-lines" in the community made that task particularly challenging.[10] The founding co-chairs of Tri-County's Implementation Team, which serves as its decision-making body, were Charles Barron, a superintendent of schools who was African American, and George Walker, a white businessman who had established a very successful wire company in the area. The team's other members included the chairs of Tri-County's three task forces and more than 30 African American and white residents involved in the local governments, schools, businesses, churches, and community-based organizations in the three counties.[11]

The chair of Tri-County's Out-of-the-Workforce Task Force was Victor Richardson, a teacher in a high school equivalency degree program who was African American and had grown up in poverty; he identified himself as being "grassroots."[12] The other members of that group included people involved in local governments, employment and job programs, schools and community-based educational programs, other community-based organizations, businesses, as well as some community volunteers.[13] Of the three task forces, Tri-County's Current Workforce Task Force had the greatest representation of people involved in area businesses.[14] Its Future Workforce Task Force was comprised almost entirely of people involved in the area's schools.[15]

Tri-County's first undertaking—after completing the training sessions with staff from the Foundation for the Mid South and other workforce alliances—was to draft an implementation plan for each of its three task forces. The idea for a minigrant program had emerged during discussions at the training sessions. The Foundation for the Mid South supported the idea because minigrants could "spark the interest and involvement of community-based groups in the change process around workforce development and get them to be a part, maintain their presence at the table as part of the entire workforce alliance."[16] By offering small grants, the workforce alliances could enhance their visibility in the community and expand their coalition of partners.

In Tri-County's original Implementation Plan, the only place that a strategy related to minigrants appeared was in the section drafted by the Out-of-the-Workforce Task Force. Victor Richardson recalled that his task force was "brainstorming about transportation, childcare, about training programs—things related to under- and un-employed people" when someone suggested that "if some people were unemployed, there might be some of them who had ideas about starting their own business, thereby creating employment for them[selves]."[17] Remembering that a Foundation representative had suggested "we could have monies to have a grant kind of program," the group proposed a "revolving loan fund or other subgrants to encourage business development."[18] In the Implementation Plan, this action was specifically linked to increasing "the amount of quality, affordable childcare services," the lack of which was widely recognized to be a barrier that was preventing poor parents from entering or staying in the workplace.[19]

Tri-County's thinking about minigrants changed after it received its Workforce Alliance grant from the Foundation for the Mid South in April 1996. By September, the group had hired Josephine Rhymes as Executive Director. Rhymes, an educator who was African American and had participated in the planning process for the grant, was well known and well connected in the area. She had spent decades teaching in the high schools and community college in Coahoma County and had played active roles bringing African American and white residents together around community issues. To help Tri-County clarify its mission and start taking action, she recalled that "the first thing that I did was to visit all of the areas and to get a lay of the land."[20]

Rhymes engaged in extensive conversations with the members of Tri-County's Implementation Team and task forces, members of the Chamber of Commerce (where she had been volunteering before taking the job as Executive Director), people involved in government agencies and community-based organizations in the three counties, and people who were unemployed. She also started handing out questionnaires to people who were seeking work in order to find out what was standing in their way and to see if she could connect them to any of the employment opportunities she heard about. Rhymes recalled how these interactions shifted the focus of minigrants from entrepreneurship to workforce development:

> We were talking about entrepreneurship because we knew ... that no big company was going to actually come and give hundreds of jobs, so we were under the impression ... that if we could start small businesses where they could catch foot and hire other people in these businesses, that this would be a means of giving people work. So that's where the idea first came up, but then after talking with people in the community and going to the Chamber of Commerce meetings and other meetings that were held around the Tri-County area, we decided that ... we would look at projects that were related to workforce development.[21]

Workforce development was central to Tri-County's mission of providing "unemployed and underemployed adults with a high degree of applicable job skills and entrepreneurial skills" and creating "an easier transition for high school students seeking to enter the job market upon graduation."[22] In her conversations, Rhymes had heard many people telling her that they had ideas about things to do, but no outlet to do them. A minigrant program could "provide seed money to people in the community to do some things that they felt were important to them."[23] Tri-County's Implementation Team approved these ideas and asked the members of the Executive Committee to develop specific procedures and guidelines for a minigrant program. In the "Operational Plan" that Tri-County submitted to the Foundation for the Mid South in 1997, the minigrant program was described in a cross-cutting section entitled "Partnering" rather than as part of the work of any of its three task forces.

Designing Tri-County's Minigrant Program

One member of the Executive Committee — the director of a health services organization in Coahoma County — had some grantmaking experience, but none had designed or managed a minigrant program before. To get some advice, Rhymes contacted Tri-County's program officer at the Foundation for the Mid South, who referred her to the Ouachita-Morehouse Workforce Alliance in Monroe, Louisiana, which had already established its own minigrant program.[24]

The program that Tri-County's Executive Committee designed — and which was later approved by the Implementation Team — was based largely on what Ouachita-Morehouse had done, with three exceptions.[25] Tri-County increased the maximum amount of their minigrant award from the $1,500 limit that was used in Louisiana to $2,000. They focused their program very specifically on workforce development projects related to "workforce training, emerging technical training, occupational enhancement, building job skills, workforce preparation, training for out-of-school youth, summer training, and internships."[26] And they targeted their program to established "businesses, community-based organizations, churches and other groups" in the three counties that had the credibility and capacity to do what they proposed.[27]

Tri-County's application was designed to be "[user]friendly, so that it wouldn't be something that was complicated, that almost anybody could apply [for]."[28] At the start, it listed the particular kinds of projects the minigrant program would support as well as additional project requirements. To be considered for funding, the workforce development project would need to be "within an established community-based organization" in one of the three countries; "have specific objectives;" "be a well-planned project using specific methods, techniques or schedules;" "demonstrate the extent to which it is needed;" "explain the impact ... on workforce development;" and "be able to evaluate project results."[29] The form, itself, asked for some basic information about the organization and the proposed project. In more detail, applicants were asked to demonstrate the extent to which the project was needed, how many people it would serve, what the project would accomplish and what impact it would have on workforce development, how the grant would be used, and how the project would be evaluated. Proposals needed to be accompanied by the organizational representative's resume and three letters of support, which could be hand written. Applicants were informed that consultants would be available for the implementation of their projects.[30]

Along with the application form, Tri-County established a process and set of criteria for evaluating minigrant proposals. Decisions about the proposals would be made by the members of the Implementation Team based on the recommendations of a group of independent, anonymous reviewers. Representatives from each of the three counties provided Rhymes with the names of people from the business, education, and religious sectors in their area who might be willing to read and review the proposals.[31] The Implementation Team sought people in these sectors because they thought they "would be familiar with what ... the needs are in the community."[32] From this group, Rhymes selected the reviewers. To protect the integrity of the process, she was the only person on the Implementation Team who knew who the reviewers were.

Tri-County developed a set of criteria for the reviewers to use in evaluating the proposals and for the Implementation Team to use in making their ultimate decisions. Overall, the objective was to identify proposals that demonstrated a "commitment to the service population in the ... area and evidence of the ability to fully implement and measure the services" that would be provided.[33] Applications were rated on a 100-point scale. Of the eight categories, the most weight was given to impact on workforce development (20 points), documentation of needs (15 points) and budget justification (15 points). Each of the remaining categories (overall project summary, organizational and administrative capability, strength of the project's goals, evaluation methodology, and community support/collaboration/coordination of services) received 10 points. As Josephine Rhymes recalled, Tri-County wanted the minigrants to support projects that went beyond the self-interest of the applicant organization. "We were really interested in: Was this a self-thing or was it that you were really interested in helping other people in the community? ... How many people will this really benefit?"[34] Tri-County was also looking for proposals that would build job skills—"soft skills" to help people get ready for work, skills to make people aware of job opportunities, and hands-on training in actual jobs.[35] Most of the minigrant award needed to be budgeted for this training.[36]

In addition to workforce development projects, Tri-County decided to use a small portion of the minigrant funds to provide $2,000 scholarships to students at Coahoma Community College. Several members of the Implementation Team, including Rhymes, were former or current faculty at the College, and the College was an active supporter of Tri-County's work.[37] The scholarships were designed to give students an education that would enable them to obtain employment or start their own business. Initially, the scholarships were targeted at graduating high school seniors in Bolivar, Quitman, or Coahoma Counties who didn't have the grades to qualify for other scholarship programs. Later, eligibility for the program was expanded to freshmen at Coahoma Community College and people who had been out of school for a while. To qualify for a scholarship, applicants had to have achieved at least a "C" average in high school. The application, itself, consisted of a short essay "expressing a proposed major and how it will realistically lead to employment or his/her idea for a sustainable business in the tri-county area..." and three letters of recommendation.[38]

Operating the Minigrant Program

Tri-County began soliciting applications for minigrants in 1997 and continued to do so about four times per year until 2003. At the start of each round, the program was publicized broadly. As Rhymes recalled, information would "be made available to our three newspapers, to our radio station that goes across about six counties that they broadcast over. Then we'd have fliers in various places like Kroger, Wal-Mart and any of the grocery stores, and over in Quitman County, the same thing — the grocery stores, the Department of Human Services, the Employment Commission and all of these different places that we'd put fliers up. On the fliers and in the newspaper, we would say that they could contact our office for an application.[39] Then the people would call in and give their name and address and we would mail the applications out. Then they would either bring the applications back to the office, or they'd mail them in."[40] Each application was read by several reviewers. Originally the reviewers met as a group to discuss the applications; later they worked individually, receiving the applications and submitting their written evaluations by mail.[41] Each quarter, Tri-County's Implementation Team met to make decisions about the latest batch of applications. Newspaper coverage of the awards provided additional publicity for the minigrant program.[42]

The number of minigrant proposals received each quarter varied over time, ranging from 0 to 12. Tri-County originally set a quarterly maximum of $3,000 for the minigrant program, although that amount was later doubled to $6,000. Since almost all of the applicants requested $2,000, the cap effectively limited the number of minigrant awards to three per quarter.[43] Overall, Tri-County received 64 applications during the period the program was in operation, 1997–2003. By the program's conclusion, 27 minigrants had been awarded.[44]

The 64 applications came from a broad range of businesses, community-based organizations, and churches in Bolivar, Coahoma, and Quitman Counties. Some were also submitted by publicly funded schools and government agencies. The projects described in the applications were targeted to three populations in the community: 27 focused on youth; 7 focused on adult welfare recipients; and 30 focused on un- or underemployed adults regardless of their welfare status.[45]

The Implementation Team's decisions relied heavily on the reviewers' evaluations and rarely involved lengthy discussions at the meetings.[46] Rhymes, who facilitated the team's meetings, presented the group with the applications and evaluations in the order in which the reviewers had scored them — highest scores first. Rhymes did not take part in any of the decisions about the applications; her role was to answer clarifying questions about the applications and the evaluations.

Different reviewers sometimes gave different scores to the same application, but the successful applications had average scores above 80. A high score alone didn't ensure that a grant would be awarded, however. Some of these were turned down because of concerns raised by reviewers in their written comments. Most of the rejections related to the project's proposed budget — in particular, budgets that were unrealistic for the project or that allocated too much of the funding for staff salaries, equipment, or construction. As Rhymes recalled, "We had several ... where the bulk of the money was going to go to the program director [and] [t]here were not enough funds for the actual project itself."[47] A project to provide pre-employment training workshops on job skills, as well as post-employment assistance to 40 welfare recipients received an average score of 97 but was turned down because the reviewers noted that the "majority of funding would be used for materials."[48]

Other proposals were rejected because they were not closely focused on building job skills or would not benefit enough people in the community. The larger the number of people who would be trained or employed through a project, the more likely it was to be funded, providing the budget was reasonable and the project itself was deemed to be feasible. As one member of the Implementation Team put it, "All things being equal, if one minigrant created two jobs and another was intended to create four jobs we would go with the four."[49] But the reviewers and the Implementation Team looked at more than just the numbers, and projects receiving a high average score were turned down when the application didn't clarify what its impact would be. One example was an application that proposed to teach work ethics to six area youths; it received an average score of 95, but was rejected because there was "not enough information on the type of jobs youth would be able to obtain."[50] Another, that proposed to provide training, skills, and employment (summer and after-school) for 25–50 local youths, received a score of 85 but was turned down because the application "does not state what type of job training or how it relates to the goals and objectives [of the project]."[51]

Rhymes followed up with applicants who were not funded. "I got a whole new feel of what it's like when you are not so much rejected, but when you have an idea and you don't get to fulfill it. Where do you go? In that light, I tried to make suggestions.... 'Try again. Reapply.' We did have some who actually did that, and on the second try got closer to what it was that they were trying to do."[52]

At the start of the minigrant program, Tri-County provided successful applicants with the full amount of their awards up front and the grantees, in turn, were required to provide Tri-County with progress reports for the Implementation Team's monthly meetings and an evaluation report after their projects were completed. After receiving the report, members of Tri-County would conduct a site visit. The process changed in 1999, however, when Tri-County failed to receive progress reports from one grantee. As Rhymes recalled, "The next thing that we heard was that the person [in charge of the project] had become very ill, and we never got our report. The Foundation for the Mid South came and actually visited this particular grantee to see the program that they had in action, and it wasn't working the way that it was described in the proposal."[53] Tri-County recovered half of the unspent grant money for this project and then changed its minigrant disbursement and evaluation policy. From this point forward, they disbursed half of the grant up front and the rest following a midterm evaluation that might include a site visit from Tri-County.[54] In addition to the grant that was terminated midstream, four grantees returned their minigrant awards when they could not implement their projects. Overall, 22 of the 27 awarded projects were fully implemented.

The Minigrant Projects

The organizations in the three counties that implemented minigrant projects included businesses, churches and faith-based organizations, schools and organizations providing community-based education and training programs, other community-based organizations, and government agencies. Some of the organizations used the minigrant funding to start something new. More commonly, since the grants were small, the organizations used the funding to support or expand a project that was already underway, combining the minigrant award with funding from other sources.

Through these projects, 199 un- and under-employed adults received training in work-related skills, and 132 of them obtained long- or short-term employment.[55] Some of the projects provided adults with general training, such as the personal and social requirements of being in the workforce, using a computer to search for jobs, problem solving, and goal setting. Others provided them with training and experience in particular jobs, such as commercial housekeeping, child care, planting and harvesting sweet potatoes, and food service. With new or newly trained employees, some of the businesses that received minigrants were able to expand their operations. Five of the adults who received training through the minigrant program subsequently opened their own businesses, two providing child care services. In a program targeted to adults who were incarcerated or had criminal records, nine of thirteen were employed, and only one returned to prison.

The twelve projects targeted to youth provided 226 of them with training in work-related skills, and with this training, 63 young people obtained summer and after-school employment.[56] Some of the projects provided young people with training in areas such as leadership, reading and good citizenship, appropriate behaviors and manners in the workplace, and how to obtain after-school employment. Others taught them how to start a business (such as lawn mowing or making and selling hair bows) that they could run while they were in school. Youth were also given training and experience to prepare them for particular jobs, such as carpentry (where they got experience building and repairing park benches and houses), financing and accounting (where they got experience working in a bank), and agricultural production and processing. Equally important, some of the projects funded by Tri-County's minigrants provided young people with a protected, unstructured environment where they could be together, hang out, socialize, and pursue their own interests.[57]

The minigrant program also enabled four students to attend Coahoma Community College. One woman, who had been out of school for 20 years and was caring for her home-bound mother, used her scholarship to obtain a cosmetology degree and license. With these credentials, she was able to start a business providing hairdressing services for other home- or facility-bound people while continuing to care for her mother. Her business continued until she left the area when her mother died.[58]

Through the minigrant program, Tri-County developed long-term relationships with some of the organizational grantees as well as some of the individuals who participated in their projects. In Jonestown, where poverty and unemployment have been particularly severe, the Durocher Service Development Program — run by the Sisters of the Holy Names of Jesus and Mary — received four awards over the course of Tri-County's minigrant program. The first two supported "carpentry for youth" programs, one for girls and the other for boys. In each, the young people also participated in Habitat for Humanity, using their newly developed skills to refurbish houses in Jonestown. The other minigrants supported two phases of a leadership and career development program called "Girls to Women." All of these programs, as well as Tri-County's relationship with the Sisters, continued after the minigrants ended. In 2005, three of the young women who had completed the Girls to Women program became members of Tri-County's Implementation Team.

Through its relationship with the Mound Bayou Community Development Corporation, Tri-County participated in introducing a new commercial crop to the Delta — sweet potatoes. With the minigrant, farmers were able to train youth and adults in a variety of skills: planting and harvesting the potatoes, grading and processing potatoes, and making crates for shipping. Many were employed as a result.[59] One of the farmers involved described his experience: "...growing sweet potatoes [commercially] was foreign to most of the farmers—well, to all the farmers except one—an elderly gentlemen who had been growing sweet potatoes on a small scale commercially. The rest of us had only grown sweet potatoes as children when we were growing up in our family gardens. So not only were the producers naïve about sweet potatoes but the workforce was totally naïve. We had to pay minimum wage so the money from Tri-County was used to supplement the training of the workforce which was a big help. The financing helped not only training but subsidizing the financing of the product."[60]

The Sweet Potato Growers Association Co-op, formed by about 20 of the farmers, has a relationship with Alcorn State University, which has an extension unit that conducts research on sweet potato farming in Mound Bayou, and with Glory Foods of Columbus, Ohio, which distributes "Mound Bayou Sweet Potatoes" around the country. One of the farmers said that the project is "kind of an uplift for the community, to have a product that's really the only product produced in Mound Bayou under the name Mound Bayou."[61]

In retrospect, Tri-County's minigrant program appears to have achieved multiple objectives. It engaged community groups in Tri-County's efforts around workforce development, which had been the Foundation for the Mid South's intention for such a program. It supported some entrepreneurship, including two new businesses providing child care services, which had been the original intention of Tri-County's Out-of-the-Workforce Task Force. And it provided practical training and jobs for people in the area who were unemployed or at risk of becoming unemployed in the future. Josephine Rhymes summed up what the experience meant to Tri-County: "We learned that we were just a small organization that if we put our monies out with other organizations, we can help more people.... Instead of us trying to run the program ourselves ... it taught us that other people in the community have ideas. In order for us to get these ideas on the table, the minigrant program to me was an ideal thing for people who wouldn't ordinarily apply for a grant."[62]

The Case Analysis

The development and implementation of Tri-County's Minigrant Program involved numerous players: the Foundation for the Mid South; the Ouachita-Morehouse Workforce Alliance; the Executive Director and members of the Executive Committee, Implementation Team, and Task Forces of the Tri-County Workforce Alliance; the people who reviewed the minigrant applications; the organizations that applied for and received the minigrants; and the youth and adults who participated in the projects that were funded by the minigrants. To understand how the ideas of these different players influenced what happened, we (1) looked at the major impacts of the case; (2) identified whose ideas were influential at the critical points that shaped Tri-County's minigrant program; and (3) explored how the accomplishments and limitations in the case were related to ideas that were, and were not, influential.

Major Impacts

Tri-County's minigrant program benefited many of the players in this case — and their communities — in important ways. The program enabled Tri-County to engage other community organizations in contributing to its mission of workforce development. Through the 22 projects these organizations carried out, hundreds of unemployed adults and youth at risk of unemployment received training in job-related skills, hands-on work experience, and employment. Five of the adults, and some young people as well, started their own businesses. The organizations that received the minigrants were able to put their own ideas into action. In some cases, the training they provided to unemployed people or their own workers enabled them to expand their business operations. The work that people did in some of the projects also improved the communities in which they lived. Houses and benches were repaired; needed services, like child care, were expanded; and a new agribusiness was supported.

Another important accomplishment in the case was the development of organizational and personal relationships that have continued beyond the duration of the minigrants. Organizational grantees developed relationships with the adults and youth involved in their projects, and Tri-County developed relationships with all of these groups. Some of the youth involved in the Jonestown projects are now on Tri-County's Implementation Team.

A major unknown in this case is the extent to which the adults involved in the minigrant projects achieved sustained employment. Another is the ultimate impact of the minigrant projects on youth.

Critical Points of Influence

Looking at the events and impacts in Tri-County's minigrant program, there appear to be four points at which the influence of players' ideas mattered: (1) deciding to institute a minigrant program; (2) designing the minigrant program; (3) deciding who would receive the minigrants; and (4) deciding how the minigrant funds would be used.

Deciding to institute a minigrant program. A minigrant program would not have been an option for Tri-County if it had not been included among the workforce alliance strategies approved by the Foundation for the Mid South. Minigrants do not appear to have been part of the core workforce alliance model that the Foundation developed with MDC. Instead, the idea appears to have emerged during the training sessions that involved Foundation staff and members of the future workforce alliances.

The members of Tri-County's Out-of-the-Workforce Task Force decided to include a form of a minigrant program in their original Implementation Plan. Although their idea to focus the program on entrepreneurial efforts around child care services did not go forward, we do not know if Tri-County would have given further consideration to minigrants if the idea had not appeared in that task force's original plan. The ultimate decision to develop a minigrant program was made by the members of Tri-County's Implementation Team.

Designing the minigrant program. All of the decisions about the design of the minigrant program were made by Tri-County's Implementation Team, but others players' ideas had a lot of influence on the team's decisions. The program's focus on workforce development was shaped by the extensive community conversations that Josephine Rhymes engaged in when she first took the position as Tri-County's Executive Director. The operational design of the program, including the application, was based largely on what the Ouachita-Morehouse Workforce Alliance had done. Tri-County's Executive Committee contributed important ideas of their own, however: the amount of the award; the kinds of organizations the program would be targeted to; the anonymous review process; and the criteria that would be most important in evaluating the proposals.

We do not know if the Executive Committee or the Implementation Team, as a whole, designed other elements of the program, including the maximum amount that could be awarded each quarter, the strategies for publicizing the program, the portion of the award that recipients would receive up front, and the timing of the site visits and evaluation reports. The redesign of the program's disbursement and evaluation policy changed after a negative experience with one grantee. The idea for the scholarship program probably originated with the Implementation Team.

It does not appear that Tri-County specifically sought the ideas of potential organizational grantees, unemployed people, or youth in designing its minigrant program. Representatives of similar types of organizations were on Tri-County's Implementation Team and task forces, however, and Josephine Rhymes had been engaging in conversations with unemployed people and reading their completed questionnaires when she was trying to find jobs for them.

Deciding who would receive the minigrants. The decisions that the Implementation Team made were largely determined by the evaluations of the anonymous reviewers. Their evaluations, in turn, were shaped by the review criteria that the Implementation Team had established.

Deciding how the grants would be used. Organizational recipients of minigrant awards had a lot of influence over what they would do with the money. To get an award, however, their proposals needed to be consistent with Tri-County's workforce development objectives and feasible with the limited amount of funding that the program provided.

Relating Impacts to Influence

The important impacts of Tri-County's minigrant program — and the lack of serious problems—suggest that needed ideas were obtained in this case. In designing the program, Tri-County tapped into multiple sources of relevant experiential knowledge — from its Executive Director and members; from Ouachita-Morehouse's minigrant program; and from the experiences of its own minigrant program, which led to the redesign of some operating procedures. Tri-County did not create an explicit process to involve the types of organizations that would receive the grants or the kinds of people who were intended to be helped by the minigrant projects in the design of the program. But some of their ideas may have been influential indirectly, transmitted by members of Tri-County's Implementation Team, who represented and interacted regularly with these kinds of organizations and individuals, and by the Executive Director, who had extensive interactions with people in the community.

The alignment and linkage of different kinds of ideas may also have contributed to the impacts of Tri-County's minigrant program. The focus of the program was closely aligned with Tri-County's workforce development mission, and Tri-County used minigrants to engage other organizations in the community in contributing to that mission. The awards enabled those organizations to put their own ideas into action in a context that could make a difference with a small amount of funding.

5

The Community Leadership
Team of Story County, Iowa

The Story

On May 18, 1996, a group of eleven women met in Ames, Iowa, to discuss their experiences with the welfare system. Seven of the women were in poverty and receiving public assistance. Three were human services professionals, some of whom had previously experienced poverty. The group leader, Lois Smidt, was also a service provider, but prior to her work as a "family development specialist" with Mid-Iowa Community Action, Inc. (MICA), she had gone through a four-year stretch when she had to rely on public assistance to make ends meet. At the first meeting, Smidt took the others through some practices of listening and relationship building that the group could use to explore their experiences, develop their own voice, and gain a sense of leadership in their own lives.[1] In Smidt's view, these kinds of practices would break the bonds of isolation and dependence that kept people in poverty, enabling the participants to form reciprocal relationships with others and, in the end, "get off welfare."

The group was created by MICA in response to a grant opportunity from the Iowa Department of Human Services. The Department wanted input from the "consumers" of public assistance services to help agencies and providers grapple with the challenges of welfare reform, which was underway around the country.[2] MICA's "Consumer Leadership Team" was established within one of its existing programs—Thriving Families—which had been bringing people from different social classes together to discuss the question, "What do families ... need in order to thrive?"[3] For Scott Miller, the MICA staff person who created Thriving Families, the new Consumer Leadership Team — later to be called Community Leadership Team — would contribute to a larger goal of transforming social service provision by providing agency staff with the input they needed to move beyond "managing poverty" toward a leadership role in "ending poverty."

Seeing Poverty in Story County

Ames is the largest community in Story County, where cornfields dominate the landscape as far as the eye can see. It's like that across much of Iowa, but looks can be deceiving, since Story County differs from the rest of the state in important ways. The county is home to about 80,000 people, which is a lot for rural Iowa and mainly accounted for by the fact that Ames is also home to Iowa State University. Of the 50,000-or-so people who live in Ames, about half are students. As with all university towns, the school creates an atmosphere all its own. The students bring down the average age (at least for nine months of the year) and provide purchasing power that sustains shops, restaurants, and other commercial activities that aren't so common in other rural counties in the Midwest.

The university also brings an influx of well-educated professors and other professionals, who account for the fact that almost half of the county's residents—and two-thirds of Ames'—have bachelor's and graduate degrees, over twice the rate in the rest of the state. The vibrancy of the university's campus, the cultural activities associated with it, and the droves of students in the coffee shops and nightspots can make it difficult to notice that the poverty rate in Ames is about twice that of Iowa as a whole. Some of that figure might be accounted for by students who have little or no income to speak of, but not all of it is. Over the last 10 years, the number of people in poverty has numbered between 9,000 and 10,000, but poor people aren't really visible in the "university town" image that the county's residents and students tend to emphasize.[4]

Lois Smidt was one of the professionals associated with the university. After growing up in rural poverty on a farm in northern Iowa, she went on to complete a master's degree in English Literature and became a temporary instructor in the Women's Studies Department at Iowa State. In 1990, her contract was not renewed because she had been employed for seven years, which was the maximum for a temporary instructor without a doctoral degree. Smidt found herself without a job, and as she struggled with her situation and desire to stay in Ames, she fell into poverty. Unlike her experience in childhood, however, Smidt was now the single mother of two young children, and she went on public assistance in order to provide for her family while she tried to make some important changes in her life.[5]

Smidt joined a network of female artists, "No Limits for Women Artists," which introduced her to Re-Evaluation Counseling. In Re-Evaluation Counseling, people learn to listen intentionally to each other to work through emotions and barriers that prevent personal growth. Both No Limits and Re-Evaluation Counseling also emphasize the role of personal leadership in overcoming internalized oppression and achieving social change.[6] While Smidt was on public assistance, a case worker from MICA visited her on a regular basis and, like many people in similar situations, it was difficult for her to see a way out. Once part of the university culture in Ames, Smidt was now a member of the relatively invisible class of people who depended on the patchwork system of state and private agencies that comprised the welfare system.

In 1995, Smidt was still on welfare when her case worker announced that she was leaving for another position. When Smidt expressed interest in her job, the caseworker said she thought Lois was qualified and pushed for her to get it. In short order Smidt was hired by MICA as a "family development specialist." Now Smidt was a case worker herself, and she began to reflect on how her position had changed:

> I went into people's homes ... and did goal-setting and support around folks who were on welfare having a plan to become economically self-sufficient ... [I] was very motivated by noticing how isolated people were, and how they sort of treated me as a friend rather than

a service provider, you know? They were ... always really excited to see me, because I was the only adult that they had seen since the last time that they saw me. I just started thinking, wow, I'm sort of contributing to this problem of poverty by helping people keep isolated.[7]

This idea stayed with Smidt as she worked at MICA, and when she found out about the new consumer team being created in the Thriving Families program, she went to her supervisor and said, "If you're going to do something around consumer leadership, how about you have somebody who's actually experienced the welfare system lead it?"[8] This suggestion led to conversations with Scott Miller, who knew Smidt from her participation in the Thriving Families forums. In those forums, Smidt had made an impression on the MICA staff as an impassioned and eloquent advocate for people on welfare, speaking from the dual perspectives of service providers and people in poverty. Miller recalls being "enamored by her skills and her personality" and supported Smidt as coordinator of the new Consumer Leadership Team.[9]

A Team to Develop Voice and Leadership

Both Smidt and Miller saw a critical need for a group that would develop the voice and leadership of people in poverty. For Lois Smidt, Consumer Leadership Team could help to counter the effects of a welfare system that was isolating poor people and trapping them in a web of dependent relationships. Her own experiences with poverty, Re-Evaluation Counseling, and No Limits had demonstrated the importance of becoming a leader in your own life — of moving away from thinking about yourself in terms of deficits or needing to be helped and developing, instead, a sense of personal worth and agency. In Smidt's view, Consumer Leadership Team could build this kind of personal leadership among people in poverty, enabling them to express their voice with confidence and to contribute their own experiences to the service provision system. By doing so, it could promote not only personal transformation, but also social change.

Scott Miller tended to emphasize the kind of change that could be driven by service providers, agency executives, and policy makers, acting as leaders in an institutional movement to end poverty. This vision of leadership is why MICA's director, Gary Stokes, brought Miller to the agency in the first place. Stokes recalls how they "spent five years [1993–98] taking a look at leadership issues around poverty agendas. Scott was [the] key staff leader in that project that we dubbed 'Move the Mountain.' So during that five-year period, we were gathering community leaders to talk about a poverty agenda, and we were interested in gaining new community commitment[s] to address poverty."[10]

It was through Move the Mountain that Miller created Thriving Families, which brought together forums of diverse participants, including people on public assistance and middle class residents, to provide information about the kinds of things agency leaders could do to create change. But something else was needed. In conversations with colleagues and friends about the issues facing service providers and how to expand their vision of what they could achieve, Miller recalls "[We were] talking about more and more how to get the voice of people in poverty to the table. We had just noticed that people that were being asked to be on these boards and in the focus groups didn't have any support to play that role, so ... the idea was just to give them a voice and some support around it."[11] For Miller, Consumer Leadership Team could play that role.

Establishing the Team's Principles and Practices

In coordinating the new group, Smidt drew on her own experiences — living in poverty as a child and adult, teaching feminist theory and women's studies, and participating in Re-Evaluation Counseling and No Limits — as well as some of the practices used in the Thriving Families forums. In April 1996, she tested her ideas with Miller's informal support group.[12]

Smidt believed that Consumer Leadership Team meetings would need to be run in a way that enabled people in poverty to participate and that respected, developed, and supported their voices and intelligence. To do that, she proposed providing members with food and child care, having people sit in a circle to demonstrate the equality of everyone in the group, hearing from people in poverty first, and using "listening pairs" to give people experience listening intentionally and respectfully to one another.[13] She emphasized the need for confidentiality to create a safe environment for people to talk and tell their stories. To model a person's ability to "choose a perspective, even if external circumstances are really difficult," she suggested having everyone mention something that was "new and good." To model the provision of support, she suggested that team members express "appreciations" of each other and that the group also include service providers to support her.[14]

Miller and his colleagues were enthusiastic about Smidt's ideas and gave her the go-ahead to organize the first meeting of Consumer Leadership Team on May 18, 1996. As she described: "...we did sort of an all day leadership development workshop. That was an invitation for the women to see what this was going to be like and did they want to be part of it."[15] The women on public assistance and service providers did, and "C-L-Team" — as the group called themselves (abbreviated CLTm hereafter) — began to put Smidt's practices into action.

At the start, the women on welfare were "shy" and didn't think anyone would listen to them. But the way the meetings were run enabled them to move past their fears and begin to use their voices to tell their stories.[16] Smidt's openly expressed need for support showed the other women in the group that it was "okay to feel like we needed support," and modeling "that very, very human style of leadership was very powerful."[17]

One of the earliest actions taken by the original women was to set down in writing the principles behind what they were doing. This became the team's statement of "Purposes and Principles," a document that members have used at every meeting to remind themselves of their reasons for coming together and what they expect of each other. Having such a statement was important when the group first decided to bring in new members. These additions were Scott Miller and Keith Schrag, a colleague of Miller's, who were invited to join about nine months after CLTm's first meeting. Miller's personal background was solidly middle class, while Schrag, like Smidt, had grown up in rural poverty as a youth. Both were very curious to experience how CLTm was working, but the eleven women had to consider carefully how bringing men into the room would affect their dialogue — particularly since much of their talk had centered around the dynamics of power and control in their relationships with men.[18] Their thoughtful consideration extended over some time, but as Smidt recalls, "I think that there was a bubbling up of awareness among the women ... of our own solid power, if you will. It's like, 'Yeah, we're strong enough to start letting in more people.'"[19]

Over time, CLTm has expanded from its original 11 members to over 100 people of different classes, races, genders, and religions. The group's meetings have become more frequent, occurring weekly instead of monthly, and begin earlier to allow more time for socializing. At intervals, the members of CLTm have added new practices, like "no gossip," and have updated their statement of Purposes and Principles, which is now printed on purple stock and referred to as "the purple paper."

In spite of these changes, however, the fundamental structure and practices of CLTm meetings have stayed pretty much the same since 1996. The group gets together every week in the early evening. After sharing a meal that some of them have prepared, they arrange themselves in a circle, and each person has an opportunity to talk about something new or good that has happened recently. The person facilitating the meeting then asks members to go over the purposes and principles in the purple paper and explain why the group adopted them. Members then have an opportunity to state things they need or have to offer, such as furniture, an appliance, a ride, or a job, which often leads to exchanges. This is often followed by listening pairs, sometimes on a chosen theme, sometimes without one. Then the meeting turns to a discussion of a particular topic or issue in the community. Before leaving, everyone expresses an appreciation of the person sitting next to her or him.

Building Cross-Class Relationships

In 1997, a local group, called the Ballard Ministerial Alliance, asked CLTm for advice on supporting families at risk of homelessness as part of MICA's project, "Home Mission." For the next six months, CLTm members held potlucks with the members of the Alliance. After dinner, "we'd all sit in a circle, and people talked about what is it like to be poor and what are some of the challenges and what are some of your gifts, and [we] did some of our processes that we used in CLTm."[20] These meetings produced the idea of pairing up a person in poverty with someone who was not in order to build intentional relationships that would accomplish two objectives: support poor people as they tried to leave poverty and enable others to learn about poverty. Developing such cross-class relationships would address a problem that had surfaced earlier in the Thriving Families forums: "Well, I need friends who are different from me, because all of my friends are in the same boat. We can't help each other get jobs, and we can't help each other figure out money because we're all poor."[21]

This idea became a program called "Family Partners," and to distinguish between the people involved, CLTm began referring to people in poverty as "participants" and those who weren't as "allies." The participants in Family Partners were members of CLTm and attended CLTm's regular meetings, but that was not the case for most of the allies, since doing so was not a requirement of the Family Partners program. As Smidt noticed, not being part of the CLTm community led to problems because:

> Middle class people had just as effective isolation patterns as poor people, so you would have like these Family Partner ally folks who would fall into isolation and be trying to fix a poor person rather being a friend.... [They] would feel ashamed because, as a middle class person, they were used to ... succeeding and doing well. It's like, "I can't fix this person. I can't solve this problem, you know?" So they would isolate and they wouldn't call for help. They wouldn't call [us] or come to a meeting and say, "I need help." So there was this mutual isolation that happened [in Family Partners].[22]

When funding for Thriving Families ended in 1997, Stokes and Miller came up with a new program to replace it, "Beyond Welfare." As a program within Move the Mountain, Beyond Welfare would provide a home for CLTm, Family Partners, and other activities related to CLTm. In Stokes' and Miller's thinking, CLTm was developing and testing ideas that would contribute to moving people off welfare and to Move the Mountain's broader agenda for social change. Miller was particularly interested in how the development of cross-class relationships through Family Partners could do both.

In 1998, Miller met Mike Green, a trainer with Asset Based Community Development (ABCD)—an organization headed by John McKnight at Northwestern University in Chicago—who took an interest in Beyond Welfare's work. Around the same time, Steve Aigner, a member of Beyond Welfare's advisory board who was a professor at Iowa State, had been teaching a course about ABCD, and there was a convergence of interest among Miller, Aigner, and Green in having Beyond Welfare work with ABCD. In 1999, Green brought Beyond Welfare into ABCD's "Neighborhood Circles" program as one of several sites he worked with around the country.[23] This was the beginning of a three year relationship in which Green traveled to Ames several times a year to meet with Smidt, Miller, and others in the Beyond Welfare community.[24]

During these visits, Smidt and Miller told Green about the problems they were experiencing in Family Partners, and he, in turn, told them about a program in the Canadian disabilities movement, called "Circles of Support," which was enabling disabled people to develop relationships with a set of other people who could help them negotiate the social service system and function more fully in everyday life. Smidt and Miller brought the idea to Beyond Welfare and CLTm, describing how Circles of Support would connect one participant (and their family) with three or four allies, as opposed to the one-on-one approach of Family Partners. Beginning in 2000, Family Partners was gradually transformed into Circles of Support, and Green introduced personal support tools for Circle members to use, including "Dream Paths," which lay out where participants want to go and how their Circle will help them get there.

"Money, meaning, and friends"

As Green worked with Beyond Welfare in Neighborhood Circles, he became more familiar with CLTm, contributing ideas that changed the way the group talked about what it was doing. Lois Smidt recalls that "what [ABCD and Mike Green] saw as our real forte was this inclusion of the people from the margins and building what they've come to call more recently 'radical hospitality'—that we create an environment of radical hospitality where there is a very open door and everyone and anyone can be welcome, regardless of your label or your station in life or your status and that kind of thing."[25] In addition, Green saw CLTm's view of poverty as going beyond the conventional material concerns of jobs and income, which seemed to resonate with ABCD's view that the "core needs with any human being" are "money, meaning, and friends."[26] In mid–2000, CLTm revised its "Purposes and Principles" document to reflect these interactions with Mike Green, adding its future vision of Story County as "a community of hospitality and caring where everyone has enough money, friends, and meaning to fulfill their dreams and potential in life, and share their contributions."

Talking about poverty as a lack of money, meaning, or friends was appealing for the members of CLTm because it explicitly recognized that people who are financially well off can also be in poverty and that more than money is required to get people out of poverty. That recognition, in turn, clarified the role of allies and cross-class relationships in CLTm meetings and Circles of Support. CLTm wanted allies to become aware of poverty in Story County that had previously been invisible to them and to provide support to participants who were trying to get out of financial poverty. But allies were also there to *be* supported — by participants and other allies who could become their friends and by a community that could add meaning to their lives.

It was during this period that CLTm decided to change its name from *Consumer* Leadership Team to *Community* Leadership Team to emphasize that both participants and allies were integral members of a mutually supportive community.[27] With this change in name, some of CLTm's practices also changed. The detailed intake process that Scott Miller had designed for CLTm participants in the early years was abandoned in 2001, and the weekly meeting adopted an "open door policy," which encourages people to come and stay if they like it.

As was the case with Family Partners, the allies in Circles of Support are not required to attend CLTm meetings. But most of them currently do, learning through practice how to develop respectful, reciprocal relationships with people who are different from them. Smidt and others in the group have observed that the Circles with allies who attend the weekly meetings tend to be more effective than the others and do not have the kinds of problems that so many of the cross-class pairings in Family Partners had.

The participants and allies involved in the weekly meetings and Circles of Support describe CLTm as a community that is very valuable to them. Many talk about developing important new relationships, which have filled a void in their lives or have changed the way they view other people. One of the participants described having "...just an incredible diversity of relationships in my life right now that has been a tremendous blessing to me. When I was young I was very, very shy and had almost no friends and now I feel like I've got a whole huge second family...."[28] An ally said that "becoming part of this diverse community breaks down my tendency to think of other people in abstract categories; meeting weekly ... with people make the people real as opposed to being stereotypes...."[29]

The supportive environment has given participants and allies more confidence in what they know and can do. One of CLTm's original members said that the constant emphasis on personal inherent leadership "was a self-confidence booster. The more I did it for myself, the more I found I was able to share with others."[30] She also noted: "Something as simple as a listening group or a listening pair and feeling that support, it made a big difference in the long run.... Even with the jobs that I have today, it's helped me have the courage to take a step in initiative when its needed."[31] Reflecting on her personal growth, a newer participant said: "Maybe now I can become an ally now that I've got this new job. Now I can help to maybe support in ways that people were supporting me before."[32]

Wheels to Work

The weekly meeting and Circles of Support are the foundation of the CLTm community, and the development of personal leadership and mutually supportive cross-class relationships within this community is CLTm's key strategy for getting participants "off welfare." In addition, CLTm provides a platform for identifying some of the practical barriers that participants face and for developing and implementing programs to address those barriers. One example is the Wheels to Work program, which supports participants in finding work and staying employed by providing them with cars.

Wheels to Work was developed early in CLTm's history and responds to an issue that was raised by people in poverty during the Thriving Families forums as well as by participants in CLTm meetings. The transit system in Ames is not highly developed and doesn't really serve the needs of poor people, many of whom also live outside the city in rural areas. When participants in CLTm brought this issue up, MICA embarked on a study of transportation programs for poor people around the country, which in some places were called "Wheels to Work," and Scott Miller brought MICA's findings to CLTm. With that information, some of the allies in CLTm proposed developing a program that would donate cars to poor people who needed them. But when CLTm took the allies' idea to participants, they said: "Well, yes. We love the idea of getting a free car, but don't give me something for nothing. At least I want to pay a dollar, or at least I want to do something."[33]

As a result, CLTm "imbedded [its culture of] reciprocity into that [program]."[34] In exchange for a car, participants would sign a reciprocity agreement, taking out a forgivable loan for a small sum that could be paid back in money or in-kind services. Over the period that Beyond Welfare measured the impact of Wheels to Work, 1999–2004, 123 cars were transferred to participants who needed transportation. During the same period, almost half of the 131 participants involved in CLTm were able to move off public assistance, and many were able to find jobs that increased their earned income.[35]

Having transportation has made a big difference in participants' lives, making it possible for them to go to job interviews, get to and from work, and run ordinary household errands, like shopping. By eliminating their need to ask for rides from others, the cars have also given participants more control over their own daily schedules. For one of the original CLTm members, receiving her car brought her back to CLTm meetings as part of the reciprocity agreement: "It was a comfortable and safe atmosphere to open up to. I was able to give back and participate in things. Little by little, a lot of what worked in the early days [of CLTm] was that there was enough to open me up and got me going again."[36]

Interacting with the Broader Community

One of the original goals of CLTm was to enable people in poverty to use their voices in forums where they might be able to influence service providers and policy makers. Through "Consumer Advisory Teams" (CATs)—supported by the Iowa Department of Human Services and the Child and Family Policy Center in Des Moines—participants in CLTm were able to do so from 1998 until 2002.

The CATs were a direct mechanism for people in poverty to provide feedback on services that the Child and Family Policy Center used in its research and advocacy publications, and the CATs were also in direct contact with Iowa state legislators. CLTm participated in the process directly, and Lois Smidt also provided training and technical assistance that was valuable in setting up other CATs around the state. In "Day on the

Hill," an annual event that took place for several years, CLTm members and people from the other CATs went to the state capitol and met with legislators. Early CLTm participants remember these occasions as very powerful experiences. Their stories and advocacy helped to ensure the creation of "Empowerment Funding" for children's welfare in 1998.[37] Even more important for some CLTm members, speaking out to powerful people who could affect policy changed the way they perceived themselves. As one participant put it: "None of us really had any self-confidence or self-esteem when we started this."[38]

CLTm members have become involved in other community issues that matter to them when opportunities have arisen. For example, allies who were members of the League of Women Voters raised the importance of livable wages with that organization. After the League studied the issue, CLTm and the League joined forces to advocate for changes in state policy. In another instance, an African American woman running for a position on the school board came to CLTm to hear members' concerns about the unequal treatment of African American children and poor children in the schools. Individually, some CLTm members supported her successful campaign. Concerns about the funding mechanisms for child welfare and social services in Story County led a group of CLTm members to study the issue, resulting in a United Way funding set-aside for transportation, which is benefiting CLTm's Wheels to Work program.

CLTm members have also extended some of their own practices to other arenas. Concerned about the school system's remedial response for problem students from poor families, CLTm participants created role-play scenarios, which helped teachers and administrators understand what the program was really like for poor mothers and their children. Participants living in the Eastwood subsidized housing development in Ames helped to organize other residents in a meeting like CLTm's, which eventually led to the development of a community garden, a new playground, and social events at the development. The experience of being involved in CLTm inspired one participant to start a program in Eastwood on her own. With donations she solicits from local businesses, "Operation Backpack" provides school supplies to low-income children there.

Extending the Reach of CLTm

Through its weekly meeting and Circles of Support, CLTm has been creating a mutually supportive cross-class community that is transforming the lives of the people involved. Since its inception in 1996, upwards of 350 people have been participants or allies in CLTm. Many more will need to be involved, however, to reach the other people — in Ames and elsewhere — who lack money, meaning, or friends in their lives and to achieve social change.

While CLTm was still with Move the Mountain, Lois Smidt and Scott Miller designed an "immersion" training program for people interested in learning about Circles of Support and CLTm. After Beyond Welfare incorporated in late 2001, Smidt, other Beyond Welfare staff, and CLTm members conducted the immersion program independently of Move the Mountain, moving the emphasis of the training to building a community like CLTm's. People from around the United States and other countries participate in the week-long programs in Ames, which cover CLTm's Purposes and Principles and many of the practices that CLTm uses in its weekly meetings and Circles of Support. Lois Smidt also provides technical assistance on-site in places where CLTm's community-building practices are being used.

As Executive Director of Move the Mountain, Scott Miller has been trying to achieve his vision of social change by developing Circles of Support in ways that could develop institutional bases to end poverty. In 2002, Miller brought the idea to a group of funders and school administrators in Des Moines, Iowa. The project, called "Name Each Child," would use the school system as a base to create over 40 Circles of Support, involving a detailed intake process for participants and over 100 allies. Allies (selected to provide support in particular areas) would help participant families move out of poverty by developing and implementing rigorous goal-setting plans. Participants and allies would take part in a "big view" meeting to differentiate the problems the Circles could solve from more systemic problems. Information from these meetings would then be relayed to a "systems change committee" composed of agency executives and policy makers.[39]

The project was funded in Des Moines, and Miller also set up a similar one in a small town called Nevada, which is in Story County, a few miles east of Ames. Smidt and another Beyond Welfare staff member were contracted by Move the Mountain to provide technical assistance for these projects, and although the projects never took root, the experience helped them appreciate why CLTm's meetings and approach to Circles of Support were so different from Miller's. The change agents in Miller's projects were allies (helping participants to change) and agency executives and policymakers (using information from participants and allies to create social change). In CLTm, by contrast, the change agents are participants, allies, and the community they create together through their weekly meetings and Circles of Support. The CLTm community develops the voice and leadership of participants so they can take more control over their lives, and it enables participants and allies to support one another in achieving their self-determined goals. Greater social change can be achieved by proliferating these kinds of communities.

The Case Analysis

The creation and development of CLTm involved numerous players: Scott Miller, Director of Thriving Families and Beyond Welfare at Mid-Iowa Community Action and later Executive Director of Move the Mountain, Inc; Lois Smidt, Family Development Specialist at Mid-Iowa Community Action and later Co-Director of Beyond Welfare, Inc.; the participants (people in poverty) and allies (people with sufficient income) involved in CLTm meetings and Circles of Support; the Iowa Department of Human Services; and Mike Green, a trainer with Asset-Based Community Development. To understand how the ideas of these different players influenced what happened, we (1) looked at the major impacts of the case; (2) identified whose ideas were influential at the critical points that shaped CLTm; and (3) explored how the accomplishments and limitations in the case were related to ideas that were, and were not, influential.

Major Impacts

CLTm's weekly meetings and Circles of Support have created a mutually supportive, cross-class community that is addressing the isolation of people who are impoverished in a variety of ways—through lack of money, meaning, or friends—and the limited influence that participants have had over their lives. Through CLTm, participants and allies have become part of a community that they own and that is very meaningful to them. Members of both groups have developed relationships with people they would not otherwise have known and have gained more confidence in what they know and can do. Many of CLTm's participants have also benefited materially — obtaining access to cars, moving off public assistance, and getting jobs that have increased their earned income.

Although the input and advocacy of CLTm members have also contributed to changing some of the policies and services affecting people in poverty, the main purpose of community engagement in CLTm is to build community among participants and allies rather than to identify, understand, and address other community problems. Nonetheless, the relationships that members develop in this community — which cut across lines of class, race, and gender — lead them to care about each others' issues and organize around them to advocate for social change. The confident voice and skills that members gain from being part of CLTm support their involvement in community problem-solving processes organized by others. In addition, CLTm's culture of reciprocity encourages participants and allies to become more involved in the communities where they live and work, "giving back" in a variety of ways.

By creating the CLTm community in Ames and by supporting the development of others like it — through immersion training — CLTm hopes to build a critical mass of cross-class relationships that will change society. Since CLTm is designed for a self-selected group of people — those who want to develop cross-class relationships and become part of this kind of community — the ultimate societal impact of CLTm will depend on the proportion of people who fall into this category.

Critical Points of Influence

Looking at the events and impacts in the development of CLTm, there appear to be four points where the influence of players' ideas mattered: (1) establishing CLTm; (2) codifying and modifying CLTm's purposes, principles, and meeting practices; (3) developing Circles of Support; and (4) designing other CLTm programs and activities.

Establishing CLTm. The Iowa Department of Human Services provided the impetus for creating CLTm; had the Department not provided MICA with a grant to get consumer input on welfare reform, it is unlikely that CLTm would ever have been established. The notion of creating a consumer leadership team came from two players who were at MICA at the time: Scott Miller, who was interested in making agency heads and policy makers more effective in addressing poverty, and Lois Smidt, who was interested in building personal leadership among people in poverty.

MICA's decision to put a person who had actually experienced the welfare system in charge of CLTm gave Smidt the opportunity to test principles and practices that she had been exposed to during her experiences with Re-Evaluation Counseling and No Limits. These principles and practices became — and continue to be — the foundation for CLTm.

Codifying and modifying CLTm's purposes, principles, and meeting practices. The decision to adopt the principles and practices that Smidt introduced was made by the original eleven women in CLTm. These women created the first "Purposes and Principles" document, which codified what they were doing and why.

Since then, CLTm's purposes, principles, and practices have continued to be owned by the members of CLTm. They have made some significant changes in CLTm's meeting practices over time — such as expanding and diversifying the people involved, making meetings more frequent, starting meetings earlier to allow more time for socializing, and adding a "no gossip" rule — and have updated the "purple paper" several times. Mike Green's influence is evident in the update in mid–2000, which included the language of "hospitality" and "money, friends, and meaning."

Developing Circles of Support. The need for cross-class relationships to support people trying to leave poverty was identified by people in poverty themselves — both in the Thriving Families forums and in potlucks involving members of CLTm and the Ballard Ministerial Alliance. Miller and Smidt translated that idea into the Family Partners program. Drawing on his experiences with the Canadian disabilities movement and ABCD, Green was very influential in helping Miller and Smidt transform Family Partners into Circles of Support, providing them not only with a name and concept (connecting a participant to multiple allies), but also tools for Circle members to use, such as the Dream Path.

Green's language of "money, meaning, and friends" helped CLTm articulate its broad definition of poverty more clearly, which, in turn, clarified the kinds of support that participants and allies can give each other. As allies were increasingly perceived to be on the receiving end as well as the giving end of their relationships with participants, the "fix-it" mentality that had characterized some of the Family Partners pairings diminished, and CLTm became a more mutually supportive community. CLTm members ended the agency-like intake process that Miller had designed for CLTm participants and adopted an open-door policy for their weekly meetings. After that, Miller had no direct influence on CLTm's Circles of Support program.

Designing other CLTm programs and activities. Decisions about developing or engaging in other programs and activities have been made by CLTm members, Lois Smidt, and other staff (in MICA, Move the Mountain, or Beyond Welfare). These players initiated and designed CLTm's structured programs: Immersion training and Wheels to Work. In the case of Wheels to Work, participants in CLTm introduced a key element of the program, the reciprocity agreement; the earlier proposal from allies for a car donation program was not influential. The ideas for local activities have come from CLTm members — both participants and allies, and most of these activities have been designed by CLTm members as well, with support from staff. CLTm's involvement in state-level policy issues has largely been in partnership with other organizations.

Relating Impacts to Influence

We can relate the important accomplishments of CLTm to the first three points of influence, since the establishment of CLTm; the codification and modification of its purpose, principles, and meeting practices; and the development of Circles of Support determined the nature of the community that CLTm has created. The ideas that serve as the foundation for the way CLTm's weekly meeting and Circles of Support are structured were contributed by Lois Smidt (influenced by her experiences with Re-Evaluation Counseling and No Limits) and Mike Green (influenced by his experiences with ABCD and the Canadian disabilities movement). Smidt's and Green's ideas were adopted by the members of CLTm, who own them and have refined them over time.

The foundation that Smidt and Green created is working well for the participants and allies in CLTm. This is due, in part, to the fact that CLTm members are self-selected — people don't join or continue with CLTm if they don't like its principles and practices. Equally important, CLTm creates domains where its members can exert influence. A fundamental objective of CLTm is to increase the influence that participants have over their own lives. The Board of Beyond Welfare is made up of participants and allies in CLTm,[40] and CLTm's members have control over maintaining or changing their community's practices. In addition, CLTm has prepared and supported its members in using their voices and putting their ideas into action in other venues.

The ideas that provided the rationale for creating CLTm in the first place came from Scott Miller and Lois Smidt, and the way CLTm was originally structured achieved both their objectives. In addition to developing personal leadership among people in economic poverty, CLTm collected information from them, both to inform human services agencies and policymakers and to document the capacity of the program to get people off welfare. After 2001, when Beyond Welfare separated from Move the Mountain, the CLTm community became an end in itself rather than a means of achieving something else, and practices like Miller's detailed intake process for participants were abandoned. At Move the Mountain, Miller developed Circles of Support along very different lines, in ways designed to create institutional bases to end poverty.

An open question about CLTm is whether its community-building practices can create enough mutually supportive cross-class relationships to change society — in Ames or elsewhere. CLTm's immersion training is extending the reach of CLTm's practices, but the self-selected group of people who want to engage in them may not comprise a sufficiently large proportion of the population to achieve societal change. At this point, ideas from other people in the community may be of value to CLTm — to discover what might make them interested in, or open to, the idea of developing cross-class relationships and to find out if different kinds of approaches for developing such relationships might be more comfortable or effective for different kinds of people.

6

Developing a "Professionalization Curriculum" in the Mississippi Delta

The Story

On August 7, 2002, the Tri-County Workforce Alliance applied for a Workforce Public Policy grant from the Foundation for the Mid-South to prepare residents of Coahoma and Quitman Counties in Mississippi "for participation in the competitive labor market and to obtain a living wage job."[1] These two counties comprised "the heartland of one of the poorest and most unindustrialized areas of the ... Mississippi Delta," and Tri-County (as the Alliance is known) had been working there and in Bolivar County since 1996 to promote "long-term economic and community development by building a competitive workforce through education and training."[2]

Over the years, Tri-County had worked closely with people and organizations in business, education, and other sectors to address the problem of "underemployment," which includes not only unemployment, but also suboptimal employment, such as having only part-time work or working multiple, low-wage jobs. Through its collaborations, Tri-County had linked employers to programs that could meet their employee training needs; created new training programs for underemployed people, like Carpentry for Women; addressed needs of youth at risk of underemployment in the future; and found jobs for many underemployed people in the area. In spite of these efforts, however, some underemployed people were still "falling through the cracks." Tri-County saw the public policy grant as an opportunity to find out why that was happening and to do something about it.

In its application, Tri-County proposed surveying employers and underemployed people to learn about the barriers to workforce development from both of their perspectives. Barriers that weren't already being addressed by existing training programs would form the basis for a "curriculum on professionalism in the workplace," which Tri-County would create "in conjunction with employers, underemployed, and educators in the target communities." The curriculum would contain "social components necessary for the world of work." After completing a pilot program that moved students into gainful employment, Tri-County would take steps to assure that everyone in the mid-south region had the opportunity to obtain these skills. The grant's policy objective was to "assure that each individual seeking employment will have an opportunity to obtain value-added, appropriate skills and knowledge to be gainfully employed, maintain employment, and work toward upward mobility."[3]

On September 11, 2002, Tri-County received $12,000 from the Foundation for the Mid-South to carry out the initial phases of its proposal. On July 15, 2003, it received an additional $32,000 to implement the Professionalization Curriculum and work toward its policy objective.

Underemployment in the Delta

Tri-County is headquartered in Clarksdale, Mississippi, known for the famous "crossroads" of U.S. Highways 61 and 49 where the legendary Delta bluesman, Robert Johnson, supposedly sold his soul to the devil in exchange for his talents. Tri-County's target area — Coahoma County, where Clarksdale is situated, and the adjacent counties of Quitman and Bolivar — differs from Mississippi as a whole in important ways. While two-thirds of Mississippi's population is white, more than two-thirds of the people living in these counties are African American.[4] One-third of the households in the tri-county area are below the poverty line, as compared to about one-fifth in the state. The proportion of people without a high school degree or equivalent is much higher in the three counties (38–45 percent) than in the state as a whole (27 percent). Within the tri-county area, the poverty rate for African Americans (33 to 46 percent) is three to four times as high as for whites (11–12 percent), and the unemployment rate is almost four times higher for African Americans (11–14 percent) than for whites (3–4 percent). The rate of underemployment is even higher, since many people who are employed have only part-time jobs, temporary jobs, or jobs that don't provide them with living wages.

The high rates of underemployment and poverty in the Delta have deep historical roots in slavery, "Jim Crow" segregation, and the plantation system that first exploited African American labor and then cast it aside with the mechanization of agriculture that began in the 1950s. Until machinery came to the plantations, the cotton fields had provided seasonal, if poorly paid and very difficult, work for African Americans who had few skills and little education. With mechanization, very few jobs were available for this large population group. Those who could leave the area to find work often went up the Mississippi River to Memphis or Chicago. For those who stayed, dependence on the welfare system became commonplace.

In the 1960's, the Civil Rights movement also began to have a profound impact on the Delta. As African Americans achieved the right to vote, more were elected to public office, and most of the mayors, city council members, and county officials in the Delta are now black. With desegregation, more educational opportunities opened up for African Americans, increasing the number of black educators and business people in the area.

Josephine Rhymes had been a school teacher and community leader in Clarksdale for many years when the opportunity to create Tri-County came about. Originally from southwest Louisiana, she was recruited by the Clarksdale school system in the mid–1960s, where she taught high school for 20 years. Subsequently, she spent 11 years on the faculty of Coahoma Community College. During that time, she became involved with a variety of nonprofit organizations and groups and helped to rally black and white residents to support a tax referendum that funded the construction of a new high school in Clarksdale.

"Why don't people work?"

When Tri-County was getting organized in the mid 1990s, Rhymes saw an opportunity to explore something she'd been interested in for a while. As she recalls:

> I volunteered a number of years at the Chamber of Commerce. I had an opportunity to also sit in on some of their meetings and the employers were always talking about that they didn't have an ample workforce. I was always curious about, "Well, why don't people work? If you say that you have jobs, then why don't people work?" I was always curious about that, so when Tri-County came on the horizon ... I looked at what the mission was [and] ... I said, "Well, this is a good time for us to find out."[5]

Rhymes became Tri-County's Executive Director, charged with supporting the work of its "Implementation Team," which functions as the group's board and active membership. The Implementation Team is made up of about 30–35 African Americans and whites from the three counties, including representatives of government, business and industry, educational institutions and community-based organizations as well as youth and "grassroots individuals."[6]

As Tri-County began its programming, employers in the Chamber and other places were telling Rhymes that people in the area didn't have specific skills for the kinds of jobs they needed to fill. So Tri-County began to link employers with training and vocational programs that would meet their needs, many of which were offered at Coahoma Community College, where Tri-County's office was located. The College's "Skill/Tech" program was tailored to employers. Its vocational courses produced skilled graduates, such as welders, whom employers could recruit. The program also worked with employers to create courses specifically designed for their company's employees. One of the Skill/Tech instructors, Charles Langford, became a member of Tri-County's Implementation Team.

Tri-County was also interested in finding out what underemployed people needed. As Rhymes ran into people who were seeking work—at local service agencies, the state jobs program, housing complexes, and other forums—she started giving them a short questionnaire. The questionnaire asked for the person's contact information, the highest grade they had completed, whether they were working, and (if they answered "no") why they weren't working. Then it asked what kind of job the person would like to have, what skills they already have, if they would need transportation or child care in order to work, and if they would be willing to take some classes to prepare for the work force.

Between 1997 and 2002, Rhymes gave these questionnaires to more than 250 people, using the information to connect them to employment opportunities that she heard about in the course of her work with Tri-County. She was successful in finding jobs for more than 100 people this way. Even though she wasn't analyzing the data in the questionnaires formally, reading them taught her and Tri-County's Implementation Team a lot about existing barriers to employment. All of these people wanted to find a job (or wanted a better job than they currently had) and many had employable skills. But they were thwarted in their efforts because they couldn't find a job, didn't have anyone to take care of their children or disabled parents, didn't have transportation, or had health problems that prevented them from working. About half were willing to take classes to prepare for the workplace.

Rhymes was particularly concerned with the underemployed people who seemed to "fall through the cracks" because they lacked job-seeking skills or experience, wanted jobs they weren't really qualified for, didn't know where to look to find a job, or didn't know which agencies could help them. When the opportunity to apply for the Workforce Public Policy grant appeared in 2002, she and the members of Tri-County's Implementation Team decided that they wanted "to come up with something that could help these people [find] a job, other than the method that we had, where we would get the printout from the employment services and try to match them with the skills" that they listed on the Tri-County questionnaires. "We were looking for something to do to help them to basically market themselves," Rhymes said.[7]

Researching the Issue

Shortly after receiving the grant, Tri-County created a research team to work to fill a "gap" that seemed to be limiting the effectiveness of programs aimed at decreasing underemployment. That gap was a lack of understanding of what "employers and people identified as underemployed have to say about this issue and possible interventions." Along with Rhymes, the research team included John Green, a new professor in the community development program at nearby Delta State University, and his graduate students. This project was the beginning of an ongoing relationship between Tri-County and Green, who later developed an Institute for Community-Based Research at the University.

The research team used different approaches to get the perspectives of underemployed people and employers. They conducted a series of focus groups with 29 underemployed people in Coahoma, Quitman, Bolivar, and Tallahatchie counties. These discussions explored the job options that underemployed people had, the features that made jobs appealing to them, the resources they had and the challenges they faced in achieving their own job goals, and what additional education or training might do for them. The members of the research team decided to interview employers individually by phone, since they thought employers would be less forthcoming about their hiring and employment practices in front of others. Thirty-two employers from Coahoma and Quitman counties were surveyed this way. Through the interviews, the team was able to learn the employers' general views about economic opportunities and challenges in the Delta and the role of education and training in improving employment and productivity. The employers were also asked about their employees' wages, benefits, job security, and job advancement, but there is no evidence that they responded to these questions.

After completing the interviews and focus groups, the research team organized separate meetings of the employers and underemployed people to go over what each group of participants had said. As the team's report describes,[8] the underemployed people related some of their problems to a lack of education or training, including their limited formal education, a mismatch between their skills and available jobs, and insufficient know-how to start their own businesses — particularly in developing business plans and in working their way through the credit system. They also talked about the limitations of acquiring more education. Even though they had received training for available jobs and had educational certificates, they weren't being hired because employers were looking for people who had work experience as well.

Training, education, and work experience were only part of the problem, however. Although they expressed a strong desire to work, the underemployed people said that many barriers were preventing them from obtaining desirable employment. Some of the issues that came up in the focus groups had surfaced before in the job-placement questionnaires that Rhymes had been distributing, such as a lack of transportation, child care, or care for dependent parents; health problems; and inexperience in applying for jobs. Other issues were new. The underemployed people talked about favoritism in hiring practices, which made it difficult for them to get a job if they weren't a friend or relative of the employer or his current employees. They spoke about the limited availability of local jobs and their reluctance or inability to leave the area to find employment elsewhere. People on public assistance said they couldn't afford to work because they would lose needed benefits, like health insurance, when they became employed. Some people said they were not considered to be employable because of previous convictions or involvement with drugs.

Discussing the jobs that were available to them, the focus group participants said that most were undesirable because the jobs only paid the minimum wage, were part-time or temporary, didn't have decent working conditions, or lacked benefits. Underemployed people thought that traditional economic development plans weren't doing much to improve the number or quality of available jobs because tax breaks and other incentives only brought companies into the area for a couple of years, after which they tended to move on. In addition, they said that barriers were preventing people like them from opening their own small businesses.

In the telephone interviews, the employers raised many of the same issues as the underemployed. The employers spoke about the limited number of jobs in the area, due, from their perspective, to the limited opportunities for business expansion and development. The employers talked about the lack of basic education among members of the local workforce, although they also stressed the lack of vocational and hi-tech training. Regarding the need for more than classroom training, employers acknowledged that they "privilege somebody who has experience and not just the education."[9] They also mentioned transportation and child care issues.

Some of the employers' perspectives were very different than those of the underemployed. In contrast to the statement by focus group participants that they really wanted to work, employers said that, in their view, many people without jobs didn't want to work, and some who had been hired didn't come to work on time, wouldn't work all day, or failed to understand the rules and regulations of their jobs. These problems with work ethics, motivation, and worker attitudes were contributing to what employers saw as "a negative atmosphere present in the existing and 'potential' workforce."[10] The extent of employer dissatisfaction with the workforce, combined with what they saw as limited opportunities for economic development and expanded job opportunities in the area, led members of the research team to report that "for some [employer] respondents, a general feeling of despair permeated their answers to most questions."[11] It does not appear that the employers raised any of the issues with wages, benefits, or job security that were of considerable concern to the underemployed people in the focus groups.

In addition to surfacing problems, the interviews and focus groups enabled employers and the underemployed to express what they thought needed to be done to address the causes of underemployment. Underemployed people talked, in very general terms, about a need to increase educational and training opportunities. They also wanted a mentorship/apprenticeship program. To create desirable jobs, they suggested pursuing employment security and new job creation from untraditional angles. In particular, they wanted to develop a small business incubator, to develop some form of cooperative industry that would entail locally dispersed ownership and provide jobs through the manufacturing of consumable goods, and to attract businesses that were willing to make a long-term commitment to the community and to provide employees with decent pay, benefits, working conditions, and training for advancement.[12]

In their interviews, the employers also noted the need to develop more jobs and industry in the area and to provide the workforce with more education and training, including "hands-on" job experience. In particular, employers believed that the workforce needed training in basic skills and work ethics and that the area needed more people with vocational skills and technologically sophisticated skills.

Bringing Employers and Underemployed People Together

After the separate meetings with employers and underemployed people had taken place, the research team organized two additional meetings to bring the groups together to discuss the findings from the telephone interviews and focus groups. In these meetings, Tri-County hoped that employers and underemployed people would listen to each other and have a conversation that could inform the development of the Professionalization Curriculum. The joint meetings, along with much of the research process that preceded them, was new to many of the participants, and they didn't know what to expect. One Tri-County member with many years of experience in workforce development said:

> I've never participated where employees were asked, "What is it that you're trying to do, and how is it that you're trying to get yourself hired?" Then in a separate meeting you've got employers being asked, "What is it that you want and need in employees?" And when it came time to bring the groups together, he said, "I had ... never seen the blending of the two."[13]

The research team organized two meetings in Quitman and Coahoma Counties, inviting the underemployed people who had participated in the focus groups, the employers who had participated in the telephone interviews, as well as educators and other stakeholders. Very few of the underemployed and employers responded, however, and members of these groups made up a small proportion of the 14 people who attended the meetings. John Green characterized the atmosphere:

> "We were very cognizant of the fact that holding together a collaboration of employers, educators, underemployed folks and all those sorts of things was difficult.... As you can imagine, the minimum wage issue was kind of considered hands-off by a lot of the employers and that sort of thing. They didn't really articulate it as such, you know? But any time that you talked about those issues, heads would go down...."[14] On some of these basic issues about pay, job security, and benefits, "neither side ever understood why the other side was the way that it was ... I guess both sides were engrained in what their attitude and opinion was, and they were not willing in that short a period of time to change."[15]

The research team tried to overcome these difficulties by focusing on the notion of professionalization and on the curriculum, itself. This strategy shifted the discussion away from most of the issues the employers didn't want to talk about. At the same time, it identified elements that both employers and the underemployed thought should be included in the curriculum, such as providing underemployed people with basic work-related skills and on-the-job training.

The team also took a strategic approach to the discussion about job advancement, which was very important to focus group participants but appeared to be off-limits for the employers. Recognizing that employers didn't see underemployed people as having much potential for advancement, the team changed the way the issue was framed. "Let's not see this as an ending point ... let's not assume that the end of their career is working a minimum wage job, but that their entry point might be working for a company like yours in that type of position. How would you like to have them trained to continue to move up in the system?"[16] Employers still resisted the idea, but "we kept asking that question.... What type of training would you want to see an employee have in order to work up through the system?"[17] When the employers finally talked about what they looked for in employees who advance to management positions in their companies, the list of characteristics sounded like "leadership skills" to the research team. Training in these leadership skills was available in the area, but not for people who couldn't find a job and lacked a high school education.

Designing the Curriculum

When the interviews, focus groups, and meetings with underemployed people and employers were completed, Tri-County decided to move forward with a Professionalization Curriculum that would cover each of the following topics in a 3-hour session: (1) how to finish adult basic education/G.E.D.; (2) finding, applying, and interviewing for a job; (3) basic computer skills; (4) money management; (5) workplace ethics and professional communication; and (6) leadership skills. The curriculum would be followed by a two-week internship to provide graduates with on-the-job training and experience to help them "work into the system."[18]

To develop the specific content of the curriculum, Tri-County created a Curriculum Design Committee composed of eight people drawn from different groups—two from the educational sector (including workforce development), two from social services (including the state jobs services office), two from local businesses, and two who were underemployed.[19] According to John Green, there "was a real effort to make sure [the committee was] diverse in terms of all of these different kind of stakeholder attributes that we talked about" in the curriculum process. One of Green's graduate students was given the job of coordinating the design committee. The committee held five weekly meetings in the summer of 2003, during which the members reviewed existing workforce development syllabi to identify components that would be appropriate to include in the Professionalization Curriculum. They also proposed their own ideas where existing material was lacking.

Tri-County believed that a committee with diverse representation was needed to give the curriculum legitimacy,[20] but in practice, the six professionals and two underemployed people had difficulty communicating and working with each other. As one of the underemployed members put it: "I wasn't comfortable [in the meetings] ... because I felt like what I said was of no concern.... It was like I was just a figurehead and just sitting there...."[21] She was frustrated because she felt that "the program was really based on a person like myself ... I was a true witness to everything" the curriculum was about.[22] She recalled "customer service" as an idea she had but did not contribute to the discussion. "That's always stuck with me because that's the most important thing that I concentrate on when I'm on the job [now]." Eventually she stopped speaking at the meetings, though she continued to attend them. "I just [sat] back and listened, took it in and watched. Some of the information that they brought, like the finance, I took it home with me and applied to my daily living.... What I learned here through this group, I applied out in the community with the people that I know are dealing with their problems."[23] The other underemployed person simply stopped coming after the second meeting.

The professionals on the committee were also aware of problems. One wasn't clear about what the underemployed members had to offer. "I can't say that they were experts in anything.... They were very intelligent girls, but they had not had the privilege of having been educated as much as I think that they wanted to be. They were pursuing, they were trying to get out of a rut, and [being on the committee] was an opportunity that they were going to take.... They were street smart."[24] Another said that the underemployed members "really felt that people ... didn't approach them [for their ideas] from the start. I guess because we stigmatize so much."[25] She concluded that "You need to have somebody in here that can focus on not just the project itself but also the members ... because if you have professionals in the group and people that are not, there are times that people can feel left out."

The curriculum that the committee developed is about 400 pages long, filling a large two-inch binder, divided into six sections, one for each of the components of the course.[26] Most of the curriculum's content is from materials that the professionals on the committee brought to the meetings, some of which was from their own syllabi. The professionals on the committee also contributed some new materials, including a small booklet on interviewing, which featured tips on punctuality, dress, and general preparation for an interview, and a list of interviewing techniques that a person could carry along (in a purse, for example), with space for writing down important information before going into an interview. According to a professional member of the committee, the underemployed members "really didn't do any of the developing of the curriculum."[27]

Once the curriculum was developed, Tri-County's Implementation Team reviewed it and gave the go-ahead to offer it at Coahoma Community College's Skill/Tech Center. Rhymes recruited six instructors from the area, some of whom were also members of Tri-County's Implementation Team. The instructors would be able to take what they wanted from the curriculum and also bring their own materials to add more specific content to their sessions.

Implementing the Curriculum and Internship

To recruit students, Tri-County distributed fliers around the area, and Rhymes made on-on-one connections with potential students during her visits to the Department of Human Services, the Clarksdale Workforce Investment Network Job Center, housing complexes, and other community forums. As in the past, she asked everyone to fill out one of her job placement questionnaires. The 75 underemployed people who expressed interest in the Professionalization Curriculum were invited to a screening interview that Tri-County would use to select the 30 students for the course. Only 33 of the 75 showed up for their screening interviews, however, and Tri-County decided to admit all of them. The vast majority of these students (94 percent) were out of work, and more than half had not completed high school or received their GED. Nonetheless, they had a variety of job-related skills and experience, such as cashiering, housekeeping, cooking, child and elder care, construction, casino work, and factory work.[28] Twenty-two of the admitted students showed up to take the first class on the evening of November 13, 2003.

During November and December 2003, the students participated in six classes at Coahoma Community College — one for each of the components of the curriculum. After each class, the students completed an evaluation focusing on the usefulness of the session to them, the effectiveness of the presenter in conveying the information, and the adequacy of the facility. All of the sessions received positive evaluations from the students.[29] In describing the overall course, students said they learned things they had wanted to know in order to find and keep a job. The skills they valued learning most related closely to the content of the work ethics session: "how to come to work ... how to dress, how to approach and talk to persons directly..." and how to bring a positive "attitude" to the workplace. The session on leadership skills also stood out for students. It taught them "how to work as a team" and develop strategy together, which was a new experience for some of them.[30]

Both the leadership skills and work ethics sessions showed students how they could communicate with employers. According to Charles Langford, who taught the work ethics portion, this was a new idea for the students. "Most of them have never even heard of the concept, you know? The employer is totally different. "You know, I can't talk to him. I've never been taught that I should talk to him. So if I've got an issue that I've got to deal with where I can't get daycare and I can't get to work or anything, I just quit ... or I don't go to work today." Langford used role playing to help students in the class understand that "until you're willing to come in and tell me [the boss] what the problem is, I can't fix it.... Go in and talk to your manager. If you're a good and dependable employee, the supervisor or manager is going to do everything he can to keep you."[31]

The leadership skills session also used role playing to help students think about talking with employers or coworkers about issues that made them uncomfortable. "Let's say that you're going in to ask for time off, or you're going in to ask for a raise. What are the different forms of interaction? What happens if there is something going on in the workplace and you're the one that's chosen to take it to your boss? You're going to be the leader, you know? How can you do that?" In the role playing, the instructor asked for volunteers, who "would get up in front of the room, and he had a video camera. The class would choose a topic for you to talk about, and you had no time to prepare for it. You just had to start talking. If it got bad, then the other participants got to throw things at you!"[32]

One of the students, who wound up working as an assistant in a hospital, said that the course had a very positive effect on her work and her life by changing the way she communicated with people.

It brought something out of me.... You know, at that time I just didn't talk to nobody, I had my head down and just walked on, you know. You got an "attitude," I got one too. But that ain't the way to carry yourself. You know you can carry yourself better than that — inside and out. And I'm talking about there's sick folks at the hospital. I'm talking about sometimes they want to call you and talk to you because they be lonely; family don't come. So, you know, I stands and talks to them, you know, with my mop in my hand so, you know, keep me from getting in trouble. And I tell them, you know, I'll come back and check on you before I leave, but I got to go on and do the rest of the [work] and, you know, they'll say, "Okay, baby, thank you for talking with me." It makes you feel better as you go on about the day.[33]

There was some attrition during the classroom sessions, so only 14 of the 22 students who began the curriculum completed it. Originally Tri-County had planned to offer two-week internships to half of the students who finished the course, but with fewer graduates, the internship was offered to all of them. Eleven of the 14 accepted the offer and received placements with local employers along with a $150 stipend.[34] Rhymes used her contacts to try to give graduates the particular kinds of job experiences they were looking for. All of the internships involved full-time work, which was important to everyone who had started the course. Graduates interested in clerical or computer work received placements as secretaries, receptionists, or office clerks; those who were interested in "keeping things clean" received placements in food preparation or organizational housekeeping; one who was interested in "using his hands" received a placement in maintenance.

At the completion of the two-week internships, the interns were evaluated by their employers. All but one of the evaluations were favorable, and the employers' remarks emphasized the professional attitudes and work habits of the interns.[35] Nine of the interns obtained full-time employment (either with their internship employer or elsewhere) and two went back to school to continue their education.

Extending the Reach of the Program

The policy objective of Tri-County's grant was to assure that everyone in the mid-south region would have the opportunity to benefit from its Professionalization Curriculum and internship program, and Tri-County's strategy for achieving that objective was to institutionalize the program as part of broader workforce development efforts. As a first step toward getting the curriculum included in other educational programs, Tri-County's Implementation Team asked Rhymes to prepare a list of the competencies students would gain from completing the curriculum. Each of these competencies had been taught before, but they hadn't been taught together for these kinds of students— under-employed individuals with limited formal education who have problems finding and keeping jobs. Leadership training, in particular, had not previously been considered to be appropriate for such people.

Tri-County has pursued several venues for extending the reach of its program. One is "Jobs for Mississippi Graduates," a state-run program for high school students who are not going on to college. Tri-County would target its curriculum and internship to students who dropped out of high school or are at risk of dropping out. Tri-County is also proposing that its Professionalization Curriculum and internship be offered at Coahoma Community College's Skill/Tech Center.

The Case Analysis

The development and implementation of the Professionalization Curriculum involved numerous players: the Executive Director and members of the Implementation Team of the Tri-County Workforce Alliance; the underemployed people who filled out Tri-County's job placement questionnaires; the members of the project's research team; the underemployed people and employers who participated in the research team's focus groups, interviews, and meetings; the underemployed and professional members of the curriculum's design committee; the curriculum's instructors; the employers who provided internship placements; and the underemployed people who participated in the curriculum and internship. To understand how the ideas of these different players influenced what happened, we (1) looked at the major impacts of the case; (2) identified whose ideas were influential at the critical points that shaped the Professionalization Curriculum; and (3) explored how the accomplishments and limitations in the case were related to ideas that were, and were not, influential.

Major Impacts

Tri-County has created a valuable program that was not previously available for its intended students—underemployed people who have been "falling through the cracks" because they have limited formal education and don't know how to find or keep a job. The program offers training in a set of skills that had not been taught as a single curriculum before. It provides leadership training for a group of people who were not previously thought to have much potential for advancement. In addition, it connects classroom teaching with on-the-job experience in the kinds of places where underemployed people want to work.

The outcomes of Tri-County's pilot program are encouraging. The first class of graduates have learned skills that they perceive to be very valuable—not only in finding and keeping a job, but also in their personal lives. Employers were satisfied with all but one of the interns. All but one of the students who completed the curriculum and internship obtained a full-time job or went back at school. At least two-thirds of the people who obtained a job have remained gainfully employed since the program ended.

The process that was used to design the program has been beneficial, as well, generating a knowledge base that is valuable for purposes that go beyond the Professionalization Curriculum, itself. The focus groups with underemployed people and the interviews with employers revealed a great deal about the problems that are contributing to underemployment in the Delta and the kinds of strategies that could be explored to address those problems. In addition to identifying issues directly related to workforce development, the ideas of employers and the underemployed highlight the importance of focusing attention on hiring and employment practices (such as wages, benefits, working conditions, job security, and job advancement), job-related supports (such as transportation and child and elder care), critical public benefits (such as health insurance), job discrimination, and the creation of desirable jobs, particularly through untraditional approaches that would attract committed businesses to the area or enable underemployed people to become owners of businesses as well as workers in businesses.

The design process did not achieve all of its objectives, however, and in some cases it created problems for certain participants. The joint meetings were not successful in getting employers and underemployed people to listen to each others' perspectives, and many of the issues that mattered to the underemployed people who participated in the focus groups were not discussed at those meetings or addressed by the curriculum and internship that Tri-County developed. The underemployed members of the Curriculum Design Committee felt alienated and unvalued; one stopped contributing and the other stopped coming to meetings.

There are also some unanswered questions about participation in the Professionalization Curriculum. We do not know why only 33 of the 75 underemployed people who showed interest in the curriculum showed up to complete the screening questionnaire, why only 22 of the 33 people who were accepted actually started the course, or why only 14 of those students completed it.

Critical Points of Influence

Looking at the events and impacts in the development of the Professionalization Curriculum, there appear to be four points at which the influence of players' ideas mattered: (1) obtaining the perspectives of underemployed people and employers; (2) creating the curriculum; (3) creating the internship; and (4) deciding to participate in the program.

Obtaining the perspectives of underemployed people and employers. Recognizing the need to hear directly from underemployed people and employers to find out why people weren't working, Tri-County created two opportunities for members of these groups to contribute their perspectives: the questionnaire that Tri-County's Executive Director gave to underemployed people to help her find them jobs; and the systematic study of underemployed people and employers that Tri-County proposed in its grant application and that the project's research team designed and carried out.

In the study, the potential for underemployed people and employers to influence what happened was largely determined by the research team, who decided how each group would be involved and what they would be asked. The process clearly differentiated the ideas of employers and the underemployed, identifying similarities and differences in their views. Participants in the interviews and focus groups were asked very broad questions, enabling employers and the underemployed to express ideas that went beyond the development of a Professionalization Curriculum. The potential influence of these ideas was limited, however, since only ideas directly related to such a curriculum (or to workforce development, in general) had any possibility of being influential in the context of this project.

Both employers and the underemployed had a lot of influence over their own participation in the process, and very few accepted the invitations to the joint meetings. The employers who came were very influential in preventing wages, benefits, and job security from being discussed, which further limited the influence of the underemployed people who cared a lot about these issues. The research team found a way to engage employers in a discussion about job advancement, however, which led to the development of the leadership component of the curriculum.

Creating the curriculum. The idea for the Professionalization Curriculum came from Tri-County, and its intended focus on "social components necessary for the world of work" was articulated in Tri-County's application to the Foundation for the Mid-South.

The six topic areas of the curriculum were determined by Tri-County based, in part, on its Executive Director's extensive experience trying to find jobs for underemployed people in the area, and on the information that the research team collected in its study of employers and underemployed people.

In its report to the Foundation for the Mid-South on October 17, 2003, Tri-County stated that it wanted to construct "a curriculum for professionalism that is considered legitimate by the underemployed and employers." In retrospect, the ideas from employers and underemployed people that appear to have influenced the topic areas of the curriculum are those that had legitimacy with both of these groups and were consistent with the project's objectives. The inclusion of the work ethics component appears to have been influenced by ideas expressed by employers. The leadership component can be traced, indirectly, to ideas that underemployed people expressed about job advancement. The adult basic education component reflects ideas expressed by both groups.

The specific content of the curriculum was determined by the Curriculum Design Committee. Although the underemployed members of this committee were "at the table" and had a potential opportunity to influence the content, that potential was not realized. The underemployed members of the committee were outnumbered, six to two, by professionals. The professionals did not seek out the views of the underemployed members, and the underemployed members stopped contributing their ideas because they perceived that the professionals on the committee did not value what they had to say. There is no evidence that the specific content of the curriculum would have been any different if the two underemployed people had not been on the committee.

The instructors for each of the six sessions had a lot of influence over the content that was actually taught. They decided what material they would use from the prepared curriculum and what they would introduce on their own.

Creating the internship. An internship was not explicitly included as part of the project Tri-County proposed in its grant application. The idea appears to have come from the underemployed people and employers who participated in the research team's focus groups and interviews. The underemployed talked about the limitations of classroom programs and expressed the need for a mentorship/apprenticeship to give them work experience. The employers acknowledged that they preferred to hire people who had "hands-on" work experience in addition to education. As with the six topic areas of the curriculum, the idea for an internship appears to have been influential because it had legitimacy with both employers and underemployed people and was consistent with the project's objectives—the internship would strengthen the Professionalization Curriculum by helping to move underemployed people into gainful employment.

The two-week internship was designed by Tri-County, and Tri-County's Executive Director was very influential in arranging placements that gave graduates the particular kinds of job experiences they were looking for. Tri-County had originally planned to split the graduates into two equal groups, with one group receiving internships and the other not. Presumably, this approach was intended to determine whether adding an internship to the curriculum actually helped people to find and keep a job. Since only 14 students completed the curriculum, this kind of experimental design was not possible.

Deciding to participate in the program. The students, course instructors, and employers providing internship placements all made their own decisions about participating in the program. Less than one-third of the underemployed people who initially expressed interest in the curriculum decided to participate, and only two-thirds of the people who started the course completed it. There was no attrition in the internship component of the program.

Relating Impacts to Influence

In order to carry out this project, Tri-County believed that it needed to hear from underemployed people and employers directly, and the first two points of influence created opportunities for members of both groups to contribute their ideas. As the case documents, however, some people chose not to participate in these opportunities—in particular, the underemployed people and employers who did not attend the research team's joint meeting and one of the underemployed members of the Curriculum Design Committee who stopped coming to meetings. The other underemployed member of the Curriculum Design Committee continued going to the meetings but stopped contributing ideas. In addition, many of the ideas that were contributed by underemployed people and employers in the focus groups, interviews, and meetings that the research team conducted were not used.

The part of Tri-County's project that reflects the ideas of underemployed people and employers most closely is the two-week internship. This idea appears to have originated in the research team's study and was proposed both by underemployed people (the kinds of people who would be interns) and employers (the kinds of people who would provide internship placements). In practice, the internship created a domain where underemployed people could exert influence, since Tri-County placed the interns in the particular kinds of job experiences they wanted to be in. The internship program was clearly of benefit to the underemployed people who participated in it. All of the interns completed their two-week placement, and many went on to gainful employment, either with their internship employer or elsewhere.

The curriculum, itself, incorporates proportionally fewer ideas from underemployed people and employers. Only three of the six topic areas of the curriculum appear to have been influenced by their ideas, and none of its specific content. Although the underemployed people who completed the course perceived the entire curriculum to be valuable, the two sessions that stood out for them had origins in the ideas of underemployed people and employers in the research team's study. The session on leadership was designed to help underemployed people advance in a job, which was an important objective of the underemployed participants in the focus groups. The session on workplace ethics and communication covered skills that employers thought underemployed people needed to learn. The underemployed students in the Professionalization Curriculum clearly found these skills to be useful, even though the underemployed people in the focus groups had not identified a need for them beforehand.

As the fourth point of influence highlights, the attrition rate in the curriculum was high, suggesting that a substantial number of its intended students may not have seen the course as being sufficiently appealing or useful to enroll or (if they did) to complete the six sessions. In retrospect, the people who seem to have been in the best position to look at the curriculum from the perspective of its intended students were the underemployed people on the Curriculum Design Committee (who were part of that population group, themselves). As the evidence shows, they had some of their own ideas about specific content that might have been particularly relevant to underemployed students. In addition, since they would have been able to look at the proposals of others on the committee from the perspective of the underemployed students who would enroll in the course, they would probably have known if the content was something those students would want to learn and if the materials would work for them. They also might have had ideas about ways to structure the screening interviews to maintain the interest of potential students. As it turned out, the Curriculum Design Committee lacked this knowledge. It was not actively sought by the professionals on the committee, in part because they do not appear to have recognized what the underemployed members had to offer.

Most of the ideas that underemployed people and employers contributed in the research team's study were not used in the context of this project. Tri-County was very interested in learning what these groups thought about the question: "Why don't people work?" Their responses identified many important issues that go well beyond a Professionalization Curriculum and internship program or even Tri-County's mission of "building a competitive workforce through education and job training."[36] As the joint meetings demonstrated, some of the issues that underemployed people care about are very sensitive to employers. Yet, these and the other ideas expressed by the participants in the research team's study — relating to hiring and employment practices, job supports, public benefits, job discrimination, and the creation of desirable jobs— deserve to be explored further because they go to the heart of the problems that are contributing to underemployment in the Delta. A future challenge for Tri-Country and other organizations in the area will be to find avenues for moving these ideas forward.

7

Revitalizing Cass Lake, Minnesota

The Story

In the spring of 1997, a group of community leaders in Cass Lake, Minnesota applied to the Minnesota Design Team (MDT) for help with "buildings and streetscapes of the downtown business district; landscapes of the town entryways; and general community development planning."[1] The MIRACLE Group — an acronym for "Moving Ideas and Relationships for the Advancement of Cass Lake's Economy" — had formed in 1996 to do something about Cass Lake's decline. As one member put it, it would "take a miracle" to prevent the city from dying.[2] Cass Lake's industrial base and private sector economy had largely vanished, and the population was less than half of what it had been when some of MIRACLE Group's members were growing up there.

Cass Lake's plight was common across rural America, but not universal. Bemidji, 15 miles west of Cass Lake and home to Bemidji State University, was becoming the area's regional economic and transportation hub, with "big box" retail stores, hotels, and an airport providing the main commuter link to Minneapolis-St. Paul and beyond. Smaller communities, like the town of Walker about 20 miles south of Cass Lake, had been able to cope with depopulation and a changing economic base by becoming an attractive stopping point for tourists on their way into north central Minnesota's beautiful lake country, which offered abundant opportunities for fishing, hunting, hiking, and snowmobiling.

Cass Lake didn't have a university, but it was well situated to take advantage of tourists in the area since it was located at the junction of major access points to Minnesota's central lake region: U.S. Highway 2 and MN Highway 371. Nonetheless, as the MIRACLE Group stated in its application to MDT, Cass Lake was failing "to capture many of the visitors and tourists passing through the area" because it "did not offer a welcome entryway to the community." The downtown business district, which the group believed was "vital to the growth of the community," was not inviting either, consisting of "vacant dilapidated buildings in need of demolition and removal or significant restoration." The MIRACLE Group applied to MDT — a state-sponsored group of planners, architects, and designers — to "bring people of the community together to generate ideas to physically improve their community" and to develop "a process for turning many of these ideas into reality."[3]

"We are losing our community"

The lake for which the city of Cass Lake is named was once thought to be the source of the Mississippi River, but the true source lies about 30 miles to the southwest, at Lake Itasca. From there, the river weaves through several connected lakes before entering Cass Lake itself, then turning east and south before settling into its regular channel. These wetlands provide a water highway that connects the Mississippi Valley to the other two major watersheds in northern Minnesota, the Great Lakes and the Red River of the North, whose basin extends across North Dakota and into Manitoba, where it empties into Lake Winnipeg. The forests hold an abundance of conifers and some hardwoods, which provide seasonal contrasts between evergreens, fall colors, and blankets of snow in the winter. Up to the nineteenth century, red cedars were a signature feature of the landscape, so much so that the Ojibwe called it *gamiskwawacagog*, which translates loosely as "place of the red cedars." As the old growth forest and cedars diminished with settlement and logging, varieties of pine and spruce have become the dominant trees, along with birch and oak. It's not mountainous or even hilly, but the terrain varies enough to provide small rises, channels, and swamps whose different habitats nurture a variety of fish and wildlife, including bald eagles and other species less common to the south.

Both of the main cultures in northern Minnesota today — Ojibwe and European — arrived there from the Great Lakes and moved west and south over these waterways. The Ojibwe, known as the Anishinabe[4] in their own language, came in the 1700s, pushing the existing residents, the Dakota people, west and south. The lakes and wetlands provided fish and wild rice as dietary staples, and today the Leech Lake Reservation has the largest natural wild rice harvest of any reservation in Minnesota. When the white settlers arrived, they gave the lake their own name, after Lewis Cass, territorial governor from 1813–31. In the nineteenth and twentieth centuries, the Great Northern Railroad brought prosperity and European immigrants, who had come mainly from Scandinavia. For decades, much of the trade going between Seattle and the Great Lakes–St. Lawrence river system passed through Cass Lake's rail terminal. U.S. Highway 2, the country's northernmost federal road, followed the railway, bringing every car, bus, and truck in the area through Cass Lake's downtown, where people would find businesses, shops, and entertainment. During this period, the city became a major logging and milling center and was home to over 2,000 residents, most of whom were white.

Although the Leech Lake Reservation has had offices in and around the city, for much of its history Cass Lake was a white enclave in the midst of the reservation. The city has served as the administrative center for the Bureau of Indian Affairs as well as the U.S. Forest Service Chippewa National Forest. These agencies have had important — and in the eyes of many, negative — impacts on the reservation; the former in its relationship to the Native people, the latter in its stewardship of Native lands. The Leech Lake Reservation, itself, comprises over 670,000 acres and wraps around Cass Lake, Leech Lake, and other wetlands, but only a third of it falls under the Tribal jurisdiction of the Leech Lake Band of the Ojibwe.[5] The remaining land is held by the county, state, and federal governments, the biggest portion being part of the Chippewa National Forest. There are also white landowners on the reservation, important among them resort owners whose lodges and cabins dot the shores of the lakes.

By the mid–1990s, Cass Lake had changed dramatically. The logging industry had disappeared as had the rail terminal. What had once been a box factory was now within a Superfund Site that was not being cleaned up. Highway 2 had been expanded into a four-lane, limited access highway and moved to the northern perimeter of town, so instead of going through the downtown business district at 20 miles per hour, drivers going elsewhere now bypassed the city at full speed.

With these changes, the economy and population of Cass Lake declined. Bemidji had established itself as the regional and economic hub, leaving few businesses in Cass Lake. The number of people living in the city decreased by more than half, from 2,100 to less than 900, and Native Americans now comprised two-thirds of the population. Twenty-nine percent of the city's residents lived at or below the poverty line, more than twice the state average. The proportion of Native Americans in poverty (34 percent) was more than twice that of whites (15 percent). In its new location, Highway 2 had become the boundary, physically and psychologically, between the city and the reservation. Cass Lake's fading downtown was now south of the highway. The reservation and most of the Native neighborhoods and reservation agencies were to the north.

By 1995, residents who felt strong ties to Cass Lake and wanted to stay in the area were increasingly in despair. The downtown area was shabby and run-down with many buildings vacant or in disrepair. People living there no longer had access to basic amenities, like a dime store, clothing store, drug store, or entertainment. The streets were unkempt and littered with trash and junk cars. Property values and the city's tax base had eroded. Only one private housing project had been built since 1976. Crimes against people and property were being committed at rates higher than those in some large metropolitan areas. Many of the youth were leaving the city to get jobs elsewhere; others were dropping out of school. As one member of the MIRACLE Group recalled, residents felt that "we are losing our community. We are losing our kids. You know, we have to try something...."[6]

People had little reason to think anything would change, however, because efforts to do anything in Cass Lake were complicated by the multiple overlapping jurisdictions in the area, the troubled historical relationship between whites and Native Americans, and the links between the two. The area within a 10 to 15 mile radius of Cass Lake includes four counties (Hubbard, Beltrami, Itasca, and Cass), the City of Cass Lake, Pike Bay Township (which surrounds the city), other townships, the Leech Lake Reservation, and the Chippewa National Forest. Officials in these different jurisdictions didn't have much of a track record of cooperating with each other. Relations between the reservation and the city were complicated by the historical mistreatment of the Ojibwe community by the white community and the continuing inequality between the two.

Developing MIRACLE Group's Agenda

In mid–1996, Bob Fitzgerald was getting used to his new job as city administrator of Cass Lake. Fitzgerald brought a unique perspective to this position because he had previously been with the Leech Lake Reservation's Planning Department, so he had a view from both sides of Highway 2, as some described it. Fitzgerald met with local officials and business owners for coffee on a regular basis to talk about the problems Cass Lake was facing and what could be done to resolve those problems. By August 1996, they had formed what they called the "Cass Lake Area Community Planning Team" with officers, an "advisory team," and regular members. The chair, vice-chair, and treasurer of the Planning Team were local business owners; the secretary was editor of the city newspaper. Fitzgerald was on the advisory team, and the "moderator" was a public official from Cass County. The mayor of Cass Lake was a member of the group, along with several other public officials, agency representatives, and business people. Overall, 26 people are listed on stationery the group used in August 1996.[7]

The group adopted its present name, the MIRACLE Group, that September when someone pointed out that what they wanted to do would "take a miracle." Ryan Christiansen, the group's secretary, responded by proposing "MIRACLE" as an acronym for "Moving Ideas and Relationships for the Advancement of Cass Lake's Economy," and the name stuck.[8] The group's early meetings were devoted to bi-weekly brainstorming sessions, which identified 48 potential priorities for action.[9] When intergovernmental cooperation emerged as one of the group's priorities, the moderator said he would he would invite representatives of the Central Minnesota Initiative Foundation to MIRACLE's September 18 meeting, since the Foundation provided financial resources for community planning and was especially interested in intergovernmental cooperation.[10]

To find out what the broader community thought about their priorities, the MIRACLE Group published them in the *Cass Lake Times*, the local newspaper of record where Christiansen was editor. The priorities that seemed to resonate the most with the readers who responded to the newspaper survey included improving cooperation among law enforcement agencies and governmental bodies, clearing away vacant dilapidated buildings, reversing negative attitudes, increasing community pride, developing a vision for the future, planning for orderly growth, increasing the number of small businesses in the area, attracting industrial businesses and jobs, improving the downtown business district, developing land use guidelines, improving existing housing, improving Cass Lake's water quality, and ensuring that the area's environment will be healthy in the future.[11]

Members of the MIRACLE Group used these priorities and others from their brainstorming sessions to form action committees. But as Christiansen pointed out to the members, the original 27 committees were far too many, and he recommended that they strongly consider reducing the number to four or five to keep things simple and enhance the group's probability of success.[12] They followed this advice, and by December 1996, the MIRACLE Group had six committees, each of which put together its own agenda.[13] The "Community Development" committee was chaired by Randy Finn, a Leech Lake Band member who had worked for the reservation and was a business and property owner in Cass Lake. Finn's family was involved in Tribal politics, and he was regarded as a community leader. One of the topic areas on his committee's agenda was "community pride/image," and one of the actions connected to this area was "obtain professional help."[14]

In December 1996, Randy Finn told the MIRACLE Group that he'd heard a news story about the Minnesota Design Team, which helped places like Cass Lake create community visioning processes and development plans. Like Christiansen, Finn thought the MIRACLE Group was trying to do too much and that MDT could help them narrow their focus. As he put it: "The MIRACLE Group ... was trying to eat an elephant.... We were trying to take on too much, it was too big, too broad, too encompassing and we didn't have enough resources and people at the table to pull it all off."[15] To bring the MDT to town, the group would need to involve the city officially, demonstrate community interest and involvement in planning for the future, and raise $3,500 to pay for the program.

The application provided the MIRACLE Group with an opportunity to lay out the area's problems and potential to outsiders—and, by doing so, to narrow their agenda into a smaller set of actionable issues. The application requested MDT's assistance in addressing the following projects: "buildings and streetscapes of the downtown business district; landscapes of the town entryways; and general community development planning." Linking the future growth of the community to the revitalization of the depressed and decaying downtown business district, the application targeted "an area approximately 2 blocks by 3 blocks, [consisting] of several service industry businesses" as the site of development and beautification. Acknowledging "vast untapped opportunities in the areas of tourism and recreation," and the city's "proximity to major highways," the application stated the need for a "town entryway image" to "capture many of the visitors and tourists passing through the area." Expressing concerns about publicly financed low to moderate income housing in the city that had "caused a gradual erosion of property valuations and in turn the tax base of the community," the application also stated a need to provide the kind of housing and services that could "capture persons working in the area and entice them to also live in the area."[16]

In addressing these projects, MDT would provide the MIRACLE Group and the city with "an uncommon opportunity to work cooperatively with neighbors and colleagues, as well as assist in planning and designing a viable, appropriate future for the community of Cass Lake that reflects the dreams and interests of the community."[17] The MIRACLE Group was planning to use the MDT process to develop its own agenda and engage more community members in its work. The city planned to use the process to develop the basis for a "Comprehensive Plan" that could carry the city into the future.

On March 21, 1997, MDT made a "screening visit" to Cass Lake—the next step in the application process.[18] Overall, the evaluation was very positive. MDT felt that "the time is right to tap the cooperative spirit that was evident in the community," highlighting the involvement of Fitzgerald. as the new city administrator, and the MIRACLE Group. The evaluators were also impressed with the "broad representation of community" they saw during their screening visit.[19] They raised a number of concerns about working in Cass Lake, however, including the numerous political jurisdictions in the area, the lack of an economic base, and the history of cultural conflict. "This will be a challenging visit. Many non-design issues that must be addressed. How to keep communication between cultures going and develop a framework for the future." The evaluators said the team would require "very sensitive leadership and distinctive expertise" and time to learn about Native American culture.[20]

MDT in Cass Lake

The first full day of the MDT program was October 3, 1997. The agenda began with a series of presentations by community leaders—public officials and MIRACLE Group members—on the area's "environments:" natural, social, economic, cultural, governmental, and youth.[21] This was followed by a luncheon with the team members and students from the Cass Lake-Bena school system, students from the Leech Lake Tribal

College, elders, business leaders, and leaders in Cass Lake government.[22] After lunch, Cass Lake Mayor Ardean Brasgalla provided the team with a guided tour of the city and the surrounding area.[23]

That evening, the MIRACLE Group and MDT hosted an open community meeting, which had been publicized around the town and reservation in newspapers, stores, and on the radio. Between 200 and 250 people showed up. After a fish-fry, MDT asked the participants to consider four questions: What do you want to see never change or is most sacred in Cass Lake? What is your vision for Cass Lake in five years? How can Cass Lake change to reach that vision? What is the most important thing to add to make Cass Lake better? Everyone at the meeting had an opportunity to write responses to these questions, and the facilitators compiled the written ideas, noting which were repeated by multiple participants. Similar ideas were grouped together under a single statement or theme. After tallying the responses, the facilitators presented the themes that were shared by the greatest numbers of participants as "consensus ideas."[24]

MDT's broad, open-ended visioning session documented that the participants valued Cass Lake's pristine natural environment, small town feeling, old historic buildings, and cultural diversity. Consistent with the projects in the MIRACLE Group's application to MDT, the participants said they wanted to improve the appearance of the community and develop an improved, thriving downtown business district with more shops providing basic amenities, specialty shops showcasing Cass Lake and its cultural heritage, elimination of slum and blighted areas, and preservation and renovation of historic and dilapidated buildings. They also wanted to improve entryways into the community, improve the city's housing stock, increase property values, and improve the local trail system so Cass Lake would become a destination for people using these trails for hiking, snowmobiling, skiing, and other recreation.

Many other ideas surfaced as well, including the establishment of zoning and property maintenance standards, environmental protections, improvements in the community's infrastructure, and improvements in the community's transportation, education, law enforcement, and judicial systems. In particular, participants said they wanted to make government more open and responsive (in part, by bringing "new blood" into the Mayor's office and City Council), and to promote intergovernmental cooperation, particularly between the Reservation Tribal Council and the City of Cass Lake. They also suggested consolidating the city and the surrounding Pike Bay Township.

The participants' positive vision of Cass Lake included more jobs and employment opportunities in the area — particularly more jobs with livable wages — and more affordable, adequate housing for people at all income levels, to be achieved, in part, by improving the existing housing stock. It also included a recreation park at the former box factory site, a youth center, a "total" community center for the entire family, family-oriented entertainment opportunities, and comprehensive recreation facilities. Participants said they wanted to develop "community pride and self-esteem" and "hard work, community commitment, and community involvement." Expressing a need to eliminate prejudices and racism in the area, they proposed creating a cultural center and a council of elders.

Since the purpose of the MDT visit was to create a shared vision of Cass Lake's future, the process was not designed to explore or identify differences in views among people in different groups. There is no record of the ideas generated at MDT's luncheon meetings with particular groups, of the demographics of the people who attended the open visioning session, or of the ideas that people in different groups proposed at that session. Consequently, there is no way of knowing if different segments of the community—for example, whites and Native Americans, residents of the city and the reservation, youth and adults, poor people and those better off—had similar or different visions of Cass Lake. If there were any disagreements, it's not something that people in the community talk about.

The next day, MDT worked on its own to turn the long list of consensus and non-consensus ideas that emerged during the public visioning session into one-, five-, and ten-year plans for Cass Lake. These plans were presented at another open community meeting on the evening of October 4, 1997, which was attended by about 50 people.

The goals and drawings in MDT's plans addressed the projects that the MIRACLE Group had proposed in its application to MDT. Improvement of the downtown business district would begin with community cleanups (which the MIRACLE Group had already initiated prior to MDT's visit), flower plantings, and a study of downtown market factors. Then it would move on to develop the "streetscape" in the geographic business area that had been specified by the MIRACLE Group. This work would include the rehabilitation of existing buildings, business development, and the establishment of ordinances and standards to preserve and extend a compact small town development pattern (as opposed to a suburban development pattern), to retain the essential elements of the existing architectural character, to remove blighting influences such as junk cars, and to provide design guidelines for signs downtown and along the highway. MDT's presentation included drawings to show people what an improved downtown streetscape might look like.[25]

The plan that MDT presented also focused on recreation and tourism, including an inventory of existing recreation facilities, the establishment of a Department of Parks and Recreation, the development of a multi-use trail system, and the development of a community park at the box factory site. Bike trails and a trailhead center were illustrated in MDT's drawings as were neighborhood parks and a new tourism center.

Other goals in MDT's plan included a leadership retreat to promote intergovernmental and community cooperation, the establishment of a comprehensive plan and sustainable development corporation, city-township consolidation, and the development of a teen center, infill residential and commercial development, and the development of an industrial site.

Early Action Steps

MDT's visit provided the MIRACLE Group and city officials with a plan of action that appeared to have community-wide endorsement. The action plan showed MIRACLE Group members how to meet many of the objectives they had laid out in their application to MDT—beautify the downtown business district, lead tourists and others downtown, and establish a structure and incentives for downtown development. It also provided the city with valuable guidance in creating its Cass Lake Comprehensive Plan, Economic Development Plan, and Economic Development Authority.

Beautification of the downtown business district did not move forward until September 2000, when the city received a $10,000 grant to develop a master plan for the

Streetscape Project. In the interim, the MIRACLE Group focused on other projects related to the overall strategy. Shortly after the MDT visit, the MIRACLE Group planted flowers in the city and organized its second community cleanup, which motivated residents to improve the appearance of their properties by painting their houses and removing trash and old cars that were no longer being used. The clean ups gave the MIRACLE Group some early successes and gave people in the community a sense of pride that they could "get together and do things and make our community look a lot better."[26]

In 1998, the MIRACLE Group sponsored a competition to develop a city logo, which was open to anyone living in Cass Lake and the surrounding reservation. The top 20 proposals were published in the *Cass Lake Times*, and residents were able to vote for their favorite at schools, City Hall, or the newspaper's office.[27] Of the ideas proposed at the MDT visioning session, two that were already used or had historical value in the community wound up being selected: "Where Eagles Soar," which had been the name of a community newsletter published in the mid–1990s, and "Gamiskwawakacog" which had been the traditional Ojibwe name for the area. With resources provided by a local business person and artist, signs incorporating the logo were placed on Highways 2 and 371 at the entrances into the city.

Together with other partners—the U. S. Forest Service, the Cass Lake Chamber of Commerce, the Leech Lake Reservation Tribal Council, the City of Cass Lake, and Pike Bay Township—the MIRACLE Group created a Tourism Partnership in 2000 to develop projects in the action plan that would attract visitors to the area and benefit residents at the same time. The partnership's early efforts focused on connecting the city directly to the system of hiking and snowmobiling trails that crisscross Minnesota, building a park-like rest area on Highway 2 at the north-east entrance to the city, and sponsoring fishing contests and festivals in Cass Lake. Later, the partnership added an interpretive center to the rest area.

As a result of these efforts, the Mi-Ge-Zi Trail has been paved in places and extended so that it now takes trail-users directly though the downtown, then to the rest area on Hwy. 2, and from there to the "Norway Beach" camping and recreation area on the shore of Cass Lake in the Chippewa National Forest. Local youth use the trail to get to the new Cass Lake High School on the south of town, which is much safer than biking or walking along the highways. In the rest area itself, the Tourism Partnership, the Chamber of Commerce, and others sponsor the "Chain Reaction Fishing Tournament" (January), the Chippewa Triathlon (June), and the "Cass Lake Rib Fest" (July), which bring hundreds of people to Cass Lake, utilizing the connections between the trails and lakes in the city.

In addition to these activities, the MIRACLE Group spearheaded a number of other projects in the MDT action plan, including the development of a Boys & Girls Club (described in more detail in the Community Voices Against Violence case study) and the involvement of Cass Lake in the Central Minnesota Initiative Foundation's Healthy Communities Partnership. Participation in this partnership provided members of the MIRACLE Group and others with leadership training in 1999 and gave the community access to significant funding through grants and loans.

The Streetscape Planning Workshops

In mid–2001, the city contracted with Richard Rose, the head of an architectural and landscape design firm, to develop guidelines for a "downtown Cass Lake Streetscape revitalization project" that would "improve the retail area adjacent to U.S. Trunk Highways

371 and 2." To "obtain essential information that will help in the design and implementation of [these] improvements," Rose conducted three planning workshops on June 12 and June 14, 2001. Rose wanted input from people who would have to "live and work with the project during and after construction" in order to understand the "problems, user needs, priorities, and potentials inherent in the project." The workshops were publicized in flyers and other media, but all of the people who turned out were community leaders—most were members of the MIRACLE Group and two were Native American. Five of the nineteen participated in more than one of the workshops.

The workshops were organized around three questions. What are the problems with downtown Cass Lake—including the specific site and economic or organizational issues—that this project should address or consider during the design and implementation stages? What are the positive conditions that exist in or near downtown Cass Lake that should be recognized or considered during the design and implementation stages? What are the changes that should be made or considered for downtown Cass Lake improvements during design and implementation? After writing their responses to each question, participants ranked their top ten items. The rankings from all participants were then tabulated to identify priority tasks and concerns.

All of the ideas that came out of Rose's workshops reiterated what people had said during the MDT visioning session. As with MDT, some of the problems and actions that people identified went beyond the scope of business district revitalization, such as the need for green space and parks, housing, a community center, library, and Ojibwe cultural center. Cultural issues were a significant concern to workshop participants—so much so that Rose stated in his report "There are a lot of negative attitudes and conflicts that must be overcome in order for real improvement to take place." Specific problems raised by participants included the lack of communication between the Native American and white cultures, the lack of Native American identification with the city, and the perceived community division at Highway 2—a boundary that was limiting cultural cooperation. Healing wounds between cultures was a highly ranked action item.

The report that Rose submitted was oriented toward the business community, and it included a number of ideas that do not appear to have been raised in the workshops. The report recommended developing a nonprofit organization—separate from the MIRACLE Group—that would be representative of, and a proponent for, the downtown business community. Drawing on ideas that Rose discussed during frequent meetings with members of the MIRACLE Group, the report emphasized the need for Cass Lake and the Leech Lake Band to invest in quality housing in and near the downtown to ensure year-round customers and economic opportunity for new business investment. It also suggested extending the project beyond the originally proposed geographic boundaries, with a minimum of two blocks of housing and commercial building upgrades along the primary Streetscape corridor and an extension to a new cultural center and park on the old high school property. The report's recommendations would have eventually extended the streetscape design and amenities north to the intersection with Highway 2.[28]

Implementing Streetscape

Rose submitted his report in October 2001, but by that time funding had run out and additional resources were needed to continue with the project. Two years later, in

2003, the Cass Lake Tourism Partnership applied for $1.7 million in funding through a federal highways transportation bill that was being drafted in the Congress.[29] In the fall of 2005, when the bill was finally passed and funds were appropriated, Cass Lake received $1.3 million for streetscape improvements and sewer and water replacement from the Federal State Transportation Improvement Program. In 2006, the city received $375,000 from the U.S. Army Corps of Engineers to replace the utilities under the streets. The City of Cass Lake and Cass County added $800,000 to the project.

After Streetscape was funded, the new mayor of Cass Lake suggested that the City Council move the project to the Highway 2–371 corridor, which had displaced the historical downtown to become the main commercial area in Cass Lake. Concerned about the budget, she stated that the city might not be able to bear the costs of maintaining the Streetscape improvements in the historical center of town. The mayor, a member of the Leech Lake Band, had been elected in 2003 and had not been part of the MDT process or the Rose workshops. The City Council voted to continue with the project in its originally planned location, maintaining that any changes would jeopardize the funding. Shortly thereafter, the city contracted the engineering firm of Widseth, Smith, Nolting (WSN) to design the Streetscape Project and begin its implementation.

WSN was not bound by the Rose report, and the firm suggested that the city form a Streetscape Planning Committee composed of government representatives, business leaders, and community residents. The city had originally planned to include only government and business representatives on the committee until community members insisted that residents-at-large be included as well. Residents living in and close to the primary redevelopment area wanted community residents to make up half of the committee. Ultimately, the committee's composition was set at seven, including five representatives from government and business and two citizens-at-large, who happened to be a former mayor of Cass Lake and the new mayor-elect. The committee later invited representatives of the Leech Lake Band to become involved in the design process, but no one from the Band ended up participating.[30] Richard Rose was also invited to participate, but illness prevented him from taking part. As far as we know, the committee never reviewed Rose's report and few, if any, of his recommendations were followed.

The Streetscape Planning Committee met monthly from October 2006 through January 2007. The meetings, which usually took place on weekday mornings, were open to the public; announcements about upcoming meetings appeared in the *Cass Lake Times*. Unlike the MDT visioning process and the workshops conducted by Richard Rose, the committee concentrated on specific Streetscape design features, such as the ornamental lighting, trees, benches, trash receptacles, planters, informational signs, sculptures, and art that would be located along the walkways.[31] Most of the committee's proposals were included in WSN's final plan. The committee members selected "Tracks and Trails" as the project's theme; they avoided specific Ojibwe themes in an effort to be cautious of cultural issues. It was not possible to incorporate an idea that had been talked about in the community for some time — placing a pedestrian crosswalk over Highway 2 to connect downtown to the other side of the highway, which would have overcome a symbolic boundary between the Native and white cultures. The site was not part of the designated Streetscape area, and the construction of such a crosswalk would have been prohibitively expensive.

The MIRACLE Group organized an informational open house for the Streetscape Project at the American Legion in downtown Cass Lake on April 12, 2007. Over 100 community members showed up to hear WSN present the final plan and timeline for the project; the Leech Lake Band did not send any official representatives. People in the audience seemed very interested and no one voiced any objections to the plan at the open house or afterwards. Construction began on April 21, 2008.

Community Participation in the MIRACLE Group

One of the reasons the MIRACLE Group brought MDT to Cass Lake was to engage more people in its community development work. But although many people turned out for MDT's visioning session, few became active members of MIRACLE Group's committees. The experience was repeated with the Healthy Communities partnership. A large number of people showed up for the visioning session at the school, voicing the same concerns that community members had with MDT, "but then you get to the committees following the visioning session and a lot of those people are lost and it's the same people that have always carried the load of doing the job that you see on the committees again."

Although the transient and limited participation of community residents has resulted in a heavy workload for MIRACLE Group members, they have managed to accomplish a lot. A representative of the Central Minnesota Initiative Foundation said that in comparison with other MDT processes, they know of none that have "come close to accomplishing what Cass Lake has done ... [which include] 80–90 percent of those goals on ... the Design Team list."[32] Nonetheless, people in the Cass Lake area who have not been active in the MIRACLE Group's work do not appear to appreciate what the group has done. As one MIRACLE Group member put it: "I personally feel that the people that live here are not gonna really see or acknowledge our changes until they themselves become involved in that change. And the majority of people that need to...have not yet become a part of it."[33]

The Case Analysis

The strategy to revitalize the downtown business district in Cass Lake — through beautification, tourism, and development — involved numerous players: the members of the MIRACLE Group; other leaders in the community, including officials in local and tribal governments and business leaders; other residents of the community; and a number of consultants, including the Minnesota Design Team, Rose and Associates, and Widseth, Smith, Nolting. To understand how the ideas of these different players influenced what happened, we (1) looked at the major impacts of the case; (2) identified whose ideas were influential at the critical points that shaped the revitalization strategy; and (3) explored how the accomplishments and limitations in the case were related to ideas that were, and were not, influential.

Major Impacts

The strategy to revitalize the downtown business district is benefiting Cass Lake in important ways. The Streetscape project brought almost $1.7 million in federal funds to the city, which will improve the physical appearance and infrastructure of the business corridor downtown. Based on the turnout and discussion at the April 2007 open house, the plan appears to be acceptable to community residents. The strategy's other projects have cleaned up the community, created clearly marked entry-points to downtown Cass Lake on the approaching highways with signage developed and designed by community members, developed a park-like rest area with an interpretive center along Highway 2, connected downtown to the broader trail system (which youth and other residents use to avoid walking or biking along the roadways), instituted a series of community festivals, and provided residents with a local retail option they wanted a lot: pizza delivery. Taken together, these actions have given members of the MIRACLE Group a sense of pride and a feeling that change can happen.

The revitalization strategy was designed to reverse Cass Lake's decline, but the extent to which it will actually do so remains an open question. Improving the physical appearance and infrastructure of the downtown business corridor and providing welcoming entryways to the city may not be sufficient to create a vibrant downtown business district. To attract businesses to the area, economic incentives and private investment may also be required.

Another uncertainty is whether a thriving downtown business district, in and of itself, can revitalize the community. The strategy that Cass Lake has implemented thus far has not included actions proposed by community members that would have revitalized the city in ways unrelated to tourism and business development. Repeatedly, in the MDT visioning session, the Rose planning workshops, and in visioning sessions organized later by the Healthy Communities partnership, community members proposed actions that would improve conditions for the people who were living in Cass Lake by renovating the existing housing stock and building more affordable housing; by expanding the transportation system; by developing neighborhood parks, community centers, libraries, and recreation facilities; and by creating more livable wage job opportunities. They also emphasized the need to take actions to heal the wounds between the Native American and white cultures.

The MDT process, itself, was intended to revitalize the community by engaging a broad array of residents in community development activities. But in spite of the large initial turnout, few have sustained their involvement. From the perspective of MIRACLE Group members, people who haven't become active members in the group are not as appreciative of the changes that have been made as those who have.

Critical Points of Influence

Looking at the events and impacts in the development of the strategy to revitalize Cass Lake's downtown business district, there appear to be four points at which the influence of players' ideas mattered: (1) identifying the strategy; (2) deciding how community members would be involved; (3) deciding which projects would move forward; and (4) designing those projects.

Identifying the strategy. The idea for this strategy came from members of the MIRACLE Group, who articulated their rationale for revitalizing the downtown business district and a basic framework for doing so in their application to MDT. When the MIRACLE Group sought community input through a newspaper "survey," readers were asked to react to a list of the group's priorities.

Deciding how the community would be involved. Over the course of this case, many intentional efforts were made to engage members of the Cass Lake community — through the MDT luncheons and visioning session, MIRACLE Group's committees and "spin-offs" (like the Tourism Partnership), the logo contest, the planning workshops conducted by Richard Rose, the WSN planning committee, and the open house where the final Streetscape plans were presented and discussed. The MIRACLE Group was very influential in creating four of these opportunities — it brought MDT to Cass Lake, sought community involvement in its own work, sponsored the logo contest, and organized the open house. The other opportunities were created by city officials, who contracted with Rose and WSN.

The way community members were involved — and their potential to influence what happened — was largely determined by the external consultants: MDT, Rose, and WSN. The MDT process involved the greatest number of community residents, which probably reflects the efforts that the MIRACLE Group made to publicize the event. Since participants at the visioning session were asked very broad questions, they were able to express ideas that went well beyond the revitalization of the downtown business district. Their potential to influence the ultimate plan, however, was limited in two respects. Since the process was not designed to identify or differentiate the ideas of people in different groups, differences in views — among Native Americans and whites, for example — could not be surfaced or addressed. In addition, MDT interpreted all of the input that participants provided and decided which ideas would be incorporated in its one-, five-, and ten-year plans.

The planning workshops conducted by Richard Rose involved far fewer participants. His report stated that he wanted input from people who would have to "live and work with the project during and after construction." While he heard from community leaders, most of whom were members of the MIRACLE Group, he did not hear directly from the city's poorer residents, whose homes were adjacent to the Streetscape development area. Like MDT, Rose posed very broad questions, but at this stage of the process such an approach limited the potential influence of participants, since only ideas related to the Streetscape project, itself, had any possibility of being influential. As with MDT, Rose decided which ideas to use. Looking at the recommendations in his report, it seems that most were drawn from his frequent meetings with people involved in the MIRACLE Group rather than from ideas raised during the workshops.

WSN's planning committee involved even fewer people — five representatives from government and business and two very prominent citizens-at-large, a former and incoming mayor. Again, members of the MIRACLE Group were well represented. Other residents — including those living adjacent to the Streetscape development area — had an opportunity to attend the committee meetings, since the meetings were open to the public. Few of them did so, however, which may have been due, in part, to the fact that most of the meetings were scheduled at times when people would need to be at work. Unlike the planning workshops conducted by Richard Rose, the WSN committee focused on specific Streetscape design issues. For the most part, their influence was limited to choosing among options presented by WSN.

Overall, the potential for influence in these various engagement processes was greatest for members of the MIRACLE Group and other community leaders. The opportunities for ordinary residents—particularly poor Native Americans living downtown—were much more limited. The area where everyone, including ordinary residents, could exert a lot of influence was in deciding whether or not to accept an invitation to become involved. Representatives of the Leech Lake Band declined invitations to participate in the WSN committee and in the Streetscape open house. Many of the community residents who participated in the MDT visioning session decided not to become involved, or not to sustain their involvement, in the MIRACLE Group's committees or work after MDT left town.

Deciding which projects would move forward. The community engagement processes described above generated a broad range of ideas for revitalizing Cass Lake. Decisions about which of these ideas would move forward were made by the MIRACLE Group, MDT, the Tourism Partnership (a spin-off of the MIRACLE Group), and city officials. MDT helped the MIRACLE Group and the city create their mutually supportive agendas, which guided their decisions. The MIRACLE Group, the Tourism Partnership, and the city also played critical roles by developing ideas into projects and by obtaining funding for projects.

Retrospectively, the ideas that were developed and implemented appear to have shared three characteristics. They were consistent with the MIRACLE Group's strategy for revitalizing the downtown business district in Cass Lake—through beautification, tourism, and development—or with other MIRACLE Group priorities. They did not require large-scale private investment. And they did not require the approval of voters in another jurisdiction. Ideas that did not satisfy these criteria—such as the mayor's proposal for relocating the site of the Streetscape project, the ideas for revitalizing Cass Lake in many other ways that came out of the MDT process and Rose workshops, and the city-township consolidation and infill developments in the MDT plan—were not implemented.

Designing the projects. The MIRACLE Group played a very influential role in the design of the various projects in this case—either directly, through its Tourism Partnership spin-off, or through the representation of its members in other groups.

The MIRACLE Group set the basic parameters for the Streetscape project, including its geographic location, and influenced Streetscape's specific design features through the involvement of its members on the WSN planning committee. WSN and the other community leaders on the planning committee were influential in the Streetscape design as well. The MIRACLE Group organized the community clean-ups, which, in turn, gave community members the opportunity to decide how they would clean up and paint their own properties. The MIRACLE Group also organized the logo contest, which enabled many people to create their own designs.

The Tourism Partnership used the winning logo to create the signage marking the entry-points to downtown Cass Lake. The members of the partnership also determined the design of their other projects, including the rest area and interpretive center, Cass Lake's connection to the trail system, and the community contests and festivals.

Relating Impacts to Influence

The important accomplishments of the downtown revitalization strategy appear to be related most closely to three of the points of influence in the case: identifying the strategy;

deciding which projects would move forward, and designing the projects. The ideas that informed decisions at each of these points came primarily from members of the MIRA-CLE Group, other community leaders, MDT, and WSN. Nonetheless, the projects that have been completed or are underway appear to be acceptable to the broader community. Most likely, this is because residents are benefiting from what was done and the projects haven't created problems for anyone.

In addition to contributing to the accomplishments in the case, the second point of influence — deciding how the community would be involved — also limited what community members could achieve. The MDT process helped to make the MIRACLE Group productive by providing it with an action plan for achieving the downtown revitalization strategy it had laid out in its application to MDT, by linking the MIRACLE Group's action plan to the city's Comprehensive Plan, and by obtaining what appeared to be broad community support and endorsement for moving these plans forward. But achieving that strategy doesn't mean that Cass Lake will be revitalized in ways that really matter to the various groups of people who live in the community. As the earlier section on "Impacts" describes, participants in the MDT visioning session and the Rose workshops repeatedly said they wanted changes that went beyond beautifying the downtown business district and promoting tourism. The changes they proposed would have revitalized Cass Lake by improving conditions for the people who were living there and by healing the wounds between the Native American and white cultures. Processes didn't emerge, however, to enable community members to develop specific and workable strategies for achieving these changes.

Some of the problems related to community participation in the MIRACLE Group's community development activities may be related to the limited amount of influence that community members had. We know from the evidence that participation dissipated shortly after the community visioning sessions conducted by MDT and, later, by the Healthy Communities partnership (during which community members raised the same issues and proposed the same changes that they had with MDT). We also know that members of the MIRACLE Group feel that people who have not been actively involved in their work do not acknowledge or appreciate the changes the group has made in the community. One possibility to consider is that participation waned because people did not have a way to explore the issues they care about the most or to develop the actions they want to take.

8

Community Centers in Southeastern Oklahoma

The Story

On June 30, 1994, the Little Dixie Community Action Agency submitted an application to the U. S. Department of Agriculture to have four economically distressed census tracts in southeastern Oklahoma designated as a rural Empowerment Zone or Enterprise Community. The centerpiece of the application was a community-based strategic plan — developed by Little Dixie with the participation and commitment of community residents, business and civic leaders, and public officials — that presented a set of strategies for revitalizing the area.

The primary focus of the rural Empowerment Zone/Enterprise Community (EZ/EC) program was to promote economic development in the poorest parts of rural America, primarily by creating new jobs, supporting entrepreneurial initiatives, expanding businesses, and providing people with education and training for jobs that offered upward mobility. Other important goals of the program included expanding affordable housing, improving the area's basic infrastructure (such as water, sewerage, and transportation), and reducing substance abuse and crime.[1]

The plan for the four census tracts in southeastern Oklahoma included actions to achieve each of these goals. It also included another kind of strategy — community centers — that was not among the specific activities listed in the federal government's instructions for completing the application. The plan budgeted almost 33 percent of the $40 million grant that would come with an Empowerment Zone designation and almost 16 percent of the $2.9 million grant that would come with an Enterprise Community designation for building or refurbishing community centers throughout the area.[2]

Rural, Poor, and in Distress

To be eligible for a rural Empowerment Zone or Enterprise Community designation, an area needed to be not only very rural, but also very poor, experiencing high rates of poverty, unemployment, and general distress.[3] From this perspective, the four census tracts in Oklahoma clearly fit the bill.

The census tracts were located in Choctaw and McCurtain Counties in the southeastern corner of the state, bordered on the south by Texas and on the east by Arkansas. This part of Oklahoma had long been among the poorest areas in the state; in the early 1990s about a quarter of the population were living below the poverty line — twice the national average. In the four census tracts, the poverty rate was even higher, ranging from 45 to 50 percent in the largely African American communities of West Idabel and Western Hugo, and from 35 to 37 percent in Western and Eastern Choctaw.[4]

Living conditions in the area reflected this poverty. There was little development along the main thoroughfare, U.S. Highway 70, which was a poorly maintained two-lane road at the time. Many of the other roads weren't even paved. Buildings in the towns were dilapidated with overgrown lawns. Beyond those perimeters, many homes didn't have electricity or running water. Some weren't connected to sewerage systems, either.[5]

With little to attract new industry and jobs, most of the young people who completed their education left, increasing the proportion of elderly and poorly educated people in the area. Residents without cars or with disabilities had difficulty accessing the few services and amenities that were available, since public transportation was very limited. Crime and violence were also serious problems. Parks and old school buildings that had closed were becoming hang-outs for people involved in drugs and other illegal activities.

The EZ/EC Planning Process

The Little Dixie Community Action Agency — a nonprofit organization that received federal funds to provide services to low-income people in southeastern Oklahoma — was among the first in the area to hear about the federal government's new rural Empowerment Zone/Enterprise Community program. The resources that came with the program were a powerful enticement to apply. Areas designated as Empowerment Zones would receive block grants of $40 million to carry out the activities in their strategic plans, and areas designated as Enterprise Communities would receive grants of almost $3 million. Areas with either designation would also be eligible for tax incentives, tax credits, and special consideration for funding under many other federal programs. Acting as the "lead entity" for an Empowerment Zone or Enterprise Community was also attractive to Little Dixie. Coordinating the efforts of people and organizations in the four census tracts to develop a strategic plan — and to implement the plan over a ten-year period if the application were successful — would provide Little Dixie with additional funding and extend its focus from service provision to economic and community development.

After a group of public officials and business and civic leaders from the four census tracts decided to go forward with the EZ/EC application in March 1994, Little Dixie's first task was to coordinate a process for developing the strategic plan. The federal government's guidelines for the EZ/EC program stated that the strategic plan would need to be developed with "the participation of the community affected ... and of the private sector, acting in concert with the State ... and local governments."[6] The guidelines didn't specify how these groups should be involved, and neither Little Dixie nor the community leaders who wanted to pursue the EZ/EC designation knew the best way to facilitate a broad community planning process. So they arranged for a team from National Training Associates, a California organization, to conduct a training workshop for about 100 people in Hugo on April 7 and 8, 1994.

At the workshop, the people being trained learned a "system" that they would later use to involve many other people in their own communities. The process began by having small groups of participants consider five questions: What are we doing now? How did it come to be this way? Whose interests are being served by the way things are? What information do we have or need that bears upon the issue? What are we going to do about all of this?[7] The purpose of these discussions was to help people recognize that things would have to be done very differently in the future to truly solve problems.[8]

After that, the participants broke into small groups to develop preliminary visions, identify needs and problems, and discuss potential solutions.[9] To encourage everyone's involvement, participants were asked to write their ideas down, in just a few words, on "sticky notes." Then the sticky notes were put on the wall for everyone to see, grouped into broad categories, such as economic development, social and human development, infrastructure, public safety, and education.

The goal of the process was to develop a list of the particular priorities that each of the four census tracts wanted to include in the strategic plan and to use that information to develop an equitable, coordinated plan for the entire EZ/EC area. Local steering committees were established to organize the work at the census tract level. Each of these five-member committees organized numerous meetings throughout the census tract to engage as many residents as possible in the planning process. They created subcommittees around different categories of the strategic plan to review relevant sticky notes from their local planning meetings and to develop specific action proposals. Other local residents with an interest or expertise in that area were sometimes appointed to the subcommittees. After reviewing all of the proposals, the local steering committee, as a whole, decided which would be the census tract's priorities. Final decisions about the local priorities that would be included in the EZ/EC strategic plan were made by an overall steering committee consisting of all of the members of each of the local steering committees plus one member each from Little Dixie, the Kiamichi Economic Development District of Oklahoma, and the Choctaw Nation.

"Everybody began wanting community centers"

The local planning meetings that took place in April and May aroused great interest among residents in the four census tracts. In some cases, several hundred people packed into a church or hall to see what the process was about. The lure was the grant for the Empowerment Zone designation. For many residents, a sense of "overall hopelessness" had been compounding the area's problems with poverty, unemployment, long-standing neglect, and crime.[10] "People couldn't envision positive things in their communities when nothing had happened before."[11] Now, with the prospect of a large federal grant, people had a reason to imagine how conditions could be different and to think about what they would want to change.[12] As one participant put it, "You take a $40 million flag and wave it in front of six hundred poor people that are mostly making minimum wage, if that, and it will cause them to dream."[13]

Most of the actions that residents proposed at the meetings—like creating jobs, building more affordable housing, paving and expanding roads, and extending water and sewerage networks—were general in nature and consistent with the options for strategic plan activities that the federal government listed in its instructions for completing the EZ/EC application. But in meeting after meeting, across all four census tracts, people voiced a strong desire for something else as well. As one participant recalled, in "all of these little towns ... everybody began wanting community centers."[14]

The sticky notes from the local planning meetings have been lost, but other written records and interviews with some of the people who participated reveal a lot about the reasons that residents in these poor, rural census tracts thought community centers were so important. Put simply, they didn't have any decent place to go to relax, socialize, engage in recreation, conduct meetings, or hold family events. Many of the older people were isolated in their homes, "existing rather than living."[15] Many of the youth were getting into trouble because they had nothing to do.[16] As one participant put it, "in our area, like I said, people don't have a whole lot of places to go after-hours and after the job to relax and just socialize together, and so community centers are pretty good down in this area."[17] Another said "We were really concerned about our young folks having something to do, and community centers would be a good way to start this. Whatever we were going to do with young folks, the community center[s] would be the ideal situations. Some community centers wanted gymnasiums in there, so that they could concentrate on basketball, which a lot of people down here like."[18]

In the steering committees for each of the census tracts, proposals for community centers were a high priority — in some cases, the committee's highest priority. The centers were referred to by different names: community center, multipurpose center, meeting center, youth recreational center, and nutrition center. Overall, they were proposed in ten sites: Western Hugo, Boswell, West Idabel, Fort Towson, Soper, Garvin, Sawyer, Swink, Bluff, and Nelson. In some places, like Western Hugo, the proposals called for refurbishing existing centers that were in dire need of repair and modernization. In places like West Idabel, where community centers did not exist, the proposals called for building a new facility.

The "Carrot" and the "Second Prize"

Once the local steering committees identified the proposals that they wanted to be included in the strategic plan, they submitted their priorities to the overall steering committee. That group was responsible for creating a coordinated area-wide plan that described all of the actions that would be taken over a period of ten years to revitalize the communities in the four census tracts. Using that plan, the overall steering committee needed to prepare two budgets: one specifying the actions that would be funded if southeastern Oklahoma received the $40 million "carrot," as Little Dixie referred to the block grant that came with the Empowerment Zone designation; another specifying the actions that would be funded if the area received the $2.9 million "second prize" that came with an Enterprise Community designation. Since only three rural Empowerment Zones would be designated in the entire country, in contrast to 30 Enterprise Community designations, everyone in the area knew that there was a much greater probability of getting the second prize than the carrot.

To receive any designation at all, Little Dixie knew that the application would need to follow the guidelines for the EZ/EC program very closely.[19] In particular, the strategic plan would need to relate each of the actions to the goals and fundable activities listed in the federal government's instructions. Equally important, the overall steering committee would need to develop a strategic plan that was supported by people across the four census tracts. To do that, each of the steering committees would need to get something out of the plan that mattered a lot to their residents—with the $2.9 million budget as well as the $40 million budget.

Many involved in the process were concerned that this would not be possible, especially if the area was designated as an Enterprise Community rather than as an Empowerment Zone. Southeastern Oklahoma was a place where old rivalries and political intrigues among mayors and other power brokers had prevented communities from collaborating in the past. Moreover, the leaders of some of the communities involved in the process weren't sure that Little Dixie would respect their local steering committee's proposals for action. Irvin Jones, from West Idabel, was doubtful when he entered the process, "...my perspective was that this is more of the same high-end diva and we're going to get a bunch of money and nothing's going to happen in my community."[20]

As it turned out, most of the concerns that people had never materialized, in large part because of the way the planning process was structured. The overall steering committee respected the recommendations made by the local steering committees, and virtually all of the local proposals were included in the area's ten-year strategic plan. This was possible because the budget for the plan was not limited by EZ/EC block grant funds. In creating a strategic plan, applicants could also assume that they could leverage hundreds of millions of dollars in tax credits, tax incentives, and special consideration for funding from other federal programs that would go along with an Empowerment Zone or Enterprise Community designation. The strategic plan could also include proposals that might be funded by the state government or private sector sources.

Southeastern Oklahoma's strategic plan included provisions for building or refurbishing all ten of the community centers that the local steering committees had proposed. Little Dixie, which was responsible for writing the application, faced a potential problem justifying these actions, however, since the instructions for the EZ/EC application didn't specifically mention community centers. The solution appears to have come from the various purposes for which community centers could be used. In the local planning meetings, the low-income people who had wanted community centers for themselves had spoken about using the centers for unstructured socializing and recreation. The people who had been running the existing centers that needed to be refurbished had also talked about programs the centers could provide, such as after-school activities and mentoring for youth. The instructions for preparing the EZ/EC application listed a number of programs that could benefit disadvantaged adults and youth in poor rural areas, and it stated that EZ/EC funds could be used for these programs as well as for purchasing or improving facilities.

In an introductory section of the strategic plan, one of the barriers to development in the area that Little Dixie listed was "Lack of Community Facilities." Describing this barrier, the document said: "It is believed by those involved in the EZ/EC planning process in virtually all areas that community facilities are needed to house youth activities, recreation, adult exercise, senior citizen health and rehabilitation activities and other services. It is believed this barrier can be solved with multi-purpose community centers."[21] In Section 21-B of the plan, which focused on actions to promote social and human development in the area, Little Dixie listed the ten centers that would be built or refurbished, describing the services they would provide, many of which were directly related to the specified goals and activities of the EZ/EC program, such as drug and alcohol abuse prevention, medical care, meals for senior citizens, job training, literacy classes, recreational and youth activities, and police sub-stations.

The overall steering committee decided to allocate one-third of the $40 million Empowerment Zone block grant — over $13 million — to constructing or refurbishing community centers, reflecting the importance of these facilities to people in the area and the lack of alternative sources of funding. Other social and human development proposals, including some of the programs the centers would provide, comprised 28 percent of this budget. Twenty-three percent of the $40 million block grant was allocated to education, 9 percent to economic development, 6 percent to program administration, and about 1 percent to infrastructure, public safety, and housing.

When the overall steering committee met to decide how to allocate the funds from the much smaller $2.9 million Enterprise Community block grant, the participants expected a long, drawn-out, and contentious process. As it turned out, however, the negotiations were easy and took only an hour and a half. As one participant put it, "Everybody knew what the first thing they wanted to do was."[22] A Little Dixie staff member recalled: "They started down using the first priorities and just went round robin and picking each one of their priorities. But each census tract got basically what they asked for as long as the money held out. So we split it up."[23] Almost 16 percent of this budget — $450,000 — was allocated for community centers. The largest proportion of the $2.9 million block grant — 46 percent — was allocated for economic development, 19 percent for other social and human development proposals, 6 percent for education, 6 percent for program administration, 4 percent for infrastructure, 3 percent for public safety, and 2 percent for housing.

On December 21, 1994, the four census tracts in Choctaw and McCurtain Counties were designated as an Enterprise Community. In the "second prize" budget, block grant funds were allocated to only two of the ten centers in the strategic plan — in West Idabel and Bluff. Little Dixie assured the local steering committees that funding for the remaining community centers could be obtained, either from the reallocation of unspent block grant funds (if some of the funded projects had been overestimated, for example) or from other sources, such as the other federal programs that gave Enterprise Communities special consideration. Ultimately, community centers were built or refurbished in all of the places that had requested one, although not always in the way community members had originally proposed.[24] Below, we tell the story of three of the centers: the Washington Community Center in Western Hugo, the Boswell Nutrition Center, and the Booker T. Washington Community Center in West Idabel.

The Washington Community Center in Western Hugo

The predominantly African American community in the western part of Hugo is one of the poorest in Oklahoma. In the late 1980's, a group of retired African American community leaders there, including long-time residents Henry and Leona Edwards, Evelyn Pointer, and Francine Morris, began an effort to create a community center.[25] With the help of Howard Turner, an African American businessman from the area, they purchased the old Washington School, which had closed when a new school had been constructed. The Washington School had "all of the physical necessities for a community center." It included several buildings on a two-block area, including a cafeteria that could seat 150 people. In 1993, the group established the Washington Community Center as a nonprofit corporation, but they were limited in what they could do as a center because they "didn't have any money to ... fix up the place."[26] In a fire that occurred shortly after incorporation, the gymnasium had burned down, and the classrooms in an adjacent wing had been seriously damaged.

When the process to develop the EZ/EC strategic plan began in 1994, Henry Edwards attended the local planning meetings to see if EZ/EC might be able to provide resources for the Washington Community Center. At that time, he was on the board of the center, and he had ideas about programs that could be conducted there if the gymnasium could be restored and the classrooms could be repaired.

> We listed various programs that we'd have over there, because we had quite a few delin-
> quents or juveniles or whatever over in this area. We are right next to a housing authority,
> a housing project and kids have nothing to do. They go down to the park there and there's
> drugs and everything down there, so we thought we'd present to the people a plan whereby
> we could develop various programs and things that would attract the young kids and the
> young people to it.... There were various after-school programs that we wanted and vari-
> ous basketball and gymnasium things, mentoring programs. We wanted things for adults
> also there. For the older people, quilting deals where older folks get together and do their
> quilting and talk and whatever.[27]

Neither Henry Edwards nor his wife were members of the Western Hugo steering committee, which was considering these ideas. But one of Henry Edwards' former students was. She was the only person on the committee who was actually from the western part of Hugo; the other members were public officials and agency heads, including the superintendent of the Hugo school system. From his participation in larger planning meetings, involving people from multiple towns, Edwards knew that community centers were being proposed throughout the EZ/EC area. He trusted his former student to move the Washington Community Center proposal forward in the local steering committee and the overall steering committee.

As the EZ/EC application was being finalized, Edwards received a phone call from Oscar Stewart, the Little Dixie staff member who was in charge of compiling all of the local priorities for the strategic plan. Stewart was wondering why the Western Hugo steering committee's list did not include a proposal for the Washington Community Center, since he knew it was one of the ideas that had emerged in the planning process. Edwards' former student had convinced the committee to put a different priority on the list. Stuart asked Edwards to prepare a community center proposal to include in the plan. At the last minute, Leona Edwards typed the following letter to the chairperson of the committee:

> This is to inform your committee of the intent for use of the facilities located at the old
> school site; our plans are to seek federal grant money to restore the gymnasium and refur-
> bish the classrooms so that we might establish a recreational facility for leisure time activities.
> The young people of this area have no place to go for relaxation and fun things to do
> except in the Goldfeder Park where they get their first dose of drug trafficking and
> exchange of dollars. Foul language and abuse of young women is the first order of the day.
> Our young people deserve better. We also plan to have drug counseling, child abuse coun-
> seling, battered women counseling, tutoring class, and many other activities which may be

of benefit to the people. We will also have a first class banquet hall and meeting rooms for small gatherings. We here at the center believe that these type[s] of programs will greatly improve the quality of life for the people of this community. So, when you are developing your goals for the long range vision for Hugo, please don't forget us over here.[28]

Because of Stewart's call and Leona Edwards' letter, the refurbishment of the Washington Community Center was included in the EZ/EC strategic plan. Action "B-21 Youth Recreational Center" followed Leona Edwards' letter closely. It proposed the "restoration of the gymnasium and refurbishing of classrooms of the old Booker T. Washington School to provide recreational areas and space for classes for tutoring, drug and teen pregnancy prevention, battered women counseling courses and other training programs."[29] Funding was estimated at $180,000. The full amount was included in the $40 million Empowerment Zone Budget, but no funding was allocated in the $2.9 million budget for the Enterprise Community designation, which the four census tracts received.

Little Dixie assured Edwards that being in the Enterprise Community would nonetheless provide other opportunities for funding. As Edwards recalled: "I won't forget that in the overall scheme of things.... We didn't get designated as a funded item [in the Enterprise Community budget], but we got put on a 'if some money is left over list, we can give it to you.' I said, 'Well, that's better than nothing.' We would certainly manage ... and that's when I became a steering committee person...."[30] When Henry Edwards became a member of the Western Hugo steering committee, replacing his former student, he became a member of the overall steering committee as well. That committee was able to support the restoration of the gymnasium and refurbishment of classrooms for the Washington Community Center by reallocating $50,000 in unused federal block grant funds to the project and by allocating $75,000 from a Community Development Block Grant that the state of Oklahoma provided to the Enterprise Community.

The Washington Community Center is run by a board, whose members pay annual dues and make decisions about the organization. Many of the kinds of programs that Leona Edwards mentioned in her letter to the steering committee were subsequently developed — mostly by government agencies and other organizations with the support of the center's board. As Leona Edwards recalled, "We partnered with every agency here in the city of Hugo, and everybody benefited from it."[31]

Just as Little Dixie had stated in the strategic plan, the Washington Community Center has served as a facility to house programs. The Department of Human Services offered parenting classes there for people who were at risk of having their children removed from their home by the courts. A staffer from that Department started the "Agape Clinic" at the center, which provided free medical services for people without health insurance. The Choctaw County Commissioners ran a community service program for convicted offenders at the center. The Hugo Independent School District provided GED classes there for people who hadn't completed high school. The Choctaw County Election Board has used the center as an election polling place. Local home health agencies have used the center to provide monthly blood pressure screening for people in the community.

The center, itself, has played a more active role in some of the programming. With resources from the Kiamichi Economic Development District of Oklahoma, the center set up a nutrition program to provide meals to the elderly three times a week. With the

Hugo Housing Authority, the center provided "rap sessions" for youth from the housing project next door, in which: "...kids would come in and talk about their problems ... whatever they wanted to talk about. They could kind of gear them into a more positive direction, because usually it was negative kinds of things. They were upset about something. This teacher did something that they didn't like, something was happening at home or something was happening in the community so we feel like we were able to sort of offset some problems that would have developed if we hadn't had that."[32]

In addition, the center has provided people in the community with a place they can use for their own purposes. As Henry Edwards put it, residents "have a place to rent of their own ... they don't have to go across the tracks and rent a place to have a family reunion, or when they have a funeral ... they usually have it up there in the center ... [along with] birthday part[ies]."[33]

For a while, the Washington Community Center was very active. As Leona Edwards recalled, it "was a vital part of the city of Hugo. We catered to everybody. We didn't cater to just the blacks and Indians. We catered to the whole city of Hugo."[34] Most of the programs were not sustained, however. Some, like the Agape Clinic, moved to another site. Other programs ended for lack of funds or other reasons. Interest on the part of the community has waned as well. As Henry Edwards put it: "The people at first, they were very interested. They were very concerned and got involved, but then as time went along, they got a little tired. It began to drop by the wayside, and the ball began to rest in the court of just a few."[35] New leadership has not yet emerged to take over the role of aging board members. Currently, the center's uses are limited to election polling, monthly blood pressure screening, three senior meals per week, and about ten family functions a year.

The Boswell Nutrition Center

In Boswell, a small town in western Choctaw County, a nutrition center had served elderly residents since the early 1970s. With federal funds disbursed through the Kiamichi Economic Development District of Oklahoma, the center served meals to people 60 years of age and older five days a week. Over the years, the center had become more than a place where elderly folks could meet their nutritional needs. It also served as a gathering place for seniors, offering them opportunities to socialize with each other and build relationships. One group of women who used the center began quilting together, and they sold their quilts to supplement the center's budget. Other people who came for a meal began playing dominos together or simply watched television together. Around the time of the EZ/EC planning process, the center's facility was very run down. Property had been donated for a new building, but additional resources were required to move ahead with construction.

One of the members of the West Choctaw steering committee recalled the discussions about community and nutrition centers during the planning process. The needs seemed obvious: "Well, the nutrition center [in Boswell] ... was very minimal. The community center, we didn't have one of those either."[36] One of the women who quilted at the Boswell nutrition center became active encouraging people to come out for the planning meetings. She recalled "we really worked hard on it ... there's no telling how many miles I walked in this town trying to get people to participate our EZ program."[37]

At the meetings, the discussions identified additional ways that a center in Boswell could be used. If the center was available to youth, "we felt like it would keep our kids off the street."[38] It could be used "for any type of family-oriented types of gatherings, you know ... such as weddings."[39] It could also be used for annual "homecoming" events, which brought people who had left the area back to their home town to visit old friends, reacquaint themselves with the community, and get back to their roots.

Action B-8 in the EZ/EC strategic plan proposed the creation of a "community-based and family-centered multipurpose community center" in Boswell and two other communities. The center would "provide a location for youth activity, senior citizen feeding programs, a library, police sub-station, and classroom space for classes on drug abuse prevention, teenage pregnancy, literacy programs, etc. The complex would also house a health clinic, media center, kitchen, multipurpose hall, physical fitness center and swimming pool."[40] The cost of the three centers was estimated at $7.2 million. In the $40 million Empowerment Zone budget, $6.75 million was allocated for this purpose. The $2.9 million Enterprise Community budget included $150,000 for nutrition sites in the target area, but nothing for the creation of the three multipurpose community centers.[41]

As with the center in western Hugo, the project went forward, nonetheless, and within a few years, a new center was built on the land that had been donated. It took a patchwork of efforts by seniors who had used Boswell's old nutrition center over the years, other residents, local businesses, and people outside the community. The reallocation of unused Enterprise Community block grant funds and grants from other sources provided almost $40,000 for the project.

The first step was to replace the unusable concrete slab on the donated site and install proper drainage for it.[42] After the slab was prepared, the frame of the building was constructed by a man who had grown up in Boswell: "Dennis Hall, well, he's made a lot of money over the years, but his mother came up here [to the nutrition center] at that time. Since [then] she's moved, but she lived here all of her life. He donated the building, just the skeleton, the metal, and had it put up."[43] Through the local corrections system "we were getting four or five prisoners a week on Friday, and they came in and finished the building. They actually did the sheet-rocking and the painting and all that."[44]

To help outfit the interior of the building, the elderly women from the old center's quilting group sold their quilts. The funds they raised "donated the floor." The Kiamichi Economic Development District of Oklahoma, which had been disbursing the federal nutrition funding for the center all along, "graciously" donated funds for the "fixtures:" a refrigerator, walk-in freezer, and other appliances. In the end, "we got a very nice place."

For the most part, the center appears to operate very similarly to the way it did before, but in a nicer environment. The nutrition program operates until about 1:00 P.M., after which the kitchen is closed. Some seniors are already on the sidewalk when the doors open at 8:00 AM, and most stay until the early afternoon; "...the quilters quilt, and some of them watch television and some of them work a puzzle." Other seniors play bingo. Many of the men whose wives send them to the center for meals stay "and play dominos all day. A lot of times they'll play dominos until 4:00 or 5:00."[45]

The social interactions are very important to the seniors who come to the center. As one of the quilters recalled: "Well, when I had cancer I couldn't go anywhere until I got well. And I was so glad to get to come back up here [to the center]. You know, it just [gave] me a lift and my doctor even told me. He said, 'now, don't you sit at home and not do anything. You go back to that nutrition center and have fellowship and quilt because that is your life. That's what you've been doing.' And he said, 'You are going to miss out if you don't do that, and I want you to [go there] because you are going to get better.' And I did."[46]

The center has been used for some other purposes, as well. The Boswell City Council holds meetings there, people come for a monthly dance or covered dish dinner, and the space is also rented for family events, like birthday parties and anniversaries, six or seven times a year.[47] The center has not developed activities for youth, but "Believers in Boswell," a local group that holds its meetings at the center, is working to establish a separate center for youth in the community. The group has raised $50,000 for its project so far, and land for the youth center has been donated by a community resident.

Booker T. Washington Community Center in West Idabel

In 1992, a group of African American residents from the west side of Idabel formed the Idabel Minority Action Committee, known locally as "IMAC." The group was led by Irvin Jones, a career military man who had returned to his home town when he retired in the early 1990s. West Idabel was where most of the African Americans in Idabel lived, and the community had changed a lot over the years Jones had been away.[48] There was little economic activity in the parts of West Idabel that had been home to black-owned businesses before. The unemployment rate was 11 percent, and half of the households were living below the poverty line.[49] The high school that Jones had attended and valued so much when he was young — Booker T. Washington — had closed when desegregation unified the school system, sending the black students across town to Idabel High School. Now the abandoned school and untended grounds had become a hang-out for people involved in drinking and drugs, as well as youth with nothing to do.

The residents involved in IMAC wanted to be a force for change in their community, and the inclusion of West Idabel as one of the census tracts in the EZ/EC application created a potential opportunity to secure resources for making that happen. When the EZ/EC planning process began in 1994, Jones was elected to lead the West Idabel steering committee and he also became vice chair of the overall steering committee for the EZ/EC.

In the local planning meetings in West Idabel, creating a community center emerged as the "number one priority."[50] In contrast to Boswell and western Hugo, West Idabel had never had a community or nutrition center. In fact, very few services or amenities were available in West Idabel at the time. The residents had to go to the east side of town or elsewhere for shopping, entertainment, sports, and recreation. There was no place to socialize or play pool in the community. IMAC didn't even have a suitable place to hold its own meetings.

The West Idabel steering committee established a Social Service Committee, headed by Darlene Lowe, a local educator, to develop the community center proposal.[51] At the time, everyone was talking about a large recreation center that had been built up the road in Broken Bow, a more prosperous town that was not part of the EZ/EC target area, and the Social Service Committee's recommendation appears to have been inspired in some ways by that center. The proposal called for a "multipurpose community center that will house a clinic, media center, kiln, kitchen, multipurpose hall, gymnasium, library, three classrooms and an office, to create jobs, training programs, and personal enrichment activities for the entire community." Additional amenities would include a snack bar, day care, a police substation, weight room, "tennis room," and swimming pool. West Idabel's center would be "self-sustaining" and involve "early to older citizens in and around the community." It would "continuously generate revenue for the community," "contribute to education," "control delinquency," address problems of "teen pregnancy" and "delinquency aggression," "establish a bond between the citizens," and "increase self-esteem and self worth."[52]

Action B-2 of the EZ/EC strategic plan provided for the planning of this multipurpose center by a local group, and Action B-3 called for its construction "within the boundaries of the West Idabel census area," estimating the cost at $2.4 million. The proposal specified that the center would provide "a variety of services, including: youth activities; feeding programs for the elderly; classes on drug prevention and abuse, teenage pregnancy, and literacy classes; a library; and a police sub-station." Action B-3 also stated that "if construction of a center is not possible, the community will seek funding for the renovation of an old school to serve some of the purposes of this action."[53] The $40 million Empowerment Zone budget included $2.25 million for the multipurpose center in West Idabel. Only $175,000 was allocated in the $2.9 million budget for the Enterprise Community designation, however — enough to renovate the old school but not to construct the new center.

The back-up plan to renovate the Booker T. Washington High School for use as a community center came from Luketta Hill, a member of the West Idabel steering committee. In 1995, when the Enterprise Community funding came through, the committee arranged for the renovation to be done by an African American construction firm headed by a man from Dallas whom Jones knew. Having this work done by a minority business person was an important achievement in the eyes of Jones and the local steering committee.[54] Funds obtained through the Enterprise Community also helped to develop the grounds of the school, creating basketball courts, ball fields, and an outdoor amphitheater named for O. W. Lee, a teacher at the old high school who had mentored many of the students there, including Jones.

Originally, the West Idabel steering committee had proposed that the Booker T. Washington Community Center be run by a partnership of local organizations, including IMAC, local churches, the Masons, and a professional women's organization known as the "Entre Nous Club." It didn't work out that way, however. As Jones recalled, "We were going to have a representative from each one of those organizations to manage it. And this worked for the first two or three meetings and then the people stopped showing up." As a result, "the IMAC member was the only one left" and "by default" IMAC was left to run the center.[55] Over time, IMAC's regular meeting, every second Wednesday of the month, also became the monthly meeting of the West Idabel steering committee. Once the Enterprise Community's block grant funds were spent, members who weren't involved in IMAC lost interest in the steering committee.

The Booker T. Washington Community Center has been used for a variety of purposes. Most of the programming has been proposed by IMAC members, although anyone in the community can suggest activities at IMAC meetings. To be implemented, programs require funding — some of which has been obtained through grants written by other organizations in the Enterprise Community — or volunteers committed to pulling a project off. Some of the center's space has been used by an Alternative School run by the Idabel school system. The school, which occupies classrooms on one side of the building, pays for the center's utilities and insurance.

Local youth are a major focus of IMAC programming at the center. IMAC has sponsored a basketball team there, which plays in tournaments in other towns around the area, as far as 120 miles away. IMAC pays half the fees and provides uniforms for the team. For Jones, the team is part of a larger effort to provide West Idabel's youth with activities and positive role models: "...the reason we do this is because these young men have finished school, and most of them were probably pretty good basketball players in high school, and they kind of are in transit with their lives. They don't know what they're going to do. They're not really working hard. Just kind of hanging out. And these are the ones the kids still watch and emulate."[56]

IMAC has also sponsored a Drug-Free Club for youth, which takes its members on field trips to a regional college or university every summer and to places like a black circus in Dallas and the Mound Bayou sweet potato farming cooperative in the Mississippi Delta, which is run by African Americans seeking to revive a tradition of independent black agriculture. Other programs for youth have included after-school tutoring and child care, a dance class, and a computer center. The computer center didn't turn out the way IMAC hoped it would. IMAC members thought that the African American youth in West Idabel needed a computer center and would want to use it. But the computers have mainly been used by white youth from Idabel. This experience taught Jones that "you can't decide what people want to do. They have to tell you themselves." In the future, he believes a higher level of "truly grassroots" involvement in developing programs is important.[57]

The meal program for senior citizens at the center is more "grassroots" in the sense that the idea came from an elderly person in West Idabel. The program serves meals on-site to about 60 or 70 seniors each month and also delivers meals to people's homes. Unlike Boswell and western Hugo, West Idabel is not a federally funded nutrition site. The program is run by volunteers, and some people provide additional support by purchasing meals.

As with the other community centers, Booker T. Washington is a place that residents and groups in West Idabel have used for their own purposes. About two to four times a month, community members rent the center for family events, funerals, and other gatherings. Groups have sponsored dances and parties for youth as well as community festivals at the center. IMAC and other groups have used the space for their own meetings. Overall, the center is a very social place — "you meet new people every time you come in the building."[58]

In retrospect, some community members think West Idabel might have been fortunate not to get funding for the big multipurpose center that the steering committee initially proposed. The large recreation center in Broken Bow ended up being taken over by the school system because it was too expensive for community groups to maintain; members of IMAC think that probably would have happened in West Idabel, too. The renovated high school is serving most of the functions of a community center that matter to people in West Idabel. Even more important, the renovation preserved a building that is an important cultural landmark in the community. One member of IMAC who had gone to school there said that when people come to the Booker T. Washington Community Center, they "are on sacred ground because it is so important to this community, the building itself ... [there] was something I got out of this school that I haven't got at any other school I ever attended."[59] Another member said, "schooling is the heart of a community. You have your churches, you have your businesses ... but every kid went to Booker T. Washington."[60] The transformation of the old high school into a community center is linking the younger generation in West Idabel to this history. It is also linking them to adults in the community who want to carry on the old high school's tradition of mentoring and supporting young people.

Maintaining the center is a challenge that West Idabel faces today. When the area's Enterprise Community designation ended in 2004, funding sources for new programs became more difficult to obtain. Jones, who recently retired as the chair of IMAC said: "I've learned that it's a lot easier to get stuff [funding to create the community center] than it is to maintain stuff.... [In the future], before we did anything, I would come up with a sure fire way [of] having some kind of income for maintaining it.... You can't rent it [the community center] in a poor neighborhood like West Idabel and make enough money to do any maintaining.... Once we start taking city money to do that, then we would eventually lose the facility." [61]

The Case Analysis

The development of community centers in southeastern Oklahoma's Enterprise Community involved numerous players: the community residents who participated in the EZ/EC process; the members of the local steering committees and overall steering committee; staff members of the Little Dixie Community Action Agency; staff members of National Training Associates; and the people who have run the centers and have organized center activities and programming. To understand how the ideas of these different players influenced what happened, we (1) looked at the major impacts of the case; (2) identified whose ideas were influential at the critical points that shaped the development of the community centers; and (3) explored how the accomplishments and limitations in the case were related to ideas that were, and were not, influential.

Major Impacts

The community centers that southeastern Oklahoma's Enterprise Community constructed or refurbished have benefited residents in important ways. As community gathering places, the centers have been addressing a serious problem in the area — the social isolation of rural poverty. Elderly people (and youth in some areas) now have safe and inviting places to go to visit with others, talk, quilt, play games or sports, have a communal meal, dance, hold family functions, have meetings, learn new skills, and work on community projects. Government agencies, private sector organizations, and individuals have facilities for running programs and providing services that they believe will benefit the residents of these communities. In West Idabel, the renovation of the Booker T. Washington High School also preserved a "sacred" cultural landmark in the community.

Getting the centers included in the EZ/EC strategic plan and obtaining the resources that were needed for their construction or refurbishment were accomplishments in themselves. Although community centers were a very high priority for the residents in the local planning meetings, this strategy was not specifically listed as a fundable activity in the federal government's instructions for completing the EZ/EC application. Some of the people involved in economic and community development in southeastern Oklahoma were concerned that the inclusion of community centers in the area's strategic plan might make the application less competitive.[62] In Western Hugo, the refurbishment of the Washington Community Center narrowly missed being included in the plan because a member of the local steering committee misrepresented the community's priorities.

Creating or improving community centers does not mean they will continue to be maintained or used, however. In Western Hugo, the community's initial enthusiasm for the Washington Community Center has waned, and most of the programs there have been discontinued. In West Idabel, IMAC was unable to get other community organizations involved in managing the Booker T. Washington Community Center and is now having difficulty obtaining resources to operate the center. Some of the programs that have been developed at the centers have not been used by the populations for whom they were intended.

Critical Points of Influence

Looking at the events and impacts in the development of community centers in southeastern Oklahoma, there appear to be five points at which the influence of players' ideas mattered: (1) deciding how the community would be involved; (2) getting community centers into the EZ/EC strategic plan; (3) constructing and refurbishing the centers; (4) deciding how the centers would be used; and (5) participating in center activities and programs.

Deciding how the community would be involved. The federal government required that the strategic plan for an Empowerment Zone or Enterprise Community designation be developed with the "participation of the community affected." In southeastern Oklahoma, the process for involving community members was designed by a team of consultants from National Training Associates in California. The process was intended to be "non-threatening," to "ensure participation and learning by everyone, including low-income individuals," and to "utilize all ideas and suggestions."[63] Large numbers of community residents participated in the planning meetings. We do not know all of the ideas they expressed or how those ideas were expressed because the sticky notes from the meetings have been lost. But the process clearly enabled people to express their desire for community centers.

A smaller number of community members were also engaged in the local steering committees, their subcommittees, and the overall steering committee. Little Dixie encouraged the five-member local steering committees to include people who represented different community interests, such as "education, infrastructure, economic development, social programs, and law enforcement."[64] But these committees—which were responsible for organizing the local planning meetings, identifying the census tract's priorities, and developing local action proposals—were not necessarily representative of the people living in their census tracts, since residence in these very low-income areas was not a prerequisite for being a committee member. Since all of the people on the local steering committees were also on the overall steering committee, ideas spread easily across communities.

Getting community centers into the EZ/EC strategic plan. The idea for community centers emerged in the planning meetings—beginning with the large training workshop and continuing in the local planning meetings across the census tracts. If these ideas had not been expressed, there is no reason to believe that community centers would have been included in the strategic plan. From what we can tell, the people who proposed community centers included residents who wanted to use the centers themselves; residents who wanted community centers for their children, parents, or friends; and people involved in programming or service provision who believed community centers could help particular populations in the community. One of these populations was youth, but since young people were not included in the planning sessions, they did not have an opportunity to speak for themselves.

To a large extent, ideas about community centers were influential because Little Dixie overcame certain shortcomings in the process and respected local priorities. The Washington Community Center would not have been included in the strategic plan if a Little Dixie staff member had not informed Henry Edwards that the Western Hugo steering committee was not representing his community's priorities. Little Dixie included all of the community center proposals submitted by the local steering committees in the plan. The available evidence suggests that the descriptions in the plan were faithful to the proposals developed locally, although the rationale for the centers and the particular uses of the centers were presented in ways that were most likely to make the EZ/EC application competitive.

Constructing and refurbishing the centers. The construction and refurbishment of the centers depended on funding, and the overall steering committee, including Little Dixie, was very influential in this regard. While only two of the centers were initially allocated funds from the Enterprise Community block grant, the overall steering committee reallocated some of these funds to other centers later on when other Enterprise Community projects were canceled or came in under budget. The overall steering committee also played an influential role in allocating funds from the Oklahoma community development block grant to the centers. Little Dixie supported the centers in obtaining funds from other sources, particularly the other federal programs that gave Enterprise Communities special consideration. In Boswell, most of the resources for constructing the new center came from community members who donated needed resources—land, labor, the skeleton of a building, appliances—and sold quilts to raise money for the floor.

The amount of resources that a community was able to garner determined the extent of what could be done. In West Idabel, for example, funding was not sufficient to construct a new center; the only feasible option was to renovate the old Booker T. Washington High School. Decisions about how the buildings would be renovated or how a new building would be designed appear to have been made by the groups running the centers—IMAC in West Idabel, the board of the Washington Community Center in Western Hugo, and the leadership of the Boswell Nutrition Center. With the exception of the "quilting ladies" in Boswell, the community residents who had expressed a desire for these centers at the local planning meetings were not involved in the design of the centers.

Deciding how the centers would be used. The unstructured uses of the centers—such as family reunions, funerals, quilting, dominos, basketball pick-up games, and organizational meetings—have been determined by the people and groups who have used the centers for these purposes. The ideas for more structured programming and service delivery—such as classes, youth clubs, and medical care—have come from the leadership of the centers, individuals who run programs or provide services, community organizations, and government agencies. There is no evidence that the people for whom these programs and services are intended have been involved in their design.

Participating in center activities and programs. Community residents have made their own decisions about participating in center activities, with the exception of a few programs where participation has been required by a child's parents or by the courts. In Western Hugo, participation and use of the Washington Community Center has waned—in part, because many of the programs have ended. We don't know how well the various programs were attended when they were running, however. In Boswell, participation in the unstructured social activities at the Nutrition Center has continued to be at least as active as before the new center was built. In West Idabel, a substantial number of community residents have been making use of the Booker T. Washington Community Center. Nonetheless, youth have declined to participate in some of the programs developed for them, and community groups have declined to participate in the management of the center.

Relating Impacts to Influence

The important accomplishments in this case appear to be related to the first four points of influence, which enabled the ideas of many different kinds of players to be contributed and used. The process developed by National Training Associates gave residents of the area an opportunity to talk about issues that really mattered to them, which documented a strong interest in community centers and identified why different kinds of people wanted community centers. The larger planning meetings and the meetings of the overall steering committee spread the idea of community centers throughout the area, broadening interest and support. That shared knowledge, in turn, helped to prevent the misrepresentation of local priorities in the process. Local proposals for community centers were presented faithfully in the EZ/EC strategic plan, and Little Dixie's knowledge about grant writing helped to align those proposals more closely to the goals and fundable activities of the EZ/EC program. Little Dixie, other members of the overall steering committee, and community members in Boswell used their knowledge about funding sources to obtain needed resources for the centers. With the construction or renovation of the centers, new domains of influence were created for various players. Residents experiencing the social isolation of rural poverty, groups in need of meeting space, and people and organizations committed to helping others in the community have all developed uses for the centers.

The problems with participation in the centers in Western Hugo and, to a lesser extent, West Idabel may be related to the fourth and fifth points of influence in the case. The people for whom structured programs and services have been developed at these centers have had little, if any, involvement in the design of those programs and services. Consequently, the programs and services have been based on assumptions about what these target populations want and need. If the assumptions are wrong, the only option for influence for the members of the target population is to choose not to participate. This dynamic may explain why African American youth have not participated in some of the programs designed for them in West Idabel. It also may contribute to the waning interest in the community center in Western Hugo, which appears to have had the most agency-driven programming of the three centers described in this case.

9

The Incorporation of Beyond Welfare in Ames, Iowa

The Story

In the summer of 2001, Lois Smidt received a call from Scott Miller, who said that he was moving to California and would no longer be working with Smidt at the Move the Mountain Leadership Center in Ames, Iowa. Miller had co-founded Move the Mountain with Gary Stokes nine years before, developing the Center's "Transformational Leadership Program" with him. Since 1996, when welfare reform started being instituted around the country, Miller had worked closely with Smidt to develop programs that engaged community residents, organizations, and agencies in assuring that families in the area had the supports they needed to leave welfare safely. These programs, which Move the Mountain referred to as "Beyond Welfare," included relationship-building strategies, advocacy, and material forms of support. Through "Community Leadership Team," a weekly evening meal and meeting, and "Circles of Support," which connected families in poverty to a group of middle class "allies," Beyond Welfare sought to develop cross-class relationships that would address the isolation of people in poverty, build their voice and confidence, give them needed connections and personal and emotional support, and educate the broader community — including policy makers — about the challenges people face trying to get out of poverty. Beyond Welfare also included a car donation program, called "Wheels to Work," a job coaching program, and a small revolving loan program.

When she received the call, Smidt was watching her son's team play baseball, and Miller's announcement that he was leaving Move the Mountain took her by surprise: "At the time it felt like it would have some potentially devastating effects on Beyond Welfare, because he did have a key role in Beyond Welfare."[1]

For five years, Smidt and Miller had been engaged in a collegial relationship at Move the Mountain, and they shared a sense of joint ownership over their work. Their roles in Beyond Welfare were different and complementary — Smidt was the day-to-day practitioner who developed and facilitated Beyond Welfare's relationship-building strategies; Miller focused on the big picture and secured the resources to operate Beyond Welfare's various programs.

141

Smidt didn't feel capable of stepping into Miller's role, and she was apprehensive about Beyond Welfare's future at Move the Mountain without Miller there. Gary Stokes, the Executive Director of Move the Mountain, had moved from Iowa to Arizona and was running the organization from there. His leadership style was very different from hers, and he was much more interested in Move the Mountain's Transformational Leadership Program than the programs of Beyond Welfare.

Smidt recalled Miller saying that "Beyond Welfare should incorporate, because then you could have access to different sources of funding and things that you would never have through Move the Mountain."[2] Shortly thereafter, Stokes came to Ames and gave her two options: she could remain at Move the Mountain, becoming the leader of Beyond Welfare, or Beyond Welfare could incorporate, becoming an autonomous organization. Stokes asked for Smidt's decision in 48 hours.

Creation of Beyond Welfare

When Gary Stokes and Scott Miller created the Move the Mountain Leadership Center in 1992, Stokes was the head of Mid-Iowa Community Action, Inc. (MICA), and Move the Mountain was a program within that organization. MICA was one of the many nonprofit "community action agencies" established under the Economic Opportunity Act of 1964 to fight the country's "war on poverty."[3] Focusing on children and families in five largely rural counties in central Iowa, MICA was established to promote citizen participation and volunteer work and to administer federal programs for people in poverty, such as Head Start, the Special Supplemental Nutrition Program for Women, Infants, and Children (commonly known as "WIC"), and maternal and child health programs. Like all community action agencies, low-income community members were required to make up at least one-third of MICA's board; one-third were required to be public officials; the remainder were leaders in the private sector.

Stokes had been active in creating MICA's Family Development and Self-Sufficiency Program, which provides "in-home support for families receiving public assistance, helping them to increase their stability and their ability to become economically self-sufficient." In the program, "Family Development Specialists meet one-on-one with families in regular home visits. Together, specialists and families address the barriers affecting their success. They complete assessment tools and develop goals around areas critical to the family's overall well-being, such as employment, substance abuse treatment, education, physical health, and mental health."[4]

Stokes and Miller first came together around the Family Development Program. Miller, who had been trained in business administration and organizational development, was first exposed to Stokes and the Family Development Program when he was working in Ohio as a social worker with Catholic Charities. He subsequently started the Ohio Center for Family Development. In 1992, when many people expected some kind of welfare reform to be imminent, Stokes brought Miller to MICA to help him establish a new leadership center to "build a collaboration of human service, healthcare, and education institutions that would reduce poverty and get better outcomes for at-risk children and families."[5] The Annie E. Casey Foundation provided the Move the Mountain Leadership Center with initial funding "to assist leaders in a five-county region of Central Iowa with strategic planning and to facilitate collaborations where those strategic plans overlapped."[6] In 1995, Move the Mountain began offering formal leadership and organizational development programs to help leaders in human services agencies, school systems, and medical institutions "make a conscious shift from management to leadership."[7]

Throughout 1996, Congress was crafting the Personal Responsibility and Work Opportunity Reconciliation Act, the massive welfare reform legislation that would achieve President Clinton's highly publicized goal of "ending welfare as we know it."[8] Throughout the debates on the bill, it was clear that welfare reform would dismantle Aid to Families with Dependent Children, a federal entitlement program started in 1935; replace it with a program that would allow the states much greater discretion in how they spent federal funding; and mandate some process to move recipients off public assistance within some specified time frame.

In advance of the act's passage, state and local government agencies, community action agencies, and other organizations began to consider what it would take to get people off public assistance and into the workforce.[9] Early in 1996, MICA received funding from Iowa's Department of Human Services to organize a group of "consumers" of public assistance, with the aim of providing agencies and service providers with information that could help them address the challenges of welfare reform. Miller and Stokes decided to make MICA's "Consumer Leadership Team" part of the Move the Mountain Leadership Center because the team would build leadership among people on public assistance, enabling them to articulate what they and others need to move out of poverty, and it would build leadership among the high-level professionals involved in Move the Mountain's leadership and organizational development programs, providing them with information they needed to create large-scale social change.

Lois Smidt, who was working at MICA as a Family Development Specialist at the time, volunteered to coordinate the Consumer Leadership Team. Smidt had grown up in poverty on a farm in rural Iowa. After teaching English Literature and Women's Studies at Iowa State University for as long as a temporary instructor without a doctoral degree could, she became unemployed and went on public assistance to provide for her two children. Smidt received in-home services from a case worker in MICA's Family Development Program for two years until, in 1995, she was hired as a Family Development Specialist, herself.

Smidt's own experiences on welfare had demonstrated the importance of assisting people in poverty to move away from thinking about themselves in terms of deficits or needing to be helped and developing, instead, a sense of personal worth and agency. With the support of Miller and other colleagues at MICA, she structured Consumer Leadership Team to meet these goals. Food and child care were provided to enable people in poverty to participate in the meetings. The meetings also incorporated a variety of listening and relationship-building practices—many drawn from Smidt's experiences with Re-Evaluation Counseling—to develop, respect, and support the voices and intelligence of people in poverty.

In 1997, MICA created a new program within Move the Mountain, called Beyond Welfare, to take a "systemic approach" to getting people off welfare and ensuring that families leaving welfare were supported by the community.[10] The idea came out of conversations that Scott Miller had with Gary Stokes. As Miller recalled, Stokes said "Why don't you get a bunch of people off of welfare? ... If you learn how to do that, and I mean seriously get them off of welfare, [funders] will [be] beating a path to your door."[11] In addition to the Consumer Leadership Team, Miller proposed that Beyond Welfare include a job development program and a "volunteer network of churches and businesses" committed to helping families "address barriers such as child care, transportation, housing, job training, education, financial crises, family isolation, job placement and retention, and job advancement."[12] Miller secured initial funding from the Joyce Foundation, the Family Preservation and Support Services Program, and the U.S. Department of Agriculture to pursue these objectives.[13] To guide Beyond Welfare, he organized a "Guiding Coalition" made up of members of his informal support group, which included Lois Smidt, professional colleagues, academics, and four women on public assistance.

Incorporation of Move the Mountain Leadership Center

In 1998, Move the Mountain Leadership Center separated from MICA, becoming an autonomous nonprofit corporation, with Stokes as Executive Director. Miller, Smidt, and Beyond Welfare went along with Move the Mountain. As Stokes explained, MICA was a local organization, primarily concerned with service provision, while Move the Mountain's "agenda quickly had become a national agenda ... [with] national implications...." Both he and Miller were interested in "transformational leadership," which meant "developing leaders of large-scale social change, particularly around poverty issues, although also around education reform.... There wasn't anybody out there in the country talking to nonprofit leaders or government leaders about how you lead large-scale change, and of course, the ending poverty framework, which Move the Mountain had adopted, was an extraordinarily large-scale social change."[14] As an independent corporation, Move the Mountain did not have to meet the board requirements of a community action agency. Its board was small, comprised of Stokes' professional colleagues. Since Stokes didn't see the need for Move the Mountain to have a local base, he moved to Arizona in 1999 and ran the organization from there. Miller, Smidt, and the rest of Beyond Welfare's staff remained in Ames.

As an autonomous organization with a national focus, Move the Mountain received funding from the Annie E. Casey Foundation to research best practices in leadership development in both the private and public sectors around the country.[15] That work, in turn, led to the creation of its Transformational Leadership Program providing training and technical assistance around "high-impact strategies to bring about long-term change."[16] Miller saw Beyond Welfare as a local laboratory for developing and testing such high-impact strategies. Building on efforts that had begun when Move the Mountain was part of MICA, Miller and Smidt created the other components of Beyond Welfare.

The "Circles of Support" program connected a person in poverty (and their family) with three or four people with sufficient means. To distinguish between the people involved, Beyond Welfare referred to people in poverty as "participants" and those who weren't as "allies." The intention of the program was to build cross-class relationships that would support poor people as they tried to leave poverty and, at the same time, educate middle-class people about the challenges that poor people face trying to get out of poverty. Along with the weekly meetings of Consumer Leadership Team, to which allies were invited, Circles of Support would contribute to Move the Mountain's larger agenda by changing the belief system of Americans about the causes and solutions of poverty and by mobilizing more people to advocate for large-scale social change.

Reciprocity was a key element in the relationships that the weekly meetings and Circles of Support sought to establish — which distinguished them from the dependent, "fixit" relationships that people in poverty had with case workers and other service providers. The members of Consumer Leadership Team, who subsequently decided to call themselves "Community Leadership Team," believed that poverty involved more than a lack of economic resources and that poor people had a lot to give people with sufficient means who lacked other things in their lives. Mike Green, a trainer with Asset Based Community Development (ABCD) who worked with Smidt and Miller in developing the Circles of Support program in Ames, helped the members of Community Leadership Team articulate the core needs of people as "money, meaning, and friends."

Over the next three years, attendance at Community Leadership Team meetings increased to about 50 participants and allies each week, and about 25 Circles of Support were formed. Beyond Welfare also developed a car donation program, called "Wheels to Work," which incorporated a reciprocity agreement that people receiving cars could fulfill by paying back a small sum of money or providing the equivalent in in-kind services. A job coaching program and a revolving loan program were initiated. Working with the Child and Family Policy Center in Des Moines and the Iowa Department of Human Services, Beyond Welfare also became involved in "Consumer Advisory Teams," which enabled people in poverty to provide input to service providers and policy makers involved in welfare reform.

Since Beyond Welfare was Move the Mountain's laboratory for testing high impact strategies to get people off public assistance and, ultimately, to end poverty, Miller needed data to evaluate the effectiveness of these strategies. A detailed intake process was used to obtain baseline data on the people who participated in Beyond Welfare's programs, and additional data were gathered thereafter.

Miller and Smidt were very committed to Beyond Welfare, but Stokes, who was living in Arizona and primarily interested in Move the Mountain's Transformational Leadership Program, was not as involved. Shortly after leaving Ames, Stokes suggested that Smidt consider finding a local institutional home for Beyond Welfare, either with MICA or another service agency in the Ames area. She recalled, "I was very adamant about that not happening, because I felt that it would compromise the community aspect [of Beyond Welfare's work]. It would be more likely to turn [Beyond Welfare] into a program of service delivery rather than a community-building entity...."[17] Beyond Welfare continued to be part of Move the Mountain; Miller and Smidt remained in Ames; and Beyond Welfare's Guiding Coalition, which later became known as the Beyond Welfare Advisory Board, continued to be comprised of people from the local area. This group provided Miller and Smidt with ideas and advice but had no formal role in the governance of Beyond Welfare.

By 2001, Miller was focusing increasing attention on extending the reach and impact of Beyond Welfare's programs. With Smidt, he instituted an "immersion" training program for people around the country who were interested in learning about Circles of Support and Community Leadership Team. He also began to work on a concept he called

"The Beyond Poverty Project," which would reduce poverty in the United States by integrating Move the Mountain's transformational leadership training with strategies developed in Beyond Welfare and other programs. He wanted to implement the components of this program in ten sites around the country to see if they would significantly reduce poverty in communities of varying sizes and socioeconomic make-up.[18]

Separation of Beyond Welfare from Move the Mountain

Lois Smidt was taken aback when Miller called her in the summer of 2001 to say that he was leaving Move the Mountain, but he had been traveling between Iowa and California a lot for the past six months, and Smidt had been wondering if he was planning to remain in Iowa, move to California, or try to live and work in both places. As Smidt recalled, Miller was "changing his mind about things, and along with that was a lot of changing on what would my role be and what would his role be."[19] As a result, she had been experiencing "a real feeling of instability and not knowing what was going on."[20]

At that point, she turned to Mike Green at ABCD for advice. Green was well acquainted with Beyond Welfare because he had been working with Smidt, Miller, and some of the members of Beyond Welfare's Advisory Board in Neighborhood Circles, one of ABCD's programs. According to Smidt, Green said, "This is really dangerous for the organization [Beyond Welfare].... It's not only unhealthy for you — and you're feeling really unstable and jerked around and you don't know what's going to happen next week, because things are changing all the time — but it's not healthy for the organization."[21]

Smidt recalled that when Miller called, he said she "should get a Board of Directors and Beyond Welfare should incorporate," since doing so would help her obtain access to funding.[22] To attract resources from local organizations, especially faith-based groups like the Catholic Campaign for Human Development, Miller suggested that the majority of Beyond Welfare's Board be comprised of people in poverty.[23] Shortly thereafter, Stokes came to Ames and met with Smidt and some of the members of Beyond Welfare's Advisory Board over dinner. He presented them with two options: Beyond Welfare could remain associated with Move the Mountain and continue its work in the Ames area with Smidt at the helm, or Beyond Welfare could incorporate and become an autonomous organization.

The day after the dinner meeting, Stokes called Smidt to inform her that the decision needed to be made within 48 hours. The deadline created problems for Smidt because it precluded thorough consultation with the people who would be most affected by the decision: the participants and allies in Beyond Welfare's Community Leadership Team and the members of Beyond Welfare's Advisory Board. Smidt was used to consulting with the members of these groups and, in this instance, she felt their advice was critical because the best course of action wasn't apparent to her — "I didn't know. I mean I was this sort of very grassroots [person], you know. I wasn't educated in nonprofits or administrative things or any of this world. It was all news to me."[24]

The deadline that Stokes imposed was consistent with Smidt's previous experience working with him, and she was concerned about continuing that relationship without Miller around to act as a buffer. Most of her concerns related to differences in the way she and Stokes thought about decision making and leadership. Smidt believed in an inclusive approach to decision making. She also believed that "all people are leaders. Given the support and environment that invites that leadership out, anybody — regardless of their status or their labels or their situation — can really do remarkable things and make remarkable contributions to the world."[25] That is what she was trying to model in Community Leadership Team and Circles of Support. Stokes appeared to practice a more executive style of decision making. In Smidt's view, he saw leadership as "sort of an exclusive thing, and that leaders are special people." As Stokes put it, Move the Mountain was looking for these "special people" who held institutional positions where they could enact large-scale social and policy change.[26] From the time that Move the Mountain left MICA in 1998, Stokes had wanted Smidt "not [to] spend as much time in direct relationship with people in poverty" and instead build relationships with "systems leaders and institutional leaders."[27] Without Miller, she worried that she would be under even more pressure to move in that direction.[28]

The 48-hour deadline would be up before the members of Community Leadership met again for their weekly meeting. As Smidt recalled, "Really, in my mind, at the moment he [Stokes] said that, the decision [to separate] was made...."[29] Nonetheless, over the next two days, Smidt talked to as many people as she could, determined not to "make that decision in isolation."[30] She was able to reach a few of the people in poverty who were active members of the Community Leadership Team, some of the members of Beyond Welfare's Advisory Board, Scott Miller, and Mike Green. All of them had reasons for Beyond Welfare to separate itself from Move the Mountain.[31]

Some of the people she consulted said that they never understood how Beyond Welfare fit in Move the Mountain. As one of the people in poverty who was a member of Beyond Welfare's Advisory Board put it "Move the Mountain was sort of so remote and mysterious ... even this Advisory Board had been set up in terms of Move the Mountain, and ... it felt secretive...."[32] Other members of the Advisory Board felt that if Beyond Welfare were to remain with Move the Mountain, it would be on Stokes' terms and "under his thumb."[33] This was cause for concern because they thought that Stokes "didn't see Beyond Welfare as ... a community development effort" — which was how Smidt and the Advisory Board saw it — "but rather as a hothouse for ways to eliminate poverty. So I don't think that he was in sympathy with what the underlying character of [Beyond Welfare] was...."[34]

Smidt shared these people's concerns with Mike Green. He recalled: "...given [that] people [in Beyond Welfare] kept talking about the tension between the direction of Move the Mountain and Beyond Welfare ... it seemed to me that it made a lot of sense to think about the incorporation and being their own separate organization."[35] According to Smidt, Green also said that she and Beyond Welfare needed "an expanded accountability loop to a board of directors that has real power ... not just this Advisory Board [while] Move the Mountain has the final say. You need to establish a local governing board and have local governance and everything."[36]

On July 24, 2001, Smidt told Stokes that Beyond Welfare would "spin out" from Move the Mountain.[37] Stokes thought it was a good decision. As he recalled, "I didn't feel that Beyond Welfare's agenda of testing this new high-impact strategy of developing relationships across class and race lines was an integral part of my own agenda, which was to develop transformational leaders around poverty issues in the United States."[38] Instead, he thought local communities needed to take ownership of the kind of work Beyond

Welfare was doing. "It just seemed strategically right to ... make [Beyond Welfare] not part of a national organization, which Move the Mountain was now, but a local organization so that it would have more access and more likelihood of gaining local resources. The United Way, the county government, and those guys weren't seeing Beyond Welfare as something that they needed to fund yet, and they hadn't even been approached, so we needed to make it a local organization."[39] Stokes also thought it would be "a growth step for Lois [Smidt] to become an executive director of a nonprofit and to take full responsibility."[40]

Stokes made a commitment to support Beyond Welfare's separation as much as possible. Smidt and the Advisory Board were given five months—until December 31, 2001—to prepare for incorporation, and Move the Mountain would hand over all of the programs associated with Beyond Welfare, all of the funding for those programs (except for a small amount of administrative overhead), and all of the office equipment that Beyond Welfare staff had been using. Move the Mountain would also support any interim grant proposals made by Beyond Welfare prior to incorporation.[41]

Formalization of Beyond Welfare's Organizational Structure

Mike Green saw incorporation as an opportunity for Beyond Welfare to define its identity. As he put it: "If you were going to be Beyond Welfare, then you should be clear about who you are and who you aren't. It's the most likely way you'd be successful, and that's what the incorporation means to me, a quest for identity."[42] In drafting Beyond Welfare's Articles of Incorporation and By-Laws, Lois Smidt and the members of the Advisory Board—most of whom were active in Community Leadership Team and/or Circles of Support—sought to formalize important principles in their work. Much of this was drawn from the statement of "Purposes and Principles" that had been developed by the members of the Community Leadership Team to codify what they were doing and why.[43]

One of the original Advisory Board members who was an ally in Circles of Support recalled the process. "When we decided to incorporate, I liked the clarity of that goal. Then you say, 'Well, we'll go out and write Articles of Incorporation.' You go and find examples, and that was kind of concrete.... What I found most invigorating about it was the discussions that we had about governance—about who's in charge, how do we vote, who's on the board, what's the relationship of the board to the whole organization. Those were very good discussions, because I think that it clarified or formalized informal norms that had been developing."[44]

The Articles of Incorporation described what the new corporation, Beyond Welfare, was being established to achieve —"a community with residents who realize that: each person has an inherent intelligence with which to mobilize their talents and gifts to face any challenge; each person's well-being is deeply connected to the well-being of all; and relationships are based on reciprocity and respect for the inherent dignity and worth of others. The Corporation seeks to develop a community where everyone has the resources to realize their sense of purpose, to fulfill their need for meaningful relationships and to contribute to the common good."[45] Beyond Welfare was described as using "a locally led strategy of building community toward the goal of eliminating systemic poverty in Story County, Iowa [where Ames is located]. To build community, the Corporation addresses dimensions of poverty, such as low income, employment insecurity, lack of voice in community affairs, and social isolation. The Corporation supports individuals and households and constructs an environment where people of all ages can build mutually meaningful, reciprocating relationships irrespective of social positions. To reduce systemic poverty in Story County, Iowa, the Corporation educates residents about the dynamics of systemic poverty and [engages in] collective actions to increase affordable housing and to raise wages to livable levels"[46]

The By-Laws assured that the governance of Beyond Welfare would be in the hands of local people who were active participants in Beyond Welfare's core programs. Specifically, the members of the Board of Directors were required to "attend regularly the weekly Community Leadership Team's meetings," "participate regularly in additional organizational and relational events within Beyond Welfare," and "meet with persons of the community one-on-one to build community involvement and support."[47] The By-Laws formalized Beyond Welfare's commitment to recognizing and incorporating the voice of people in poverty in its work by stating that a "majority" of the Board of Directors "shall be people who are, or recently have been, marginalized by poverty."[48]

On December 15, 2001, Beyond Welfare filed its papers and became an independent non-profit organization with Lois Smidt as its Executive Director. Most of the original Board members had been on Beyond Welfare's previous Advisory Board. One month later, on January 15, 2002, the By-Laws were revised to state that a majority of the Board of Directors "shall be people who were raised in poverty, or are, or recently have been, marginalized by poverty."[49] The change was made because only three members of Community Leadership Team who were living in poverty, or had been living in poverty recently, responded to the invitation to join Beyond Welfare's Board — less than the five needed to comprise a majority of the nine-member Board. Three years later, Beyond Welfare revised its By-Laws once again to stipulate that the Board be led by Co-Chairs, "of which one must be currently experiencing poverty or has recently experienced poverty."[50]

One of the people in poverty who served on Beyond Welfare's Board from the start said that she "learned a lot of skills" as a result of "serving on the Board and working with the budget committee." Her experience made her realize "how much planning, thought and processing ... we have to go through to come to being able to carry out the work that we did."[51]

Further Clarification of Beyond Welfare's Identity

As Beyond Welfare began to operate on its own and concentrate on its primary purpose, its programmatic emphasis changed. More attention was paid to Community Leadership Team and Circles of Support, which formed the foundation of Beyond Welfare's community- and relationship-building efforts. Scott Miller's detailed intake process for new members was abandoned, and Community Leadership Team adopted an "open door policy" that allowed people to come to weekly meetings without answering questions or filling out a lot of forms. Wheels to Work continued as it had when Beyond Welfare was part of Move the Mountain, but the revolving loan program became more informal, and job coaching was incorporated into Circles of Support, provided on a volunteer basis by allies rather than by paid staff in a separate program. Beyond Welfare's participation in the state's Consumer Advisory Teams ended when funding for that initiative was discontinued in 2002.

Beyond Welfare continued to interact with Move the Mountain after the two organizations were structurally independent, and these interactions helped Beyond Welfare to clarify its identity further. Less than a year after he left, Scott Miller returned to Ames and rejoined the staff of Move the Mountain. As he had expressed a year before in his "Beyond Poverty" concept paper, he was still interested in using Beyond Welfare's strategies, particularly Circles of Support, as part of a comprehensive program to reduce — or even end — poverty.[52] He contracted with Beyond Welfare to participate in some of his projects, and from 2003 until 2005, about 20 percent of Beyond Welfare's budget came from Move the Mountain subcontracts.

The largest of these projects, in Des Moines, Iowa, was called "Name Each Child." The overall objectives of this project were to: "(1) redesign the way in which services and supports are delivered and connected to a test group of families to increase their earned income so they are out of poverty, and to increase the academic achievement performance of their children" and (2) "use this test group as the centerpiece to facilitate a learning agenda for system leaders, managers, line staff, and the public at large on what changes in both the community and system are necessary to help more people out of poverty."[53] To accomplish these goals, the project would implement a number of strategies: Circles of Support; weekly "grassroots leadership" and peer support meetings; case management; plans for family asset development; plans for children's academic achievement; comprehensive job development and job placement; car donation; revolving loans; substance abuse prevention and treatment; and a "systems change" team.[54]

Some of the staff of Beyond Welfare were contracted to provide technical assistance, particularly around the Circles of Support and weekly meetings. Initially, it seemed that the contract would be good for all parties. Beyond Welfare staff had the greatest experience with Circles of Support and weekly Community Leadership Team meetings, and Miller saw Name Each Child as an opportunity to incorporate those strategies in a project to create large-scale social change.[55] He also saw the Des Moines project as "a way to support Beyond Welfare, because they were going to get a contract out of this, so it seemed like a win-win-win for everybody."[56]

Tensions arose, however, because the way Miller wanted to implement Circles of Support and the weekly meetings differed from Beyond Welfare's practices, and the context in which he wanted these practices to be implemented was at odds with some of Beyond Welfare's values and principles. Unlike Community Leadership Team meetings, the weekly meetings in Des Moines incorporated a "curriculum for grassroots leadership," through which people in poverty would learn how to "articulate their own story, interact with community leaders with confidence and in a non-accusatory style, develop and articulate a leadership agenda, and run a well-organized meeting."[57] Unlike the "Dream Path" that Beyond Welfare used in its Circles of Support, each family in poverty in the Des Moines project would be required to prepare a written "academic achievement" plan laying the academic goals for each of their children as well as an "asset development" plan laying out the family's "net worth," "balance sheet," "goals statement," "development plan," "community building plans," and "talents and time plan." Instead of developing the voice and leadership of people in poverty so they can take more control over their lives — which is one of the central objectives of Beyond Welfare's practices — the primary change agents in the Des Moines project were the members of the "Systems Change Team" who were to communicate system barriers identified by Circle members to the "Human Services Planning Alliance."[58]

The subcontracts with Move the Mountain created other problems for Beyond Welfare as well. They took Smidt away from Ames and Beyond Welfare's core activities.[59] Some of the subcontracts put pressure on Beyond Welfare to expand its activities — doubling the number of Circles of Support in Ames — and to change its practices, for example, by creating a more formal, case management-style process for tracking its members and their progress, including psychological assessments and the recording of household economic data over time. To compare outcomes in Ames with outcomes in Move the Mountain's other project sites, Beyond Welfare would be required to track income, jobs, and school grades for the poor families involved in its weekly meetings and Circles of Support.[60] Other subcontracts would require Beyond Welfare to work with organizations whose values — such as intolerance for same-sex families and families headed by single mothers — were in opposition to those of many of the people involved in Beyond Welfare.[61]

On the recommendation of the members of Community Leadership Team, the Board of Beyond Welfare refused to go along with most of these requirements. Concerned about the pressure Smidt was under, the Board decided that she "should not have meetings with [Miller] in isolation ... that there should always be at least one other person present in those meetings so that we have an accountability structure support."[62] By 2005, Beyond Welfare had terminated all of its contracts with Move the Mountain, returning any remaining funds. The two organizations entered into negotiations to develop a "memorandum of understanding" covering ownership of the names of practices that Smidt and Miller had developed together, like Circles of Support, and a framework for working together that would limit Move the Mountain's influence on Beyond Welfare.[63] These negotiations were unsuccessful, however, and in 2006, the relationship between Beyond Welfare and Move the Mountain ended.

In 2007, the two organizations presented themselves very differently on their web sites. Scott Miller had become Chief Executive Officer of Move the Mountain, and that organization emphasized its goal of inspiring and equipping communities to "end poverty." The web site stated that Move the Mountain "provides training, technical assistance, consulting and coaching to leaders and communities who are focused on ending poverty" and draws its "theories and examples from our own work in the field, serving hundreds of leaders across the country each year." Highlighted programs included "Transformational Leadership" training for individuals, "Transformational Planning" for community action agencies, and "Circles," which was described as "bringing community volunteers (known as Allies) to partner with families who are pursuing economic well-being to end poverty in their communities."[64]

Beyond Welfare's web site emphasized the kind of community the organization was trying to create. "In order to effectively build relationships and community across socioeconomic, class, race, ability, age, gender, life experience, and other 'differences,' it is necessary to have some common values to guide us. Those who are marginalized from the community often feel 'less than' those who are more central to community life. Below are the values that guide the work of Beyond Welfare, an organization committed to building communities of caring across lines of difference so that everyone has enough Money, Friends, and Meaning. In this way all will be invited to give of their gifts to the community and all are treated as leaders. Beyond Welfare strives to build community where:

- Each person's inherent intelligence is supported to mobilize their talents and to face any challenge;
- Each person's well-being is deeply connected to the well-being of all and caring relationships are critical to our well-being;
- Our relationships are based on deep, reciprocal caring, and nonjudgmental respect for the inherent dignity and worth of others;
- Everyone has the resources to realize their sense of purpose, to fulfill their relationships and to contribute to the common good."[65]

The Case Analysis

The incorporation of Beyond Welfare involved numerous players: Gary Stokes, head of Mid-Iowa Community Action and, later, of the incorporated Move the Mountain Leadership Center; Scott Miller, co-founder and, later, Chief Executive Officer of Move the Mountain; Lois Smidt, Family Development Specialist at Mid-Iowa Community Action, Community Resource Coordinator of Beyond Welfare when it was part of Move the Mountain, and Executive Director (later, Co-Director) of the incorporated Beyond Welfare; other staff involved in Beyond Welfare, before and after incorporation; the members of Beyond Welfare's Guiding Coalition, Advisory Board, and Board of Directors; other participants (people in economic poverty) and allies (people with sufficient income) involved in Community Leadership Team meetings and Circles of Support; and Mike Green, a trainer with Asset Based Community Development. To understand how the ideas of these different players influenced what happened, we (1) looked at the major impacts of the case; (2) identified whose ideas were influential at the critical points that shaped the incorporation of Beyond Welfare; and (3) explored how the accomplishments and limitations in the case were related to ideas that were, and were not, influential.

Major Impacts

The incorporation of Beyond Welfare enabled the organization to clarify its own identity, protect its culture, and diminish its dependence on institutions not aligned well with its purposes and principles. Move the Mountain provided a nurturing environment, in which Beyond Welfare's core elements—Community Leadership Team and Circles of Support—were able to develop, and by the time of incorporation, Beyond Welfare was ready to become a distinct and autonomous entity. Through its Articles of Incorporation and By-Laws, Beyond Welfare clarified its goals, which were different in important ways from those of Move the Mountain, and formalized its values and principles. The experience of doing so, and of serving on the Board, benefited the individuals involved as well as the organization.

Beyond Welfare's structural independence from Move the Mountain relieved tensions that Lois Smidt, members of the Advisory Board, and members of Community Leadership Team had been experiencing prior to incorporation. Most of these tensions related to differences in the way executives at Move the Mountain approached decision making and leadership. The subcontracts that Beyond Welfare received from Move the Mountain after incorporation provided Beyond Welfare with a source of revenue. But Move the Mountain's attempt to use Beyond Welfare's strategies as part of its comprehensive programs to end poverty created serious problems for Beyond Welfare's staff and Board because they felt they could not protect the integrity of their work in that context. Severing the working relationship between Beyond Welfare and Move the Mountain appeared to be the only way to resolve those problems.

Initially, Move the Mountain believed that the incorporation of Beyond Welfare would enhance its own agenda since, as a local organization with local funding sources, Beyond Welfare would represent community commitment to ending poverty. Moreover, even if it were an independent organization, Beyond Welfare could continue to serve as Move the Mountain's laboratory for testing high-impact strategies to end poverty. Beyond Welfare did not see its role in these ways, however. For Beyond Welfare, the primary purpose of Community Leadership Team and Circles of Support is to build a certain kind of community rather than to end economic poverty. Both organizations are now pursuing their own goals independently. The societal impacts of their work remain to be seen.

Critical Points of Influence

Looking at the events and impacts in the incorporation of Beyond Welfare, there appear to be four points where the influence of players' ideas mattered: (1) creating Beyond Welfare; (2) deciding to separate Beyond Welfare from Move the Mountain; (3) designing Beyond Welfare's operating procedures; and (4) deciding to accept or reject subcontracts from Move the Mountain.

Creating Beyond Welfare. The development of the core elements of Beyond Welfare — Community Leadership Team and Circles of Support — are described in detail in another case: The Community Leadership Team of Story County, Iowa. Many of the principles and practices in these programs were introduced by Lois Smidt and Mike Green, based on their experiences elsewhere. Scott Miller's support made it possible for Smidt and Green to do so, and the three of them worked closely together during this development period.

It was Miller's idea to bring multiple programs together as Beyond Welfare. Both he and Gary Stokes were interested in doing something that could get a lot of people off welfare — in part, because that would open the door to additional funding. Miller believed that a systemic approach was needed to accomplish that goal. Through Beyond Welfare, he sought to develop and test high-impact strategies and coordinate these strategies in large-scale, comprehensive programs. Miller established an Advisory Board for Beyond Welfare in order to support him and his work; he did not give the group a formal role in the governance of Beyond Welfare.

Miller also appears to have been influential in making Beyond Welfare part of Move the Mountain — both initially, when Move the Mountain was a program of Mid-Iowa Community Action and later, when Move the Mountain incorporated and took Beyond

Welfare with it. Miller was actively involved in Move the Mountain's Transformational Leadership Program as well as Beyond Welfare and saw real synergy between the two. That connection was not as apparent or compelling to Stokes.

Deciding to separate Beyond Welfare from Move the Mountain. The first person who suggested that Beyond Welfare separate from Move the Mountain was Gary Stokes. He didn't believe that Beyond Welfare's community-based programs belonged in an organization committed to a national transformational leadership agenda. In fact, he believed that Move the Mountain's agenda would be enhanced if Beyond Welfare became part of a locally funded organization, since that would demonstrate a substantial community commitment to address poverty. Miller still wanted Beyond Welfare to be part of Move the Mountain, however, and Smidt thought the community aspect of Beyond Welfare's work would be compromised if it became part of a service agency.

The need to make a decision was precipitated by Miller's departure, which removed the most powerful advocate for keeping Beyond Welfare within Move the Mountain as well as the buffer in the relationship between Stokes and Smidt. The deadline that Stokes imposed precluded Smidt from involving all of the people who would be affected by the decision. Ultimately the decision to incorporate was made by Smidt, after speaking with some of the members of Beyond Welfare's Advisory Board, some of the members of Community Leadership Team, Scott Miller, and Mike Green. For various reasons, all of these people supported the decision to incorporate. In setting the terms of the separation, Stokes provided Beyond Welfare with many of the supports it would need to establish itself as an independent organization.

Designing Beyond Welfare's operating procedures. Beyond Welfare's Articles of Incorporation and By-Laws were developed by Smidt and individuals who had been on Beyond Welfare's Advisory Board, most (if not all) of whom were active in Community Leadership Team and Circles of Support. The drafting process gave these people an opportunity to clarify the goals of the new organization and to formalize important principles of their work in Beyond Welfare's operating procedures. In doing so, they made Community Leadership Team's "Purposes and Principles"—codified by the members of that group — the foundation for the new organization.

Incorporation gave the Board of Directors real power and influence over the structure and operation of Beyond Welfare, which had not been the case for Beyond Welfare's previous Advisory Board. The By-Laws assured that the governance of the organization would be in the hands of people who were members of Community Leadership Team and that people in poverty would have a substantial voice in that governance. Although the idea of having a Board comprised of a majority of people in poverty is consistent with Community Leadership Team's purposes and principles, it was originally suggested by Scott Miller as a means of securing funding from certain types of local organizations. There is no evidence that members of Community Leadership Team who were living in poverty wanted, or asked for, this kind of board composition. They influenced the first revision of Beyond Welfare's By-Laws, however, when an insufficient number of people living in poverty responded to Community Leadership Team's invitation to join the Board.

Deciding to accept or reject subcontracts from Move the Mountain. Offers of subcontracts from Move the Mountain began when Scott Miller rejoined that organization.

Decisions to accept them were made by Lois Smidt and the Beyond Welfare Board, based on the new organization's need for financial resources and Smidt's and Miller's prior close working relationship. Concerns about undue pressure prompted the Board to take action to prevent Smidt from meeting with Miller alone. Concerns about requirements being imposed by Move the Mountain that had the potential to undermine the integrity of Beyond Welfare's work were expressed by Smidt, other Beyond Welfare staff members, members of Community Leadership Team, and the Board. Ultimately, the Board made the decision to terminate all contracts with Move the Mountain and, after unsuccessfully attempting to negotiate a Memorandum of Understanding, to end the working relationship between the two organizations.

Relating Impacts to Influence

The important accomplishments of this case appear to be related to all of the points of influence, which created opportunities for many of the players to learn from their experiences and put their experiential knowledge to use. The core elements of Beyond Welfare were deeply informed by Smidt's personal and professional experiences, and, later, by Green's experiences as well. The decision to incorporate Beyond Welfare was grounded in problems that people in a variety of positions had been experiencing when Beyond Welfare was part of Move the Mountain. Beyond Welfare's operating procedures were based on a set of purposes and principles derived from the experiences of the participants and allies in Community Leadership Team. Most important, the clarification of the key differences in the way Move the Mountain and Beyond Welfare viewed Community Leadership Team's weekly meetings and Circles of Support—the last step in Beyond Welfare's "quest for identity"—came out of the tensions and problems that people in the two organizations experienced when they tried to work together after Beyond Welfare's incorporation.

The many players who contributed and used their experiential knowledge in this case were able to do so because domains were created where they could exert influence. Initially, Move the Mountain created such a domain for Smidt. Through Smidt's consultations, some of the members of Beyond Welfare's Advisory Board and some members of Community Leadership Team were able to influence the incorporation decision and the development of Beyond Welfare's Articles of Incorporation and By-Laws. With incorporation, a Board was created that had real influence over the governance of Beyond Welfare, and the specified composition of the Board assured that this governance would be in the hands of people who were active in Community Leadership Team, including those with a direct experience of economic poverty.

10

Saving a Mural in Humboldt Park, Chicago

The Story

On November 7, 2002, three organizations completed a proposal for restoring a 31-year old Puerto Rican mural near Humboldt Park and developing the adjacent lot into a community space and garden that would enhance and preserve the view of the mural.[1] The lead organization, the Near Northwest Neighborhood Network — known locally as NNNN — was committed to improving conditions for the lower income people who had been living in the area around Humboldt Park for a long time, many of whom were Puerto Rican. In developing the proposal, NNNN had teamed with the Juan Antonio Corretjer Puerto Rican Cultural Center and archi-treasures, an organization that involved community members in designing and creating urban spaces.

The mural they wanted to restore, *La Crucifixion de Don Pedro Albizu Campos*, was the oldest surviving Puerto Rican mural in Chicago.[2] It had been painted in 1971 by founding members of the Puerto Rican Art Association on a 24 by 60 foot wall overlooking a vacant lot seven blocks east of Humboldt Park. In the mural, three figures involved in Puerto Rico's struggle for independence from the United States hang from crosses. Dr. Pedro Albizu Campos, the leader of the Puerto Rican Nationalist Party in the 1930s, is in the center flanked by Lolita Lebrón and Rafael Cancel Miranda on either side. Luis Muñoz Marín, the first Puerto Rican elected governor of the island who was an ardent opponent of the independence movement, thrusts a spear toward Campos' chest. Portraits of six other patriots from Puerto Rico's history witness the event. The crucifixion is set against a backdrop of Puerto Rico's first flag, the "Tiger of Liberty," which was used by Puerto Rican nationalists and abolitionists in an unsuccessful insurrection against Spain in the town of Lares in 1868.[3]

The mural has a strong and specific political theme, but that was not the group's primary justification for restoring it. Instead, their proposal emphasized the mural's historic and artistic value as well as its more general connection to Puerto Rican history and to the Humboldt Park community as a whole. Saving the mural was also consistent with a broader effort to control the gentrification that was displacing long-standing Puerto Rican families, organizations, and businesses from the area east of Humboldt Park. With the support of a land use plan created by community organizations and residents in the mid–1990s and the designation of some parts of the community as a Redevelopment Area, NNNN and its many member organizations had obtained some control over future development. In 1995, they began to challenge the process of gentrification by using architecture, public art, and space to imprint Puerto Rican culture and aesthetics on the community's landscape.

Repeated Cycles of Displacement

At the time the mural was created, in 1971, lower income Puerto Rican families who had been displaced from other parts of Chicago were moving into the surrounding neighborhood in droves.[4] Many of these families had migrated to Chicago in the 1950s. Attracted by jobs in the steel mills and other industries, they had originally settled in ethnically diverse neighborhoods just west of downtown. They were forced to move in the 1960s, however, when Chicago began implementing its "Development Plan for the Central Area," which relocated the University of Illinois at Chicago to the Near West Side neighborhood.[5] Most relocated to Lincoln Park, which had been abandoned by middle-class white families moving to the suburbs. Within a decade, the "Chicago 21 Plan," including a major expansion of DePaul University, brought an influx of white professionals and students to Lincoln Park. As rents and property values rose, and manufacturing companies closed their plants, the poorer Puerto Rican population was displaced to neighborhoods farther west. They moved to Wicker Park, Bucktown, West Town, and Humboldt Park — economically depressed areas plagued by gang violence and drugs.[6]

Division Street, an east-west thoroughfare marking the course of this displacement, has long served as the heart of the Puerto Rican community in Chicago. On June 12, 1966, it was the route for the city's first Puerto Rican Parade. During the parade, a white police officer shot a Puerto Rican youth, and rioting erupted across the area for three days. Dozens were injured and three police cars were overturned and set ablaze. For many in the Puerto Rican community, this was a call to action. New organizations were created to support Puerto Ricans who were being forced to move to more western neighborhoods. Some focused on meeting basic needs, such as housing. Others, like the Juan Antonio Corretjer Puerto Rican Cultural Center, were committed to the "study and creation of Puerto Rican culture through social activism."[7]

In 1971, a group of students at Malcolm X College, including one who had just arrived from Puerto Rico, organized themselves as "La Asociación de Arte de Puerto Rico" [the Puerto Rican Art Association] and decided to paint murals. Chicago had a long history of mural painting, beginning with murals commissioned as part of the Works Progress Administration Program in the Great Depression and continuing, in the 1960s, with murals created in the community mural movement.[8] Mexico and other Caribbean countries had strong mural traditions as well.

The artists found an appropriate wall not far from Humboldt Park, on a building on North Avenue, just east of Artesian Avenue. It was two stories high and ran the 60-foot length of the adjacent vacant lot, providing good exposure to people passing through the area. After a month and a half of discussion, the artists obtained permission from the building owner as well as some funding for materials from Association House (a local settlement house created over 100 years ago to aid immigrants) and other community organizations. Mario Galan, a member of the group, recalled that the artists didn't know what they were going to paint on the wall until they met a man named Carlos who "was looking for people who painted murals" to paint his "dream."[9] According to a community organizer in the area, *La Crucifixion de Don Pedro Albizu Campos*, which provides strong illustrations of historical Puerto Rican resistance, "captured ... the spirit of resistance of the youth at that time."[10]

Galan didn't expect this mural to survive more than a few years, with good reason. Paint has a difficult time standing up to Chicago's severe weather, and murals rarely survive when neighborhoods change and property changes hands. All of the murals on the Near West Side and Lincoln Park are gone, along with most of the blue collar and immigrant populations who used to live there.[11] Since the 1980s, many of the murals on buildings farther west of downtown have been lost as well. As middle and upper class white families began moving back to the city, these neighborhoods have been undergoing progressive gentrification. Murals have been destroyed when developers have demolished buildings to create new houses or condominium apartments. They have been painted over when the people who cared about them have left and newly arrived residents consider them to be "eyesores." This is what happened to many Puerto Rican murals in Wicker Park and Bucktown as Puerto Rican families who had moved there in the 1960s and 1970s were displaced farther west toward Humboldt Park.

In the 1990s, the area around Humboldt Park began to face encroaching gentrification too, threatening to dislocate the Puerto Rican community once again. Because of rising rents and property taxes, it became increasingly difficult for renters and homeowners with limited incomes to stay there. As one resident put it, "apartments are very expensive, they have gone up five times what they used to cost, so people only earn enough to eat and pay rent and they have had to leave."[12] For some, leaving the violence and poverty of Humboldt Park was a good thing, a small personal victory in a longer struggle for a peaceful life. But many others saw Humboldt Park as their community, and they wanted to stay — "there was all these bad conditions, but at the same time there was still a sense of community ... even though it was poor, there was still a sense of home and there's still a sense of belonging."[13] After having been moved from neighborhood to neighborhood, pushed out as middle class residents came in, Puerto Ricans and other long-standing residents in Humboldt Park decided to take a stand and hold onto their "pedacito de Patria" [a little piece of the homeland]."[14]

The Community's Response

Around 1990, NNNN — which had been established a few years before to coordinate community efforts around crime prevention — began to shift its organizing focus to the interconnected themes of poverty and gentrification. The challenge was to address poverty, which fueled gentrification by depressing land values, in ways that wouldn't make it too expensive for long-standing residents to stay in the area around Humboldt Park — an increasingly common pitfall of community development efforts around the country. A growing number of Puerto Ricans from the area were in positions to lend support to these efforts. By 1993, Puerto Rican community members had been elected to the United States Congress and the Illinois State Senate. In city government, Billy Ocasio, who had grown up in the neighborhood in the 1960s and 70s and had worked there to create more affordable housing, was Alderman in the 26th Ward, which included much of the area around Humboldt Park where NNNN was active.

In 1994, NNNN started a new organizing initiative, the Humboldt Park Empowerment Partnership, to unite area organizations in a cooperative grassroots planning process. With a grant from the city, the partnership engaged community organizations and residents in developing a "Community Land Use Plan." For NNNN organizers, the plan was about community control over development in the area around Humboldt Park: "Part of the Land Use Plan was the understanding that he who owns the land has the power in the community and that the Humboldt Park community was going slip away, slip away ... to, you know, what I call upper-middle class people, if the people in the community were not organized together. And we had some understanding of who owned the land and also how the community wanted the land used. So it was really an effort to create a power block."[15]

In 1998, with the assistance of Alderman Ocasio, parts of the community were designated as a "Redevelopment Area." This designation gave the community access to tax incentives and other mechanisms to bring investment into the area. It also gave the city control over vacant land and properties that had been abandoned or were in arrears on their taxes, providing up to $2 million to secure these lots for redevelopment. Much of the city's control in Redevelopment Areas is exercised by the relevant Aldermen.[16]

During the same period, NNNN, the Division Street Business Development Association, and the many other organizational members of the Humboldt Park Empowerment Partnership developed a strategy to challenge the process of gentrification that was threatening to displace Puerto Ricans and other lower income residents from the area. In the late 1980s, the Division Street Business Development Association had begun to explore the feasibility of making the area east of Humboldt Park Chicago's "Puerto Rican destination."[17] At that time, the Association's goal had been to promote economic development in the neighborhood. Now, with encroaching gentrification, making the area distinctly Puerto Rican — by imprinting Puerto Rican culture and aesthetics on the landscape — also appeared to be a way to claim the neighborhood from outsiders who wanted to take it over.

The community established "Paseo Boricua" on Division Street, marking the area from Western Avenue to Mozart Avenue as the heart of the Puerto Rican barrio in Chicago. Two huge steel Puerto Rican flags were installed at each end of the Paseo, crossing over Division Street as arches. Planters were placed on the Paseo depicting the flags of Puerto Rico's 78 municipalities. A Paseo Boricua Walk of Fame was created. Lampposts, benches, and commercial and residential buildings were modeled after Spanish and Puerto Rican architecture. With the help of archi-treasures, the community built "La Casita de Don Pedro," to celebrate the Puerto Rican nationalist leader through cultural and political events.

The Juan Antonio Corretjer Puerto Rican Cultural Center, which had relocated three times since 1973 as the Puerto Rican community was displaced to the west, moved to the Paseo. The Center, named after a Puerto Rican poet and political leader, established the Albizu Campos Alternative High School, a Family Learning Center to help single mothers in the area complete their high school education, and the Café Teatro Batey Urbano, a grassroots space dedicated to Puerto Rican/Latino youth. Students at the Alternative

High School restored *La Crucifixion de Don Pedro Albizu Campos* in 1990, adding an inscription on the left side of the mural commemorating the fortieth anniversary of the Puerto Rican nationalists' attack on Harry Truman at Blair House in 1950.

The Proposal to Restore the Mural

In 2001, Eduardo Arocho observed foundation being poured on the vacant lot adjacent to *La Crucifixion de Don Pedro Albizu Campos*.[18] Arocho, a poet and community organizer, had lived near the mural all his life. He was attached to the mural and was concerned that the construction would prevent people from seeing it anymore. For Arocho, each of the faces in the mural represented a great story in Puerto Rico's history, and he had been bringing groups to the corner of North Avenue and Artesian Avenue to talk about those stories.[19] The mural was meaningful to others in the community as well. A woman who lived on Artesian Avenue recalled how her father took her to mural when she was five years old, "[h]e was trying to tell me about ... Puerto Rico and ... something that I should know more about[,] because of my heritage...."[20] Parents continued to bring their children to the mural, in some cases to expose them to aspects of Puerto Rican history that were not taught in school.[21] The mural was also a landmark that children in the neighborhood used to find their way home.[22]

In 1999, a developer had bought the 16,000 square foot lot adjacent to the mural to build condominium apartments there, but Arocho had not been aware of the developer's plans until work on the foundation started. He felt that he couldn't take any action at the time because he was working for the Division Street Business Development Association, and the mural was four blocks north of the Association's jurisdiction. Shortly thereafter, however, he took a position as economic development coordinator for NNNN, whose territory included the block where the mural was located. On the first day of his new job he proposed that NNNN do something to prevent the mural from being obscured by the new condominium building.

Arocho arranged for NNNN to contract with John Pitman Weber, a veteran Chicago muralist and Professor of Art at Elmhurst College, to assess the condition of the mural. His report emphasized the mural's significance as "probably the first in the Midwest (and possibly the first on the mainland USA) devoted entirely to Puerto Rican subject matter and Puerto Rican historical themes," adding that the mural "has been a Chicago landmark for 30 years and has been published in several books."[23] He assessed the cost of restoring the mural in places where the stucco on the wall had been repaired or replaced to be about $5,000. Arocho also met with José Lopez, Director of the Puerto Rican Cultural Center, and Joyce Fernandes of archi-treasures to develop a concept drawing for creating a community space and garden in the adjacent lot to enhance the visibility of the mural.[24]

While Arocho was working on a formal proposal, Eliud Medina, the Executive Director of NNNN, met with the owner of the lot. The owner offered to sell the lot at market rates, but NNNN did not have the money to buy it.[25] As an alternative, the owner offered to reduce the height of the proposed condominium from four to three stories and recreate a smaller version of the mural on the outside wall of the new building.[26] This option was not acceptable to NNNN because the original mural would still be obscured from view. Medina wrote to Alderman Ocasio, asking him to meet with the owner and "recommend that he use another lot within the Redevelopment Area or the 26th ward for his project."[27] This proposal would entail a land swap using city-owned lots.

While these negotiations were going on, Arocho worked on a formal proposal — on behalf of NNNN, the Puerto Rican Cultural Center, and archi-treasures—for restoring the mural and creating a community space and garden in the adjacent lot. He had changed his relationship with NNNN from employee to consultant on the mural project and was working at the Family Learning Center teaching a class in community development. The proposal he submitted on November 7, 2002, to be presented to the members of the Humboldt Park Empowerment Partnership for approval, included the results of a survey that Arocho and the students at the Family Learning Center had conducted to assess the "general sentiment toward the mural" of the residents who lived nearby.

The students surveyed 30 people living on Artesian Avenue door-to-door, asking them — in English or Spanish — "What do you know about the mural? What do you think the mural represents? Do you think the mural should be restored? Do you think a recreational area on the lot would enhance the mural?" The respondents also told the interviewers their names, how old they were, and how long they had lived in the neighborhood.[28]

Based on their names, most of the people surveyed were Latino. Their ages ranged from 19 to 86. One-third had lived in the neighborhood for at least 10 years; seven for 18 to 28 years. Some of the respondents said they didn't know much about the mural or what it represented. Some saw it as an interesting or beautiful painting. Others talked about the mural's religious connotations, saying that it represented three martyrs, religious leaders or saints, church art, or (in a negative context) "someone imitating God." Most talked about the mural's connection to Puerto Rican people and history, saying that it represented Puerto Rico's struggles or historic Puerto Ricans who did something important with their lives. Only two people talked about the specific political imagery in the mural — the independence figures being crucified or the flag of Lares.[29]

Most of the respondents supported restoring the mural and enhancing it with a recreational area on the lot. A common underlying reason was to hold onto something that mattered to them and that was in danger of being taken away. Some of the respondents said that the mural "is all that remains of Puerto Ricans," "benefits Puerto Ricans," "is good for the Hispanics," or "makes us Puerto Ricans feel more proud." One said that it was important to make the mural look beautiful "so the Americans won't want to get rid of the little culture we have." Another said she wanted to make sure that nothing bad would happen to the mural because she is Puerto Rican and "the whites want to take everything we have." A number of respondents talked about how the restoration and recreational area would benefit children, by passing on the beauty of the mural to them, by giving youth a chance to see the mural and realize what Puerto Rican people did, or by cleaning up the trashy vacant lot and creating a park where children could play. A few of the respondents did not support restoring the mural. One hedged (saying the decision would depend on what was done); one felt it was just a "typical mural;" one thought it was "an ugly picture with a negative presentation meaning people trying to be God;" and one thought it should be replaced with something "to promote education to better the Hispanic culture."[30]

In the November 2002 proposal, Arocho summarized the residents' responses by noting that "40 percent said the mural represented some aspect of Puerto Rican history; about 30 percent said that the mural had some sort of religious representation. Another 13 percent classified the mural as interesting art." Among the people who understood the question, "73 percent said that they would like to see the mural restored." "Exactly 90 percent said yes to repairing the lot for the use of the residents." He concluded that "although the mural was dedicated to Puerto Rican heritage, it has transcended its original meaning and now represents the Humboldt Park community as a whole — across ethnic lines."[31]

The proposal included detailed sketches from archi-treasures of the garden that would be created in the lot adjacent to the mural. The proposal's stated objectives for this development were "to preserve the historic Puerto Rican mural; add greenery to the commercial corridor of North Avenue; enhance the view of the mural; provide for a new community gathering space; provide activities during the summer for youths in the surrounding area; and retain mural visibility." The cost of the restoration and lot development were estimated at $243,430, of which $200,000 was for the acquisition of the lot.[32]

While negotiations for the lot continued, Arocho organized a Mural Restoration Committee, including representatives of NNNN, the Puerto Rican Cultural Center, archi-treasures, and the Division Street Business Development Association.[33] NNNN included the mural in plans for a "North Avenue Business Corridor" modeled on Division Street's Paseo Boricua.[34]

Breakdown in Negotiations

On April 16, 2003, the owner of the lot began building a cinder block wall under *La Crucifixion de Don Pedro Albizu Campos*.[35] That morning, Eliud Medina called Alderman Ocasio, and NNNN faxed a flyer to people and organizations around the community. A photograph of the mural and the cinder block construction appeared below the following text:

Save our Mural
Help stop the destruction of our history & community!!!!

An illegal development has taken control of a lot on Artesian and North Avenue adjacent to the historic community mural, "La Crucifixion de Don Pedro." The developer wants to build a condo unit without the proper permits. If this development occurs it will not only cover the mural but will also gentrify our community. Join us on Wednesday, April 16 at 10:00 A.M. on the corner of Artesian and North Ave. to say NO to gentrification and YES to equitable and responsible development without displacement[36]

A group of about ten people, including Latino youth involved in Batey Urbano, pitched a tent under the mural and carried signs in what they called an "act of civil disobedience."[37] The signs, some of which were hand-lettered and others print-shopped, were captured in newspaper photographs of the demonstration: "Stop Building Condos, Stop Gentrification;" "Save Our Mural, Stop Gentrification;" "Destroy Our Art, Destroy Our Memories;" and "Boricua ¡Si!, Yuppie ¡No!."[38] A priest from the nearby Catholic Church came out to support the action. Community members at the scene were reported as saying that the crucifixion of Campos was "a reflection ... of Puerto Ricans' struggle to survive in cities like Chicago." A woman who had watched the painters creating the mural 32 years before remembered that she had "cried; it was all we had at the time."[39]

To make sure the owner didn't start construction again the next morning, a few of the protestors stayed the night.[40] The work didn't resume, however, because some in the construction crew "were not licensed.... We got the city department of buildings to come out and ticket them and stop the project."[41]

NNNN went back into negotiations with the owner's attorney. On June 19, the attorney wrote to Eliud Medina stating that they had been working with the community and the city to try to identify a fair and equitable resolution, but were now "questioning whether your organization and the City have acted in good faith." Specifically, the attorney said that his client had offered to sell the property to NNNN or the city at market value but had never received a written offer. His client had also been willing to swap the property for another lot or lots of similar value, character, and zoning, but had encountered nothing but delays in receiving lists and appraisals of potential lots even though they had provided every piece of information requested of them. If an agreement could not be reached by the end of the month, interest on the construction loans would give them "no choice but to resume construction at the project site."[42]

At 7:00 A.M. on August 29, residents on Artesian Avenue called NNNN's office to alert the staff that construction on the lot had begun again.[43] Enrique Salgado, Director of the Division Street Business Development Association recalled how quickly the work was advancing: "They had already built ... the corners of the building.... There were like 14 guys that were working, and of the 14 ... 10 of them were masons and four were laborers. They had a whole crew, and they were focusing heavily on the one wall where the mural was. On that wall they actually got maybe about two or three feet high."[44]

Eliud Medina and Alderman Ocasio were on Division Street that morning, placing a new star for salsa artist Andrés Jimenez on the "Paseo Boricua Walk of Fame."[45] Immediately thereafter, they went to the lot. Some of the young people involved in Batey Urbano met with the staff of the Puerto Rican Cultural Center and then started calling everyone they knew. "Basically we just started going through our phones and asking those people to call so we were giving the number out. So those people started calling on their own as well as when we finished with our list of people on our phones we had kind of run out of people to call. Then we just started calling ourselves directly. But I can imagine at least, it was probably a good 20–25 people maybe even more."[46]

In the period since the first protest in April, the city's Aldermanic Wards were redistricted and the lot adjacent to the mural was now in the 1st Ward, where Manny Flores was Alderman, instead of Ocasio's 26th Ward. Organizers in the area had worked to elect Flores as Alderman. Although he was out of town at the time, he made a statement saying "I want the Puerto Rican community to know that Manny Flores supports the mural and would like to see the mural stand."[47]

No one recalls how many people participated in the protest, but photographs show about two dozen people walking around with signs similar to the first demonstration: "Stop Destroying Our Mural"; "Honk Your Horn, Save Our Mural"; and "Save Our Mural, Stop Gentrification." The columns around the lot had risen a full story, and in the background the wall was about six feet high, already obscuring the bottom third of the mural. Scaffolding was placed against the wall and the construction site was surrounded by a six foot tall chain-link fence.[48] The youths involved turned the demonstration into a "cultural act." "Groups started coming out to perform Bomba and Plena," which are drum and percussion-based forms of Puerto Rican folk music and dancing.[49]

The protest appears to have been intimidating to the construction workers at the site, many of whom were Polish immigrants who spoke little or no English. People were honking on North Avenue, which is a two-way, four-lane avenue that is heavily used. As the drums beat around the lot, one of the workers troweled cement or mortar on the mural across the face of Lolita Lebrón. This made the youths who were protesting "real mad."[50] One said they should "stone" the worker who defaced the mural, but the others told him, "No, that's not what we do."[51] By the time the press showed up, work at the site had stopped.

The next day, more people came back to continue the protest, but construction had not resumed. The owner's attorney was there, however, photographing the lot. He was telling the protesters they would be arrested for trespassing when Aldermen Ocasio and Flores arrived, along with Eliud Medina of NNNN. They acknowledged that the owner now had all of the necessary permits for construction and that they were still interested in negotiating a swap. But Medina said that the owner "wants four lots in exchange for the one lot on Artesian ... [and] we're not going to give them four lots."[52]

Ocasio told the lawyer that if construction resumed, the protesters would just come back. Further, Ocasio said that they would have to arrest him in order to clear the site.[53] This was not the kind of publicity the owner wanted, and when he arrived he took a short walk with his attorney, the Aldermen, and Medina.[54] By the end of the walk, the owner agreed to stop construction and restart the negotiations.

In December 2003, when Ocasio and Flores were still unable to reach a land swap agreement with the owner, the two Aldermen proposed an ordinance in the City Council "authorizing the acquisition of a vacant parcel of property, through negotiated purchase or condemnation proceedings, located at 2425 West North Avenue, to be used as a public open space."[55] This set in motion a legal process whereby a judge would decide if the city could appropriate the lot through eminent domain. At the same time, the Mural Restoration Committee that Arocho had formed began to make plans to have the mural designated as a "historical site," to start an archive of all of the Puerto Rican murals in the city, and to obtain funding for their projects.[56]

Another protest took place on June 4, 2004.[57] On that day, community residents were preparing for the annual Puerto Rican Day Parade, and a lot of people showed up or honked to show their support. Young people from Batey Urbano came with signs and flags, and people played music. One of the youths recalled that construction workers were "sort of sitting against the wall across the street in a row ... not knowing what to do." An African American worker "pointed at the wall and said, 'What's the big deal?'" The protesting youths replied, "That would be like a mural of Rosa Parks, Martin Luther King, Malcolm X, Marcus Garvey. Famous, famous African American leaders having a wall built over it. You know what I'm saying? So when we told him that, he said, 'Oh, we can't do this then. We can't keep building.'"[58]

Enrique Salgado described how the protest came to an end: "Alderman Ocasio came out.... Then Alderman Flores came out, and he actually stood there with us for a long time. He came out to basically bring us the news that ... there was a stop work order put on them and just for us to stay there. He was going to stay with us until the inspector showed up.... Then when the inspector came out, he put out the big orange stickers for the stop work order. They had to stop."[59]

Resolution

The June 4, 2004, protest was over in just a few hours, and it marked the end of the owner's attempt to build condominiums on the lot. As the demonstration was going on, the court case for eminent domain concluded in favor of the community. A ruling on November 2, 2004, placed the lot in the hands of the city.[60] The owner received more than $500,000 in compensation for the lot, loan costs, and legal fees.

In 2006, Eduardo Arocho presented an updated Mural Restoration Project proposal to NNNN, which included an educational curriculum to support six high school or college level art students who would work as apprentices on the restoration as well as video documentation of the project.[61] The Mural Restoration Committee also began to generate momentum for restoring other murals and painting new murals.[62] In September 2006, several organizational members of the Humboldt Park Empowerment Partnership published a glossy brochure with photographs and historical information on 27 Puerto Rican murals (eight of which had been painted after 2002), 9 Puerto Rican cultural institutions, and 10 Puerto Rican cultural events in the neighborhood. Under a map of the area around Humboldt Park, which shows where each of these are, the brochure states: "The community has claimed this space with the imprinting of a Puerto Rican aesthetic upon the urban landscape.... As the spread of gentrification casts doubts on the future of Puerto Ricans in Humboldt Park, a stubborn hope continues to radiate from Paseo Boricua.[63]

On February 20, 2007, the founder of Union Estadista of Illinois—a statehood organization that educates Puerto Ricans in Chicago about the benefit of Puerto Rico becoming the fifty-first state—held a small press conference in front of *La Crucifixion de Don Pedro Albizu Campos*.[64] He said that the mural "has nothing to do with our Puerto Rican heritage.... This is a guy who used to be a terrorist.... It is an embarrassment to the Puerto Rican community to have this mural here." A former Hispanic assistant to the Lieutenant Governor of Illinois said that honoring Campos in a mural "would be sending the wrong message to our youths, enticing them to engage in criminal acts against the most hospitable, safe, and powerful nation in the world ... that has given Puerto Ricans the freedom to come and go as we please and the social and economic status that we still cherish." The founder of Union Estadista of Illinois blamed Aldermen Ocasio and Flores for supporting the mural. The Aldermen responded by saying that the project was something the community rallied around; they had made it very clear what they wanted. As Ocasio put it: "This is art. We preserve art throughout the whole city of Chicago.... It is a place where people can go and read ... take their kids and let them run around. It's a part of a bigger plan that residents asked for.... Hundreds of people came together to make this decision." A member of United Blocks of West Humboldt Park said she thought the funds used to purchase the lot and restore the mural could have been better used elsewhere. Supporting the appropriation, Jon Pounds of the Chicago Public Art Group said that "it is entirely appropriate for city money to be spent to create spaces in which dialogue and disagreement can occur, especially one that respects complex histories.... There is nothing wrong with a little friction, a little controversy."[65]

On November 3, 2007, another protest was held in front of the mural. This time, over 100 people, mainly Puerto Rican, showed up with NNNN to protest gentrification and the continuing displacement of community residents as property values in the Humboldt Park area continue to climb. The venue was chosen because the process of saving *La Crucifixion de Don Pedro Albizu Campos* had made the mural a symbol of the community's resistance to gentrification. A local organizer involved in the original protests said the "mural became the community's defiance to allowing [gentrification] to happen. That's where you started to see ... broad support start to come out."[66] One of the youths involved recalled that the protests to save the mural "brought gentrification for us ... up in the front for people to see. That ... is what gentrification is. It's not something creating beautiful [things], you're talking about destroying. And sure it's a mural, but it could well have been a whole block of people that live there, making condos out of their houses."[67] Another youth said that although the mural is "very political ... about Puerto Rico and Puerto Rican independence ... at the same time it has been adopted as a more popular expression of Puerto Rican resistance or the presence of Puerto Ricans in that area.... It is all of those things to me."[68]

The preserved mural has also become a symbol of the continuing presence of Puerto Ricans and their culture in the area around Humboldt Park. As a young Puerto Rican in the neighborhood put it: "If we start painting over our murals, how much of our history goes away with that?"[69] Considering the relationship of Puerto Rican murals to the issues of gentrification and displacement, he said "This is our history, this is our roots, this is our culture, you know, where does it stop? If ... not at this mural, then where? Next mural, or the next one after that, then the flags, until what? Until no one remembers that Humboldt Park was a place Latinos— you know — where we gathered, where we celebrate."[70]

The Case Analysis

The process of saving the mural, *La Crucifixion de Don Pedro Albizu Campos*, involved numerous players: the Executive Director and organizers of the Near Northwest Neighborhood Network; consultants working for NNNN (Eduardo Arocho, John Pitman Weber, and archi-treasures); organizational members of the Humboldt Park Empowerment Partnership, including the Juan Antonio Corretjer Puerto Rican Cultural Center and the Division Street Business Development Association; elected officials, particularly the Aldermen of the 1st and 26th Wards; young people in the community, including students in Eduardo Arocho's community building course at the Family Learning Center and youth associated with the Batey Urbano; community members who responded to the survey and participated in the protests; and the owner of the lot adjacent to the mural, his construction workers, and attorneys. To understand how the ideas of these different players influenced what happened, we (1) looked at the major impacts of the case; (2) identified whose ideas were influential at the critical points in saving the mural; and (3) explored how the accomplishments and limitations in the case were related to ideas that were, and were not, influential.

Major Impacts

By saving *La Crucifixion de Don Pedro Albizu Campos*, community members preserved a landmark that was valuable to them in a number of ways: as a representation of the Puerto Rican presence in the area around Humboldt Park; as a resource for educating young people and adults about Puerto Rican culture and history; as a distinctive expression of the Puerto Rican nationalist struggle; and as an historically important work of art. Saving *La Crucifixion de Don Pedro Albizu Campos*— which was accomplished in spite of the mural's controversial subject matter — has created a momentum for preserving other murals and creating new murals in the neighborhood.

The process of saving *La Crucifixion de Don Pedro Albizu Campos* gave the mural new meaning, making it even more valuable to people in the community than it had been before. The mural became a symbol of the community's resistance to gentrification and displacement. It also became integrally linked to the community's strategy to resist gentrification and displacement by imprinting Puerto Rican culture and aesthetics on the community's landscape. Through the protests to save the mural, many more young people and adults became aware of, and engaged in, the community's struggle against gentrification and displacement.

Critical Points of Influence

Looking at the events and impacts in saving the mural, there appear to be four points at which the influence of players' ideas mattered: (1) making the community aware of the threat to the mural; (2) linking the mural to the community's struggle against gentrification and displacement; (3) developing and implementing actions to halt construction on the lot adjacent to the mural and to take control of the lot; and (4) developing plans to restore the mural and create a community space and garden in the adjacent lot.

Making the community aware of the threat to the mural. Eduardo Arocho played a key role in making NNNN and the Puerto Rican Cultural Center aware of the initial threat to the mural. Had he not done so, construction on the lot might have proceeded to the point where it could not have been stopped. NNNN, in turn, spread news of the threat to all of the organizational members of the Humboldt Park Empowerment Partnership, and the Puerto Rican Cultural Center informed the young people associated with Batey Urbano. NNNN was informed about later threats to the mural — in April and August 2003 and June 2004 — by residents in the neighborhood who noticed that the owner of the adjacent lot had resumed construction.

Linking the mural to the community's struggle against gentrification and displacement. Resisting gentrification and displacement is a central focus of NNNN and the organizational members of the Humboldt Park Empowerment Partnership, including the Puerto Rican Cultural Center and the Division Street Business Development Association. The strategy to challenge gentrification in the area east of Humboldt Park by using architecture, public art, and space to imprint Puerto Rican culture and aesthetics on the community's landscape came from the members of these groups.

Prior to 2001, it does not appear that murals played a role in this strategy or that the community linked *La Crucifixion de Don Pedro Albizu Campos* to the struggle against gentrification. The connection appears to have been made by NNNN and the other organizations involved in the strategy when the mural was threatened. *La Crucifixion de Don Pedro Albizu Campos* is the first Puerto Rican mural in the city, and it is located on a street that these groups wanted to develop into a "North Avenue Business Corridor" modeled after Paseo Boricua.

Developing and implementing actions to halt construction on the lot adjacent to the mural and take control of the lot. A broad range of players were involved in the actions that were taken to prevent the owner of the lot adjacent to the mural from constructing condominium apartments there. Eduardo Arocho and his students at the Family Learning Center conducted the survey, which documented that a majority of residents on Artesian Avenue wanted the mural to be preserved and to have the adjacent lot developed as a public recreational space.

Staff at NNNN and the Puerto Rican Cultural Center, as well as young people associated with Batey Urbano, played central roles in organizing the three protests. These individuals and other community residents, including elected officials, participated in the protests. All of the signs in the protests connected saving the mural with efforts to stop gentrification. According to the people involved, that linkage was responsible for the community's broad support for the protests.

Eliud Medina, Executive Director of NNNN, and Aldermen Ocasio and Flores played key roles in the land swap negotiations with the lot owner and his attorneys and in taking control of the lot through eminent domain. The protests and negotiations delayed construction, providing needed time to achieve the ultimate solution in this case.

Developing plans to restore the mural and create a community space and garden in the adjacent lot. Plans to restore the mural and create a community space and garden in the adjacent lot were developed by Eduardo Arocho, John Pitman Weber, and Joyce Fernandes— on behalf of NNNN, the Puerto Rican Cultural Center, and archi-treasures— in 2001, two years before the first protest. In 2006, Arocho and Weber proposed involving six high school or college level art students as apprentices on the project. Final decisions about these plans will be made by members of the Humboldt Park Empowerment Partnership.

Relating Impacts to Influence

The important accomplishments of this case appear to be related to all of the points of influence, which created a broad constituency for saving *La Crucifixion de Don Pedro Albizu Campos* and brought together the many different kinds of ideas and knowledge that were needed to achieve that goal — residents' perspectives about the mural and the adjacent lot as well as a broad array of experience and expertise in community organizing, community surveys, mural restoration and art history, politics, real estate law, and landscaping. The process for saving the mural created multiple opportunities for players to act on their ideas, through the development of the proposal for restoring the mural and creating a community garden on the adjacent lot, the three protests, the land-swap negotiations, and legal efforts to appropriate the lot through eminent domain. All of the players involved in the process cared about the mural, although their reasons varied. By working to save the mural, they were doing something for themselves as well as others.

The linkage of ideas also appears to have been critical in this case, particularly the linkage of community members' ideas about the mural to the community's struggle against gentrification and displacement (the second point of influence in the case). There is no evidence that the community, at large, connected the mural to issues of gentrification and displacement prior to the protests, but the perceptions of the residents who participated in the survey provided a strong foundation for making the connection. A commonly held perception among people in the neighborhood was that the mural represented something Puerto Rican that mattered to them, which was in danger of being taken away. This perception is very consistent with the notion of displacement, and the condominium apartments that the owner was planning to build on the adjacent lot were a vivid example of gentrification.

The linkage was important because the threats of gentrification and displacement were high priority issues among a large number of people and organizations in the community, including the area's Aldermen. Making the connection increased community support for saving the mural and may have helped to overcome some people's concerns about the mural's controversial subject matter. At the same time, it increased the number of people who were aware of, and involved in, the community's struggle against gentrification and displacement.

Linking the mural to the community's aesthetic strategy for challenging gentrification created a momentum for saving other Puerto Rican murals in the area around Humboldt Park and creating new ones. These murals, in turn, are marking more outdoor space with Puerto Rican imagery, furthering all of the other efforts to imprint Puerto Rican culture on the landscape of the community.

11

The Pathway of Ideas

The stories and individual case analyses reveal a lot about influence under particular circumstances. But the Workgroup had a larger goal — to see if we could draw any generalizable conclusions about influence in community participation processes by looking at the ten cases as a whole. In designing the study, we intentionally selected a set of cases that varied in the extent to which different kinds of people, or "players," had been involved and in the ways they had been involved. By doing so, we hoped to be able to identify broadly applicable factors that affect the potential for different players' ideas to be influential in participation processes — especially the ideas of residents who have a long history of having been marginalized and excluded from decision making in communities.

As we conducted the cross-case analysis, we made an unexpected discovery. By comparing and combining findings in the cases, we uncovered a pathway that players' ideas need to travel in order to become influential in community participation processes. This pathway — which explains how participation processes give players an influential voice — appears to be the same in all of the cases, regardless of the particular approaches that were used to promote community participation. So it is likely to be applicable to a broad array of community participation processes.

The pathway (illustrated on the following page) consists of four steps, and players' ideas need to get through each of the steps, in sequence, in order to be influential:

The pathway begins with the opportunity to participate. The cases demonstrate that players need to have certain kinds of participation opportunities in order to have any potential to influence what happens. They need opportunities to contribute their ideas in important areas. These opportunities need to be timely and feasible for them to participate in.

The second step is the expression of ideas. The cases demonstrate that opportunities to contribute ideas are only meaningful if players can actually express what they want to say. Their ability to do so depends on the conditions under which they participate and the questions they are asked.

The third step is the communication of ideas. The cases demonstrate that the potential for players' ideas to influence what happens depends on who else in the community knows about their ideas and how well these other players understand their ideas. Communication is particularly important when players can't act on their own ideas or when acting on an idea requires the efforts of multiple players.

The final step in the pathway is the use of ideas. In our study, ideas that were used

Opportunity to Participate → **Expression of Ideas** → **Communication of Ideas** → **Use of Ideas** *(Influence)*

Pathway to Influence

to make something happen were considered to be influential; other ideas were not. The cases demonstrate that only some of the ideas that are expressed and communicated in participation processes are actually used, and these are the ideas that determine which issues are addressed and how issues are addressed. Acting on a particular player's ideas often requires the support of other players.

Below, we discuss the pathway in detail, presenting the case evidence on which it is based. We begin by discussing the different kinds of players, who are the sources of all of the ideas in the cases. After that, we describe each of the steps of the pathway in turn, identifying the factors that determined whose ideas moved forward at that point and how that mattered. Finally, we relate the impacts in the cases to the movement of different players' ideas along the pathway. The cases demonstrate that the accomplishments and limitations of community participation processes are related to the extent to which the process generates— and uses— all of the ideas that are needed to identify, understand, and address issues. Addressing complex and challenging issues requires many kinds of ideas from a broad range of players. When needed ideas are prevented from being influential — because they are blocked somewhere along the pathway —community participation processes are less effective in identifying, understanding, and addressing complex issues and participation, itself, is adversely affected.

To make our findings concrete, we will be using the analogy of a track meet to describe how the ideas in the cases moved along the pathway. The rules of the game are:

- The players in the cases are the athletes in the track meet.
- Each player's opportunities to contribute ideas are the track lanes that the athlete can run in.
- The ideas that players express are batons that the athletes hold.
- The communication of ideas among players is equivalent to the passing of batons among athletes (much like a relay race).
- The obstacles that players encounter moving their ideas forward are hurdles that the athletes need to jump over.
- The ideas that influence what happens (i.e., the ideas that move through all of the steps of the pathway) are the batons that athletes succeed in carrying over the finish line.
- The goal of the track meet — unlike a competitive race — is to bring all of the needed "idea batons" across the finish line.

The Players in the Cases

When we looked at the various kinds of players who were involved in the cases, they appeared to fall into three groups: lead players; other people with clout, resources, or acknowledged expertise; and marginalized and ordinary residents (people who have been historically excluded from community decision making). These players were the source of all of the ideas in the cases. In the track meet analogy, they make up the pool of athletes.

By "lead players," we mean the people who stimulated and ran a lot of what happened in the cases. The Pathways to Collaboration partnerships were lead players in each of their cases, but people associated with other community organizations functioned as lead players in many of the cases as well, such as the Latin United Community Housing Association (Housing for Single Mothers), the Little Dixie Community Action Agency (Poor Man's Bank and Community Centers), Mid-Iowa Community Action and Move the Mountain (Community Leadership Team and Incorporation of Beyond Welfare), the Cass Lake Family Resource Center and the Leech Lake Tribal Council (Community Voices Against Violence), and the Puerto Rican Cultural Center (Saving a Mural). In the track meet analogy, the lead players were the organizers of the athletic event, inviting most of the athletes and audience and setting the rules of the game. They also participated actively on the field as athletes.

The cases focused on serious and challenging issues that the lead players cared about and felt they were in a position to do something about — crime and violence; unemployment; poverty; lack of affordable housing; displacement and gentrification; and the survival of a community and an organization. Each of these issues affected disadvantaged residents in the community who had been marginalized because of their income, race, ethnicity, employment status, and/or marital status, such as Native American adults and youth living in the poorest section of the Leech Lake reservation (Community Voices Against Violence), poor single mothers (Housing for Single Mothers), poor people who needed business funding but did not qualify for traditional loans (Poor Man's Bank), and un/underemployed adults and youth at risk of un/underemployment (Minigrants).

By addressing the issues in the cases, the lead players were trying to do something that would help the members of these groups. In more than half the cases, some or all of the lead players and other people in the community were also directly affected by the issues, although not necessarily in the same way as the marginalized population. In these cases, the lead players were doing something for themselves as well as others.

The impetus for involving other people in the cases usually came from the lead players. Many of these other participants were people from within and beyond the community who had clout, resources, and/or acknowledged expertise. Some were involved in local and tribal governments, local businesses, schools, social service agencies, law enforcement agencies, and other community organizations and groups. Others included advisors and consultants — both local and from outside the community — as well as people at state, regional, and national levels who were associated with foundations, government agencies, and large-scale programs and initiatives.

Other community residents also participated in the cases. These people included members of the marginalized groups who were directly experiencing the problem in the case as well as members of the general public — "ordinary" residents without clout, resources, or acknowledged expertise about the issue at hand. The involvement of such residents was a requirement in three of the cases. In the Oklahoma cases (Poor Man's Bank and Community Centers), the federal government mandated broad community involvement in developing the Empowerment Zone/Enterprise Community strategic plan. The origin of Community Leadership Team was a contract from the state government to obtain input from people on public assistance. The marginalized and ordinary residents who were involved in the cases were predominantly adults. Youth were active participants in only three cases: Community Voices against Violence, Minigrants, and Saving a Mural.

First Step in the Pathway: Opportunity to Participate

To have any potential to influence what happened in the cases, players needed to have certain kinds of participation opportunities. They needed opportunities to contribute their ideas in areas that were related to the critical points of influence in the cases, and these opportunities needed to be timely and feasible for them to participate in. The extent to which different groups of players had such opportunities varied substantially, which determined whether they were ever able to express potentially influential ideas in the next step of the pathway.

In the track meet analogy, this step of the pathway determines if athletes get on to the field at all and, if they do, which lanes they can run in and when they can start to run.

Opportunities for participation did not necessarily give players opportunities to contribute their ideas.

The players in the cases participated in a variety of ways—through visioning sessions, planning workshops, summits, forums, organizational meetings, rallies, protests, interviews, focus groups, surveys, questionnaires, conversations, and programs. While most forms of participation gave players opportunities to contribute their ideas, some of the opportunities for marginalized and ordinary residents did not. In educational forums,

Watching vs. Playing

such as the law enforcement forums organized by Community Voices against Violence, the residents in the audience were there to learn from the presenters' ideas rather than to contribute ideas of their own. The people who participated in the various programs that were developed to help members of marginalized target populations—such as the Professionalization Curriculum, training programs funded by minigrants, and structured programs at the community centers—did not have opportunities to contribute their ideas to identifying, understanding, or addressing any of the issues in the cases.

Players who participated only in ways like these had no potential to influence what happened in the cases. In the track meet analogy, it would be equivalent to inviting them to watch the event rather than to participate on the field as one of the athletes.

Some players lacked opportunities to contribute ideas in important areas.

To have any potential to influence what happened in the cases, players not only needed opportunities to contribute ideas, they needed opportunities to contribute ideas in areas that mattered. Looking at the critical points of influence in the cases, players' ideas appear to have mattered in five areas, where they determined:

- The particular issues, problems, and needs that came to light
- Which of these issues, problems, and needs moved forward to be developed into "doable" projects and programs
- How the projects and programs were designed and carried out
- How success was envisaged and defined
- How community members were involved in the process.

Some groups of players in the cases had opportunities to contribute ideas in all of these areas. The opportunities for others focused on only one or two areas, which limited the domains where they could potentially exert influence. In the track meet analogy, it would be as though some of the athletes could run in all of the lanes on the field, while others were allowed to run only in certain lanes but not others.

In several of the cases, the timing of opportunities differed among players as well. In the track meet analogy, it would be as though some athletes were allowed to start the race earlier than others.

Running in One Lane vs. Multiple Lanes

Starting Late vs. Early

The lead players and many of the other participants with clout, resources, or acknowledged expertise had opportunities to contribute ideas in all of the critical areas in the cases, usually at very early stages in the process. In a number of cases, such as Revitalizing Cass Lake and Professionalization Curriculum, the lead players had well developed ideas about the issues they wanted to address and the way they wanted to address those issues before involving other people in their work. Lead players often sought the ideas of consultants to help them construct activities to involve the broader community. Opportunities to contribute ideas about which of the many issues, problems, and needs that came to light should be developed into projects and programs were largely limited to the lead players, other community leaders, and consultants.

For the most part, marginalized and ordinary residents only had opportunities to identify issues, problems, and needs and, less frequently, to contribute ideas to the design or implementation of projects and programs. With the exception of two cases where marginalized residents went to talk to lead players on their own (Community Voices Against Violence and Housing for Single Mothers), all of these opportunities were created by the lead players and their consultants. In three cases (Community Voices Against Violence, Community Leadership Team, and Incorporation of Beyond Welfare), entities were created that gave marginalized residents opportunities to contribute some ideas in the other critical areas, as well.

Most of the projects and programs in the cases were developed to benefit members of marginalized groups. Those residents had opportunities to contribute their ideas to the design or implementation of the projects and programs in only half the cases, however. Such opportunities occurred early in the design stage for the Professionalization Curriculum, the Wheels to Work program in the Community Leadership Team case, and the youth summits in the Community Voices against Violence case. In the Housing for Single Mothers case, the opportunity for single mothers to contribute their ideas about the design of the housing that was being developed for them came late in the process; the lead player's initial housing proposals were developed by staff alone.

In the rest of the cases, opportunities for the intended beneficiaries of projects and programs to contribute design and implementation ideas were either limited or absent. In the Community Centers case, residents had opportunities to propose their own unstructured uses of the centers, but neither adults nor youth had opportunities to contribute to the design of the many structured programs that the community centers developed for them. In the Poor Man's Bank case, potential loan recipients did not have opportunities to contribute any ideas about how the program should be designed or run, although the application process gave them opportunities to propose what they wanted to do with their loans. In the Revitalizing Cass Lake case, the residents who lived downtown near the proposed Streetscape project — and would therefore be affected by it — had very limited opportunities to contribute their ideas to the design of that project. In the Minigrants case, underemployed people did not have explicit opportunities to contribute their ideas to the design or operation of that program.

Two other groups with potentially valuable design and implementation ideas also had variable opportunities in the cases: people other than the intended beneficiaries of the project or program who would also be affected by the actions being taken; and people who had experience running similar kinds of projects or programs in other places. In designing the minigrant program, the lead player created opportunities for members of these groups to contribute ideas, by engaging in conversations with many people in the community, some of whom were associated with the kinds of organizations that would be potential grantees, and by seeking advice from members of another Workforce Alliance who were already running a similar program. In the Poor Man's Bank case, representatives of the local steering committees, who would be running the loan program in their census tracts, were appointed to the Poor Man's Bank Committee. But the committee did not seek ideas from people who had operated successful revolving loan programs elsewhere in the country or internationally. In the Housing for Single Mothers case, the lead player's initial proposals were developed without the involvement of community groups in the neighborhoods where the housing would be built.

Participation was more feasible for some players than others.

In at least some of the opportunities in each of the cases, the lead players made special efforts to overcome barriers that made it difficult for marginalized and ordinary residents to take advantage of opportunities to contribute their ideas. They did so by publicizing the opportunities in multiple ways, going to residents rather than asking them to go somewhere else, scheduling opportunities at convenient places and times, organizing multiple opportunities at different places and times, and providing participants with transportation, food, and child care.

In two cases, the investigation revealed barriers that prevented marginalized and ordinary residents from participating in opportunities to which they were invited. It became more difficult for residents to participate in Community Voices Against Violence meetings after the meetings were rescheduled to be held during work hours, which was more convenient for the professionals who were participating as representatives of their agencies. The same problem prevented residents from participating in public meetings of the Streetscape Planning Committee in the case about Revitalizing Cass Lake. In the track meet analogy, it would be as though some of the athletes who were invited to participate in the event could not get to the stadium to take part in it.

The extent to which different players had timely and feasible opportunities to contribute ideas in important areas mattered.

The progression of ideas through the first step of the pathway had important implications for what ultimately happened in the cases. For one, ***the opportunities brought players into the process who otherwise would not have had ways to contribute their ideas***. Marginalized and ordinary residents were given opportunities to contribute their ideas about community issues, problems, and needs as well as the design of some of the projects and programs that were being developed to benefit them. Efforts to overcome barriers made it possible for large numbers of these residents to participate in some of the opportunities, such as the Empowerment Zone/Enterprise Community planning meetings in the Oklahoma cases, the youth summits and the community survey in the Community Voices Against Violence case, and the community visioning session in the case about Revitalizing Cass Lake.

Other players who later played important roles in the cases became involved at this step in the pathway as well. These players included the local economic development advisor who was given an opportunity to introduce his idea for a Poor Man's Bank, the people who were given opportunities to contribute their ideas about Tri-County's minigrant program, and the numerous consultants who were brought in to involve the broader community and to design the projects and programs in the cases.

In a number of cases, the contribution of ideas from certain groups of players was blocked at this stage of the pathway. As a result, ***lead players and others lacked ideas and knowledge that were needed to develop effective projects and programs***.

- Without hearing from potential loan recipients or people with experience running successful revolving loan programs elsewhere, the Poor Man's Bank Committee had no way of knowing how much funding poor people needed in order to start or expand businesses, how much they could afford to pay back monthly, or how to make peer pressure work. The lack of this knowledge accounted for the unsustainability of the program (Poor Man's Bank).
- Without asking single mothers and community groups about design issues before developing its initial housing proposal, the lead player had no way of knowing what kind of housing single mothers really wanted or what kinds of housing would and wouldn't work for other people living in the neighborhood. Without that knowledge, the lead player initially developed housing proposals that were 'out of sync' with the single mothers and community groups, which resulted in delays and conflict (Housing for Single Mothers).
- Without hearing from the youth and adults for whom they were developing structured programs at the community centers, the programmers had no way of knowing what those people really wanted. Programs created without that knowledge may have accounted for the limited use of some center programs by their intended target populations and the waning use of one of the centers (Community Centers).
- Without hearing from people living downtown near the proposed Streetscape project, the lead player and consultants involved in the design of the project had no way of knowing how those residents would be affected by what they

planned to do. Since Streetscape has not yet been completed, the consequences of designing the project without that knowledge are unknown (Revitalizing Cass Lake).

The lack of opportunities for marginal and ordinary residents to contribute ideas in other important areas created problems for them in later steps of the pathway. Without opportunities to contribute ideas about which issues, problems, and needs should move forward, these residents had no way to further the ones they wanted the community to address. Without opportunities to contribute ideas about how the community would be involved in the process, these residents had no way to affect the extent or nature of their involvement.

Second Step in the Pathway: Expression of Ideas

To have any potential to influence what happened in the cases, players' ideas needed to be expressed. But having opportunities to contribute ideas did not necessarily mean that players could express what they wanted to say. Their ability to do so depended on the conditions of the opportunities in which they participated and the questions they were asked. The extent to which different players could express their ideas varied substantially, which determined if their ideas could be communicated to anyone else in the next step of the pathway.

In the track meet analogy, expressed ideas are the batons that athletes carry in their hands. This step of the pathway determines if athletes get to carry full-size batons, small batons, or no batons at all. Athletes with small batons have very little to bring or pass on to the finish line. Athletes with no batons are out of the game.

The ability of players to express what they wanted to say depended on the conditions of their participation.

In a number of cases, we have evidence of conditions that enabled players to express their ideas freely. Marginalized residents in the Housing for Single Mothers case and the

Need "Idea" Batons to Play

Community Voices Against Violence case felt comfortable enough with the lead players to talk to them on their own.

In some of the opportunities created to engage marginalized and/or ordinary residents in the cases, special efforts were made to create safe, comfortable environments where they could express ideas that mattered to them, even if those ideas were painful, difficult, or contentious. The Empowerment Zone/Enterprise Community planning meetings in the Oklahoma cases were designed to be non-threatening and to ensure participation by everyone, including low-income individuals. A major focus of Community Leadership Team and Community Voices Against Violence was to build supportive communities, and the meetings of these groups created conditions where people trusted each other and could tell their personal stories.

Conditions encouraging free expression were not sustained in Community Voices Against Violence, however. When the group was restructured around "stakeholder" representatives of local agencies, the participation of ordinary residents waned. In addition to changing the time of the meetings, which made attendance less feasible for people who were not participating as part of their jobs, the nature of participation became less inviting for marginalized and ordinary residents. Story telling ended, and the focus of meetings shifted to priority setting and the development of action plans.

For the most part, any ideas that players wanted to express but couldn't or wouldn't express during opportunities in the cases are unknown. Through interviews in the investigations, however, we learned of two opportunities where conditions prevented people who had a 'seat at the table' from expressing their ideas. Of the two unemployed members of the design committee in the Professionalization Curriculum case, one stopped coming to meetings, and the other continued to attend but stopped contributing her ideas. The unemployed members were outnumbered, six to two, by professionals; their views were not sought by the professionals; and they perceived that the professionals on the committee did not value what they had to say.

Members of the Poor Man's Bank Committee included representatives of the local steering committees, who were responsible for operating the Poor Man's Bank in their communities and applying the necessary peer pressure to assure the repayment of loans. Ideas about the problems they might face — or were facing — were not sought, however, and the representatives deferred to the committee members associated with the lead player, who were assumed to have more expertise about revolving loans. Even when the Chair of one of the local steering committees (who was also Vice-Chair of the overall steering committee) was fairly certain that many loan recipients would not be able to meet the proposed payback terms, he chose not to express those ideas for fear that the committee's response would have adverse consequences for people in his community.

The ability of players to express what they wanted to say depended on the questions they were asked.

In quite a few of the opportunities in the cases, players' ideas were elicited by asking them questions. In some of these opportunities, players were asked very broad, open-ended questions, which placed few constraints on what they could say. Examples include the Empowerment Zone/Enterprise community planning meetings in the Oklahoma cases, the first two youth summits in the Community Voices Against Violence case, the community visioning session in the case about Revitalizing Cass Lake, and the focus groups and interviews to develop the Professionalization Curriculum. Although players could express their ideas freely during all of these opportunities, the timing of the opportunities varied, which affected the advancement of players' ideas in later steps in the pathway. The Oklahoma planning meetings were held at the start of the process, before any community priorities were identified. The opportunities in the other cases occurred after the lead players already had well-developed ideas about what they wanted to do.

Questions were more targeted in other opportunities in the cases. Open-ended questions about a narrow topic were posed to local residents in the survey in the Saving a Mural case and to grant and loan applicants in the Minigrant case and Poor Man's Bank case. In the survey about violence and law enforcement in the Community Voices Against Violence case, residents were asked a series of specific, close-ended questions. In three opportunities—the newspaper survey and the Streetscape Planning Committee in the Revitalizing Cass Lake case and the architect's survey of single mothers in the Housing for Single Mothers case—players were presented with a predetermined set of options, which enabled them to express their preferences but not introduce new ideas.

In opportunities with more targeted questions, the extent to which players were constrained depended on how well the questions were aligned with the ideas they wanted to express. There was a very close alignment in the Community Voices Against Violence survey, which explored issues about the police that had initially been raised by marginalized and ordinary residents, and in the architect's survey of single mothers, which included design options that the mothers wanted. Applicants for loans from the Poor Man's Bank or for minigrants could propose anything they wanted to do with the funds within the constraints set by those programs. The mural survey enabled residents living close to the mural to express what the mural meant to them and to react to the lead player's proposal to turn the adjacent lot into a recreational area. Constraints appear to have been greater in the newspaper survey and Streetscape Planning Committee in Cass Lake, since all of the options were ideas contributed by lead players and consultants.

The way ideas were elicited and the conditions under which ideas were elicited mattered.

The progression of ideas through the second step of the pathway had important implications for what ultimately happened in the cases. ***Broad, open-ended questions and safe, comfortable conditions enabled marginalized and ordinary residents to identify important issues, problems, and needs that the lead players had not raised or been aware of before.*** These kinds of opportunities surfaced:

- Problems that Native Americans were experiencing with inadequate police response and abuse by police (Community Voices Against Violence)
- Problems that youth were experiencing with poverty, racism, and the dysfunctional behavior of adults in their lives (Community Voices Against Violence)
- The need for youth to have a "rec center" where they could "hang out" and engage in unstructured activities after school, in the evenings, and on weekends (Community Voices Against Violence)

- The need for more suitable housing for poor single mothers in Humboldt Park (Housing for Single Mothers)
- The need for places where people in southeastern Oklahoma could go to relax, socialize, engage in recreation, conduct meetings, and hold family events (Community Centers)
- The need to improve conditions for the people living in Cass Lake by renovating the existing housing stock and building more affordable housing; by expanding the transportation system; by developing neighborhood parks, community centers, libraries, and recreation facilities; by creating more livable wage job opportunities; and by healing the wounds between Native American and white cultures (Revitalizing Cass Lake)
- The need to address underemployment in the Mississippi Delta by providing "on-the-job" training in addition to education and by focusing attention on hiring and employment practices (such as wages, benefits, working conditions, job security, and job advancement), job-related supports (such as transportation and child and elder care), critical public benefits (such as health insurance), job discrimination, and the creation of desirable jobs, particularly through nontraditional approaches that would attract committed businesses to the area or enable underemployed people to become owners of businesses as well as workers in businesses (Professionalization Curriculum)
- The need for people in poverty to have friends of sufficient means (Community Leadership Team)
- The need for poor people in Story County to have cars and the importance of incorporating reciprocity in a car donation program (Community Leadership Team).

Opportunities with more targeted questions also elicited valuable ideas from community members. Some provided information that helped to move forward issues that were important to marginalized residents. In the Community Voices Against Violence case, the community survey documented and quantified the problems that Native Americans were experiencing with the police. In the Housing for Single Mothers case, the architect's survey revealed the housing design features that were important to single mothers.

Other opportunities with targeted questions helped to move lead player ideas forward. In the case about Revitalizing Cass Lake, the newspaper survey told the lead player what respondents thought about the group's priorities, and the responses of members of the Streetscape Planning Committee helped the consultant choose among potential design options for the lead player's project. The survey in the case about Saving a Mural documented that residents supported what the lead player wanted to do—preserve the mural and have the adjacent lot developed as a public recreational space.

When conditions prevented people with a "seat at the table" from expressing their ideas, those people experienced negative emotional consequences and other players lacked ideas and knowledge that were needed to develop effective programs. In the Professionalization Curriculum case, the experience of serving on the design committee made the unemployed members feel alienated and unvalued. Without their ideas, the other members of the committee had no way to look at the content they were developing from the perspective of the curriculum's intended students (unemployed people) to see if the subject matter would be relevant to them or if the materials would work for them. They also had no way of knowing how to structure the screening interviews to maintain the interest of potential students. Screening interviews and curriculum content developed without these ideas may have contributed to the high attrition rate of the program.

Unrealistic payback terms and ineffective strategies for applying peer pressure accounted for the unsustainability of the Poor Man's Bank. Lack of opportunities in the first step of the pathway prevented potential loan recipients and people with experience running successful revolving loan programs elsewhere from contributing their ideas to the design of the program. When the representative from a local steering committee could not express his ideas, members of the Poor Man's Bank Committee had no way to recognize serious flaws in the program's operating procedures.

When the conditions of participation changed, marginalized and ordinary residents lost their only means of expression. The restructuring of Community Voices Against Violence was designed to enable agency stakeholders to contribute their ideas to accomplishing something achievable. The value of ideas from marginalized and ordinary residents does not appear to have been explicitly recognized, however, and the meetings stopped providing them with opportunities to share their experiences in the form of stories. This was a critical loss for those residents because the group's rallies and early meetings had provided them with their only means of expression.

Third Step in the Pathway: Communication of Ideas

To have any potential to influence what happened in the cases, players' ideas needed to be communicated to other players who could help move the ideas forward and act on them. This was particularly important when players couldn't act on their own ideas or when acting on an idea required the efforts of multiple players.

The effectiveness of communication in the cases depended on who knew about each player's ideas and how well their ideas were understood. That, in turn, depended on whom each player interacted with directly in their participation opportunities, the circumstances and period of time over which those interactions occurred, how clearly and specifically players expressed their own ideas, how faithfully and completely their ideas were recorded and reported by others, and how widely the reports of players' ideas were disseminated. When communication was not effective in the cases, players' ideas were misinterpreted or lost, which prevented them from being used in the next step of the pathway.

In the track meet analogy, this step of the pathway determines the chances athletes have of passing their batons to other athletes who can carry the batons across the finish line. It also determines if batons are passed successfully or dropped and if the batons that are successfully passed are faithful to the originals or not.

Opportunities for direct communication and discussion of ideas varied substantially among players.

Passing "Idea" Batons

In the cases, the direct communication of ideas occurred among players who were involved in the same opportunity. Many of these opportunities were one-time interactions, such as a conversation or interview between two people, the submission of a grant or loan application, the completion of a survey or questionnaire, or participation in a single group meeting or event. Others were ongoing, usually in the form of meetings that brought players together repeatedly over time.

The purpose of most of the one-time opportunities was to provide the lead players with information from other people in the community, and almost all of the opportunities for marginalized and ordinary residents fell into this category. In some of these opportunities, the residents participated with members of other player groups—lead players and other players with clout, resources, or acknowledged expertise. Examples include the Empowerment Zone/Enterprise Community planning meetings in the Oklahoma cases, the rallies and forums organized by Community Voices Against Violence, the community visioning session in the case about Revitalizing Cass Lake, the protests to save the mural, and the meetings of underemployed people and employers in the Professionalization Curriculum case. In other one-time opportunities—such as the youth summits in the Community Voices Against Violence case and the focus groups of underemployed people that were conducted to develop the Professionalization Curriculum—participation was largely limited to members of a particular marginalized group.

Lead players and other players with clout, resources, or acknowledged expertise participated in most of the ongoing meetings in the cases, which gave them opportunities to get to know each other, hear each others' ideas repeatedly, and discuss ideas. In addition to lead player meetings, which occurred in all of the cases, ongoing meetings in which these two player groups participated included the various Enterprise Community steering committee meetings in the Oklahoma cases, meetings of the Humboldt Park Empowerment Partnership in the Housing for Single Mothers case, meetings of the research team in the Professionalization Curriculum case, and meetings of the Streetscape Planning Committee in the case about Revitalizing Cass Lake. In some cases, many of the same players participated in multiple meetings. In the Revitalizing Cass Lake case, for example, members of the lead player group participated in most of the meetings in the case. In the Oklahoma cases, many of the same players were involved in the various Enterprise Community committees, and those players organized and attended most of the community planning meetings as well.

Marginalized and ordinary residents were involved in few of the ongoing meetings in the cases and very rarely in meetings where the ideas that they and others had contributed in the one-time opportunities were discussed. In some of the ongoing meetings in which marginalized residents participated, such as meetings of Mothers United in Action in the Housing for Single Mothers case, they only interacted among themselves. Participation was more diverse in meetings of Community Leadership Team, meetings of the Board of Beyond Welfare, early Community Voices Against Violence meetings, and meetings of the Professionalization Curriculum design committee. The design committee meetings did not foster meaningful communication, however, since (as pointed out in the previous step of the pathway) conditions did not enable marginalized residents to express their ideas.

In the track meet analogy, these differences in players' opportunities for direct communication mean that some of the athletes (lead players and other players with clout, resources, or acknowledged expertise) have very good chances of passing their batons—and receiving batons from other athletes—because they can run in many lanes alongside many other athletes for prolonged periods of time. The remaining athletes (marginalized and ordinary residents) are not as well positioned to pass their batons. Most of them are only allowed to run in one of the lanes. Some of these lanes are limited to athletes just like them. When different kinds of athletes are running in their lane, they are within passing distance for only a short period of time.

In the course of articulating, recording, and reporting ideas, some of the ideas that players expressed were misinterpreted or lost.

Players in the cases had the most control over the communication of their ideas when they had opportunities to talk to other players face-to-face or to record their own

Chances for Passing

ideas in writing. When they did not express their ideas clearly or specifically, however, their ideas were not necessarily understood as intended. If their written notes were not transmitted to other players, their ideas could be lost.

In the Housing for Single Mothers case, single mothers went to the lead player — Latin United Community Housing Association, or LUCHA — to express a general need for more suitable housing. At the time, it does not appear that LUCHA staff explored what the single mothers actually had in mind. They probably assumed that they knew what the single mothers wanted, and the single mothers probably assumed that LUCHA staff knew what they wanted, too. LUCHA staff created a solution for the single mothers, basing their initial housing proposals on strategies they had been using for other groups. The case documents major discrepancies, however, between LUCHA's initial proposals and the desired housing features that the architect later elicited from single mothers.

In the Empowerment Zone/Enterprise Community planning meetings in the Oklahoma cases, players wrote their ideas on "sticky notes," which were posted on the walls. The sticky notes have been lost, but from what participants recalled in interviews, most of the ideas were written very succinctly. Some of the terms people wrote down — like "jobs" or "community centers" — didn't clarify exactly what they had in mind. We don't know what happened to the sticky notes after the meetings, but it does not appear that lists of all of the ideas were ever prepared. So it is not possible to know if all of the ideas that people recorded at the planning meetings were actually transmitted to the local steering committees to use in making decisions about community priorities.

Players in the cases had a number of other opportunities to make a written record of their own ideas — in applications for minigrants and Poor Man's Bank loans, in the signs they carried in the protests to save the mural, and in their written responses to questions posed at the community visioning session and planning workshops in the Revitalizing Cass Lake case. In all of the other opportunities in the cases, the recording of players' ideas depended on someone else. In many of the conversations, rallies, and meetings in the cases, no one documented what the participants said. Further transmission depended on whatever the people who were at the opportunity chose to pass on to others and whether they understood and relayed those ideas accurately or not. All of the other ideas from these opportunities were lost. Since the lost ideas were never documented, it is not possible to know what they were.

When players' ideas were documented — in meeting notes or minutes and in records of survey responses — the further communication of those ideas depended on whether the ideas were reported to people who did not participate in the opportunity and how accurately, specifically, completely, and widely the ideas were reported. The effectiveness of this communication varied substantially across opportunities in the cases.

- The ideas generated at the youth summits in the Community Voices Against Violence case were not compiled or reported, even though a broad range of issues, problems, and needs were recorded by note-takers at the events. (The ideas that were documented in these notes were analyzed for the first time in the course of the case investigation.)
- In the case about Saving a Mural, responses to the survey were summarized in a proposal to have the adjacent lot developed as a public recreational space, but

much of the specificity of the respondents' ideas was lost in the way their ideas were reported.

- In the case about Revitalizing Cass Lake, ideas from the community visioning session were reported to the public as one-, five-, and ten-year plans for Cass Lake. These plans included only a portion of the ideas that were expressed by the people who had participated in the visioning session.
- In the same case, the report that Rose and Associates submitted to city officials included brief descriptions of the ideas that participants in the planning workshops expressed. Most of the recommendations in the report were not based on those ideas, however. They were drawn from other meetings that Rose had with MIRACLE Group members.
- In the Professionalization Curriculum case, the report prepared by the research team — for its own use in developing the curriculum and for the project's funder — presented the team's analysis of the ideas that were expressed in the focus groups with underemployed people and in the interviews with employers. Prior to the preparation of the report, participants in each group had an opportunity to go over and discuss what they and others in their group had said.
- In the Community Voices Against Violence case, the report of the community survey included the responses of all of the participants to all of the questions in the survey. The findings were presented at a highly publicized and well-attended public forum.

In the track meet analogy, problems with the interpretation and transmission of ideas are reflected in the nature of the batons that are passed from athlete to athlete and the extent to which they are passed. Some batons are dropped when athletes try to pass them on. Some batons are passed successfully, but don't get into the hands of athletes who can take them across the finish line. Some batons— representing ideas that are expressed differently when they are transmitted by others— are changed by the athletes who receive them so they no longer resemble the baton that the original athlete wanted to pass on.

The ideas of different kinds of players were rarely differentiated in records or reports.

The players in all of the cases were very diverse, and it is likely that different kinds of players had different ideas— at least about some areas. The way ideas were recorded and reported in the cases made it difficult or impossible to identify these differences, however. In the track meet analogy, it means there is no way of knowing which athlete passed a baton once the baton is received by another athlete.

The ideas that players contributed were differentiated in only three cases. In the Community Voices Against Violence case, responses to the community survey were differentiated based on where people lived, so it was possible to compare experiences and perceptions of people living in the poorest Native American neighborhoods on the reservation with those of people living in more affluent white areas. In the Professionalization Curriculum case, the research team's report differentiated the views of underemployed people and employers. In the Community Voices Against Violence case, the ideas of young people were differentiated in the youth summits.

Dropping and Changing "Idea" Batons

Records and reports from the other opportunities did not differentiate ideas among the people involved. For example, in the case about Revitalizing Cass Lake, ideas of participants in the community visioning session were not differentiated according to whether they were Native American or white, whether they were poor or better off, or whether they lived on or off the reservation. In the Oklahoma cases (Community Centers and Poor Man's Bank), ideas of the community members who participated in the Empowerment Zone/Enterprise Community planning meetings were not differentiated according to whether they were African American, Native American, or white; where they lived, or their income level. In the Saving a Mural case, the ideas of survey respondents were not differentiated according to whether they were Puerto Rican or not.

The extent to which players' ideas were communicated accurately, specifically, completely, and widely mattered.

The progression of ideas through the third step of the pathway had important implications for what ultimately happened in the cases. For one, opportunities that brought diverse people together to hear and discuss each other's ideas contributed to the case accomplishments in important ways. ***These kinds of opportunities broadened support for some ideas by making more people aware of issues, problems, and needs that community members wanted to be addressed and by identifying different reasons for wanting a particular action to be taken.***

- The Empowerment Zone/Enterprise Community planning meetings and the meetings of the overall steering committee (which included the members of all of the local steering committees) spread the idea of community centers throughout the area. People involved in the process recognized that large numbers of residents wanted community centers for themselves and their families and that people involved in developing programs and providing services for marginalized adults and youth in the area supported community centers, too. This broad interest and support played a critical role in getting community centers into the Empowerment Zone/Enterprise Community strategic plan (Community Centers).

- The protests to save the mural brought together people who valued the mural for different reasons. Linking the mural to the community's struggle against gentrification increased community support for saving the mural and increased the number of people who were aware of, and involved in, the community's struggle against gentrification (Saving a Mural).

Sharing ideas broadly prevented the substitution of ideas. Because of the way the overall and local steering committees were structured, a lead player in the Community Centers case was aware that the Western Hugo steering committee was not representing the community's priorities. Without this recognition, the Washington Community Center would not have been included in the Empowerment Zone/Enterprise Community strategic plan.

Bringing diverse people together on an ongoing basis led to the development of relationships that made concerted actions possible.

- Through its meetings, rallies, and forums, Community Voices Against Violence brought people together across racial, sectoral, and jurisdictional divides. The meetings and rallies enabled residents to express their painful feelings about the escalating problems of crime and violence in the community, share their personal stories, demonstrate their support for others, and start a community healing process. The meetings began to make law enforcement officials and others aware of problems that Native American residents were experiencing with the police, which was a prerequisite for developing actions to address these issues. The forums brought law enforcement professionals from multiple jurisdictions together to share ideas, which contributed to the development of the cooperative law enforcement agreement (Community Voices Against Violence).
- Through its meetings, Community Leadership Team has developed a mutually supportive, cross-class community. The relationships that members have developed, and the ideas they have shared, have led them to care about each others' issues and work together to address those issues (Community Leadership Team).

Through ongoing meetings where they could share and discuss ideas, participants—particularly members of marginalized groups—gained voice and skills and a sense of power over their own lives. These impacts are documented in interviews with people who participated in Community Leadership Team, the Board of Beyond Welfare, Mothers United in Action (Housing for Single Mothers), and Batey Urbano (Saving a Mural).

The careful recording and reporting of ideas supported difficult and controversial actions to address issues that mattered a lot to marginalized residents. The community survey in the Community Voices Against Violence case quantified the extent to which poor Native Americans were having problems with the police and documented the specific nature of those problems. By doing so, the survey transformed people's stories—which some officials might previously have considered to be anecdotes or the complaints of marginalized residents—into data that needed to be taken seriously. Conducting the survey under the auspices of a policing organization, and having the data presented by members of local law enforcement agencies, gave further credibility to the survey's findings, which ultimately led to the replacement of the Cass Lake police chief and other officers.

In a number of the cases, the communication of some players' ideas was blocked at this stage of the pathway, with serious consequences. ***The lack of reports, or the nature of the reports that were prepared, limited the broader community's awareness of issues, problems, and needs that mattered a lot to marginalized residents.***

- Because ideas from the youth summits in the Community Voices Against Violence case were not reported publicly, few people in Cass Lake were made aware of the serious problems that Native American youth were facing with poverty, racism, and the adults in their families or the kinds of strategies they wanted to be taken to address those problems. The problems the youth raised continue to persist and are contributing to problems with crime and violence in the community.
- The one-, five-, and ten-year plans that came out of the community visioning session in the case about Revitalizing Cass Lake did not include most of the actions that community residents wanted to be taken to improve conditions for them. Without taking these steps, it may not be possible to revitalize Cass Lake, even if efforts to promote tourism and downtown business development are successful.
- The report of the focus groups with underemployed people and the interviews with employers in the Professionalization Curriculum case revealed a great deal about the problems that are contributing to underemployment in the Delta and the kinds of strategies — going beyond workforce development — that could be explored to address these issues. The broader community was not made aware of these ideas, however, and none of them were further developed.

The lack of clarity or specificity in the communication of ideas created serious problems in some of the cases, particularly when one party was acting on ideas expressed by another.

- In the Housing for Single Mothers case, the lead player's initial housing proposals differed in important ways from the features that single mothers wanted. If community groups had not blocked those proposals, the housing would have lacked features that mattered a lot to single mothers and would have incorporated features they did not want.
- After residents in the Empowerment Zone/Enterprise Community planning meetings expressed a general desire for community centers, the local steering committees created centers for them — without necessarily knowing what the residents in their communities had in mind. The variation with which community centers are currently being used may reflect, in part, the extent to which the ideas of the people designing the centers and the people using them were aligned.

In some of the cases, opportunities that didn't differentiate ideas among people in different groups created a false semblance of consensus and limited what the lead players

and others could accomplish. None of the opportunities in the Cass Lake cases enabled Native Americans and whites to surface differences in their views, and without such opportunities, it was not possible to address these differences. Although the community visioning session in the case about Revitalizing Cass Lake obtained what appeared to be broad community support and endorsement for moving the downtown redevelopment plan forward, representatives of the Leech Lake Band of the Ojibwe declined invitations to participate in the Streetscape Planning Committee and in the subsequent open house. As the Community Voices Against Violence case demonstrates, longstanding racial divisions in the community have not been overcome. Native Americans and whites were able to come together around an extreme case of cross-race violence, but that has not been repeated as successfully in cases of "Indian against Indian" violence.

Fourth Step in the Pathway: Use of Ideas

Only some of the ideas that were expressed and communicated in the cases were actually used, and those were the ideas that influenced what happened. The use of ideas from players in different groups varied substantially. When players could not act on their own ideas, the use of their ideas depended on the support of other players.

In the track meet analogy, this step determines if athletes accept batons from athletes who are trying to pass them on and if batons are carried across the finish line. Only certain athletes (equivalent to players who can act on an idea) can bring batons over the finish line.

Ideas contributed by lead players were very influential.

Many of the ideas that were acted upon in the cases came from lead players. This finding is not surprising since the lead players had opportunities to contribute ideas in all of the areas related to the critical points of influence in the cases, and they had the

Carrying Batons Across the Finish Line

fewest hurdles to overcome in expressing and communicating their ideas to players who could make things happen — the lead players, themselves, and other leaders in the community.

Of the ideas that lead players contributed in the cases, the vast majority were used. In more than half the cases, the lead players introduced key issues, problems, and needs that were ultimately addressed. In all but one of the cases (Housing for Single Mothers), the lead players set the parameters that guided how key projects, programs, and strategies were carried out. In several cases, ideas for refining programs reflected what key players had learned from their experiences.

When the ideas of lead players were not used, the cases identify three reasons. There were differences in ideas among individuals within a lead player group or across lead players in the case (Incorporation of Beyond Welfare; Minigrants). The lead player could not garner the resources or political support that was needed to carry out the idea (Revitalizing Cass Lake). The idea was opposed by influential groups in the community (Housing for Single Mothers).

Many of the other influential ideas came from other players with clout, resources, or acknowledged expertise who could help move the lead players' ideas forward.

Much of what the lead players wanted to accomplish in the cases went beyond their own capacities. To put their ideas into action, they needed the knowledge, assistance, and support of other players.

When lead players sought ideas from consultants with acknowledged expertise in particular areas, those consultants' ideas were almost always used. Consultants designed most of the formal community engagement activities in the cases and helped the lead players design many of the projects in the cases. In the Cass Lake cases, they helped lead players organize and structure their work and figure out what to do next. In the Poor Man's Bank case, the central idea came from a local advisor brought in by a lead player.

In half the cases, ideas from funders and other players were used when they provided resources to support what the lead players wanted to do. In one case (Incorporation of Beyond Welfare), a lead player discontinued funding from an organization that was pressuring it to do something it did not want to do.

The ideas of elected officials and other community leaders and groups were influential when their knowledge, assistance, or support was needed to accomplish what the lead players wanted to do. In one case (Housing for Single Mothers), the ideas of elected officials and community groups blocked what a lead player wanted to do.

The use of ideas from marginalized and ordinary residents depended on the alignment of their ideas with the ideas of other players.

In many of the cases, the lead players had well developed ideas about what they wanted to do before they involved community residents in their work. When the ideas that marginalized and ordinary residents contributed were closely aligned with what lead players were planning to do — or when residents raised issues with lead players that were aligned with what the lead players were interested in doing — the residents' ideas were always used. Examples include:

- Unstructured uses of community centers; selling quilts to pay for the floor of one of the centers (Community Centers)
- The need for cross-class relationships and cars; refinement of Community Leadership Team practices; reciprocity in the Wheels to Work program; personal and community activities (Community Leadership Team)
- Community Voices Against Violence meeting practices and peace rallies; design of the first two youth summits (Community Voices against Violence)
- Reasons for Beyond Welfare to separate from Move the Mountain; basing Beyond Welfare's operating procedures on Community Leadership Team's Purposes and Principles; severing the working relationship with Move the Mountain (Incorporation of Beyond Welfare)
- The need for more suitable housing for single mothers; activities of Mothers United in Action; and, later in the case, design features of housing for single mothers (Housing for Single Mothers)
- Meanings of the mural; features of the protests to save the mural (Saving a Mural)
- Inclusion of hands-on experience and a component to address job advancement in the Professionalization Curriculum; preferences for internship placements (Professionalization Curriculum)
- Use of loans from the Poor Man's Bank (Poor Man's Bank).

Ideas from marginalized and ordinary residents that were not closely aligned with what the lead players were planning to do were *not* acted upon. The most striking examples are from the youth summits in the Community Voices Against Violence case, the community visioning session in the case about Revitalizing Cass Lake, and the focus groups that were conducted for the Professionalization Curriculum.

In each of these opportunities, marginalized and ordinary residents were asked very broad questions (as described in the second step of the pathway). But the potential for their responses to influence what happened was limited, since the lead players were looking for ideas that would support and strengthen what they were planning to do—establish a Boys & Girls Club and Tribal Youth Division for youth in Cass Lake, revitalize Cass Lake's downtown business district, and create a Professionalization Curriculum focusing on social components necessary for the world of work. Residents' ideas that were consistent with the lead players' plans were used. Ideas about issues, problems, and needs that went beyond the focus of the lead players' plans were not acted upon in the context of the cases:

- The need for places where youth in Cass Lake could "hang out" and engage in unstructured activities after school, in the evenings, and on weekends; problems youth were experiencing with poverty, racism, and the dysfunctional behavior of adults in their lives (Community Voices Against Violence)
- The need to improve conditions for people living in Cass Lake by renovating the existing housing stock and building more affordable housing; expanding the transportation system; developing neighborhood parks, community centers, libraries, and recreation facilities; creating more livable wage job

opportunities; and healing the wounds between Native American and white cultures (Revitalizing Cass Lake)

• The need to address underemployment in the Delta by focusing attention on issues beyond workforce development, including hiring and employment practices (such as wages, benefits, working conditions, job security), job-related supports (such as transportation and child and elder care), critical public benefits (such as health insurance), job discrimination, and the creation of desirable jobs, particularly through nontraditional approaches that would attract committed businesses to the area or enable underemployed people to become owners of businesses as well as workers in businesses (Professionalization Curriculum).

The use of ideas contributed by marginalized and ordinary residents also depended on their alignment with what other players wanted to do. Some of these ideas moved forward because players with more clout than marginalized and ordinary residents wanted the same thing for similar or different reasons. This kind of alignment was a factor in getting community centers into the Empowerment Zone/Enterprise Community strategic plan, since programmers as well as residents wanted the centers. It also played a role in the Housing for Single Mothers case. Although no one knew it at the time, housing features that were important to single mothers were also important to certain community groups, for very different reasons. Fortuitously, the objections of community groups to the lead player's initial housing proposals led to the development of housing that was more 'in sync' with the preferences of single mothers. In the Professionalization Curriculum case, by contrast, some of the ideas contributed by underemployed people — related to wages, benefits, and job security — did not go forward because employers refused to discuss them.

The use of ideas from marginalized and ordinary residents depended on the support of other players in moving residents' ideas forward.

In the cases, four types of support provided by lead players and other players with clout, resources, or acknowledged expertise appear to have been important in determining the use of ideas contributed by marginalized and ordinary residents. One form of support was to respect the community participation process. In the Community Centers case, the lead player respected local priorities for community centers and overcame shortcomings in the process that would have prevented the Washington Community Center from being included as a priority. In the case of the Poor Man's Bank, the inclusion of West Idabel's priority in the strategic plan demonstrated respect for the process on the part of the lead player. But in this case, a local consultant's idea supplanted any ideas that residents may have expressed about economic development priorities in the local planning sessions.

In three cases, lead players and other players with clout, resources, or acknowledged expertise developed strategies to move forward controversial ideas that mattered to marginalized and ordinary residents.

• Community centers were not specifically listed as a fundable activity in the federal government's instructions for completing the Empowerment

Zone/Enterprise Community application. In drafting the strategic plan, the lead player presented the rationale and uses of the centers in ways that were most likely to make the application competitive (Community Centers).

- The controversial problems that marginalized residents raised about police abuse and responsiveness were ultimately addressed because the community survey transformed their anecdotal experiences into accepted knowledge that needed to be taken seriously. Having the findings presented by members of local law enforcement agencies gave these ideas even more credibility (Community Voices Against Violence).
- Members of the research team working on the Professionalization Curriculum developed a strategy to get employers to discuss the issue of job advancement, which was very important to the underemployed people who participated in the focus groups. The discussion about the kind of training that employees would need in order to work their way up led to the leadership component of the curriculum (Professionalization Curriculum).

One of the hurdles that marginalized and ordinary residents faced in the cases was that they were rarely in a position to act on their own ideas. Many of the ideas from the youth summits in the Community Voices Against Violence case, the community visioning session in the case about Revitalizing Cass Lake, and the focus groups that were conducted for the Professionalization Curriculum did not move forward because the people involved had no way to transform their ideas into doable actions. In some cases, however, lead players created domains where marginalized and ordinary residents could act on their ideas to some extent. In the track meet analogy, it would be equivalent to opening up lanes where athletes can carry their own batons to the finish line.

- Community centers have given residents places where they can engage in self-identified activities: hold family functions, have meetings, socialize with other people, quilt, watch TV, play games and sports (Community Centers).
- In Community Leadership Team, members have raised, and helped each other with, personal issues; they have also supported each other in "giving back" to the communities where they live in ways that are meaningful to them (Community Leadership Team).
- The incorporation of Beyond Welfare gave the Board real power and influence over the structure and operation of the organization. People who have experienced economic poverty have a substantial voice in that governance since they comprise a majority of the Board members (Incorporation of Beyond Welfare).
- Minigrant awards enabled community-based organizations to put their own ideas into action. With the training they received in minigrant-funded programs, some unemployed people started their own businesses (Minigrants).
- The loosely organized process for saving the mural made it possible for many kinds of players to act on their ideas. Youth from Batey Urbano had such opportunities during the protests (Saving a Mural).
- In the Professionalization Curriculum, the preferences of unemployed students

guided the internship placements they received (Professionalization Curriculum).

- The Poor Man's Bank program enabled loan recipients to use the funds for their own business purposes (Poor Man's Bank).

A final form of support related to the resources that were needed to act on residents' ideas. Assistance in securing resources was critical to refurbish and construct the community centers that were included in the Empowerment Zone/Enterprise Community strategic plan. The overall steering committee, including the lead player, played important roles in this regard, as did community members in Boswell. In West Idabel, insufficient resources for constructing a new center led to the renovation of the Booker T. Washington High School, which had the unintended benefit of preserving a "sacred" cultural landmark in the community. In the Housing for Single Mothers case, resource constraints prevented some of the design features desired by single mothers from being incorporated in the housing that was built.

Impacts and Influence

The pathway enables us to distinguish ideas in the cases that that were influential (i.e., advanced through all of the steps); were contributed but not used (i.e., were blocked in the third or fourth step); and were missing (i.e., were blocked in the first or second step of the pathway). When we look at the impacts of the cases in terms of which ideas moved forward and which did not, we see that the extent to which a community participation process generates, and uses, all of the ideas that are needed to identify, understand, and address issues relates closely to what the process is able to accomplish.

The accomplishments in the cases depended on many kinds of ideas from a variety of players.

The ideas that advanced through all of the steps of the pathway were the foundation for the important accomplishments in the cases. Looking across all of these accomplishments, the study demonstrates that many different kinds of ideas were required and that these ideas came from a broad range of players.

Some of the ideas were drawn from what the players had learned through their formal education or training. These ideas covered many areas of acknowledged expertise, including community organizing, community development, economic development, community engagement, advocacy, politics, law, law enforcement, counseling, social services, education, qualitative and survey research, land use, architecture, landscaping, art restoration, art history, leadership, management, and philanthropy.

Other ideas were drawn from the players' life experiences. These ideas reflected what they had learned from having experienced problems directly, from having engaged in certain kinds of actions, from having seen what worked and didn't work in various situations, from knowing what matters to themselves and the people they care about, and from having lived in their community and worked with particular people, organizations, or groups.

Ideas from marginalized and ordinary residents played important roles in most of the case accomplishments.

Some of the actions in the cases that were of substantial benefit to marginalized residents were developed solely with ideas from the lead players and other players with clout, resources, or acknowledged expertise. Examples include the minigrant program; the workplace ethics and communication component of the Professionalization Curriculum, which was proposed by employers; and the Boys & Girls Clubs in the Community Voices Against Violence case. Ideas from marginalized and ordinary residents contributed to most of the other accomplishments, however.

A number of important issues and problems that were addressed in the cases were initially raised by the marginalized and ordinary residents who were experiencing them directly. It is unlikely that problems with police abuse and responsiveness in Cass Lake, the lack of suitable housing for single mothers in Humboldt Park, the need for community centers in southeast Oklahoma, or the need for cross-class relationships in Ames would have been addressed if marginalized and ordinary residents had not brought these issues to light through the process.

Ideas from marginalized and ordinary residents contributed to the understanding of problems that other players raised. In the Incorporation of Beyond Welfare case, their ideas identified reasons that Beyond Welfare's relationship with Move the Mountain wasn't working. In the Saving a Mural case, their ideas showed how the mural mattered to people in the neighborhood and why they didn't want it to be covered or destroyed.

Ideas from marginalized and ordinary residents also contributed to the success of many of the projects and programs that were carried out in the cases.

- All of the ideas for unstructured uses of the community centers have come from the residents who have used the centers for these purposes. These uses were the primary reasons residents wanted community centers and what they appear to value most about the centers. In Boswell, women using the old center came up with the idea of selling their quilts to pay for the floors of the new center (Community Centers).
- Members of Community Leadership Team refined their meeting practices based on their experiences with those practices over time; doing so contributed to the development of the group's community, which the members value and own (Community Leadership Team).
- After the murder of the resort owner, residents knew that story telling, mutual respect, and mutual support would be needed to enable community members to deal with their anguish and begin a healing process. Their ideas shaped the way Community Voices Against Violence originally functioned (Community Voices Against Violence).
- The process of incorporation formalized Community Leadership Team's values and principles, which helped to clarify the organizational identify of Beyond Welfare (Incorporation of Beyond Welfare).
- Single mothers knew the design features that would make housing suitable for them. Many of the reasons current tenants feel better off than they did before relate to the use of these ideas (Housing for Single Mothers).

- When neighborhood residents observed construction on the lot next to the mural, they passed that information on to others who could do something about it. The ideas of the protesters, many of whom were young people, helped to draw community and media attention to the protests (Saving a Mural).
- Problems that underemployed people were facing as they tried to move beyond minimum wage jobs informed the leadership component of the Professionalization Curriculum, which was one of the most valuable sessions for the students. Issues that underemployed people raised about the need for on-the-job experience in addition to educational credentials led to the inclusion of the internship (Professionalization Curriculum).
- The way some of the recipients of Poor Man's Bank loans used their funds made certain services more locally available to residents in West Idabel (Poor Man's Bank).

The use of ideas from people with acknowledged expertise was not always helpful.

While most of the ideas that were used in the cases were helpful in identifying, understanding, or addressing issues, some were not. In two of the cases, the use of ideas from people with acknowledged expertise led to serious problems.

- After the law enforcement forums were completed, the members of Community Voices Against Violence didn't know what to do next, so they looked to outside experts for advice. Assistance from the Upper Midwest Community Policing Institute turned out to be very helpful. But the restructuring of Community Voices Against Violence by the organizer from the Center for Reducing Rural Violence was not. The organizer's intention was to enable stakeholders representing agencies to work together to accomplish something achievable. But marginalized and ordinary residents stopped coming to meetings when it became inconvenient for them to do so and when issues and activities that were important to them were eliminated from the group's "achievable" agenda. The stakeholders who continued to participate as part of their jobs didn't have their hearts in it and the group took very few actions. With these changes, the founding members of Community Voices against Violence felt something important had been lost. Marginalized and ordinary residents lost their only means of expression (Community Voices Against Violence).
- The members of the West Idabel steering committee assumed that the economic development consultant who encouraged them to create a Poor Man's Bank knew a lot about revolving loan programs. The representatives of the local steering committees on the Poor Man's Bank Committee assumed that Little Dixie (a lead player) had expertise in this area as well and deferred to Little Dixie in the development of the Bank's operating procedures. As later events made clear, these assumptions of expertise were not justified (Poor Man's Bank).

Some of the problems and limitations in the cases were related to ideas that were needed but not used because they were blocked somewhere along the pathway.

In two cases, missing or unused ideas limited the effectiveness of programs and contributed to delays, tension, and conflict.

- In the Poor Man's Bank case, three kinds of ideas were missing: the ideas of people who had run successful revolving loan programs elsewhere and knew what it would take to make peer pressure work; the ideas of the local steering committee representatives who were responsible for operating the program locally; and the ideas of potential loan recipients about the amount of funding they would need to start or expand businesses and how much they could afford to pay back monthly. The lack of this knowledge accounted for the unsustainability of the Poor Man's Bank.
- In the Housing for Single Mothers case, two kinds of ideas were missing early on when the original concept for the housing was being developed: the ideas of single mothers for whom the housing was being built and the ideas of community residents who would be living near the housing. As a result, there was no way to recognize the alignment in the ideas of single mothers and community residents or the lack of alignment of their ideas with the housing that the lead player originally had in mind. Without this knowledge, the lead player initially developed housing proposals that were 'out of sync' with the single mothers and community groups, which resulted in delays and conflict.

In three cases, important issues that mattered a lot to marginalized and ordinary residents were not addressed.

- Young people in Cass Lake still lack places to hang out and engage in unstructured activities after school, in the evenings, and on weekends. Poverty, racism in the community, and serious problems with the adults in their families persist. (Community Voices Against Violence).
- Issues that underemployed people in the Delta raised and care about — related to hiring and employment practices, job supports, public benefits, job discrimination, and the creation of desirable jobs — have not been addressed (Professionalization Curriculum).
- Cass Lake's revitalization strategy has not included actions that residents repeatedly proposed to improve living conditions for them and to heal the wounds between the Native American and white cultures (Revitalizing Cass Lake).

When hurdles in the pathway prevented players' ideas from being influential, their participation in the process was adversely affected.

In four of the cases, players who were unable to move their ideas forward exerted the only influence they could — they stopped participating in the process.

The Unlevel Playing Field

- When members of the West Idabel Steering Committee were unable to prevent or correct structural problems with the Poor Man's Bank, they ended their community's participation in the program (Poor Man's Bank).
- The underemployed people on the Professionalization Curriculum design committee stopped contributing and coming to meetings when other members did not value their ideas or act on them (Professionalization Curriculum).
- Marginalized and ordinary residents stopped participating in Community Voices Against Violence after the restructuring of the group made it impossible for them to express their ideas (Community Voices Against Violence).
- The participation of marginalized and ordinary community residents in the MIRACLE Group's community development activities may have waned because these activities haven't given them a way to explore the issues they cared about the most or to develop the actions they wanted to take (Revitalizing Cass Lake).

The relationship of influence to participation creates a feedback loop that brings the pathway full circle. The pathway identifies the many hurdles that ideas need to overcome in community participation processes in order to become influential. It also reveals that some players— particularly marginalized and ordinary residents—face considerably more hurdles than others. In the track meet analogy, we see that the athletes are not playing on a level playing field. Some of the athletes never get onto the track in the first place. Of those that do, some don't have batons or only have small ones. Others aren't allowed to carry their own batons to the finish line and can't pass their batons to athletes who are. Athletes get tired trying to overcome such hurdles, especially when they lack supports. After a while, they walk off the track. Remembering the experience, they are less likely to go to the next meet, even if they are invited.

12

Realizing the Promise of Community Participation

The Pathways to Collaboration Workgroup embarked on this case investigation to answer four questions that go to the heart of realizing the promise of community participation:

- How can we tell if participation processes are giving historically excluded groups an influential voice about issues that affect their lives?
- Does it matter if processes are doing that or not?
- If it does matter, what is hindering and supporting the influence of historically excluded groups in participation processes?
- How can practitioners improve their processes to realize the promise?

These questions loomed large for our Workgroup when we recognized that we didn't really know the extent to which the Pathways partnerships were doing what they were committed to doing or what they could learn from each other to improve their work. The extensive literature in the field suggested that many other people and organizations— in the United States and internationally — also needed answers to these questions to make their community participation processes "genuine," "meaningful," and "real."

When we completed the study, we returned to these questions to see what we had learned, looking for ways that we and others who aspire to realize the promise of community participation could apply our findings in practice. As it turned out, by opening up the "black box" of community participation and looking at influence directly, we learned a lot more than any of us expected, and that learning came from every phase of the study: developing the methods, investigating and analyzing the individual cases, writing the case narratives, analyzing the ten cases as a whole, and relating the cross-case analysis to the literature.

With the findings and tools from our study, we and other practitioners are in a much better position than we were before to use our processes to promote the voice and influence of historically excluded groups. We now know how participation processes give people an influential voice, the barriers that have been preventing that from happening for members of historically excluded groups, what we need to do to overcome those barriers, and how to tell if we've actually done that or not. We also know that applying what we've learned involves changes in mindset as well as changes in practice. We've been going through some fundamental shifts in thinking since the start of our study. That hasn't been easy, but it's been a worthwhile journey because seeing our work in new ways is making it possible to realize the promise of community participation.

How Can We Tell If We're Doing What We Want to Be Doing?

Practitioners who want to promote the voice and influence of historically excluded groups have been working at a distinct disadvantage. Without methods to assess the influence of the various people — or "players" — in a community participation process, they have had no way of knowing whether, or to what extent, their process is accomplishing what they want it to accomplish.

The methods we developed for our case study show that it is possible to determine whose voices are influential in a community participation process — by ***tracking the ideas of different players over time***. Our approach distinguishes opportunity, voice, and influence. Players have an opportunity to participate in the process when they are invited or when they initiate an opportunity on their own. They have a voice when the opportunity enables them to express their ideas to others. They have an influential voice when their ideas are used to make something happen (for example, when actions are taken to address issues they raise or when their ideas shape actions that are taken).

Although our study was retrospective, the methods can be applied prospectively as well. Practitioners can determine whose voices are influential in their community participation process by keeping track of:

- Who is involved in each of the opportunities in the process
- What different participants say
- How their ideas are reflected in decisions that are made and actions that are taken.

To see how well a process is working to promote the voice and influence of historically excluded groups, the ideas of marginalized and ordinary residents need to be differentiated from those of the lead players who initiate and organize the process and those of other players with clout, resources, or acknowledged expertise.

Does It Matter If We're Doing It or Not?

Community participation processes are time- and resource-intensive, so before investing even more effort to assure that historically excluded groups have an influential voice in their processes, practitioners and funders are justified in asking: "Is it worth it?" We believe that it is, for the following reasons.

Our study shows that the pattern of influence relates closely to what a community participation process is able to accomplish. Many kinds of ideas — including those of marginalized and ordinary residents — were needed to identify, understand, and address the serious community issues in our cases. This finding is consistent with a substantial literature documenting the importance of both lay and expert knowledge in technology assessment, environmental risk assessment, emergency preparedness, policy development, and other areas.[1]

Community participation processes play important roles in generating those ideas and putting them to use in developing and taking effective actions—in other words, in making sure that all needed ideas are influential. Ideas from marginalized and ordinary residents have little chance of being contributed or used without such a process. The ideas of different kinds of players—such as marginalized residents and professional experts—have little chance of being exchanged and combined without a participatory process. By enabling the ideas of diverse players to be influential, participation processes support the co-production of knowledge, the generation of new knowledge, and the creation of synergy.[2]

Looking more closely at historically excluded groups, we found that the extent of their influence is related to three desired outcomes of community participation processes. When the ideas of marginalized and ordinary residents were influential in the cases, issues they cared about got on the community's agenda and were addressed in ways that worked for them; other players had access to knowledge they needed to develop effective projects and programs, which were often being designed to help a marginalized target population; and marginalized and ordinary residents were actively engaged in the process. When the ideas of marginalized and ordinary residents were not influential, important issues that mattered to them were not addressed; programs developed for them by other players were compromised by incorrect assumptions, delays, tension, and conflict; and they stopped participating in the process.

What Is Hindering and Supporting the Influence of Historically Excluded Groups?

When we analyzed the ten cases in our study, we uncovered a pathway of steps that players' ideas need to travel in order to be influential in community participation processes. This pathway explains how participation processes give players an influential voice—through opportunities that enable them to express ideas they care about, to communicate their ideas to others who can help move them forward, and to have their ideas be used as a basis for decisions and actions. Ideas need to get through all of the steps of the pathway in order to be influential; if they are blocked at any step along the way, they lose their potential for influence. The path-dependence of ideas

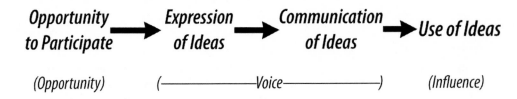

The Pathway of Ideas

explains some of the limitations of community participation described in the literature, such as having a seat at the table without having a voice, and having your voice heard but not heeded.[3]

In the previous section of the book, we used the analogy of a track meet to describe the pathway, and our study shows that the playing field is not a level one. The ideas of marginalized and ordinary residents are far less likely to get through all of the steps in the pathway than the ideas of lead players and other players with clout, resources, or acknowledged expertise. This is ironic because it shows that ***community participation processes are inadvertently recreating the inequities that they were intended to address in the first place.*** To realize the promise of community participation to give historically excluded groups an influential voice, we need to level the playing field.

Hurdles in the Pathway

The hurdles we identified at each step of the pathway, which are summarized in the table on pages 204–206, show us why the playing field isn't level. While these hurdles can block the ideas of any player, marginalized and ordinary residents face many more hurdles than other players do.

Step I: Opportunity to Participate. In our study — as in the broader literature — we found that opportunities for participation are usually organized by lead players and other players with clout, resources, or acknowledged expertise.[4] Consequently, those players know about, and have access to, most of the opportunities in the process. That is not the case for marginalized and ordinary residents, however.

We found that marginalized and ordinary residents are not invited to participate in important opportunities in the process. For the most part, their opportunities are limited to "participation exercises" — such as visioning sessions, summits, or focus groups— that are specifically created for the purpose of engaging particular target populations or the broader community in the process. They are rarely included in opportunities that are not organized for this purpose but play critical roles in the pathway to influence, such as meetings of the lead players and other community organizations and groups.

Marginalized and ordinary residents also face hurdles that prevent them from participating in the opportunities to which they are invited. Members of these groups don't know about available opportunities when announcements are not designed for them or disseminated in ways that reach them. Participation isn't feasible when opportunities are scheduled at times and places that are more convenient for other players than for them or when needed transportation or childcare isn't provided. These hurdles account, in part, for the challenge of "recruiting" historically excluded groups, which is reported frequently in the literature.[5]

Step II: Expression of Ideas. In our study — as in the broader literature — we found that the issues, questions, and discussion in the opportunities that comprise a participation process are usually framed by lead players and other players with clout, resources, or acknowledged expertise.[6] It isn't surprising, then, that these players face few, if any, hurdles expressing their ideas. The hurdles in this step of the pathway apply almost exclusively to marginalized and ordinary residents.

We found that the opportunities available to marginalized and ordinary residents limit the kinds of ideas they can express. Through participation exercises, they have

Hurdles and Supports in the Pathway

Hurdles	*Supports*

Step I: Opportunity to Participate

Some players do not have an opportunity to participate because:

(1) They are not invited.

In addition to the "usual suspects," invite the following groups with critically needed ideas:
- People who are experiencing problems directly
- People for whom plans, programs, policies are being developed
- Other people who are likely to be affected by those plans, programs, and policies
- People who have experience with similar kinds of problems, plans, programs, and policies elsewhere.

(2) They are not aware of the opportunity.

Enable marginalized and ordinary residents to initiate opportunities on their own.

Provide marginalized and ordinary residents with understandable, useful, and timely information about oppportunities that are available to them

(3) The opportunity is not feasible for them.

Provide marginalized and ordinary residents with needed supports:
- Choose times and venues that are convenient for them
- Provide transportation, food, and child care.

Step II: Expression of Ideas

Some players can't express ideas that matter to them because:

(1) The opportunity limits the kind of ideas they can express.

Give marginalized and ordinary residents opportunities to contribute their ideas in all of the areas that matter:
- Identifying important issues, problems, and needs
- Determining which issues, problems, and needs move forward to be developed into plans, programs, and policies
- Contributing to the design and implementation of these actions
- Defining what success looks like and means
- Deciding how they and other community members are involved in the process.

Include marginalized and ordinary residents in ongoing meetings of lead players and other community organizations and groups.

Hurdles	Supports
(2) Their ideas are not valued by other participants.	Discuss why different kinds of players are involved in the process and why their ideas are needed.
	Recognize and appreciate what marginalized and ordinary residents know from their life experiences that other participants don't know.
(3) They defer to other participants with presumed expertise.	Actively seek out the ideas of marginalized and ordinary residents.
	Recognize the need for different kinds of expertise (drawn from formal education and life experiences) and the limitations of any particular kind of expertise.
(4) They cannot express their ideas in a voice that is meaningful to them.	Enable players to express their ideas in a variety of ways, including by telling personal stories.
(5) They are afraid of speaking out.	Create safe, comfortable conditions where marginalized and ordinary residents can express their ideas without fear of adverse consequences.
(6) They are constrained by the questions they are asked.	Involve marginalized and ordinary residents in framing the issues and the questions they will be asked.
	Ask questions that are broad and open-ended or closely aligned with the ideas that marginalized and ordinary residents want to express.
Step III: Communication of Ideas *Some players' ideas are not heard by other players who can help move the ideas forward or act on them because:* (1) They are involved in "one-time" opportunities or "single player" opportunities that limit their interactions with other kinds of players.	Identify venues where marginalized and ordinary residents can interact with other kinds of players repeatedly over time.
	Create conditions that enable diverse players to get to know each other and to hear and discuss each others' ideas.
(2) Their ideas are dismissed or misinterpreted by other players.	Encourage all players to express their ideas clearly and specifically so that other players don't make assumptions about what they mean to say.
(3) Their ideas are not shared with the broader community.	Record and report the ideas that all players express in each opportunity faithfully and completely.
	Disseminate players' ideas widely–to players in other opportunities and in the broader community who can help to move them forward.

Hurdles	*Supports*
(4) Their ideas are not differentiated from those of other players.	Document differences in the ideas of different players.
	Avoid creating a semblance of consensus where consensus does not exist.
Step IV: Use of Ideas *Some players' ideas are not used because:* (1) Their ideas are contributed after important decisions have already been made.	Focus on problems before developing actions or solutions.
	Involve marginalized and ordinary residents early in the process—before proposals and plans have been developed and before deciding what to do.
(2) Other players in subsequent opportunities decide whether their ideas will be used or not.	Involve marginalized and ordinary residents in opportunities where decisions about their ideas are made.
(3) Their ideas are not aligned with those of more influential players.	Respect the commitment of the process to give marginalized and ordinary residents an influential voice about issues that affect their lives by taking action on what they say.
(4) Their ideas are not acknowledged to be relevant or important by more influential players.	Transform the ideas of marginalized and ordinary residents into accepted knowledge (for example, by conducting surveys based on their ideas and by preparing reports that translate their ideas into data and language that experts respect and understand).
(5) They can't act on their own ideas.	Bring marginalized and ordinary residents together with players who have the resources and capacity to act on their ideas.
	Provide marginalized and ordinary residents assistance in developing their ideas into "doable" projects.
	Develop projects, programs, and policies that create opportunities for marginalized and ordinary residents to act on their own ideas.

opportunities to identify issues, problems, and needs and sometimes to contribute to the design and implementation of projects and programs. But they are rarely included in the meetings of lead players or other groups that determine what the participation process is about, how the broader community is involved, or which of the many ideas generated in the process move forward and which fall by the wayside. As a result, marginalized and ordinary residents have no way to influence the nature or extent of their own involvement or to further the ideas they care about the most.

Our study identified a number of other hurdles that prevent marginalized and ordinary residents from expressing what they want to say in participation opportunities, many of which have also been reported in the literature. Societal norms that equate professional expertise with knowledge devalue the ideas of marginalized and ordinary residents in the eyes of acknowledged experts in the process and sometimes in the eyes of the residents, themselves.[7] In this kind of environment, some residents defer to participants with presumed expertise.[8]

When the accepted form of expression is to articulate ideas in ways that mirror those of professionals, marginalized and ordinary residents can't express their ideas in a voice that is meaningful to them, such as by telling personal stories.[9] Residents are afraid of speaking out when expressing their ideas puts them or others they care about at risk of adverse consequences.

Marginalized and ordinary residents are also constrained by the questions they are asked in participation opportunities.[10] Since they are rarely involved in framing these questions, the ideas being solicited tend to be more closely aligned with what the organizers of the process want to know than with what marginalized and ordinary residents want to say. When this occurs, residents have difficulty raising issues or problems that really matter to them, challenging the assumptions of experts, introducing new options for addressing problems, or shifting the focus of a participation exercise from solving a problem to preventing the problem in the first place.[11]

Step III: Communication of Ideas. This step of the pathway is very important for marginalized and ordinary residents because they need the assistance of other players to move their ideas forward and act on them. But a number of hurdles prevent their ideas from being communicated to the players who can do that.

We found that the opportunities available to marginalized and ordinary residents limit their interactions with other kinds of players. The participation exercises in which they are involved are usually "one-time" events or "single player" opportunities where they only get to interact with people like themselves. They are rarely involved in ongoing meetings that enable participants to get to know different kinds of players and to discuss ideas repeatedly over time.

Consistent with the literature, we found that marginalized and ordinary residents are less likely to be listened to than other kinds of players. When their forms of expression appear to be unreasonable, emotional, irrational, or irrelevant to lead players and other players with clout, resources, or acknowledged expertise, the ideas they express tend to be dismissed.[12] When marginalized and ordinary residents don't have an opportunity to express their ideas clearly and specifically, other players misinterpret or make incorrect assumptions about what they mean to say.[13]

To reach players who can help to move their ideas forward and act on them, marginalized and ordinary residents need to communicate their ideas beyond the players who are directly involved in their opportunities. But we found that the ideas of marginalized and ordinary residents are rarely shared with the broader community. In some opportunities, the ideas that participants express are not differentiated from each other or not documented at all. When reports are prepared, the ideas of marginalized and ordinary residents run the risk of being condensed, reinterpreted, or cut. When marginalized and ordinary residents express ideas that are "beyond the scope of the exercise," those ideas are not disseminated to other players in the community who could help to move them forward.

Step IV: Use of Ideas. In our study, we found that the vast majority of ideas contributed by lead players and other players with clout, resources, or acknowledged expertise are used in community participation processes, which isn't surprising since these players are in positions to make things happen. That isn't the case for marginalized and ordinary residents, however.

A number of hurdles prevent the ideas that marginalized and ordinary residents are able to contribute from being used as a basis for action and decision making. The participation exercises in which these residents are involved often occur after important decisions have been made—for example, after lead players have already developed proposals or plans for what they want to do. Consistent with the literature, we found that ideas not closely aligned with those plans—or with the interests of other influential players—have little chance of being acted upon because they aren't considered to be relevant or important by the players who are in positions to take action.[14] These are critical hurdles for marginalized and ordinary residents because their status precludes them from putting their ideas into action on their own.[15]

Strategies for Overcoming Hurdles

To realize the promise of community participation processes to give marginalized and ordinary residents an influential voice about issues that affect their lives, we not only need to understand the hurdles that are preventing their ideas from becoming influential, but also how those hurdles can be overcome. The variation in the cases we selected to study was very helpful in this regard. For every hurdle we identified in the cases, we found examples in other cases—or other opportunities in the same case—where supportive strategies moved ideas across the barrier.

These supports demonstrate that it is possible to overcome the hurdles in the pathway to influence and, by doing so, to make the playing field of community participation far more level for historically excluded groups. The supports also show us what we need to focus our attention on to make that happen.

In the table on pages 204–206, *Hurdles and Supports in the Pathway*, the supportive strategies are presented next to the particular hurdles they overcome in each step of the pathway. Another way to look at them is from the perspective of the opportunities that comprise a community participation process. ***Opportunities are where changes can be made in these processes***. The supports overcome hurdles in the pathway by changing who is involved in opportunities, the kinds of opportunities in which they are involved, the conditions of those opportunities, and the relationship among the opportunities that comprise the process.

Who is Involved. The pathway to influence clarifies the purpose of involving diverse people in community participation processes—to generate all of the ideas that are needed to identify, understand, and address issues. It isn't possible to know what those ideas are in advance, which is why processes that support the entry and exchange of a broad range of ideas are so important. But it is possible to identify the kinds of people who have needed ideas.

The ideas of lead players and other players with clout, resources, or acknowledged expertise are obviously needed, and our study shows that these players have broad access to the opportunities in participation processes. But considerably more attention needs to be paid to assuring opportunities for other groups with critically needed ideas:

- People who are experiencing problems directly
- People for whom plans, programs, and policies are being developed
- Other people who are likely to be affected by those plans, programs, and
   policies
- People who have experience with similar kinds of problems, plans, programs,
   and policies elsewhere.

Many of these people are marginalized and ordinary residents, and their ideas are critical for a variety of reasons. They have the most accurate and direct knowledge about the problems they are facing and the extent to which different issues matter in their lives. They have valuable insights about the causes of the problems they are experiencing and the roles they can play in addressing those problems. They know what they want solutions to look like and achieve and have ideas that can help to design interventions that meet those objectives. They know what has worked and hasn't worked in similar situations. And they can anticipate how proposed plans, programs, and policies are likely to affect their lives.

The hurdles in the first step of the pathway that block their entry to the process can be overcome in two ways: by inviting members of these groups to participate in opportunities organized by others; and by enabling them to initiate opportunities on their own.

Kinds of Opportunities. The opportunities in community participation processes are the venues where players express their ideas, but opportunities vary substantially in the kinds of ideas they enable players to express. The pathway to influence draws attention to this important characteristic of opportunities and to the range of ideas that different players can express in the opportunities that are available to them. Marginalized and ordinary residents face serious hurdles in this regard, which limit the domains where their ideas have any potential to be influential. But these hurdles can be overcome if steps are taken to assure that marginalized and ordinary residents have access to opportunities covering all of the areas that matter in participation processes:

- Identifying important issues, problems, and needs
- Determining which issues, problems, and needs move forward to be developed
   into plans, programs, and policies
- Contributing to the design and implementation of plans, programs, and policies
- Defining what success looks like and means
- Deciding how they and other community members are involved in the process.

Providing marginalized and ordinary residents with this range of opportunities is important not only for the residents, but also for the process at large. The opportunities give marginalized and ordinary residents the potential to influence which issues get on the agenda and how those issues are addressed. By giving them this potential for influence, the process is more likely to focus on issues that historically excluded groups really care about and to develop actions that will work for them.

One way to give marginalized and ordinary residents this range of opportunities is to include them not only in specially constructed participation exercises—where their ideas have a limited potential for influence—but also in ongoing meetings of lead players and other community organizations and groups. These meetings are not generally considered to be part of community participation processes in the literature because they are not created for the specific purpose of promoting community engagement. Nonetheless, we found that these meetings play critical roles in the pathway to influence by giving participants the opportunity to develop initial plans and proposals, design the community participation process, discuss the ideas that the broader community contributes through participation exercises, and decide which ideas move forward and what should be done.

Conditions of Opportunities. Having access to the full range of opportunities is critical, but the conditions of each opportunity determine the extent to which marginalized and ordinary residents are able to take advantage of them and to express and communicate their ideas when they do. Our study shows that it is possible to create supportive conditions that enhance the potential for the ideas of these residents to be influential within an opportunity. One of the reasons that marginalized and ordinary residents need to be involved in designing participation processes is that their ideas are required to create such conditions.

Participation supports *(first step of the pathway).* To give marginalized and ordinary residents real opportunities for participation, members of these groups need to be aware that they are invited. In addition, participation needs to be feasible for them.

Participation processes can create such conditions by working with marginalized and ordinary residents to prepare understandable and useful information about available opportunities for members of these groups, get this information to them in a timely manner, select times and venues that will be convenient for them, and provide the kinds of assistance that some of them will need, such as transportation and child care.

Expression supports *(second step of the pathway).* Having a seat at the table doesn't mean much for marginalized and ordinary residents unless the opportunity enables them to express what they want to say.

Participation processes can play a very supportive role in this regard by creating conditions where the ideas of marginalized and ordinary residents are valued by everyone involved in each opportunity — the facilitator, the other kinds of players, and the residents, themselves. One way to achieve this objective is to discuss why different kinds of players are involved in the process and why their ideas are needed. Such a discussion can help the group recognize that the process requires expertise drawn from life experiences as well as formal education and training. It can also help participants appreciate what marginalized and ordinary residents know from their life experiences that players with clout, resources, or acknowledged expertise don't know, but that the process, as a whole, needs to know.

To address other hurdles that prevent marginalized and ordinary residents from expressing their ideas during an opportunity, participation processes can work with members of these groups to create conditions where residents feel safe and comfortable and are able to express their ideas in a voice that is meaningful to them, such as by telling personal stories. They can develop nonthreatening ways to seek out the ideas of residents who feel inhibited speaking up on their own. And they can pay close attention to the framing of issues and questions to make sure that marginalized and ordinary residents are able to think about issues in ways that are meaningful to them and to express the ideas that really matter to them. In some community participation processes, achieving these objectives may require the use of different frames of reference for different kinds of players or the creation of opportunities that enable particular kinds of players to come together on their own.

Communication supports *(third step of the pathway)*. To be influential, the ideas that marginalized and ordinary residents express during an opportunity need to be communicated to players who can help move the ideas forward and act on them.

The most direct way to support the communication of marginalized and ordinary residents' ideas is to involve them in opportunities where they can interact and discuss ideas repeatedly with other kinds of players over time. A support mentioned earlier — involving marginalized and ordinary residents in ongoing meetings of lead players and other community organizations and groups—can be very helpful in this regard. Creating conditions where the ideas of marginalized and ordinary residents are valued by players with clout, resources, or acknowledged expertise not only makes it easier for residents to express their ideas in this kind of opportunity, but also makes it less likely that their ideas will be dismissed.

The ideas of all players in an opportunity run the risk of being misunderstood, particularly when they come from diverse backgrounds. To overcome this hurdle — and to prevent players with clout, resources, or acknowledged expertise from making assumptions about what marginalized and ordinary residents mean to say — participation processes can encourage everyone involved in each opportunity to express their ideas clearly and specifically. The use of common language and concrete examples, and the avoidance of jargon, acronyms, and sound bites can help to promote more accurate communication.

The other barriers to communication in participation processes can be overcome by paying attention to the way expressed ideas are recorded and reported in opportunities. Ideas are the most valuable asset that any participation process produces, but if the ideas that are generated in an opportunity aren't documented well, they run the risk of being lost. This is a serious hurdle for marginalized and ordinary residents, who often have few opportunities to express their ideas directly to players who can move them forward or act on them. To preserve ideas for later use, and to make it possible for ideas to be disseminated more broadly, participation processes need to record and report the ideas that players express in each opportunity faithfully and completely. To assess the voice and influence of different kinds of players in the process, their ideas need to be differentiated from each other and documented as clearly and specifically as they were expressed.

Relationship among Opportunities. Participation processes are comprised of multiple opportunities, and interactions among these opportunities play a critical role in moving ideas along the pathway to influence.

Our study found that influence is rarely achieved in a single opportunity. Instead, ideas move from opportunity to opportunity as they advance along the pathway. Players often need more than one opportunity to be able to express what they want to say to players who need to hear them. When the players who hear an idea directly do not carry it forward, the idea needs to be relayed or reported to players in other opportunities. After decisions are made to move ideas forward, additional opportunities are usually required to bring ideas from different players together, transform them into "doable" plans, and put those plans into action.

Some of the hurdles that block the communication and use of marginalized and ordinary residents' ideas are related to interconnections among opportunities. Participation processes can overcome these hurdles through supports that focus on the dissemination of ideas generated in opportunities, the sequencing of opportunities, and the addition of opportunities.

Dissemination of ideas (*third step of the pathway*). A support mentioned above — the faithful and complete recording and reporting of ideas generated in an opportunity — is a prerequisite to disseminating those ideas further to players who can help move the ideas forward or act on them. Participation processes can promote the influence of ideas contributed by marginalized and ordinary residents by assuring that they will be transmitted to players in other opportunities in the process. Ideas that matter to marginalized and ordinary residents, but go beyond the scope of the process in which they participated, can still be influential if they are shared with interested players in the broader community.

Sequencing of opportunities (*fourth step of the pathway*). The use of ideas contributed by marginalized and ordinary residents is often limited by decisions made by other players in opportunities that occur before and after the ones in which the residents are involved. For example, if the lead players have already decided what they want to do before other community members are engaged in the process, any ideas that residents raise about serious problems they are facing or about actions that are not closely aligned with the lead players' plans are unlikely to be considered to be relevant by the lead players. Decisions about the use of residents' ideas tend to be made by lead players in meetings that occur after the community participation exercises.

Participation processes can overcome these hurdles in three ways: by focusing on problems before developing actions or solutions; by assuring that opportunities for marginalized and ordinary residents begin early in the process— before proposals and plans have been developed; and by assuring that residents are involved in opportunities subsequent to their participation exercises where decisions about the ideas they have contributed will be made.

Addition of opportunities (*fourth step of the pathway*). Our study found that participation processes evolve over time and that the addition of new opportunities— not envisioned at the outset—can play important roles in promoting the use of ideas contributed by marginalized and ordinary residents.

Opportunities, such as surveys and public forums, can be introduced to transform the ideas of marginalized and ordinary residents into accepted knowledge that powerful players take seriously. For example, by conducting surveys based on residents' ideas and preparing reports of the findings, researchers can turn residents' anecdotal experiences into data and language that experts and decision makers respect and understand.

New opportunities can be created to bring marginalized and ordinary residents together with interested players who can help them develop their ideas into "doable" plans and put those plans into action. Participation processes can also work to develop projects, programs, and policies that create opportunities for marginalized and ordinary residents to act on their own ideas.

How Can We Use These Findings to Improve Our Participation Processes?

Our study generated a lot of the information we were seeking at the outset. As a result, we now know how to tell if our participation processes are doing what we want them to be doing. We know the types of hurdles that stand in the way and the kinds of strategies that can overcome them. We also know that working to level the playing field for marginalized and ordinary residents is worth the effort. That's all well and good, but how do we — and everyone else who aspires to realize the promise of community participation — use this information to improve what we do in practice?

Acting on what we've learned seems daunting at first because influence is path-dependent. Consequently, if we want to realize the promise of community participation, we need to pay attention to all of the steps in the pathway. Overcoming hurdles at only some of the steps but not others is not likely to be effective. For example, if marginalized and ordinary residents don't have opportunities to express what they want to say, introducing supports to promote the communication of ideas or the use of ideas won't matter for them, since their ideas won't have entered the process in the first place. Introducing supports to assure that marginalized and ordinary residents have opportunities to participate and to express what they want to say won't result in their ideas being influential if hurdles that prevent the communication or use of their ideas haven't been addressed as well.

While there is a lot to keep in mind, the good news is that we and other practitioners don't have to start from scratch. Our processes already incorporate practices that support the influence of historically excluded groups. To move forward, we need a way to distinguish these practices from those that are inadvertently hindering influence — in other words, to distinguish what we want to keep on doing from what we need to change. The ***Table of Hurdles and Supports in the Pathway*** can be helpful in this regard, since it provides us with a framework for identifying the particular hurdles and supports in our processes. Reflecting on our work, we can conduct a "process scan" that not only tells us which hurdles and supports have characterized our processes in the past, but also how consistently they have been in play. Process scans are likely to be more accurate if some of the players who participated in these processes are involved — particularly marginalized and ordinary residents, since most of the hurdles and supports apply to them.

The table also provides a framework that can enable practitioners to learn from each other. The key to this kind of learning is to find, and link up with, other practitioners who are using supportive strategies that address the particular hurdles that our own processes need to overcome. By conducting a process scan, we automatically identify the supportive strategies we have been using that we can share with others, and we also identify the hurdles in our processes for which we need supports. If practitioners have a way to share this information and communicate with each other, we can learn from each other and institute the particular supports we need. Our goal is to create a web-based platform that would promote cross-process learning among the many practitioners around the world who share our aspiration to realize the promise of community participation. With contributions based on all of our experiences, the field's knowledge of hurdles and supportive strategies is sure to grow.

Going over the table, we realized that a number of important attributes of participation processes were not high on our radar screens before. To keep them in mind in planning new community participation processes, we developed two questionnaires for us and other practitioners to use. The first, *Identifying People with Needed Ideas*, poses a set of questions to help us clarify who will need to be involved in the process and the

---

Identifying People with Needed Ideas

(1) Is the process starting with a problem or an action?
- If it is starting with an action, what problem is the action trying to address?

(2) Who is experiencing the problem directly?
- How do these people characterize the problem?
- Is it a problem for them? If so, how?
- What are their ideas about the causes of the problem?
- How much does this problem matter to them? What problems matter more?

(3) Who else is affected by the problem?
- How do people in these groups characterize the problem?
- How does the problem affect them?
- What are their ideas about the causes of the problem?
- How much does the problem matter to them? What problems matter more?

(4) What is the problem that needs to be addressed?
- Based on ideas generated in (2) and (3), was the original framing of the problem correct or does it need to be changed?

(5) What can be done to address the problem?
- What do people who are experiencing the problem directly think they or others can do? What does a solution to the problem look like to them?
- What do other people who are affected by the problem think they or others can do? What does a solution to the problem look like to them?
- What are the views of people who have relevant expertise and/or have dealt with similar kinds of problems elsewhere? What does a solution to the problem look like to them?

(6) Whose ideas are needed to design the actions?
- Who are the actions intended to help?
- Who else will be affected by the actions?
- Who will be involved in carrying out the actions?
- Who has had success implementing similar kinds of actions elsewhere?
- Who else has relevant knowledge or experience?

kinds of ideas these players will need to contribute. The second questionnaire, ***Optimizing Opportunities for Marginalized and Ordinary Residents*** (on pages 216–217), is designed to help us anticipate hurdles in the process that are likely to constrain the voice and influence of members of these groups so we can institute needed supports beforehand.

The table and questionnaires show us what we need to do to promote the voice and influence of historically excluded groups in our participation processes. But we won't make much progress in taking those steps unless we also change the way we think about what we're doing. In the course of conducting our study and reflecting on the findings, we recognized that certain patterns of thinking—common among practitioners of community participation—were preventing us from doing what we want to be doing. To apply what we learned, we found that our thinking about community participation needs to change in four ways:

- From involving marginalized and ordinary residents in the process to giving them influence through the process
- From seeking to speak in one voice to eliciting many voices
- From making assumptions about the people we want to help to hearing their ideas directly
- From giving historically excluded groups influence at the margins to assuring they have influence that counts.

From involvement to influence

Before we began our study, we thought about community participation in terms of involving community members in the process and their participation in the process. Now, we no longer see participation as an end in itself. Instead, we think about what we want it to accomplish—give people who have been excluded from decision making an influential voice. Voice and influence are all about ideas, and we discovered that the key to being able to achieve these objectives is to make players' ideas the central focus of our participation processes.

When we pay close attention to the ideas of different players, we see our work in new ways. We understand how community participation processes give players an influential voice—by enabling them to contribute, combine, and use their ideas to address issues that matter to them in ways that work for them. We appreciate the broad range of ideas that are needed to identify, understand, and solve problems as well as the kinds of players who have that knowledge. Our notion of opportunities expands to include all of the venues where players can express, communicate, and act on their ideas—not just participation exercises—and we become aware of conditions within opportunities, and relationships among opportunities, that determine whose ideas are able to advance along the pathway to influence. Our notion of success becomes clearer, too, because we can gage the influence of historically excluded groups by looking at the extent to which their ideas shape the issues the process takes on and the way the process addresses those issues.

Once this shift in thinking occurs, it's hard to be complacent about what we are doing. We no longer feel content when marginalized and ordinary residents are invited to participate in a process or even when they are given a seat at the table. We want to make sure that they can express ideas that really matter to them, that their ideas are documented specifically and completely, that they can exchange and combine their ideas with

Optimizing Opportunities for Marginalized and Ordinary Residents

1. What opportunities will they have to participate in the process?

- Will they be invited to participate in ongoing meetings of lead players and other community organizations and groups as well as exercises created for the specific purpose of promoting community engagement?
- Will they be able to initiate opportunities on their own?

2. Will these opportunities enable them to:

- Identify issues, problems, and needs that matter to them?
- Determine which issues, problems, and needs move forward in the process to be developed into plans, programs, and policies?
- Contribute to the design and implementation of plans, programs, and policies?
- Define what success looks like and means?
- Decide how they and other community members are involved in the process?

3. At what stage in the process will their opportunities take place?

- What decisions will have been made prior to their opportunities?
- Will proposals and plans have been developed before their first opportunity?

4. Will they be able to take advantage of their opportunities?

- What will be done to make sure they are aware of the opportunities?
- Will the places and times be convenient for them?
- Will they have access to needed assistance, such as transportation and child care?
- Will any other barriers need to be overcome?

5. Will they be able to express what they want to say during their opportunities?

- What will be done to assure that all participants understand why marginalized and ordinary residents are involved and why their ideas are needed?
- Will their ideas be actively sought out?
- Will they be able to express their ideas in ways that are meaningful to them, such as by telling personal stories?
- What will be done to create conditions that are safe and comfortable for them?
- What will be done to assure that the opportunities allow them to think about issues in ways that are meaningful to them and express ideas that really matter to them?
- Will they be involved in the framing of issues and questions in their opportunities?

6. Will their ideas be communicated to other players who can move them forward or act on them?

- Will their opportunities enable them to interact and discuss ideas repeatedly with other kinds of players over time?
- What will be done to assure that they and other participants express their ideas clearly and specifically?
- How will the ideas that are expressed in the opportunities be documented?
- Will the ideas of participants be differentiated?
- What will be done to assure that the records and reports of ideas are accurate and complete?
- Who will see the records and reports?
- Will they be transmitted to players in other opportunities?
- Will they be shared with interested players in the broader community?

7. How will the process promote the use of their ideas?

- Will they be involved in deciding how the ideas generated in their opportunities are used or will those decisions be made by other players?
- Will they have opportunities to work with other players who can transform their ideas into data and language that experts and decision makers will respect and understand?
- Will they have opportunities to work with other players who have the resources and capacity to act on their ideas?
- Will the process develop projects, programs, and policies that enable them to act on their own ideas?

those of other players, and that their ideas are used to make something they care about happen. We also feel less satisfied with reports of participation processes in the literature, which frequently describe who was invited and sometimes who came, but very rarely tell us what the different players said, whose ideas were included in the product of the process, whose ideas were acted upon, and whose fell by the wayside. Our new focus on the influence of ideas makes it clear that we and others who want to realize the promise of community participation have a way to go before we are consistently doing what we want to be doing. But now we also have a way to think about our work that makes the achievement of that goal possible.

From one voice to many voices

Making ideas the central focus of our practice means that we need to elicit and document the ideas of the different players in a participation process. That may sound straightforward, but as we discovered in the early stages of our study, the strong tendency of some participation processes to speak with a unitary voice makes the differentiation of players' ideas difficult.

Community-driven partnerships, like those in the Pathways Workgroup, tend to speak with one voice — the voice of the community — which masks the ideas of different kinds of players in their participation processes. When participation processes seek to achieve consensus, as many do, they explicitly avoid identifying differences in players' ideas. To conduct our investigation, we needed to introduce a prism to reveal the rich spectrum of ideas of the various players in each case. We found that a prism is needed in practice, too, because we can't promote the voice and influence of historically excluded groups unless our processes differentiate the ideas of members of these groups from the ideas of other players.

There is no reason to believe that putting a prism in the process will prevent the development of community voice or consensus. In fact, by eliciting and recording different players' ideas, identifying where their ideas are aligned, and combining their ideas to generate new knowledge about problems and potential solutions, a participation process can facilitate the development of a genuine consensus and identify areas where speaking in a unitary community voice is justified. In practice, this is akin to using a prism in reverse (if that were possible). The process starts with the differentiated ideas of its players and uses the prism to bring some of their ideas together. When we work in this way, community voice and consensus occur as an outcome of the process rather than as a predefined requirement or goal.

From making assumptions to going to the source

To investigate the cases in our study, we needed to become idea detectives, not only looking for evidence about who said what, but also seeing if we could learn the ideas of players who were experiencing the problems in the case or who would be affected by the actions that were being proposed or undertaken. Going to the source turned out to be a critical strategy in the investigation. It led us to important ideas of marginalized and ordinary residents that would otherwise have been overlooked. It also revealed when other players in the cases were basing decisions on incorrect assumptions.

Our experiences conducting the study highlight the importance of going to the source in practice. Community participation processes can't avoid generating incorrect ideas or preventing players from speaking on behalf of others. At a societal level, marginalized residents are often spoken for by others, and since we don't know what we don't know, everyone runs the risk of making mistaken assumptions. What processes can do is make sure that all players—especially members of "target populations"—speak for themselves so that incorrect assumptions are identified before they become influential.

The questionnaire, *Identifying People with Needed Ideas*, shows us whose voices need to be heard directly and what the other players in the process need to learn from them. Using this questionnaire to "go to the source" changes the way we think about ideas in the process. When an issue or problem gets raised, we want to hear from the people experiencing the problem directly to make sure that it actually is a problem for them and, if so, how and to what extent. When an action is proposed, we want to hear from the people the action is intended to help to make sure that it is something they actually want and need and, if so, what would make it work well for them. As the process applies what is learned by going to the source, problems are reframed and action proposals are modified or discarded. We begin to recognize what we don't know and to appreciate what the people we have been making assumptions about know.

From influence at the margins to influence that counts

Thinking about our work in terms of the influence of ideas raises a challenging issue for practitioners who want to realize the promise of community participation. We want our processes to give historically excluded groups an influential voice about issues that affect their lives. But how much influence do our processes actually give them?

Optimally, community participation processes should enable marginalized and ordinary residents to raise issues that matter to them a lot and to get those issues addressed in ways that work for them. Yet our study and the broader literature suggest that this doesn't happen very often in practice.[16]

When processes give marginalized and ordinary residents opportunities to raise issues they care about, these issues either tend to be addressed by other players—not necessarily in the way the residents intended—or not addressed at all. When processes begin with a plan or proposal for action, the actions are rarely based on ideas proposed by marginalized and ordinary residents, themselves. In some cases, residents have a lot of influence designing these actions, but the action may not be something they care about or want. In others, they have little influence, especially when the lead players start with well-developed ideas about the actions they want to carry out.

In many processes, the role of marginalized and ordinary residents is limited to providing information for other players to use, which means that the influence of their ideas depends entirely on decisions made by those players. In this role, residents have no way to move forward ideas they care about, to exchange and combine their ideas with other kinds of players, or to work with other players to develop their ideas into "doable" plans and put them into action.

If we want to realize the promise of community participation, we need to become less content with giving historically excluded groups influence at the margin and work to create processes that give them influence that counts. Some of the supportive strategies identified in our study can be helpful in this regard. The influence of marginalized and ordinary residents in participation processes can be enhanced dramatically by including them in ongoing meetings of lead players and other community organizations and groups—but only if the conditions of these meetings enable their voices to be influential. Ideas of marginalized and ordinary residents that go beyond the scope of a process can still be influential if the process takes responsibility for sharing those ideas with interested players in the broader community and for bringing residents together with those players.

Ultimately, however, we believe that new kinds of participation processes will be required to achieve this goal, such as processes that are initiated by marginalized and ordinary residents, and processes that use their ideas as a basis for action and funding. Moving in this direction will involve an even bigger shift in thinking. We hope that practitioners, funders, members of historically excluded groups, and others who share our aspirations will join us on that journey.

Chapter Notes

For chapters 1 through 10, the codes (e.g., CV-D-050) refer to documents and interview transcripts from the case investigations. If not otherwise specified, web sites were accessed from September 2007 to January 2008.

Introduction

1. Arnstein, 1969; Barber, 1984; Beierle, 1998; Carr & Halvorsen, 2001; Chaskin 2001; Corburn, 2005; Creighton, 2005; Crosby & Nethercut, 2005; Fischer, 2000; Francis, 2001; Fraser, Lepofsky, Kick & Williams, 2003; Gastil & Levine, 2005; Gibson, 2006; Lasker & Weiss, 2003; Minkler & Wallerstein, 2003; Pateman, 1970; Perlman & Susskind, 1983; Pimbert & Wakeford, 2001; Rowe & Frewer, 2000; Skocpol, 2004.

2. Arnstein, 1969; Barber, 1984; Carson & Hartz-Karp, 2005; Cornwall & Gaventa, 2001; Fraser, 1992; Gibson, 2006; Guidry & Sawyer, 2003; Highlander Research and Education Center; Pateman 1970; Mansbridge 1980 and 2001; Pimbert & Wakeford, 2001; Skocpol, 2004.

3. Bruner, 2000; McKnight 1985 and 1995.

4. Chrislip, 1994; Creighton, 2005; Pew Research Center for the People and the Press, 2003; Pimbert & Wakeford, 2001.

5. Gibson, 2006; Lukensmeyer, Goldman & Brigham, 2005.

6. Camerer, Loewenstein & Weber, 1989; Creighton, 2005; Pimbert & Wakeford, 2001; Stirling & Gee, 2002.

7. Arnstein, 1969; Beierle, 1998; Briggs, 2002; Chiu, 2003; Collins, 2005; Corburn, 2003 and 2005; Creighton, 2005; Cunningham-Burley, Kerr, & Pavis, 2001; Fischer, 2000; Fraser, Lepovsky, Kick, & Williams, 2003; Geertz, 1983; Hendriks, 2005; Khakee, Barbanente, & Borri, 2000; Lasker, 2004; Lenaghan, 2001; Lindblom & Cohen, 1979; Mirenowicz, 2001; Nader, 1996; Rowe, Marsh, & Frewer, 2004; Sclove, 2001.

8. Arnstein, 1969; Beierle, 1998; Caine, Salomons & Simmons, 2007; Cheatham & Shen, 2003; Corburn, 2003; Creighton, 2005; Fraser & Lepofsky, 2004; Lasker, 2004; Lasker, Hunter, & Francis, 2007; Pimbert & Wakeford, 2001; Stirling, 2006; Tau Lee, Krause & Goetchius, 2003.

9. Bohman & Rehg, 1997; Vox, 1998; Button & Ryfe, 2005; Creighton, 2005; Denhardt & Denhardt, 2000; Gibson, 2006; King & Stivers, 1998; Pateman, 1970.

10. Mill, 1859.

11. Anderson & Jaeger, 2001; Annenberg Institute for School Reform, 1998; Arnstein, 1969; Barber, 2001; Beierle, 1998; Bgeholz, 2006; Bonner et. al, 2005; Briggs,

2002; Button & Ryfe, 2005; Caine, Salomons & Simmons, 2007; Carr & Halvorsen, 2001; Carson, 2006; Charles, Sokoloff & Satullo, 2005; Chaskin 2001; Cheatham & Shen, 2003; Cheng & Fiero, 2005; Chiu, 2003; Clements-Nolle & Bachrach, 2003; Coelho, Pozzoni & Montoya, 2005; Cohen, 2005; Connell & Kubisch, 1998; Corburn, 2005; Cornwall & Gaventa, 2001; Creighton, 2005; Crosby, Kelly & Schaefer, 1986; Crosby 1995; Crosby & Nethercut, 2005; Cunninghan-Burley, Kerr & Pavis, 2001; Delap, 2001; Fawcett et. al, 1996; Fischer, 2000; Fishkin & Farrar, 2005; Francis, 2001; Fraser, Lepofsky, Kick & Williams, 2003; Fraser, 2004; Fraser & Lepofsky, 2004; Fraser & Kick, 2007; Frediani, 2007; Gastil & Kieth, 2005; Gibson, 2006; Hart & Rajbhandry, 2003; Hendriks, 2005; Holmes & Scoones, 2001; Irwin, 2001; Israel et. al, 2001; Karpowitz & Mansbridge, 2005; Khakee, Barbanente & Borri, 2000; Lasker & Weiss, 2003; Lasker, 2004; Lasker, Hunter, & Francis, 2007; Lavalle, Acharya & Houtzager, 2005; Lenaghan, 2001; Lukensmeyer, Goldman & Brighan, 2005; Mansbridge, 2006; Melville, Willingham & Dedrick, 2005; Minkler & Wallerstein, 2003; Mirenowicz, 2001; Morello-Frosch et. al, 2005; Murty & Wakeford, 2001; Pateman, 1970; Perlman & Susskind, 1983; Peterson et. al, 2006; Pimbert, 2001; Pimbert & Wakeford, 2001; Potapchuk, Carlson & Kennedy, 2005; Rowe & Frewer, 2004; Schultz et. al, 2003; Schwinn, Kesler & Schwinn, 2005; Sclove, 2001; Scully & McCoy, 2005; Sokoloff, Steinberg & Pyser, 2005; Stirling, 2001; Tau Lee, Krause & Goetchius, 2003; UN-HABITAT, 2006; Wakeford, 2001(a&b); Wallace, 2001; Weiksner, 2005.

12. Arnstein, 1969.

13. Holmes & Scoones, 2001.

14. Bonner et. al, 2005; Levine, Fung & Gastil, 2005; Melville, Willingham & Dedrick, 2005; Murty & Wakeford, 2001.

15. Cornwall & Gaventa, 2001.

16. Caine, Salomons & Simmons, 2007; Cook & Kothari, 2001; Corburn, 2003; Cornwall & Gaventa, 2001; Frediani, 2007; Fraser, Lepofsky, Kick & Williams, 2002; Fraser & Lepofsky, 2004; Gibson, 2006; Hendriks, 2005; Irwin, 2001; Levine, Fung & Gastil, 2005; Pimbert & Wakeford, 2001.

17. Carson & Hartz-Karp, 2005; Cornwall & Gaventa, 2001.

18. Fraser and Lepofsky, 2004; Levine, Fung & Gastil, 2005.

19. Cornwall & Gaventa, 2001; Fraser, Lepofsky, Kick & Williams, 2002.

20. Beierle, 1998; Button & Ryfe, 2005; Carson & Hartz-Karp, 2005; Levine, Fung & Gastil, 2005; Pimbert & Wakeford, 2001; Rowe, Marsh & Frewer, 2004; Scully & McCoy, 2005; Wakeford, 2001(a&b).

21. Karpowitz & Mansbridge, 2005.

22. Abelson et. al, 2003; Carson & Hartz-Karp, 2005; Creighton, 2005; Levine, Fung & Gastil, 2005; Rowe, Marsh & Frewer, 2004; Wakeford, 2001.

23. Abelson et. al, 2003; Beierle, 1998; Francis, 2001; Fraser, Lepofsky, Kick & Williams, 2002; Gibson, 2006; Levine, Fung & Gastil, 2005; Pimbert & Wakeford, 2001.

24. Francis, 2001.

Chapter 1

1. CV-D-050.
2. CV-D-050.
3. CV-I-003, p. 11.
4. This and much of what follows about the loss of land and resources comes from CV-D-112, Larry Oakes, "Key events in tribe's troubled history," Minneapolis-St. Paul *StarTribune* (21 February 2005).
5. This and much of what follows about the loss of culture comes from CV-D-113, "Beacons of Hope" by Larry Oakes. Minneapolis-St. Paul *StarTribune* (April 26, 2004).
6. CV-I-004, pp. 12–13. See also CV-D-113.
7. CV-I-005, p. 11.
8. CV-I-002, p. 6.
9. CV-G-001, p. 9.
10. CV-I-009, p. 2.
11. CV-G-003, pp. 7–12.
12. CV-I-002, p. 6.
13. CV-D-050, p.2.
14. CV-D-032.
15. CV-I-004, p. 4.
16. CV-D-024.
17. CV-D-050, p. 1.
18. CV-I-004, p. 14.
19. CV-I-009, p. 3.
20. CV-I-004, p. 6.
21. CV-D-056 for Louise Smith's knowledge about police corruption and abuse.
22. CV-I-012, p. 7; CV-I-004, p. 12.
23. CV-I-012, p. 5.
24. CV-I-004, p. 10.
25. CV-D-024.
26. Cass Lake City Juvenile Statistics 1997–June 30, 2007.
27. CV-I-002, p. 5.
28. CV-I-001, p. 14.
29. CV-I-001, p. 2.
30. CV-G-001, p. 17.
31. CV-D-111.
32. All information that follows on the two November youth summits is derived from the analysis of CV-D-074 (CL-B summit) and CV-D-077 (LL Res summit) unless otherwise noted.
33. CV-D-077.
34. CV-D-080 2/18/99.
35. CV-D-081.
36. CV-D-082.
37. CV-G-001, p. 14.
38. CV-I-010, p. 15. This quote is attributed (heard by

the director of the Boys & Girls Club), but it is confirmed in other interviews.

39. CV-D-075.
40. CV-I-004, p. 14. Corroborated in CV-D-050 (Randy Fisher [Cass County Sheriff's Department] to Dennis Cusick [Upper Midwest Center for Community Policing]); the letter is not dated but content shows it to have been written in late April 1999.
41. From the organization website, *www.umcpi.org*.
42. CV-I-005, p. 3.
43. CV-D-050.
44. CV-I-004, p. 14.
45. CV-D-091.
46. CV-I-004, p. 16.
47. CV-I-005, pp. 5–6. A former police officer from Cass Lake stated that some members of CVAV were "against the police" and that the survey was "tainted" because CVAV used people who had police records to administer it in the community [CV-I-011, p. 2].
48. CV-I-004, pp. 16–17.
49. CV-D-008.
50. CV-I-004, p. 18.
51. CV-D-056.
52. CV-I-005, p. 7.
53. CV-I-005, pp. 8–9.
54. CV-D-132.
55. CV-I-005, p. 15.
56. CV-I-005, p. 10.
57. CV-I-007, p. 6.
58. CV-I-012, part 2, p. 14.
59. CV-D-121.
60. CV-D-121.
61. CV-I-006, p. 7.

Chapter 2

1. In this narrative, the "Humboldt Park area" refers to the neighborhoods around the park. The city of Chicago designates community areas based on census information, while neighborhoods are defined by residents according to more natural boundaries. The city calls the east side of the park West Town, and the area west of the park, Humboldt Park. The official "Humboldt Park" extends well west of the "Humboldt Park area" that the Humboldt Park Empowerment Partnership services. Demographically, official "West Town" is about 50 percent Latino, and official "Humboldt Park" is about 50 percent African American. But the "Humboldt Park area" that is served by the partnership is mostly Latino.
2. HPEP Round 1 Pathways to Collaboration Workgroup Report, pp. 3–4.
3. LU-I-006, p. 2 and LU-I-015 p. 3.
4. LU-D-042, LU-D-020 February 1998 and September 1999 tax credit applications. The developments are 1414 North Washtenaw, the Borinquen Apartments, and the SRO.
5. HPEP Round 1 Pathways to Collaboration Workgroup Report, p. 11.
6. HPEP Round 1 Pathways to Collaboration Workgroup Report, p. 21.
7. LU-D-020, p. 15; September 1999 tax credit application (selection criteria section).
8. LU-I-001, p. 15.
9. LU-I-001, p. 2.
10. LU-G-002, p. 1.
11. LU-I-013, p. 2.
12. LU-I-005, p. 3. The investigation could not find the women who met with Ocasio on that occasion. However,

the conversation is corroborated by several people who were involved with LUCHA at the time, and the previously cited conversations from the 1980s and 1990s confirm that these kinds of issues were known in the community. Though there were conversations between Ocasio and some of the mothers, there is no evidence that the mothers participated in generating the ideas in his concept for a large development with services. See LU-I-017, p. 4.

13. LU-D-042; see also LU-I-004, p. 4.

14. LU-I-004, p. 18.

15. LU-I-004, p. 18.

16. LU-I-001, p. 18.

17. LU-I-017, p. 2.

18. According to the HUD website: "The Section 8 Rental Voucher Program increases affordable housing choices for very low-income households by allowing families to choose privately owned rental housing. The public housing authority (PHA) generally pays the landlord the difference between 30 percent of household income and the PHA-determined payment standard–about 80 to 100 percent of the fair market rent (FMR). The rent must be reasonable. The household may choose a unit with a higher rent than the FMR and pay the landlord the difference or choose a lower cost unit and keep the difference." See *http://www.hud.gov/progdesc/voucher.cfm.*

19. LU-I-011, pp. 2–6, 9, 14.

20. LU-D-042, February 1998 Tax Credit application. The Low-Income Housing Tax Credit (LIHTC) is a program that benefits housing development corporations who build affordable housing. The LIHTC is a 10-year credit to the income tax assessment of the project owner equal to 70 percent of the present value of any new project, or 30 percent of the present value of a previously constructed project (U.S. Title 26 Internal Revenue Code, Section 42: *http://frwebgate.access.gpo.gov/cgi-bin/get doc.cgi?dbname=browse_usc&docid=Cite:+26USC42*) A project owner in Chicago first submits an application to the city DOH, who then enters it to the Illinois Housing Development Authority, which allocates a limited number of tax credits each year. The application includes estimates of the expected cost of the project and a commitment to comply with either of the following conditions, known as "set-asides." For Illinois, these are defined as "a rental project in which at least 25 percent of the units that have rents (including tenant-paid heat) that do not exceed, on a monthly basis, 30 percent of the gross monthly income of a Household earning the maximum income for a Low-Income Household in the geographical area in which the Affordable Housing Project is located and that are occupied by persons and families who qualify as Low-Income Households; or a unit for sale to Low-Income Households and who will pay no more than 30 percent of their gross household income for mortgage principal, interest, property taxes, and property insurance upon the purchase of the unit." (Illinois Joint Committee on Administrative Code, *http://www.ilga.gov/com mission/jcar/admincode/047/04700355sections.html*).

21. LU-D-003. There is no evidence from this document review that anyone from MUA attended this meeting.

22. LU-D-031, LU-D-032.

23. Handwritten notes on the fact sheet (LU-D-032).

24. An agenda from the meeting contains the following handwritten notes for the key players, which are consistent with all evidence the investigation has found. "United Blks of [West] H.P. we do supp concept of project + work w/. LUCHA for alt. site"; the Chair of HPEP "Does not support project housing site on Spaulding +

Division"; "Block Club [Federation] not at this site, don't want this in their neighborhood, no more social services in the area"; "Ex Dir" [of NNNN] "Supports project but not the site." [LU-D-031].

25. A member of United Blocks characterized the reaction of long time owners, "it was everybody else who had lived there for years and years and years, black and Hispanic, that were like, 'We're not having this. We just got rid of this garbage. We don't want more'" [LU-I-015, p. 10].

26. LU-I-006, p.10.

27. LU-I-006, pp. 6–10.

28. LU-I-015, pp. 9–10.

29. LU-I-015, p. 6.

30. LU-I-015, p. 9. Receiving the housing for "free" was United Blocks' characterization of the issue; in fact, single mothers would pay rent, but subsidies and support for the project would keep their rent below market levels.

31. LU-I-018.

32. LU-D-018.

33. LU-D-031.

34. LU-D-020.

35. All information in this paragraph is from LU-D-020.

36. LU-I-001.

37. LU-D-028.

38. LU-I-001, p. 4.

39. LU-D-005.

40. LU-D-006.

41. LU-I-016, p. 4.

42. LU-D-046.

43. LU-I-004, p. 13.

44. LU-I-011, p. 10.

45. LU-I-003, p. 7.

46. LU-I-017, p. 6. A letter from MUA to Billy Ocasio also described the organization's role of "advocat[ing] to get the political support needed to acquire the land and ... tax credits" for the project" [LU-D-013].

47. LU-I-010, p. 4.

48. LU-I-010, p. 4.

49. LU-I-011, pp. 24, 32.

50. LU-I-018, p. 4.

51. LU-I-011, pp. 10–11 and LU-I-001, p. 27.

52. LU-I-011, p. 34.

53. LU-I-001, p. 24.

Chapter 3

1. In 1998, when the area was awarded a "Champion Community" designation in the second round of the Empowerment Zone/Enterprise Community program, the EC expanded to include census tracts in Pushmataha County, immediately to the north of Choctaw County.

2. From the Aspen Institute Roundtable on Comprehensive Community Initiatives, *http://www.commbuild. org/html_pages/showresults.asp?topic_search=primary& logic=or&template=69.htm&box=69* (accessed February 6, 2008).

3. USDA, Designation of Empowerment Zones and Enterprise Communities; Interim Rules and Notices [7 CFR Part 25] *http://www.epa.gov/fedrgstr/EPA-IMPACT/ 1998/October/Day-07/i26542.htm* (accessed February 6, 2008).

4. For additional information about the process, see the "Community Centers" case.

5. PB-D-013; questions asked included, "What are we doing now?" "How did it come to be this way?"

"Whose interests are being served by the way things are?" "What are we going to do about all of this?"

6. PB-I-002, pp. 15–16; the "peer pressure" idea is corroborated in PB-I-001, p. 2.

7. The others were for an "industrial business district," and "residential improvements (housing, renovation, landscaping, and upkeep)." See PB-D-071.

8. PB-D-071. Spelling has been corrected.

9. See http://www.grameen-info.org and Joel L. Fleishman, *The Foundation* (New York: Public Affairs, 2007), pp. 131–33.

10. The Rotary International *Revolving Loan Fund Guide* describes how to create a revolving loan fund. Its description of the process is similar to Jones's description of Dr. Frey's idea. (See http://www.rotary.org/news room/downloadcenter/pdfs/163en.pdf.)

11. We were not able to interview Dr. Frey for this investigation.

12. Though the Choctaw Nation had a member on the committee at this point, it was not very active in the Empowerment Zone process until 1998. In March 1995, after the EC had been designated but before the funding was dispersed, a fifth local census tract was added, Central Choctaw. This comprised an area outside of Hugo in Choctaw County. Central Choctaw was left out of the original application because it was thought that it didn't fit the EZ requirements. But once they had the designation, they learned that Central Choctaw did, in fact, fit the poverty profile in the EZ application guidelines, so a local steering committee was formed then.

13. Federal Register, January 18, 1994, Department of Agriculture 7 CFR Part 25, "Designation of Empowerment Zones and Enterprise Communities; Interim Rules and Notices."

14. PB-D-069 (A-21 document from the strategic plan).

15. From the two budgets in the application.

16. PB-K-011.

17. SEEDS loans were small business development loans financed through a State of Oklahoma program.

18. PB-D-024.

19. PB-I-002, p. 26.

20. PB-I-001, p. 6. The respondent does not clarify when he began to do this and doesn't provide much detail about what he did. His recollection is mainly that he had authority at some point to develop loan programs for clients from Little Dixie's various resources.

21. PB-D-016.

22. PB-I-002, p. 25.

23. PB-I-002, p. 30.

24. PB-I-002, pp. 20–21.

25. Jones was only asked to collect payments in West Idabel. We don't have any evidence on whether or not the steering committee in Central Choctaw was asked to do the same for their loans.

26. PB-I-003, p. 4.

27. PB-K-011, p. 1.

28. PB-I-002, p. 28.

29. PB-D-014, PB-D-023. The PMBC "tabled" Little Dixie's suggestion for a loan fee to offset the agency's costs in managing Poor Man's Bank loans. The issue was not taken up again.

30. PB-I-002, p. 24.

31. PB-I-002, p. 27.

32. The West Idabel steering committee, however, continued to meet for the entire duration of the EC. It evolved into the regular monthly meeting of IMAC.

33. PB-K-006, p. 2.

34. The records on the last six Poor Man's Bank loans are incomplete. Loan number 25 was made in Central Choctaw, but the loan file is not dated, so we are not treating it as part of the last set of loans. This loan was repaid in full. Also, the file for loan 29 is missing, so there is no information on it, although its place in the sequence of loan numbers (next to last, of 30 loans), indicates it was made between June and November of 2000. We can't be sure it was made in Central Choctaw, but this conclusion is the best fit for the evidence.

35. PB-K-006, p. 1, PB-K-001.

36. PB-K-002, p. 2.

37. PB-K-010, p. 2.

38. PB-K-004, p. 2.

39. PB-K-004, p. 1.

Chapter 4

1. From Bridges Summer 1998 (St. Louis Federal Register).

2. MDC web site; the organization is now known as MDC rather than "Manpower Development Corporation." http://www.mdcinc.org.

3. MG-I-005, p. 6.

4. MG-I-005, p. 3.

5. From Bridges Summer 1998 (St. Louis Federal Register) and TC-0122.

6. One of Tri-County's members, Lillie V. Davis, has written the story of her own town's founding by ex-slaves and the autonomous society and economy they developed; see *Drifting into Falcon* (Darling, Mississippi: Richardson's Writing Service, 2007). See also Cobb, pp. 72–73, quoting a plantation owner from the era named George Collins.

7. A website collecting work and features related to Mound Bayou's history may be found at http://www.madison.k12.wi.us/shabazz/Trips/Moundbayou/index.html. See also Agricultural Marketing Resource Center, "Mound Bayou Sweet Potatoes, MAC, and Glory Foods" (Iowa State University, March 2004).

8. Peter Applebome, "Deep South and Down Home, But It's a Ghetto All the Same," *New York Times* (August 21, 1993).

9. MDC web site: http://www.mdcinc.org and TC-0122.

10. The first Tri-County application was developed by a group from Coahoma, Quitman, and Tunica counties, but it was turned down because the team did not match the Foundation's diversity requirements. For the second application, the Tunica County members dropped out and were replaced by people from Bolivar County.

11. MG-D-109: Attachment to TCWA 1997 Operation Plan; also see MG-D-007.

12. MG-I-011, p. 4.

13. MG-D-109: Attachment to TCWA 1997 Operation Plan.

14. MG-D-109: Attachment to TCWA 1997 Operation Plan.

15. MG-D-109: Attachment to TCWA 1997 Operation Plan.

16. MG-I-005, p. 2.

17. MG-I-011, p. 3.

18. MG-I-011 and MG-D-102.

19. MG-D-102. Two of the strategies created entrepreneurship training and opportunities, another supported developing better public transportation services in the three county area, and another developed a "career awareness campaign." None of these strategies included "subgrants" among the actions.

20. MG-I-007, p. 13.
21. MG-I-007, p. 52.
22. MG-D-109: Mission Statement from Tri-County's 1997 Operational Plan.
23. MG-I-007, p. 69.
24. Rhymes conversation with Roz Lasker, December 13, 2007.
25. Rhymes conversation with Roz Lasker, December 13, 2007.
26. MG-D-109: Minigrant guidelines from Tri-County's 1997 Operational Plan.
27. MG-D-001.
28. Cover sheet from TCWA Minigrant Application in the 1997 Operational Plan and MG-I-007, p. 59.
29. The application also provided examples of appropriate workforce development ideas, including "issues related to workforce training," "emerging technical writing," "occupational enhancement," "building job skills," "workforce preparation," "training for out-of-school youth," "summer training," and "internships/student/teacher/business/industry." MG-D-109 (Mini-Grant Guidelines).
30. MG-D-001.
31. MG-I-007, p. 62.
32. MG-I-007, p. 63. The Foundation for the Mid South built a multi-sectoral approach into most aspects of the Workforce Alliance model, and Tri-County builds it into most of the decision-making committees that it creates for its own work, as well. Corroborated by MG-I-011, p. 14, "We knew that we wanted a diverse group of readers." This respondent adds, however, that another group beyond the educators and business persons was "grassroots people," though he isn't completely sure.
33. MG-D-094: Tri-County Workforce Alliance, "Mini-Grant Evaluation/Ratings Criteria" (no date).
34. MG-I-007, p. 56.
35. MG-I-007, p. 58.
36. MG-I-007, p. 65.
37. Tri-County offered some programs through the Skill/Tech Center and other units at the college; for more information, see the Professionalization Curriculum case.
38. MG-D-111 (Tri-County Workforce Alliance Scholarship criteria, first (1998) and second (1999) versions).
39. Quote clarified by Josephine Rhymes on January 9, 2008.
40. MG-I-007, p. 60.
41. MG-I-007, p. 63.
42. See, for example, "Tri-County announces mini grant recipients," *Clarksdale Press Register* (October 19, 2001); or "Workforce Alliance to award mini-grants," *Clarksdale Press Register* (May 1, 2002).
43. The Implementation Team deviated from this rule only once, in the spring of 2003, which was the last quarter that grants would be available.
44. Five of the awarded proposals were not fully implemented.
45. MG-D-087.
46. MG-I-007, p. 66.
47. MG-I-007, p. 65.
48. MG-D-087.
49. MG-I-011, p. 11.
50. MG-D-087.
51. MG-D-087.
52. MG-I-007, p. 71.
53. MG-I-007, p. 62.
54. MG-D-093. The specific language of the "Grant Agreement" is "Grantee will receive 50 percent of the grant award before the project begins, the remaining 50 percent to be paid during the course of the project when deemed necessary by the grantee after evaluation and approval by the monitoring committee of Tri-County Workforce Alliance (WFA)."
55. MG-D-087.
56. MG-D-087. Reporting on the direct employment in the mini-grant projects did not specify how long the jobs lasted, although in some cases it was short-term or summer employment.
57. MG-I-013, p. 13.
58. MG-I-006, p. 3.
59. MG-I-001; MG-I-002.
60. MG-I-002, p. 1.
61. MG-I-002, pp. 2–3. See also Agricultural Marketing Resource Center, "Mound Bayou Sweet Potatoes, MAC, and Glory Foods." In addition to support from Tri-County, the sweet potato growers in Mound Bayou also received assistance from the Mid-Delta Empowerment Zone, which includes Bolivar County (but not Coahoma or Quitman); see *www.ezec.gov/ezec/ms/mdeza.html*.
62. MG-I-007, p. 68.

Chapter 5

1. CO-D-003.
2. CO-I-001, pp. 1–2.
3. CL-0102, p. 1.
4. Unless otherwise noted, the population, demographic, and income figures cited in this chapter are compiled from U.S. Census data, 1999–2005, available at *www.quickfacts.census.gov* and *www.factfinder.census.gov*.
5. CO-K-001.
6. See *www.rc.org/theory/index.html*. Co-Counseling is also known as "Re-Evaluation Counseling," or "RC." It was founded by Harvey Jackins in the 1950s and is used by thousands or people in over 40 countries around the world. "No Limits for Women Artists" was founded by Betsy Damon in 1984, who was also involved with Re-Evaluation Counseling.
7. CO-I-005, p. 2.
8. CO-I-005, p. 5.
9. CO-I-001, p. 3.
10. CO-I-006, p. 2.
11. CO-I-001, pp. 3 and 5.
12. CO-I-005, p. 5.
13. "Listening pairs," as used in No Limits, developed the "intentionality of breaking up the time equally" between the members of the pair.
14. CO-I-005, pp. 5–7.
15. CO-I-005, p. 5.
16. CO-G-001, p. 2.
17. CO-G-001, p. 6.
18. CO-I-005, p. 12.
19. CO-I-005, p. 12.
20. CO-I-005, p. 14.
21. CO-I-005, p. 12.
22. CO-I-005, p. 16.
23. See *www.northwestern.edu/ipr/abcd/abcdneighcircle.html*.
24. CO-I-009, p. 1.
25. CO-I-005, p. 19.
26. CO-I-009, p. 4.
27. The CATs also changed their names at this time to "community advisory teams," and it seems that CLTm's name change was linked to that.
28. CO-G-003, p. 7.
29. CO-G-004, p. 5.
30. CO-I-012, p. 2.
31. CO-I-012, p. 8.

32. CO-G-002, p. 5
33. CO-I-005, p. 13
34. CO-I-005, p. 13.
35. CO-D-091.
36. CO-I-012, pp. 6–7.
37. CO-I-011, p. 11.
38. CO-G-001, p. 17
39. CO-D-181.
40. For more information, see "The Incorporation of Beyond Welfare" case.

Chapter 6

1. PC-D-009. "TCWA Grant Proposal to Foundation for the Mid South, Workforce Public Policy Mini-Grant," August 7, 2002.
2. PC-D-004.
3. PC-D-009.
4. All statistics from census data as reported in Workforce Report II, PC-D-031.
5. PC-I-007, p. 3.
6. MG-D-007.
7. PC-I-007, p. 32.
8. PC-D-031, pp. 14–16.
9. PC-I-003, p. 9.
10. PC-D-031, p.12.
11. PC-D-031, p. 11.
12. PC-D-031.
13. PC-I-008, p. 4.
14. PC-I-003, p. 12.
15. PC-I-003, pp. 12–13.
16. PC-I-003, p. 13.
17. PC-I-003, p. 13.
18. PC-D-111, TCWA "Workforce Development and Professionalization Curriculum."
19. The cross-sectoral composition of committees was a regular feature of Tri-County practice, which was part of the Workforce Alliance structure that the Foundation for the Mid South built into each of the seven alliances it supported.
20. PC-D-040.
21. PC-G-001, p. 7.
22. PC-G-001, pp. 13–14.
23. PC-G-001, pp. 14–15.
24. PC-I-002, p. 8.
25. PC-G-005, p. 14.
26. PC-D-011.
27. PC-I-002, p. 6.
28. PC-D-082.
29. PC-D-103, PC-D-104, PC-D-105, PC-D-106, PC-D-107, student evaluations of PC sessions.
30. PC-I-005, pp. 3, 4, 6.
31. PC-I-008, p. 14.
32. PC-I-003, p. 14.
33. PC-I-005, p. 6.
34. Two of the students didn't want to take the internships, and one dropped out because of illness.
35. C-D-108.
36. PC-D-004.

Chapter 7

1. MD-D-002.
2. CV-I-002, pp. 2–3.
3. MD-D-002.
4. Also spelled Anishinaabe.
5. The surface area of the Leech Lake Ojibwe Reservation is 677,099 acres. Of this, 212,000 acres are lakes, leaving 465,099 acres of land. Government-owned portions total 332,804 acres, leaving 132,295 acres under Tribal jurisdiction. Of this, less than 30,000 acres are actually owned by Ojibwes or the Band; the rest is owned by non–Band members, including white residents and resort owners. See *www.llojibwe.com/llojibwe/History.html.*
6. MG-0104-1, p. 1.
7. MG-1118-1.
8. CV-I-002, pp. 2–3.
9. MG-1118-1.
10. MG-1119-1. Central Minnesota Initiative Fund, which later became the Initiative Foundation, is one of the regional funding institutions that the McKnight Foundation created around the state.
11. CV-D-003.
12. MG-1127-1, September 25, 1996.
13. MD-D-007. The committees were General Development, Economic Development, Community Development, Education and Cultural Development, Recreation and Natural Development, and Transportation Development.
14. MD-D-010.
15. MG-0109-1, p. 18.
16. MD-D-002.
17. MD-D-002.
18. Except as noted, all content in this paragraph is from MD-D-008.
19. MD-D-008.
20. MD-D-023.
21. MD-D-058.
22. The area school system is "Cass Lake-Bena." Bena is about 15 miles east of Cass Lake, also within the Leech Lake Reservation, and has a population of just over 100 residents.
23. MD-D-065, MD-D-075.
24. MD-D-009.
25. MD-D-001.
26. MG-0125-2, p. 18.
27. MD-D-052.
28. All information in this section is from MD-D-105, unless otherwise noted.
29. MD-D-063.
30. The investigation could not determine why the Leech Lake members did not participate.
31. *Cass Lake Times* article from October 2006.
32. MD-I-002, p.16.
33. MD-G-001 p. 55.

Chapter 8

1. Federal Register, January 18, 1994, Department of Agriculture 7 CFR Part 25, "Designation of Empowerment Zones and Enterprise Communities; Interim Rules and Notices."
2. CC-D-025.
3. Federal Register, January 18, 1994, Department of Agriculture 7 CFR Part 25, "Designation of Empowerment Zones and Enterprise Communities; Interim Rules and Notices."
4. CC-D-017.
5. SEOK Round I Pathways to Collaboration Workgroup Report.
6. Federal Register, January 18, 1994, Department of Agriculture 7 CFR Part 25, "Designation of Empowerment Zones and Enterprise Communities; Interim Rules and Notices."
7. CC-D-008.

8. CC-D-008.
9. CC-D-008.
10. SE-0502-1, p. 13.
11. SE-1195-2, p.8
12. SE-1195-2, p. 8.
13. SE-0503-1, p. 17.
14. CC-I-001, p. 6.
15. SE-0113 and SE-0111.
16. SE-0111 and SE-0115.
17. CC-I-001, p. 7.
18. CC-I-001, p. 9.
19. From Jerry Pool (via John Guidry).
20. SE-0502-1, p. 4.
21. CC-D-003.
22. SE-0105-1, p. 26.
23. SE-0112, pp. 10–11.
24. Jeanie Butler confirmed that even Nelson (B-15, which doesn't appear to have been allocated any block grant funds in either of the budgets) has a community center located in an old school building, but she isn't sure when it was established or how it was funded.
25. According to Jeanie Butler, Henry retired in 1990; Leona worked for a short time as a Head Start teacher, at the local Vocational School, and as a consultant for Head Start teachers. She retired in 1999.
26. CC-I-001, pp. 5–6.
27. CC-I-001, pp. 6–8.
28. CC-D-022.
29. CC-D-030.
30. CC-I-001, p. 11.
31. CC-G-003, p. 19.
32. CC-G-003, p. 13.
33. CC-I-001, p. 30.
34. CC-G-003, p. 19.
35. CC-I-001, p. 30.
36. CC-I-004, pp. 4.
37. CC-G-002, p. 4.
38. CC-I-004, p. 5
39. CC-I-004, pp. 4–5.
40. CC-D-030.
41. The strategic plan also proposed a "sports complex" in Boswell, which would have included fields for baseball, track, and football; the plan stated that "children of this distressed area should not be deprived of activities that children in other communities enjoy."
42. CC-D-014, CC-D-028.
43. CC-I-002, p. 2.
44. CC-I-002, p. 2.
45. CC-I-002, pp. 8–9.
46. CC-G-002, p. 8.
47. CC-I-002, pp. 2–4.
48. "West Idabel" is not a separate municipality; it is simply the west side of Idabel. The railroad tracks that divided east and west in the town served as a boundary between different communities— white, on the east side, and black and Native American on the west side.
49. CC-D-029.
50. CC-D-030.
51. CC-D-021.
52. CC-D-029.
53. CC-D-030.
54. SE-0105-2, p. 17.
55. CC-I-003, p. 3.
56. CC-I-003, p. 12.
57. CC-I-003, p. 13.
58. CC-G-001, p. 20.
59. CC-G-001, pp. 20–21.
60. CC-G-001, p. 21.
61. CC-I-003, p. 13.
62. SE-0107-2, p.9
63. CC-D-008.
64. SE-0107-2, p. 5.

Chapter 9

1. IN-I-005, p. 20.
2. IN-I-005, p. 21.
3. MICA web site (*http://www.micaonline.org*) and Wikipedia (*http://en.wikipedia.org/wiki/War_on_Poverty*) entries for "War on Poverty" and "Community Action Agencies" (*http://en.wikipedia.org/wiki/Community_Action_Agencies*).
4. MICA web site. We do not know if "self-sufficiency" was part of the program language before welfare reform, but the current description of the role of Family Development Specialists seems consistent with what Lois did in 1995. *http://www.micaonline.org/services_families/services_families.htm.*
5. IN-D-185, p. 2.
6. IN-D-185, p. 2.
7. IN-D-185, pp. 2–3.
8. The phrase, "ending welfare as we know it," goes back to a campaign advertisement that Clinton ran on September 9, 1992. See Demetrios James Caraley, "Ending Welfare as We Know It: A Reform Still in Progress," *Political Science Quarterly* 116 (4) (2001–02), 525–58, p. 527.
9. The Personal Responsibility and Work Opportunity Reconciliation Act was passed in August 1996.
10. IN-D-009.
11. IN-I-001, p. 3.
12. IN-D-009.
13. IN-D-116.
14. IN-I-006, pp. 4, 8.
15. IN-D-185.
16. MTM web site *http://www.movethemountain.org/index.cfm* (Transformational Leadership).
17. IN-I-005, p. 26.
18. IN-D-185.
19. IN-I-005, p. 20.
20. IN-I-005, p. 20.
21. IN-I-005, pp. 20–21.
22. IN-I-005, p. 21.
23. IN-I-001, pp. 10–11; IN-I-005, pp. 20–21.
24. IN-I-005, p. 21.
25. IN-I-005, p. 25.
26. IN-I-005, p. 25.
27. IN-I-005, p. 25.
28. IN-I-005, p. 25.
29. IN-I-005, p. 28.
30. IN-I-005, pp. 28–29.
31. IN-I-005, p. 30.
32. IN-I-005, p. 26. As noted, Miller was not involved in CLTm's activities, though he was a Family Partner.
33. IN-G-005, p. 2.
34. IN-G-005, pp. 1–2.
35. IN-I-009, p. 3.
36. IN-I-005, p. 21.
37. IN-D-060.
38. IN-I-006, p. 8.
39. IN-I-006, p.6.
40. IN-I-006, p. 8.
41. IN-D-060.
42. IN-I-009, p. 8.
43. IN-D-035, IN-D-036, IN-D-037.
44. IN-G-005, pp. 5, 6.
45. IN-D-066.

46. IN-D-066.
47. IN-D-095.
48. IN-D-095.
49. IN-D-096.
50. IN-D-096.
51. IN-I-004, p. 3, 6.
52. IN-D-185.
53. IN-D-179.
54. IN-D-179.
55. On Smidt, see IN-I-001, p. 22; on the testing of Beyond Welfare's methods, see IN-D-185 and IN-D-179.
56. IN-I-001, p. 13.
57. IN-D-179.
58. IN-D-179.
59. IN-I-001, p. 14.
60. See, IN-D-089; see also IN-I-007, pp. 16–19; and IN-I-001, pp. 16–19.
61. This refers to a project that was supported by the Compassion Iowa Fund. It involved Focus on the Family, the organization led by James Dobson, whose views were regarded by the Beyond Welfare Board and members of CLTm as hostile to families with same-sex parents and families headed by single mothers, who were a significant component of CLTm's *participant* membership.
62. IN-I-005, p. 36. At this time, Miller offered Smidt a job with Move the Mountain, along with a raise, which she declined; at another point, he offered her the job of managing the Name Each Child project in Des Moines, which she also declined, although she agreed to provide an external evaluation of the project as a consultant [IN-I-005, p. 36].
63. See IN-D-099 "Beyond Welfare and Move the Mountain Collaboration Meeting" (August 9, 2005; notes from Lois Smidt); and IN-D-098 "Draft notes from MTM meeting that will lead to MOU being created" (August 2, 2005; notes from Scott Miller).
64. MTM web site, *http://www.movethemountain.org.*
65. BW web site, *http://www.beyondwelfare.org/.*

Chapter 10

1. MU-D-007.
2. MU-D-008, MU-D-007, and MU-D-020.
3. MU-D-007.
4. MU-D-027.
5. From "The Plan of Chicago," *Encyclopedia of Chicago* (www.encyclopedia.chicagohistory.org/ pages/ 300009.html) and Jessica Rodriguez, "Uncertain fate of mural mirrors the history of local Latino community" (June 2003, *www.prcc-chgo.org*).
6. Rodriguez article, June 2003,
7. PRCC web site mission statement (*http://www. prcc-chgo.org/prcc_mission.htm*).
8. MU-D-001 and "Politics and Practice of Community Public Art: Whose Murals Get Saved" by John Pitman Weber, 2003; *http://www.getty.edu/conservation/pub lications/weber.pdf.*
9. MU-D-032.
10. MU-I-003, p. 2.
11. "Politics and Practice of Community Public Art: Whose Murals Get Saved" by John Pitman Weber, 2003. *http://www.getty.edu/conservation/publications/pdf_publi cations/weber.pdf.*
12. MU-G-004, p. 5.
13. HP-0104-1, p. 1.
14. Rodriguez, Jessica "Uncertain Fate of Murals: The History of Local Latino Community"(Lerner News 6/ 2003) 2003.

15. HP-0124-1, p. 14.
16. *http://nnnn.org/redevelopment_area.html.*
17. Information from Noah Temaner Jenkins on January 16, 2008.
18. Information about Arocho comes from MU-I-005.
19. MU-D-001.
20. MU-G-009, p. 4.
21. MU-G-009, pp. 6–7; MU-I-002.
22. Chicago *Tribune* article: "A Wall that Builds Bridges," February 8, 2004.
23. MU-D-008.
24. MU-D-018.
25. MU-D-001.
26. MU-D-001; MU-D-003.
27. MU-D-004.
28. The survey [MU-D-002], with the raw data, was attached to Arocho's proposal for the lot [MU-D-007]. The interviewers sometimes used "improved" or "renovated" instead of "restored" for the question about what should be done with the mural. A Spanish translation was also offered — "Que es lo que usted conose del mural?" "Cree que el mural deberia ser restaurado?" "Cree que un parque privado debe ser construido en el lote vacante?"
29. MU-D-002.
30. MU-D-002.
31. MU-D-007, p. 2.
32. MU-D-007, p. 4; the project would also need to meet the guidelines of the Humboldt Park Tax Incremental Finance District, since it fell within the Redevelopment Area.
33. MU-I-005 and MU-D-021.
34. MU-D-028.
35. MU-D-014.
36. MU-D-017.
37. Brian Smith, "Neighbors demonstrate to save Puerto Rican mural," *Chicago Sun-Times* (April 17, 2003).
38. MU-D-014.
39. MU-D-014.
40. MU-I-002, p. 2.
41. MU-I-007, p. 10.
42. MU-D-006.
43. MU-D-026.
44. MU-I-008, p. 4.
45. MU-D-026.
46. MU-I-002, p. 3.
47. MU-D-026.
48. MU-D-022; MU-D-027.
49. MU-I-002, p. 2.
50. MU-I-002, p. 3.
51. MU-I-011, p. 11.
52. MU-D-026.
53. MU-I-008, p. 7.
54. MU-I-008, p. 7; MU-I-002, pp. 3–4.
55. MU-D-011.
56. MU-D-021.
57. MU-D-036.
58. MU-G-010, p. 4.
59. MU-I-008, p. 9.
60. MU-D-033.
61. MU-D-029.
62. MU-I-008, p. 13.
63. MU-D-020.
64. MU-D-031.
65. MU-D-031.
66. MU-I-008, p. 8.
67. MU-I-011, p. 16.
68. MU-I-002, p.6.
69. MU-G-004, p. 6.
70. MU-G-004, p. 11.

Chapter 12

1. Arnstein, 1969; Beierle, 1998; Briggs, 2002; Caine, Salomons & Simmons, 2007; Cheatham & Shen, 2003; Chiu, 2003; Collins, 2005; Corburn, 2003 and 2005; Creighton, 2005; Cunninghan-Burley, Kerr, & Pavis, 2001; Fischer, 2000; Fraser, Lepovsky, Kick, & Williams, 2003; Fraser & Lepofsky, 2004; Geertz, 1983; Hendriks, 2005; Khakee, Barbanente, & Borri, 2000; Lasker, 2004; Lasker, Hunter, & Francis, 2007; Lenaghan, 2001; Lindblom & Cohen, 1979; Mirenowicz, 2001; Nader, 1996; Pimbert & Stirling, 2001; Rowe, Marsh, & Frewer, 2004; Sclove, 2001; Stirling, 2006; Tau Lee, Krause & Goetchius, 2003.

2. Andersen & Jaeger, 2001; Corburn, 2005; Lasker, Weiss & Miller, 2001; Lasker & Weiss, 2003; Lindblom & Cohen, 1979; Nader, 1996.

3. Arnstein, 1969; Cornwall & Gaventa, 2001.

4. Arnstein, 1969; Caine, Salomons & Simmons, 2007; Cook & Kothari, 2001; Corburn, 2003; Cornwall & Gaventa, 2001; Fraser, Lepofsky, Kick & Williams, 2002; Fraser & Lepofsky, 2004; Gibson, 2006; Hendriks, 2005; Irwin, 2001; Levine, Fung & Gastil, 2005; Pimbert & Wakeford, 2001.

5. Bonner et al., 2005; Coelho, Pozzoni & Montoya, 2005; Levine, Fung & Gastil, 2005; Melville, Willingham & Dedrick, 2005; Murty & Wakeford, 2001; Pimbert & Wakeford, 2001.

6. Bushe & Kassam, 2005; Corburn, 2005; Delap, 2001; Hendriks, 2005; Irwin, 2001; Melville, Willingham & Dedrick, 2005; Mirenowicz, 2001; Pimbert & Wakeford, 2001; Wallace, 2001.

7. Ahmed, Beck, Maurana & Newton, 2004; Button & Ryfe, 2005; Cunninghan-Burley, Kerr & Pavis, 2001; Gastil & Kieth, 2005; Hendriks, 2005; Lasker & Weiss, 2003; Lindblom & Cohen, 1979.

8. Hart & Rajbhandry, 2003.

9. Corburn, 2005.

10. Arnstein, 1969; Bushe & Kassam, 2005; Corburn, 2005; Delap, 2001; Fraser, Lepofsky, Kick & Williams, 2002; Fraser & Lepofsky, 2004; Hendriks, 2005; Mirenowicz, 2001.

11. Arnstein, 1969; Bushe & Kassam, 2005; Corburn, 2005; Delap, 2001; Fraser, Lepofsky, Kick & Williams, 2002; Fraser & Lepofsky, 2004; Hendriks, 2005; Irwin, 2001; Lasker, Weiss & Miller, 2001; Mirenowicz, 2001; Wallace, 2001.

12. Coelho, Pozzoni & Montoya, 2005; Corburn, 2005; Cunninghan-Burley, Kerr, & Pavis, 2001; Hendriks, 2005; Levine, Fung & Gastil, 2005; Pimbert & Wakeford, 2001.

13. Arnstein, 1969; Irwin, 2001; Lasker, Hunter, & Francis, 2007.

14. Caine, Salomons & Simmons, 2007; Corburn, 2005; Fraser, Lepofsky, Kick & Williams, 2002; Fraser & Lepofsky, 2004; Gibson, 2006; Karpowitz & Mansbridge, 2005.

15. Coelho, Pozzoni & Montoya, 2005; Fraser, Lepofsky, Kick & Williams, 2002.

16. Arnstein, 1969; Caine, Salomons & Simmons, 2007; Cook & Kothari, 2001; Corburn, 2003; Cornwall & Gaventa, 2001; Frediani, 2007; Fraser, Lepofsky, Kick & Williams, 2002; Fraser & Lepofsky, 2004; Gibson, 2006; Hendriks, 2005; Irwin, 2001; Levine, Fung & Gastil, 2005; Pimbert & Wakeford, 2001.

References

Abelson, J., P. Forest, J. Eyles, P. Smith, and E. Martin (2003). Deliberations about deliberative methods: Issues in the design and evaluation of public participation processes. *Social Science & Medicine, 57*(2), 239–242.

Ahmed, S. M., B. Beck, C. A. Maurana, and G. Newton (2004). Overcoming barriers to effective community-based participatory research in U.S. medical schools. *Education and Health, 17*(2), 141–151.

Andersen, I., and B. Jæger (2001). Scenario workshops and urban planning in Denmark. *Participatory Learning and Action, SPECIAL ISSUE: Deliberative Democracy and Citizen Empowerment*(40), 53–56.

Annenberg Institute for School Reform (1998). *Reasons for hope, voices for change: A report of the Annenberg Institute on public engagement for public education.*

Arnstein, S. R. (1969). A ladder of citizen participation. *Journal of the American Institute of Planners, 35*(4), 216–224.

Barber, B. R. (1984). *Strong democracy: Participatory politics for a new age.* Berkeley: University of California Press.

_____. (2001). How to make society civil and democracy strong. In A. Giddens (Ed.), *The global third way debate.* Cambridge, UK: Polity Press.

Beierle, T. C. (1998). *Public participation in environmental decisions: An evaluation framework using social goals.* Washington, DC: Resources for the Future.

Bogeholz, S. (2006). Nature experience and its importance for environmental knowledge, values and action: Recent German empirical contributions. *Environmental Education Research, 12*(1), 65–84.

Bohman, J., and W. Rehg (1997). *Deliberative democracy: Essays on reason and politics.* Cambridge, MA: The MIT Press.

Bonner, P. A., R. Carlitz, R. Gunn, L. E. Maak, and C. A. Ratliff (2005). Bringing the public and the government together through on-line dialogues. In J. Gastil, and P. Levine (Eds.), *The deliberative democracy handbook: Strategies for effective civic engagement in the twenty-first century* (pp. 141–154). San Francisco: Jossey-Bass.

Box, R. C. (1998). *Citizen governance: Leading American communities into the 21st century.* Thousand Oaks, CA: Sage Publications.

Briggs, Xavier de Souza. (2002). *The will and the way: Local partnerships, political strategy and the well-being of America's children and youth.* John F. Kennedy School of Government, Harvard University.

Bruner, C. (2000) *Social systems reform in poor neighborhoods: What we know and what we need to find out.* Des Moines, IA: National Center for Service Integration.

Bushe, G. R., and A. F. Kassam (2005). When is appreciative inquiry transformational? A meta-case analysis. *The Journal of Applied Behavioral Science, 41*(2), 161–181.

Button, M., and D. M. Ryfe (2005). What can we learn from the practice of deliberative democracy? In J. Gastil, and P. Levine (Eds.), *The deliberative democracy handbook: Strategies for effective civic engagement in the twenty-first century* (pp. 20–35). San Francisco: Jossey-Bass.

Caine, K. J., M. J. Salomons, and D. Simmons (2007). Partnerships for social change in the Canadian north: Revisiting the insider-outsider dialectic. *Development and Change, 39*(3), 441–471.

Camerer, C., G. Loewenstein, and M. Weber (1989). The curse of knowledge in economic settings: An experimental analysis. *Journal of Political Economy, 97*(5), 1232–1254.

Carr, D. S., and K. Halvorsen (2001). An evaluation of three democratic community-based approaches to citizen participation: Surveys, conversations with community groups, and community dinners. *Society & Natural Resources, 14*(2), 107–126.

Carson, L. (2006). Improving public deliberative practice: A comparative analysis of two Italian citizens' jury projects in 2006. *Journal of Public Deliberation, 2*(1), Article 12.

_____, and J. Hartz-Karp (2005). Adapting and combining deliberative designs: Juries, polls, and forums. *The deliberative democracy handbook: Strategies for effective civic engagement in the twenty-first century* (pp. 120–139). San Francisco: Jossey-Bass.

Charles, M., H. Sokoloff, and C. Satullo (2005). Electoral deliberation and public journalism. In J. Gastil, and P. Levine (Eds.), *The deliberative democracy handbook: Strategies for effective civic engagement in the twenty-first century* (pp. 59–68). San Francisco: Jossey-Bass.

Chaskin, R. J. (2001). Building community capacity. *Urban Affairs Review, 36*(3), 291–323.

Cheatham, A., and E. Shen (2003). Community based participatory research with Cambodian girls in Long Beach, California: A case study. In M. Minkler, and N. Wallerstein (Eds.), *Community-based participatory research for health* (pp. 316–331). San Francisco, CA: Jossey-Bass.

Cheng, A., and J. D. Fiero (2005). Collaborative learning and the public's stewardship of its forests. *The deliberative democracy handbook: Strategies for effective civic engagement in the twenty-first century* (pp. 164–174). San Francisco: Jossey-Bass.

Chiu, L. F. (2003). Transformational potential of focus group practice in participatory action research. *Action Research, 1*(2), 165–183.

Chrislip, D. D. (1994). American renewal: Reconnecting citizens with public life. *National Civic Review*; 83:26–31.

Clements-Nolle, K., and A. Bachrach (2003). Community-based participatory research with a hidden population: The transgender community health project. In M. Minkler, and N. Wallerstein (Eds.), *Community-based participatory research for health* (pp. 332–345). San Francisco, CA: Jossey-Bass.

Coelho, V.S.P., B. Pozzoni, and M. C. Montoya (2005). Participation and public policies in Brazil. *The deliberative democracy handbook: Strategies for effective civic engagement in the twenty-first century* (pp. 174–185). San Francisco: Jossey-Bass.

Cohen, J. (2005). Global justice. *National Convention of the Democratici*, Di Sinistra, Florence, Italy.

Collins, S. B. (2005). An understanding of poverty from those who are poor. *Action Research, 3*(1), 9–31.

Connell, J. P., and A. C. Kubisch (1998). Applying a theory of change approach to the evaluation of comprehensive community initiatives: Progress, prospects, and problems. In K. Fulbright-Anderson, A. C. Kubisch and J. P. Connell (Eds.), *New approaches to evaluating community initiatives,*

vol.2: Theory, measurement, and analysis (pp. 15–44). Washington, DC: The Aspen Institute.

Cooke, B., and U. Kothari (Eds.). (2001). *Participation: The new tyranny?*. London: Zed Books.

Corburn, J. (2003). Bringing local knowledge into environmental decision making: Improving urban planning for communities at risk. *Journal of Planning Education and Research, 22*: 420–433.

_____. (2005). *Street science: Community knowledge and environmental health justice.* Cambridge, MA: MIT Press.

Cornwall, A., and J. Gaventa (2001). Bridging the gap: Citizenship, partnership and accountability. *Participatory Learning and Action, SPECIAL ISSUE: Deliberative Democracy and Citizen Empowerment*(40), 32–35.

Creighton, J. L. (2005). *The public participation handbook: Making better decisions through citizen involvement.* San Francisco, CA: Jossey-Bass.

Crosby, N. (1995). Citizen juries: One solution for difficult environmental questions. In O. Renn, T. Webler and P. Wiedemann (Eds.), *Fairness and competence in citizen participation: Evaluating models for environmental discourse* (pp. 157–175). Boston, MA: Kluwer Academic Publishers.

Crosby, N., J. M. Kelly, and P. Schaefer (1986). Citizens panels: A new approach to citizen participation. *Public Administration Review, 46*(2), 170–178.

_____, and D. Nethercut (2005). Citizens juries: Creating a trustworthy voice of the people. *The deliberative democracy handbook: Strategies for effective civic engagement in the twenty-first century* (pp. 111–120). San Francisco: Jossey-Bass.

Cunningham-Burley, S., A. Kerr, and S. Pavis (2001). Focus groups and public involvement in the new genetics. *Participatory Learning and Action, SPECIAL ISSUE: Deliberative Democracy and Citizen Empowerment*(40), 36–38.

Delap, C. (2001). Citizen juries: Reflections on the UK experience. *Participatory Learning and Action, SPECIAL ISSUE: Deliberative Democracy and Citizen Empowerment*(40), 39–42.

Denhardt, R.B. and J.V. Denhardt (2000). The new public service: Serving rather than steering. *Public Administration Review*; 60:549–559.

Fawcett, S. B., A. Paine-Andrews, V. T. Francisco, J. A. Schultz, K. P. Richter, R. K. Lewis, et al. (1996). Empowering community health initiatives through evaluation. In D. M. Fetterman, S. Kaftarian and A. Wandersman (Eds.), *Empowerment evaluation: Knowledge and tools for self-assessment and accountability* (pp. 161–187). Thousand Oaks, CA: Sage.

Fischer, F. (2000). *Citizens, experts, and the environment: The politics of local knowledge.* Durham, NC: Duke University Press.

Fishkin, J., and C. Farrar (2005). Deliberative

polling: From experiment to community resource. In J. Gastil, and P. Levine (Eds.), *The deliberative democracy handbook: Strategies for effective civic engagement in the twenty-first century* (pp. 68–80). San Francisco: Jossey-Bass.

Francis, P. (2001). Participatory development at the World Bank: The primacy of process. In B. Cooke, and U. Kothari (Eds.), *Participation: The new tyranny?* (pp. 72–87). London: Zed Books.

Fraser, J., and J. Lepofsky (2004). The uses of knowledge in neighbourhood revitalization. *Community and Development Journal, 39*(1), 4–12.

Fraser, J. C. (2004). Beyond gentrification: Mobilizing communities and claiming space. *Urban Geography, 25*(5), 437–457.

_____, and E. L. Kick (2007). The role of public, private, non-profit and community sectors in shaping mixed-income housing outcomes in the U.S. *Urban Studies, 44*(12), 2357–2377.

_____, J. Lepofsky, E. L. Kick, and J. P. Williams (2003). The construction of the local and the limits of contemporary community building in the United States. *Urban Affairs Review, 38*(3), 417.

Frediani, A. A. (2007). Amartya Sen, the World Bank, and the redress of urban poverty: A Brazilian case study. *Journal of Human Development, 8*(1), 133–152.

Gastil, J., and W. M. Keith (2005). A nation that (sometimes) likes to talk: A brief history of public deliberation in the United States. In J. Gastil, and P. Levine (Eds.), *The deliberative democracy handbook: Strategies for effective civic engagement in the twenty-first century* (pp. 3–20). San Francisco: Jossey-Bass.

_____, and P. Levine (Eds.). (2005). *The deliberative democracy handbook: Strategies for effective civic engagement in the twenty-first century*. San Francisco, CA: Jossey-Bass.

Geertz, C. (1983). *Local knowledge*. New York: Basic Books.

Gibson, C. M. (2006). *Citizens at the center: A new approach to civic engagement*. Washington, DC: The Case Foundation.

Guidry, J. A., and M. Q. Sawyer (2003). Contentious pluralism: The public sphere and democracy. *Perspectives on Politics, 1*(3), 273–289.

Hart, R. A., and J. Rajbhandry (2003). Using participatory methods to further the democratic goals of children's organizations. *New Directions for Evaluation, 98*(Summer), 61–75.

Hendriks, C. M. (2005). Consensus conferences and planning cells: Lay citizen deliberations. In J. Gastil, and P. Levine (Eds.), *The deliberative democracy handbook: Strategies for effective civic engagement in the twenty-first century* (pp. 80–111). San Francisco: Jossey-Bass.

Highlander Research and Education Center. (n.d.). *Constructing democracy; creating democratic space; base-building*. Retrieved October, 2007, from *http://www.highlandercenter.org/.*

Holmes, T., and I. Scoones (2001). Participatory environmental policy processes: Experiences from north and south. *Participatory Learning and Action, SPECIAL ISSUE: Deliberative Democracy and Citizen Empowerment*(40), 76–78.

Irwin, A. (2001). Citizen engagement in science and technology policy: A commentary on recent UK experience. *Participatory Learning and Action, SPECIAL ISSUE: Deliberative Democracy and Citizen Empowerment*(40), 72–75.

Israel, B. A., A. J. Schulz, E. P. Parker, and A. B. Becker (2001). Community-based participatory research: Policy recommendations for promoting a partnership approach in health research. *Education for Health: Change in Learning & Practice, 14*(2; 2), 182–197.

Karpowitz, C. F., and J. Mansbridge (2005). Disagreement and consensus: The importance of dynamic updating in public deliberation. *The deliberative democracy handbook: Strategies for effective civic engagement in the twenty-first century* (pp. 237–254). San Francisco: Jossey-Bass.

Khakee, A., A. Barbanente, and D. Borri (2000). Expert and experiential knowledge in planning. *Journal of the Operational Research Society, 51*, 776–788.

King, C.S., and C. Stivers (1998). *Government is us: Public administration in an anti-government era*. Thousand Oaks, CA: Sage Publications.

Lasker, R. D. (2004). *Redefining readiness: Terrorism planning through the eyes of the public*. New York: The New York Academy of Medicine.

_____, N. D. Hunter, and S. E. Francis (2007). *With the public's knowledge, we can make sheltering in place possible*. New York: The New York Academy of Medicine.

_____, E. S. Weiss, and R. Miller (2001). Partnership synergy: A practical framework for studying and strengthening the collaborative advantage. *Milbank Quarterly, 79*(2; 2), 179.

_____, and E. D. Weiss (2003). Broadening participation in community problem solving: A multidisciplinary model to support collaborative practice and research. *Journal of Urban Health, 80*:14–47.

Lavalle, A. G., A. Acharya, and P. P. Houtzager (2005). Beyond comparative anecdotalism: Lessons on civil society and participation from São Paulo, Brazil. *World Development, 33*(6), 951–964.

Lenaghan, J. (2001). Participation and governance in the UK department of health. *Participatory Learning and Action, SPECIAL ISSUE: Deliberative Democracy and Citizen Empowerment*(40), 64–65.

Levine, P., A. Fung, and J. Gastil (2005). Future directions for public deliberation. *The deliberative democracy handbook: Strategies for effective civic engagement in the twenty-first century* (pp. 271–289). San Francisco: Jossey-Bass.

Lindblom, C., and D. K. Cohen (1979). *Usable knowledge: Social science and social problem solving.* New Haven, CT: Yale University Press.

Lukensmeyer, C. J., J. Goldman, and S. Brigham (2005). A town meeting for the twenty-first century. *The deliberative democracy handbook: Strategies for effective civic engagement in the twenty-first century* (pp. 154–164). San Francisco: Jossey-Bass.

Mansbridge, J. (1980). *Beyond adversary democracy.* Chicago: University of Chicago Press.

_____. (2001). *Oppositional consciousness: The subjective roots of social protest.* Chicago: Chicago University Press.

McKnight, J.L. (1985). Health and empowerment. *Canadian Journal of Public Health*; 76:37–38

_____. (1995). *The careless society: Community and its counterfeits.* New York: Basic Books.

Melville, K., T. L. Willingham, and J. R. Dedrick (2005). National issues forums: A network of communities promoting public deliberation. In J. Gastil, and P. Levine (Eds.), *The deliberative democracy handbook: Strategies for effective civic engagement in the twenty-first century* (pp. 37–59). San Francisco: Jossey-Bass.

Mill, J. S. (1859). *On liberty.* J. W. Parker: London.

Minkler, M., and N. Wallerstein (Eds.). (2003). *Community-based participatory research for health.* San Francisco, CA: Jossey-Bass.

Mirenowicz, J. (2001). The Danish consensus conference model in Switzerland and France: On the importance of framing the issue. *Participatory Learning and Action, SPECIAL ISSUE: Deliberative Democracy and Citizen Empowerment*(40), 57–60.

Morello-Frosch, R., M. Pastor, J. L. Sadd, C. Porras, and P. Michele (2005). Citizens, science, and data judo: Leveraging secondary data analysis to build a community-academic collaborative for environmental justice in southern California. In B. A. Israel, E. Eng, A. J. Schulz and E. A. Parker (Eds.), *Methods in community-based participatory research* (pp. 207–325). New York: Jossey-Bass.

Murty, D. S., and T. Wakeford (2001). Farmer foresight: An experiment in south India. *Participatory Learning and Action, SPECIAL ISSUE: Deliberative Democracy and Citizen Empowerment*(40), 46–51.

Nader, L. (1996). *Naked science: Anthropological inquiry into boundaries, power, and knowledge.* New York: Routledge.

Pateman, C. (1970). *Participation and democratic theory.* Cambridge, UK: Cambridge University Press.

Perlman, J., and H. Spiegel (1983). Copenhagen's black quadrant: The facade and reality of participation. In L. Susskind, and M. Elliot (Eds.), *Paternalism, conflict, and coproduction: Learning from citizen action and citizen participation in western Europe* (pp. 35–69). New York: Plenum Publishing.

Petersen, D., M. Minkler, V. B. Vásquez, and A. C. Baden (2006). Community-based participatory research as a tool for policy change: A case study of the southern California environmental justice collaborative. *Review of Policy Research, 23*(2), 339–353.

Pew Research Center for the People & the Press. (2003). *Evenly divided and increasingly polarized: 2004 political landscape.*

Pimbert, M. (2001). Reclaiming our right to power: Some conditions for deliberative democracy. *Participatory Learning and Action, SPECIAL ISSUE: Deliberative Democracy and Citizen Empowerment*(40), 81–84.

_____, and T. Wakeford (2001). Overview — deliberative democracy and citizen empowerment. *Participatory Learning and Action, SPECIAL ISSUE: Deliberative Democracy and Citizen Empowerment* (40), 23–28.

Potapchuk, W. R., C. Carlson, and J. Kennedy (2005). Growing governance deliberatively: Lessons and inspiration from Hampton, Virginia. *The deliberative democracy handbook: Strategies for effective civic engagement in the twenty-first century* (pp. 254–271). San Francisco: Jossey-Bass.

Rowe, G., R. Marsh, and L. J. Frewer (2004). Evaluation of a deliberative conference. *Science, Technology and Human Values, 29*(1), 88–121.

_____, and L. J. Frewer (2000). Public participation methods: A framework for evaluation. *Science, Technology & Human Values, 25*(1), 3–29.

_____, and L. J. Frewer (2004). Evaluating public-participation exercises: A research agenda. *Science, Technology & Human Values, 29*(4), 512–557.

Schulz, A. J., B. A. Israel, E. A. Parker, M. Lockett, Y. R. Hill, and R. Wills (2003). Engaging women in community based participatory research for health: The east side village health worker partnership. In M. Minkler, and N. Wallerstein (Eds.), *Community-based participatory research for health* (pp. 293–316). San Francisco, CA: Jossey-Bass.

Schwinn, C. J., J. T. Kesler, and D. R. Schwinn (2005). Learning democracy centers: Where the public works. *The deliberative democracy handbook: Strategies for effective civic engagement in the twenty-first century* (pp. 228–237). San Francisco: Jossey-Bass.

Sclove, D. (2001). Telecommunications and the future of democracy: Preliminary report on the first U.S. citizens' panel. *Participatory Learning and Action, SPECIAL ISSUE: Deliberative Democracy and Citizen Empowerment*(40), 52.

Scully, P. L., and M. L. McCoy (2005). Study circles: Local deliberation as the cornerstone of deliberative democracy. *The deliberative democracy handbook: Strategies for effective civic engagement in the twenty-first century* (pp. 199–213). San Francisco: Jossey-Bass.

Skocpol, T. (2004). Voice and inequality: The transformation of American civic democracy. *Perspectives on Politics, 2*(1), 3–20.

Sokoloff, H., H. M. Steinberg, and S. N. Pyser (2005). Deliberative city planning on the Philadelphia waterfront. *The deliberative democracy handbook: Strategies for effective civic engagement in the twenty-first century* (pp. 185–197). San Francisco: Jossey-Bass.

Stirling, A. (2001). Inclusive deliberation and scientific expertise: Precaution, diversity and transparency in the governance of risk. *Participatory Learning and Action, SPECIAL ISSUE: Deliberative Democracy and Citizen Empowerment* (40), 66–71.

_____. (2006). Analysis, participation and power: Justification and closure in participatory multi-criteria analysis. *Land Use Policy 23*(1), 95–107.

_____, and D. Gee (2002). Science, precaution, and practice. *Public Health Reports, 117*(6), 521.

Tau Lee, P., N. Krause, and C. Goetchius (2003). Participatory action research with hotel room cleaners: From collaborative study to the bargaining table. In M. Minkler, and N. Wallerstein (Eds.), *Community-based participatory research*

for health (pp. 390–409). San Francisco, CA: Jossey-Bass.

UN-HABITAT (2006). Habitat jam. Vancouver, Canada. *World Urban Forum* (Third).

Uyesugi, J., and R. Shipley (2005). Visioning diversity: Planning Vancouver's multicultural communities. *International Planning Studies, 10*(3/4), 305–322.

Wakeford, T. (2001a). Evaluating DIPs. *Participatory Learning and Action, SPECIAL ISSUE: Deliberative Democracy and Citizen Empowerment*(40), 79–80.

_____. (2001b). A selection of methods used in deliberative and inclusionary processes. *Participatory Learning and Action, SPECIAL ISSUE: Deliberative Democracy and Citizen Empowerment*(40), 29–31.

Wallace, H. (2001). The issue of framing and consensus conferences. *Participatory Learning and Action, SPECIAL ISSUE: Deliberative Democracy and Citizen Empowerment*(40), 61–63.

Weiksner, G. M. (2005). e-thePeople.org: Large-scale, ongoing deliberation. *The deliberative democracy handbook: Strategies for effective civic engagement in the twenty-first century* (pp. 213–228). San Francisco: Jossey-Bass.

Index

Acevedo, William 44
Aigner, Steve 85
Albizu Campos Alternative High School 159
Alinsky, Saul 42
archi-treasures 156, 159–162, 166, 168
Arnstein, Sherry 7, 8
Arocho, Eduardo 160–162, 165–168
Asset Based Community Development (ABCD) 85, 89, 145
Association House 157

Baker, Catherine 48
Ballard Ministerial Alliance 84, 91
Barron, Charles 70
Batey Urbano 159, 162–163, 166–168, 188, 194
Beyond Welfare 85, 88–89, 91–92; Board of Directors 92, 147, 149, 151–155, 184, 194, 188; Guiding Coalition/Advisory Board 144–148, 152–155; incorporation 141–155, 175, 191–192, 196
Bickerdike Redevelopment Corporation 41, 50
Block Club Federation 41, 44–46, 49–50, 52
Booker T. Washington Community Center 133–140, 195
Boswell 56, 131–133, 138
Boswell Nutrition Center 131–133, 139, 195–196
Boys & Girls Clubs 28, 32, 35, 37, 39, 115, 192, 196
Brasgalla, Ardean 113

case analyses 34–39, 50–53, 63–67, 77–79, 89–92, 103–107, 118–122, 136–140, 152–155, 166–169
case impacts 14, 15, 34–35, 38–39, 50–51, 63–64, 78, 89–90, 103–104, 118–119, 136–137, 152–153, 166–167; relation to influence 38–39, 52–53, 65–67, 79, 91–92, 106–107, 121–122, 139–140, 155, 168–169, 195–199
case narratives 16, 21–39, 40–53, 54–67, 68–79, 80–92, 93–107,

108–122, 123–140, 141–155, 156–169
case study methods 9–15
Cass Lake area 22, 23, 31, 108–110; revitalization 108–122, 175–178, 180–181, 183–187, 189–194, 198–199
Cass Lake/Bena school system 27, 29, 32, 36, 112
Cass Lake Family Resource Center 21, 24–25, 29, 35
Cass Lake Tourism Partnership 115, 117, 121
Center for Reducing Rural Violence (CRRV) 29–30, 32, 35–36, 38, 197
Center for the Advancement of Collaborative Strategies in Health 6
Central Minnesota Initiative Foundation 111, 115, 118
Chicago Public Art Group 165
Child and Family Policy Center 87, 145
Choctaw (central, western, eastern) 60–61, 63–64, 66, 124
Choctaw Nation 58, 125
Christiansen, Ryan 111
Circles of Support 85–86, 88–89, 91–92, 141, 144–145, 149–155
Coahoma Community College 73, 76, 94–95, 100–102
Colom, Vilma 44
community 12, 217–218
Community Action Programs 7
community centers 123–140, 172, 174–175, 177, 181, 187–189, 192–196
Community Leadership Team (CLTm) v, 6, 80–92, 141–155, 172, 175, 179, 181, 184, 188, 192, 194, 196; distinction between participants and allies 84, 89, 91; Purposes and Principles 83–84, 90–91,148, 153–155, 192, 196
community participation 6–9; evaluation criteria 9, 215; forms 6; process 11, 208, 215–219; promise 1, 6, 203, 208, 213, 217, 219; uses of, 7

Community Voices Against Violence (CVAV) 21–39, 172, 174–177, 179–186, 188–192, 194, 196–199
consensus 8, 113–114, 189, 206, 218
Consumer Advisory Teams (CATs) 87, 145, 150
cooperative law enforcement agreement 31–32, 34, 37, 38
cross-case analysis 16–17, 170–199

Delta State University 96
del Valle, Miguel 47
Division Street Business Development Association 159–160, 162–163, 166–167

Edwards, Henry 128–131, 138
Edwards, Leona 128–131
Empowerment Zone 42, 54–56, 58–59, 123–134, 137–139, 173
Enterprise Community 54–56, 58–59, 123–139, 173
Enterprise Corporation of the Delta 69

Family Learning Center 159, 161, 166, 168
Fernandes, Joyce 160, 168
Finn, Randy 24, 26, 28, 33, 37–38, 111
Fisher, Randy 31
Fitzgerald, Bob 110, 112
Fleming, Elaine 34
Flores, Manny 163–166, 168
focus groups 96, 103–106, 180, 183, 186, 189, 192, 194
forums 25–6, 31, 35–36, 38, 83–84, 87, 91, 173, 183, 186, 188, 197
Foundation for the Mid South 68, 70–72, 75, 77–78; workforce alliances 69–71, 78, 93–94, 104–105
Frey, Walter 56, 58–59, 64

Gabrielle, Gina 31
Galan, Mario 158
gentrification 156–169, 188
Grameen Bank 57–58

Granato, Jesse 47
Green, John 96, 99
Green, Mike 85, 89, 91, 145–148, 152–155

Hall, Dennis 132
Hill, Luketta 134
Hispanic Housing Development Corporation 41
housing for single mothers 40–53, 172, 175–178, 180–181, 183–185, 189, 191–193, 195–196, 198
Hugo (western) 56, 61, 124, 126, 128–131
Humboldt Park area 41; Puerto Rican displacement 157–158
Humboldt Park Empowerment Partnership vi, 6, 40–53; 156–169, 183
Hunt, Eli 25
Hurdles and Supports in the Pathway (table) 204–206, 213

Idabel (west) 55–56, 60–61, 63–64, 66, 124, 126, 133–136, 197
Idabel Minority Action Committee (IMAC) 55, 61, 133–138
ideas 7, 11–15, 215–216; blocked 195; communication 182–190, 205–207, 211–212; differentiation 12–14, 186–187, 201, 217–218; expression 178–182, 203–207, 210–211; incorrect 218; influential 11, 170–171, 195; kinds 195; missing 12, 195, 201–202; needed 208–209, 214; use 190–195, 206–208, 212
Identifying People with Needed Ideas (questionnaire) 215
influence 8, 11–15, 170; assessment 8, 11–12, 15, 201; barriers 203–208; critical points 35–38, 51–52, 64–65, 78–79, 90–91, 104–106, 119–121, 137–139, 153–155, 167–168, 173–174, 209; extent 219; pathway 170–199, 202–203; relation to outcomes 38–39, 52–53, 65–67, 79, 91–92, 106–107, 121–122, 139–140, 155, 168–169, 195–199, 201–202; strategies to support 208–212
interviews 14, 96, 103–106, 180, 186, 189
Iowa Department of Human Services 80, 87, 89–90, 143, 145

Johnson, Larry 31–32
Jones, Irvin 55–57, 59, 61–63, 65–67, 127, 133–136
Jonestown 70, 76
Juan Antonio Corretjer Puerto Rican Cultural Center 156–157, 159–163, 166–168

Kiamichi Economic Development District (KEDDO) 58, 125, 130–132

Landon, Peter 44, 47
Langford, Charles 95, 101

Latin United Community Housing Association (LUCHA) 40–53, 172, 177, 185
League of Women Voters 88
Leech Lake Band of the Ojibwe 21, 22–23, 26, 34, 109–110, 112, 116–118, 121, 190
Leech Lake Tribal Council 26–29, 32, 35, 37–39, 113
Levy, Jonathan 44
Little Dixie Community Action Agency 55, 58–66, 123–130, 136, 138–139, 172, 197
Lopez, José 160
Lowe, Darlene 133

marginalized and ordinary residents 2, 6–7, 172, 175–180, 182–184, 188–189, 191–194, 196–197, 199, 202; barriers to influence 203–208; optimizing influence 208–219
Martinez, Magdalena 49
McKnight, John 85
MDC 68, 70, 78
Medina, Eliud 45–47, 160, 163–164, 166, 168
Mid-Iowa Community Action (MICA) 80–82, 84, 87, 89–91, 142–145, 152–153, 172
Mill, John Stuart 7
Miller, Scott 80, 82–83, 85, 87–92, 141–155
minigrants 68–79, 172, 174, 176–177, 180, 185, 191, 194, 196
Minnesota Design Team (MDT) 108, 111–116, 118–122
MIRACLE Group vi, 6, 21–39; 108–122, 175, 186, 199
Mississippi Delta 69–70, 94–95
Model Cities 7
Morris, Francine 128
Mothers United in Action (Madres Unidas en Acción; MUA) 43, 46–51, 53, 184, 188, 192
Mound Bayou 69, 76–77
Move the Mountain Leadership Center 82, 85, 88–89, 91–92, 141–148, 150–155, 172, 192, 196
murals (saving of La Crucifixion de Don Pedro Albizu Campos) 156–169, 180–181, 183, 185, 187–188, 192, 194, 196–197; Mural Restoration Committee 162, 164–165

Name Each Child 150–151
National Training Associates 56, 124, 136–137, 139
Near Northwest Neighborhood Network 40, 42, 45–46, 50–52, 156–168
New York Academy of Medicine 6
No Limits for Women Artists 81, 90–91
Nogueras, Miguel 46

Ocasio, Billy 42–44, 46–47, 51–52, 158–160, 163–166, 168

opportunities for involvement 14, 15, 173–178, 201, 208–212; conditions 210–211; kinds 209–210; participants 208–209, 211–212; see also focus groups; forums; interviews; meeting conveners; protests; questionnaires; rallies; summits; surveys; visioning sessions
Optimizing Opportunities for Marginalized and Ordinary Residents (questionnaire) 216–217
Ouachita-Morehouse Workforce Alliance 72, 77, 79

participation in the process 198–199, 203
Pathways to Collaboration Workgroup v, 1, 5, 10, 200, 217
pathway of ideas 16–17, 170–199, 202–203; communication of ideas (third step) 182–190, 205–207, 211–212; expression of ideas (second step) 178–182, 203–207, 210–211; hurdles and supports 203–212; opportunity to participate (first step) 173–178, 203–204, 210; use of ideas (final step) 190–195, 206–208, 212
Pelton, Mary Helen 25
players in the cases 14, 34, 50, 63, 77, 89, 103, 118, 136, 152, 166, 171–173
Pointer, Evelyn 128
Poor Man's Bank 54–67, 172, 176–177, 180, 182, 185, 187, 191–193, 195, 198–199; Poor Man's Bank committee (PMBC) 59, 61–63, 65–67, 177, 179–180, 182, 197
Pounds, Jon 165
poverty: CLTm definition 85–86, 145; relationship to gentrification 42, 158
Professionalization Curriculum 93–107, 174–175, 180–181, 183, 189, 192–194, 196–198; Curriculum Design Committee 99–100, 103–107, 179, 181–182, 184, 199; research team 96–99, 103–107, 183, 186, 194
protests 162–166, 183, 185, 188, 192, 197
Puerto Rican Art Association (La Asociación de Arte de Puerto Rico) 156–157

questionnaires 95–96, 101, 104, 214, 216–217

rallies 21, 24–25, 35–36, 38, 46, 51, 183, 188, 192
Redevelopment Area 42, 49, 159
Re-Evaluation Counseling 81, 90–91
Rhymes, Josephine 71–74, 77–79, 94–97, 100, 102–103, 105
Richardson, Victor 70–71

Rose, Richard 115–118, 120, 186

Salgado, Enrique 163–164
Smidt, Lois 80–83, 85, 87–92, 141–155
Smith, Louise 24–25, 29–32, 35
Southeast Oklahoma Champion and Enterprise Community vi, 6, 54–67, 123–140, 184; local census tract steering committees 56–59, 61–63, 65, 67, 125–127, 129–134, 136–139, 183, 188–189; local planning meetings 56, 125, 127, 137–139, 177, 179–180, 183, 185, 187, 189; overall steering committee 59, 62–64, 125–128, 130, 133, 136–139, 183, 187–188, 195
southeastern Oklahoma area (Choctaw and McCurtain Counties) 123–124
Stewart, Oscar 129–130
Stokes, Gary 82, 85, 141–148, 152–154
Story County 80–81
Streetscape Project 108–122, 177; Planning Committee 117, 120–121, 176, 180–181, 183, 190;

planning workshops 116, 119–122, 185–186
summits 26–29, 36–38, 177, 179, 183, 185–186, 189, 192, 194
surveys 27, 30–31, 35, 36–37, 38, 48, 52, 111, 119, 161–162, 177, 180–181, 185–188, 194

track meet analogy (illustrating the movement of ideas along the pathway to influence) 171–176, 178, 182, 184, 186, 190, 194, 203
Tri-County Workforce Alliance vi, 6, 68–79, 93–107; Executive Committee 72, 77, 79; Implementation Team 70–79, 95–96, 100, 102–103; task forces 70–71, 77–79
Turner, Howard 128

un/underemployment 93–107, 193
Union Estadista of Illinois 165
United Blocks of West Humboldt Park 41, 44–46, 49–50, 52, 165
Upper Midwest Community Policing Institute (UMCPI) 29–31, 35–36, 38, 197

Victor, Sonny 59
violence 21–39
visioning sessions 113–115, 119–122, 177, 180, 183, 185–187, 189–190, 192, 194
voice 11, 201, 217–218

Walker, George 70
Washington Community Center 128–131, 137–140, 188, 193
Weber, John Pitman 160, 166, 168
Weed & Seed 33, 36
West Choctaw steering committee 131–132
West Idabel steering committee 56–67, 133–134, 193, 197, 199
Western Hugo steering committee 61, 129–130, 188
Wheels to Work 86–87, 91, 141, 145, 149, 175, 192
Widseth, Smith, Nolting (WSN) 117–118, 120–122
W.K. Kellogg Foundation v, 6

youth involvement 26–29, 76–78, 112, 131, 135–136, 138–140, 159–164, 166, 168, 173, 180, 183, 185–186, 189, 192, 194, 197–198